Inventory Optimization with SAP®

 **PRESS**

SAP PRESS is a joint initiative of SAP and Galileo Press. The know-how offered by SAP specialists combined with the expertise of the publishing house Galileo Press offers the reader expert books in the field. SAP PRESS features first-hand information and expert advice, and provides useful skills for professional decision-making.

SAP PRESS offers a variety of books on technical and business related topics for the SAP user. For further information, please visit our website: www.sap-press.com.

Jörg Thomas Dickersbach, Gerhard Keller, Klaus Weihrauch
Production Planning and Control with SAP
2007, 477 pp., ISBN 978-1-59229-106-9

Martin Murray
SAP MM—Functionality and Technical Configuration
2006, 504 pp., ISBN 978-1-59229-072-7

Gerd Hartmann, Ulrich Schmidt
Product Lifecycle Management with SAP
2005, 620 pp., ISBN 978-1-59229-036-9

Michael Hölzer, Michael Schramm
Quality Management with SAP
2005, 538 pp., ISBN 978-1-59229-051-2

Marc Hoppe

Inventory Optimization with SAP®

Galileo Press

Bonn • Boston

ISBN   978-1-59229-097-0

1st edition 2006, 1st reprint 2007

Translation Lemoine International, Inc., Salt Lake City, UT
Copy Editor Nancy Etscovitz, UCG, Inc., Boston, MA
Cover Design Silke Braun
Layout Design Vera Brauner
Production Steffi Ehrentraut
Typesetting SatzPro, Krefeld
Printed and bound in Germany

Contents at a Glance

For logisticians all around the world:

I have heard of thee,
... that excellent knowledge,
and understanding, and wisdom
are found in thee.

But I have heard of thee,
that thou canst interpret obscure things, and
resolve difficult things.
... thou shalt be clothed with purple,
and shalt have a chain of gold about thy neck,
and shalt be the third prince in my kingdom.

The Book of Daniel, 5:14 + 5:16

Contents

5   Material Requirements Planning 207

8   Production   365

You can optimally tune your supply chain and save a lot of money by reducing your inventory without compromising the level of your customer service and the utilization of your internal capacities.

Introduction

An important objective in a company's supply chain management is to ensure an efficient inventory management. If you examine the way in which companies are actually handling inventory management, the methods employed appear to be good; however, the way in which all aspects integral to inventory management interact is often far from ideal, that is, there needs to be a better system of internal controls for inventory to be managed efficiently. So, you frequently hear statements like the following:

> *"We define the high quality of our services as being our competitive edge, but our service levels are insufficient despite our high stock levels."*

> *"Our machine assignments change five times a day, but we have no idea of the number of sales orders that we are actually putting on hold because of that."*

These statements describe only some of the many problems inherent in supply chains today. Despite all the uncertainties and the corresponding countermeasures taken to address these uncertainties, a company's top priority is still to ensure as high a service level as possible to customers. On the other hand, the overall costs must be kept to a minimum.

An important key to success in supply chain management is the optimization of inventories, because stock surplus quantities result in an increase in costs and lower profit margins, while inventory bottlenecks cause problems in production and poor service levels. Warehouse stocks are subject to different influencing factors. This book describes these factors and what you can do to efficiently counteract them.Inventory Causes Costs

Decisions made regarding inventory management can have a direct influence on the success of a company. Until a few years ago, it was generally assumed that a high volume of stocks guaranteed a successful future for the company. Today, increasing costs force companies to reduce their inventories and warehouse stocks. Therefore, the optimization of a company's inventory becomes an increasingly important tool for helping companies to save costs. The importance of those inventory costs becomes clearer when you look at the following financial statements:

Table 1 contains the financial statement of EPCOS AG, a manufacturer of passive construction elements. The inventory, which is summarized as "Net stocks," represents an amount of 205,123 Euro in 2003. This corresponds to 14.35% of the entire amount of the company's assets and is the second biggest cost item.

ASSETS (09/30/2003)	in €
Liquid assets	195,797
Receivables from goods and services, net	185,292
Net stocks	205,123
Accruals, deferrals, and other assets	38,884
Deferred income taxes	7,523
Current assets, total	**632,619**
Fixed assets, net	649,527
Intangible assets, net	39,940
Deferred income taxes 1	83,022
Other long-term assets	23,922
Total assets	**1,429,030**

Table 1 High Inventory Costs in the Financial Statement of EPCOS AG in 2003

In Table 2, the financial statement of Beiersdorf AG, a producer of consumer goods, shows that the stocks assume an even bigger portion of the total assets (672 m Euro), namely 19.89%.

ASSETS (12/31/03)	in m €
Intangible assets	97
Fixed assets	912
Financial assets	22
Total assets	**1,031**

Table 2 Financial Statement of Beiersdorf AG in 2003—672 Million Euro of Inventory Costs Represent 19.89% of the Total Assets

ASSETS (12/31/03)	in m €
Stocks	672
Receivables from goods and services	688
Other receivables and assets	94
Current-asset securities and liquid funds	842
Current assets	**2,296**
Deferred taxes	28
Accruals and deferrals	23
Total	**3,378**

Table 2 Financial Statement of Beiersdorf AG in 2003 — 672 Million Euro of Inventory Costs Represent 19.89% of the Total Assets (cont.)

These examples show that a company's inventory represents a considerable percentage of the total assets and the business volume of a company. This inventory-total assets ratio applies to some industries more than to others. For example, in mechanical engineering and plant construction, the long project runtimes and the increasing value of the products over time have a strong impact on a company's financials. In the chemical industry, the values are significantly smaller, which is due to the shorter project runtimes and the cheaper material components used; however, even here, you can save a lot of money by optimizing the inventory.

Inventory Cost Elements and Portions

A prerequisite for a long-term inventory optimization is the availability of precise information on the inventory costs in your company, and an efficient process design and ownership taken for the individual inventories.

Depending on the industry, the stockholding costs can vary considerably. Table 3 contains some general indicators for the different cost portions of stockholding costs including their value ranges (Hartmann 1999).

The entire amount of stockholding costs represents approximately 16–26% of the average valuated stock. The interest that accumulates on the working capital (fixed capital) is the biggest portion of the entire stockholding costs.

Cost Elements	Cost Portions in % (in relation to the average valuated stock)
Working capital interest	8–10
Loss, breakage	2–5
Inventory management	1–2
Depreciation	1, 5–2
Plant maintenance	1–2
Disposal	1–2
Taxes	1–2
Insurance	0, 5–1
Total stockholding costs	**16–26**

Table 3 Stockholding Costs and Their Cost Portions (Source: Hartmann)

Since the list in Table 3 does not contain the stockout costs, the entire amount will be even higher. You can find more information on this topic in Chapter 2, *Factors Influencing Inventory*.

Calculating a Cost Reduction

The key figure diagram from DuPont illustrates how an inventory reduction influences the return on investment (ROI) of a company. DuPont was the first company to implement this calculation method to determine the ROI. That was back in 1919. Since then, it has been improved several times, and today it is an integral part of the performance measurement system in every company.

The performance measurement system displays the relationships between the individual cost elements and the fixed and current assets. The inventories are part of the stocks, which, in turn, are part of the current assets.

In other words, if you can reduce the stock levels, you can also reduce the current assets. A decrease in current assets reduces the amount of total assets. Therefore, if the revenue doesn't change, the asset turnover will increase. The product resulting from the operating margin (profit-sales ratio) and Mthe asset turnover is the ROI. Therefore, in the above example, an inventory reduction of 10% results in an increase of the ROI by 3.6% for your company (see Figure 1, bottom line).

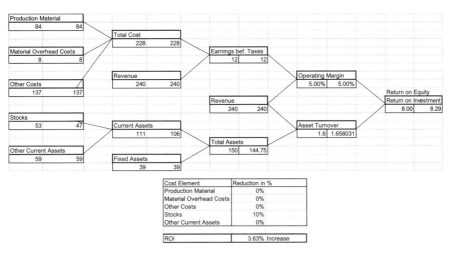

Figure 1 Example of an Inventory Reduction of 10% According to the Performance Measurement System Implemented by DuPont

The entire capital of a company consists of the shareholders' equity and the outside capital. While the shareholders' equity is already a part of the company's property, the outside capital must, for example, be borrowed from a bank. The total ROI consists of the return on equity and the return on investment. It is the goal of every company to maximize its profits. One important aspect here is to invest as little equity and outside capital as possible. Therefore, an inventory reduction will reduce the amount of equity and outside capital you have to invest. Consequently, the return on equity or investment increases, because the return on equity (return on investment) is the ratio between the operating profit and the equity (outside capital). In summary, we can make the following statements: Inventories are a major cost factor in the company. An inventory optimization can essentially help to reduce costs, which results in a considerable improvement of the company's performance indicators.

Inventory Management Using mySAP

Two SAP solutions that enable you to control your inventory management and optimize your inventory are mySAP Enterprise Resource Planning (mySAP ERP) and mySAP Supply Chain Management (mySAP SCM). mySAP ERP is the successor to the R/3 system and it controls all business-relevant accounting, HR, and logistics processes as a backbone system. mySAP SCM is a complementary solution that enables you to equip your company to meet the challenges of the supply chain management area.

In this book, you'll learn how to optimize mySAP ERP by modifying existing settings and leveraging the interaction between your specific processes and the SAP system. And you will learn how to do this without incurring any additional costs or investments.

You'll learn how to optimize mySAP SCM by leveraging the inventory management potentials that you can utilize using the SAP APO component.

Structure of this Book

Chapter 1 explains why inventories are necessary in a company, and it describes the different inventory concepts that are currently being used. The end of the chapter describes actual measures that you can implement to counteract uncertainties in the supply chain.

Chapter 2 describes the effect that individual areas—such as lot sizes, production planning, and demand planning—have on the inventory, and provides some optimization potentials. These potentials are described in further detail in the subsequent chapters, which mainly illustrate ways for you to optimize your inventories using mySAP ERP and mySAP SCM.

Chapter 3 focuses on the options available for analyzing inventories and describes the measures that you should undertake based on the analysis results.

Chapter 4 describes the inventory optimization options involved in demand planning processes. It explains how you can improve the exactness of your forecasts in your demand planning process.

Chapter 5 focuses on the material requirements planning strategies and their impact on the inventory, and it describes how you can optimize the material requirements planning (MRP) processes.

Chapter 6 focuses on how inventories impact the service level and security policy. Based on some real-life examples, this chapter explains how you can reduce safety stocks without compromising the service level.

Chapter 7 describes and evaluates the different lot-sizing procedures. In addition, it shows you the options available when working with lot sizes, and tells you what you should consider when selecting lot sizes to reduce inventories.

Chapter 8 describes the difference between the MRP planning logic and the simulation of a material and capacity requirements planning. It also defines the requirements of a good and feasible production plan, after which it describes the potentials that you can implement by using SAP Advanced Planner and Optimizer (SAP APO) for the production planning.

Chapter 9 describes the options available for implementing a practical inventory and logistics controlling process. In this chapter, you'll find concrete key figures and analysis options for your inventory management using mySAP ERP and mySAP SCM.

Chapter 10 describes a tried-and-tested inventory optimization process. It provides useful advice on what you can do to optimize the inventories and inventory management processes in your own company. The described process is designed in such a way that you can implement the inventory optimization by merely optimizing your processes, or by optimizing the mySAP ERP and mySAP SCM solutions.

Hamburg, Germany, May 2006
Marc Hoppe

A supply chain is prone to errors and involves many uncertainties. Inventories are a means of ensuring a certain degree of security and of minimizing the risk of stockout situations; however, you can do much more with your inventories. This chapter introduces you to different inventory concepts and to the options and risks involved.

1 Why Inventory Is Necessary

A supply chain involves the interaction of many different partners, such as customers, manufacturers, suppliers, suppliers of suppliers, and so on. In addition, the role of service providers such as shipping companies is constantly increasing due to the growing specialization of those providers in their core businesses. Globalization enables companies to extend their own supply chain and to establish distribution centers, storage locations, production centers, and sales offices throughout the world. The result of these growing supply chains is a significant increase in complexity, which means that the decisions a company has to make also become more complex and multi-faceted. You have to find answers to new questions: Where are inventories stored within the supply chain network? Which capacities must be extended in the long run? Which products does a company want to use to respond to different trends in different markets? Because of the many different influencing factors, the basis for making a decision is rarely free of uncertainties.

The more partners that are involved in the supply chain processes, the greater the potential for more errors and the more uncertainties exist. Here are just a few examples:

▶ Will the supplier deliver on time?

▶ Did the shipping agent calculate the best route?

▶ Will the subcontractor be able to ensure a production with a satisfactory quality?

▶ Is my own production running smoothly, or are there any important rush orders that require a change in plans?

▶ Will the customer order the notified quantity at the scheduled points in time?

These are only some of the many questions that you must consider, which make it apparent that you can never exactly forecast and proactively address all the uncertainties involved in the supply chain.

1.1   Different Inventory Concepts

How do you use the inventories in your company? Do you consider them as being integral to enabling you to act with a high degree of flexibility on the market, thereby ensuring that you keep your delivery promises, regardless of what it takes? Or do you regard them as cost drivers for your company so that you constantly try to reduce the inventory costs and optimize the profit margin? Before you introduce a strategic inventory management in your company, you should consider two basically different inventory concepts.

1.1.1   Inventories as Enabling Agents

Inventories enable smooth processes in your company and a sufficiently high degree of flexibility that is needed to react to exceptional situations. But inventories also generate costs.

They enable a smooth production, because you can absorb disruptions with other orders or inventories. This way you can avoid production standstills.

To ensure your ability to deliver at any time and to guarantee that your deliveries are always prompt, the stocks in your warehouse must be sufficient. Your ability to deliver depends directly on your safety stocks: The greater the demand for your ability to deliver, the greater the need for you to maintain an appropriate amount of safety stock.

Deviations of any kind—whether in production, procurement, or logistics—can be balanced by a sufficiently high quantity of buffer or safety stock.

Large buffer stocks in production enable cost-optimized manufacturing that doesn't require frequent set-up changes and can constantly utilize existing resources. This reduces the variable production costs.

The reasons for building up stocks are both logistical and economic.

Logistical Reasons for Building Up Stocks

The logistical reasons for building up stocks are mainly related to the stocks of *finished goods*:

▶ **The existence of finished goods stocks is a necessary prerequisite for the development of make-to-stock strategies.**
If you pursue a make-to-order strategy, you don't start production until a concrete sales order exists. In a customer-independent make-to-stock concept, you must produce the finished goods and hold them in stock so that, if necessary, the customer sales order can be processed much faster than in a make-to-order concept. Consequently, you need to have a finished goods stock.

▶ **Without finished goods stocks, you cannot implement a consistent utilization of your resources in your rough-cut capacity planning.**
To utilize production capacities as consistently as possible, you must carefully plan the production process far ahead. For this purpose, it may be necessary to build up buffer stocks so that you can compensate short-term fluctuations in sales without encountering any problems.

▶ **Finished goods stocks reduce costs because they prompt a separation of market and production.**
Market fluctuations can result in suboptimal order quantities and in fluctuations regarding the utilization of production resources. To stay independent of those market fluctuations and to implement optimal setups for ideal production schedules, as well as to procure quantities from your suppliers that are optimized for your specific lot sizes, you may have to build up stocks that enable you to reduce costs in other areas of the supply chain.

▶ **Finished goods stocks make products presentable.**
Sometimes it can be an advantage if you're able to present a product to the customer before you receive the purchase order. For this purpose, you need finished goods stocks. The quantity of the stocks then depends on the customer's quality requirements.

The logistical reasons for building up stocks are also related to the stocks of *semifinished goods*:

▶ **Semifinished goods stocks are required for implementing a process-oriented production.**
Keeping semifinished goods stocks can be mandatory in the process manufacturing area. The reason for this is that sometimes wait times must be observed due to the processes used (for example, to cool goods) so that buffer stocks become necessary.

▶ **Semifinished goods stocks enable a separation of production stages.**
To ensure a smooth production across all production stages and to compensate short-term disruptions, it may be necessary to keep buffer stocks at specific intermediate stages.

▶ **Semifinished goods stocks increase planning flexibility and reduce planning efforts.**
If you keep buffer stocks, you can increase your planning flexibility, particularly with regard to short-term disruptions.

▶ **The transport of bigger lots increases stocks and can also reduce logistics and production costs.**
If the transport costs represent a large portion of the entire supply-chain costs, it may be useful to produce stocks for the warehouse to optimize the transport and transport costs that will follow at a later stage. In this case, you should ensure that the trucks or other transport units you use are fully loaded.

Other logistical reasons for building up stocks include the stocks of *raw materials and components.*

▶ **Safety stocks ensure that goods can be ordered and delivered at any time.**
Your suppliers can also experience bottlenecks, or they may have fixed delivery times due to cost reasons. Nevertheless, short-term changes to your production process can cause changes in the requirements dates or quantities for raw materials. For this reason, you should have safety stocks that enable you to absorb those fluctuations.

▶ **Stocks enable volume discounts in purchasing.**
Although large orders cause an increase in raw materials stocks, they can result in volume discounts or decreased shipping and handling costs so that the overall costs are reduced despite the increase in stocks.

Monetary Reasons for Building Up Stocks

Building up stocks can also result in cost reductions. The following sections provide an overview of the financial benefits:

▶ **Large quantities reduce ordering costs.**
Each individual order of raw materials from a supplier generates costs for order processing, delivery, accounting, and the physical storage of the materials in your own warehouse. The same applies to production orders in your own company. Those production orders generate costs for order processing and the new production setup (setup costs). The bigger the

scope of an individual production order, the higher the increase in stocks and the lower the number of reissues of an order so that the overall annual order reissue costs are reduced. In other words: Bigger lot sizes in production orders reduce the setup costs, whereas small lots increase the setup costs.

► **Inventories reduce stockout costs.**
The stockout costs can be divided into three areas:

   ► *Reduced revenues:* For finished products, these are mainly lost profits due to sales that haven't taken place due to stockouts, or the customer not having purchased the products because the delivery date was exceeded. The reduced revenues can also include sales deductions that occur when a customer demands a price reduction because of poor product quality or a late delivery.

   ► *Lost contribution margins:* A loss in revenues due to a non-adherence to agreed-on delivery dates means that the product costs, which have already been generated, cannot be compensated. A non-delivery or poor delivery can also result in opportunity costs due to unsatisfied customers or spillover effects on other customers.

   ► *Additional stockout costs:* If raw materials are missing, the resulting production disruptions generate costs, lead to unsatisfied customers, and even to a loss in sales orders. The outcome can be additional costs in logistics due to rush deliveries, or increased costs in production because of short-term changes to the production program, which require non-optimal set-up changes. Moreover, additional costs might be generated on the suppliers' side due to rush deliveries of new raw materials. Contractual penalties and the payment of damages are also possible and part of the additional stockout costs.

► **Stocks reduce acquisition cost.**
The purchase of large quantities of raw materials reduces the portion of each individual part in the fixed ordering costs. With regard to your own production, it is the reduction of changeover costs that results from the increased lot sizes.

► **Inventories minimize the costs of quality losses in startup phases.**
During the startup phase of productions, the risk of using defect parts is higher than in tried-and-tested processes. Bigger production lots result in a substantial reduction of scrap figures and therefore in reduced costs.

1.1.2   Inventories as Concealers of Weak Processes

Contrary to the concept of advantageous inventories, you can also maintain that inventories, while they provide safety, can also conceal suboptimal processes in your company. In addition, if you reduce your inventories, you can invest your fixed capital in something more lucrative to maximize your profits.

A sufficient quantity of inventories enable a smooth flow of the supply chain; however, the downside of this is that the weaknesses of sensitive processes, which haven't yet been entirely reasoned, are hidden. Small quantities of inventory cause companies to constantly optimize their processes. Weak processes can be more easily identified if the inventory optimum has been reached.

For example, if a production process involves multiple stages and there are no buffer stocks available, the production process can quickly run into problems due to insufficiently coordinated capacities, so that suddenly the actual costs are higher than the target costs. Here, too, a minimal inventory requires an optimal coordination of the individual production steps.

A loss in quality, for example, in manufacturing, generally results in scrap. This can be neglected when you store a high quantity of inventories. However, if your stocks are not that high, too much scrap can result in production delays. In any case, it increases the production costs, which means you will soon realize which of the production processes need optimization.

A high quantity of inventories means that the supply chain is very flexible. Low quantities, on the other hand, demonstrate clearly where this flexibility is actually missing.

You can rapidly improve your ability to deliver by maintaining high inventories. But by increasing your inventories, you also increase the overall costs, which means that you pay a high price to ensure customer satisfaction. Low inventories, on the other hand, clearly show you the products for which your ability to deliver is insufficient. With low inventories, it is easier to examine the supply chain processes and thereby ensure a long-term deliverability based on improved processes instead of simply an increase in inventory.

Logistical Reasons for Not Building Up Stocks

The following sections describe the logistical reasons for not building up stocks:

▶ **The supplier is made responsible for inventory management.**
In today's business, customers increasingly require the suppliers to take on the inventory management responsibility. In this way, they can reduce their own inventories and improve their service level. The suppliers, in turn, benefit from this added responsibility by increasing their revenues with specific customers, which enables them to reduce their production costs.

▶ **Smaller lots reduce the replenishment lead times.**
Customers increasingly tend to require small lots and therefore shorter replenishment lead times. As a rule, smaller lots lead to inventory decreases; however, in order to keep a constant level of supply and customer satisfaction, goods must be ordered and delivered more frequently. Companies sometimes tolerate higher transport costs in these circumstances, because the overall amount of cost savings is even higher.

▶ **The willingness to tolerate stockouts decreases. Stockouts become visible with a low inventory.**
Stockouts or bad quality of the goods delivered have always accounted for bad supplier ratings; however, today the willingness to accept stockouts or a poor quality—which often results in the termination of relationships between customers and their suppliers—is almost nonexistent. Since customer tolerance for poor quality has declined, you should no longer include stockouts in your initial calculations. The impact of stockouts and poor quality become particularly obvious when you keep your inventory as low as possible. This enables you to take corrective actions much more rapidly.

▶ **Low inventories increase your flexibility regarding changes in the market.**
Markets and therefore the requirements change swiftly. Due to the increase of the changing market influences, you must ensure a high degree of flexibility to respond quickly to the changes. With unforeseen changes of requirements, it can happen that products, which used to be sold in high quantities in the past, are no longer demanded to the same extent today, for example, because of technical innovations. The inventories that remain in the warehouse must often be sold at very low prices, or even be scrapped. This is another reason for optimizing your inventories.

Monetary Reasons for Not Building Up Stocks

On the financial side, inventories generate many costs, which justify why you should reduce rather than increase your inventory:

▶ **Costs generated by a capital tie-up**
Inventories tie up capital. The interest charges generated by this capital tie-up and the lost interest from profits represent a loss for the company (see also Table 1.1 in the *Introduction* chapter regarding the high inventory costs).

▶ **Costs generated by maintaining inventories**
The inventory maintenance costs—for example, for air conditioning, lighting, plant maintenance, renting additional warehouse space, logistics, taxes, insurance, and so on—can be restricted by reducing the inventories.

▶ **Costs generated by a decrease in flexibility**
High work-in-progress inventories block the production progress. If the average volume of inventories increases, the average lead time increases as well while the ability to react quickly to changes in the customer demand will decrease.

▶ **Costs generated by the production coordination**
High work-in-progress invetories require an extensive control process, for example, because of the necessity to accelerate individual orders when dealing with record chasers.

▶ **Costs generated by a capacity tie-up**
A production that is not tailored to the actual requirements ties up production capacities that may be needed for products, which must be produced instead, and which leads to delayed deliveries. Therefore, the company must also bear the opportunity costs generated by materials that are not used in production.

▶ **Costs generated by a reduced ROI**
In terms of accounting, inventories are part of the current assets in the financial statement and therefore have a direct impact on the ROI. The ratio between the profit and the invested capital worsens if the inventory increases. A reduced ROI increases the financial costs due to increased interest rates and a decreasing stock price.

▶ **Costs generated by process errors with big lots**
Big production lots result in high finished goods stocks. Non-recognized process errors can affect the quality of all finished parts. The effects become more apparent if you deal with big lot sizes.

▶ **Costs generated by production problems**
Higher work-in-progress inventories conceal problems within the production process. Sensitive processes, such as machine malfunctions, bad quality, or problems related to the material flow, are easily concealed.

So far, we've described many reasons and influencing factors that are for or
against inventories. Therefore, it's obvious that there is not one universally
valid inventory strategy. On the contrary, inventories must be accurately
analyzed in the context of their relationship to a specific company and product in order to find their optimization potentials. Ultimately, you may conclude that keeping a high stock of a specific product and virtually no stock of
another product may make sense. Finding the right individual strategy is the
challenge you have to face.

1.1.3 Inventory as an Adjusting Screw

Figure 1.1 illustrates the impact of inventory changes. The ship represents
the company; the water represents the inventory.

The figure shows what happens if you turn the inventory screw, in other
words, the water level, up or down, depending on whether you have to solve
short-term problems (by raising the water level), or want to achieve long-
term improvements (by lowering the water level).

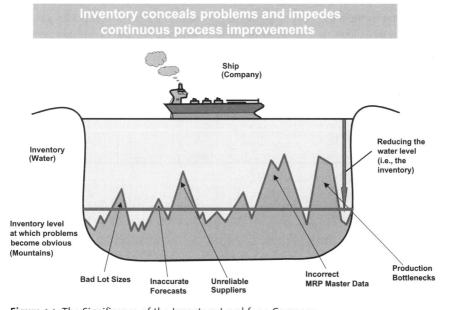

Figure 1.1 The Significance of the Inventory Level for a Company

For this reason, you should never reduce your inventory radically as this can lead to information and material flow problems, causing the ship to run aground. That situation would result in a lot of effort and you would have no time to get a hold of the rudder and trigger strategic countermeasures. So, make sure you turn this screw with great care and solve the problems that occur one by one before they turn into an emergency situation. After all, you are looking for a long-term solution to the inventory and process problems. You should implement an inventory management that covers the entire supply chain to avoid the creation of individual inventory optimums for each functional area. This is the only way to achieve an overall optimum for your company.

You can only counteract the pressure of a permanent cost reduction by constantly analyzing your inventories. ABC and XYZ analyses are useful analysis tools that enable you to permanently monitor your inventories and instigate cost-reduction measures. In this context, it is important that the analyses be carried out even at the most detailed level, that is, at the level of individual materials, because the aggregated view cannot reveal the actual problems.

1.2   Uncertainties in the Supply Chain

Big warehouses generate high costs. A considerable portion of those costs is determined by the safety stock. Safety stock is necessary to ensure a certain customer service level. The volume of the safety stock, which holds a significant potential for cost reduction, is determined by uncertainties. Consequently, the company should consider reducing the uncertainties. According to Wagner (2000), there are basically two sources of uncertainties in the supply chain:

▸ Process uncertainty (e.g., unreliable production processes, fluctuating lead times, and so on)

▸ Demand uncertainty (e.g., the discrepancy between the planned demand and the actual demand)

Because Wagner describes only the demand side (and not the supply side), this differentiation is somewhat imprecise. For this reason, we'll separate the uncertainties according to their relevance to the demand and supply sides, and in this way cover the entire supply chain. The process uncertainties are relevant to the supply side (fluctuating lead times, as described by Wagner), but also to the demand side (unreliable demand planning processes, which is contrary to Wagner's conception of demand uncertainty).

1.2.1 Demand-Side Uncertainties

Consumption Variances

Consumption variances describe why the actual demand per period deviates from the planned demand. The reasons for this deviation can be new trends, the introduction of new products, or simply a change in the customer's behavior. The primary goal of the safety stock is to ensure that the variances in consumption or replenishment lead times don't cause an undersupply of the distribution department or downstream production areas with the material in question.

The goal of demand planning is to enable you to forecast the demand as accurately as possible. To do that, mathematical forecast models are used. Unfortunately, these models can provide only an approximation of the actual demand. A degree of uncertainty still remains regarding whether the customer will actually purchase the forecast or ordered products, and if so, when this purchase will occur. The goal of the forecast is to keep the deviation as small as possible, which is why the accuracy of the forecast is so critical. Deviations in forecasted demands are also regarded as consumption variances, because the inaccurate forecasts result in a planned demand that is either too high or too low.

1.2.2 Supply-Side Uncertainties

Delivery Date Variances

Differences can occur between the planned replenishment lead time (RLT) and the RLT that was actually needed for procuring external goods. These differences in the replenishment lead times are referred to as *delivery date variances*. There are numerous reasons for those variances, which must be subdivided into the following two scenarios: *Orders from external suppliers* and *Internal orders*. While you can forecast the RLT for internal orders with relative precision, the uncertainties for external supplies will increase in accordance with the growing complexity of the logistic processes.

Other differences can occur for in-house produced goods between the planned lead time and production quantity, and the actual values. In other words, the planned lead time does not correspond to the actual lead time. These differences are also referred to as delivery date variances with the only difference being that they refer to the delivery dates in production. There can be various reasons for the fluctuations, for example, a machine can fail or someone in personnel becomes ill, or urgent rush orders disturb the production plan.

If the production volume is reduced during certain periods of the year, for example, during the summer vacations, or if the entire production is discontinued, the goods must be produced in advance; otherwise, the customers cannot be sufficiently supplied. This situation leads to a buildup of inventory before the summer break begins. We could observe such a high volume of advance production in the consumer goods industry before the turn of the century, as many companies feared losing their ability to deliver due to Y2K problems with their computers. Such situations are planned delivery date variances that will be compensated by specific safety stocks.

Delivery Quantity Variances

Variances can be caused by incomplete or partly incorrect delivery quantities. These quantity variances result in a deviation of the actual inventory volume once the orders have been received and posted in the warehouse. The deviations are referred to as *delivery quantity variances*.

To fully utilize the production resources and to avoid expensive and time-consuming machine changes, a set-up optimization is often carried out. For this purpose, the lots must have a certain size, which may result in a postponement of other sales orders. To avoid such a situation, smaller lots are often used. This, however, causes many set-up changes and an increase in the amount of scrap. The term "scrap" describes a subset of a production order that has been produced in bad quality and cannot be sold. A particularly large amount of scrap may indicate that the sales order cannot be fulfilled to its full extent, because it is impossible to deliver the entire quantity that has been ordered. This situation is referred to as delivery quantity variances in production.

Price Variances

Discounts granted by the supplier or price changes can result in a situation whereby a customer suddenly demands larger quantities of goods, or a supplier cannot deliver because other customers have unexpectedly ordered larger quantities as well. In addition, the price changes affect the inventory values, which means that the *price variances* predominantly influence the inventory value.

Inventory Variances

Inventory variances are another factor that you must consider. Inventory variances represent the differences between the book value and the actual existing inventory. These differences can result in premature or late orders of material. For example, if the actual inventory in the warehouse were higher than what is shown in the books, the resulting order would be premature.

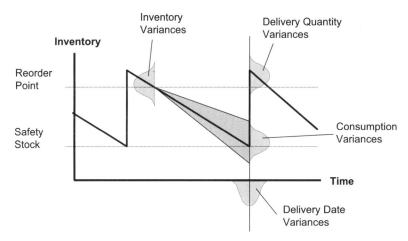

Figure 1.2 Potential Supply-Side VarianTces and Their Effects (According to Fraunhofer Institut für Rationalisierung—FIR)

Figure 1.2 provides an overview of the different types of variances. The variance categories, *inventory variances*, *delivery date variances*, *delivery quantity variances*, and *consumption variances*, are represented by the inventory sawtooth curve. The statistical probability regarding whether the variance is positive or negative (i.e., too early or too late, too big or too small) is illustrated according to the Gaussian distribution. The actual statistical distribution can—without a doubt—differ from this one. For this reason, companies should determine their own statistical distribution on a regular basis.

1.3   How to Deal With Uncertainties

There are various ways to counteract the aforementioned uncertainties; you can either resort to using individual measures or a set of combined measures. You can take action on the demand side or on the supply side. If you consider the current situation in your company, you'll soon find yourself employing the measures described in the next section. Because you're already probably responding to the uncertainties in your supply chain, in addition to needing a list of the various countermeasures, you'll also need to know where you can find optimization potentials in your company for processes and inventories. Here, we'll supply you with both.

1.3.1 Demand-Side Optimization Potentials

To counteract the uncertainties on the demand side, you must always slightly overestimate the actual *customer requirement*. This leads to slightly higher requirements in your calculation, which results in an inventory buildup in the form of safety stocks. Safety stocks also reflect an overestimated customer requirement. The difficulty here lies in being able to forecast the customer requirement as accurately as possible so you can keep the inventory buildup as low as possible. This results in the following inventory optimization potentials:

▸ **Improving the forecast accuracy**
By improving the forecast accuracy, for example, by optimizing your demand planning process, you can minimize the delta between planned and actual requirements.

▸ **Reducing the number of forecast errors**
By improving the selection of mathematical forecasting methods and the combination of the demand planner's experience with mathematical forecasting methods, you can reduce the number of forecast errors and thus improve the forecast accuracy.

▸ **Streamlining the range of goods**
By streamlining your range of goods, you can focus your demand planning process on fewer different products and thereby improve your planning accuracy by dedicating more time to each product in this process.

▸ **Collaborative planning, forecasting, and replenishment (CPFR, VMI)**
A demand planning in collaboration with your customers usually results in a more accurate forecast of the requirements, because, by doing so, you can minimize the bullwhip effect. In other words, your customer can either actively participate in the planning process (CPFR), or provide the forecast as a data file to you, while you are responsible for supplying the customer with goods (vendor-managed inventory, VMI).

▸ **Shortening the planning cycles**
By shortening the planning cycles (e.g., weekly instead of monthly plannings), you can reduce the uncertainties in the replenishment process and therefore react faster to demand fluctuations.

1.3.2 Supply-Side Optimization Potentials

To compensate for uncertainties on the supply side (purchasing or material requirements planning), you must slightly overestimate the *procurement lead times* or the *procurement quantities*. The replenishment lead times of suppliers and the transport times are rounded up or complemented with a little buffer. You also need to add some leeway to the safety ranges or safety stocks in your planning. For one-time stockout situations, that is, in situations where you are unable to deliver, your material requirements planning (MRP) controllers must slightly increase the safety stocks. In this way, you don't eliminate weaknesses in your process; instead, you compensate for them with higher safety stocks. This results in the following inventory optimization potentials:

▶ **Reducing the safety stocks**
You must define safety stocks for each individual material. It is absolutely necessary that you find the cause of a stockout. Your safety stocks should only compensate for uncertainties that you have not caused. You should, of course, avoid using all stockouts in the future.

▶ **Reducing the transport times**
Transport times can be optimized via route optimizations, or by using a different number of shipping companies.

▶ **Improving the distribution resource planning**
The cross-plant delivery between production plants and distribution centers and off-premises warehouses must be optimized within the company network.

▶ **Reducing the replenishment lead time**
The replenishment lead times of your suppliers should be maintained as accurately as possible. Don't forget to include this factor in your plannings.

▶ **Increasing the MRP quality in materials management**
Your MRP controllers should be supported as much as possible. This requires a perfected MRP process, an optimizing MRP tool, and clearly defined areas of responsibility. If you select and use the right analysis processes (e.g., ABC and XYZ analyses), your MRP controller should get the best possible support.

▶ **Improving the vendor performance**
You should be able to include the capacities of your vendors in your plannings, as well as the ability to flexibly select your vendors.

▶ **Supplier-managed inventory (SMI)**
Planning the inventory in collaboration with your supplier, and the resulting inventory and storage responsibility of your supplier, can lead to a substantial improvement of the procurement process since exceptional situations are much less likely to occur.

▶ **Optimal lot-size creation**
The use of optimized lot-sizing procedures such as the Groff reorder procedure (see Section 7.4.5) enables you to reduce your lot sizes and therefore your inventory.

▶ **Shortening the MRP cycles**
By implementing a real-time MRP, you can identify the effects of changes immediately, and then proactively respond to them. This ensures transparency. Furthermore, you no longer have to wait for the result of the MRP run that is carried out during the night. You don't lose any time and can quickly respond to your customers' requests or fix bottlenecks.

Underestimating the *production output* is another way of minimizing uncertainties on the supply side. For this purpose, the planned working times for production orders contain a little buffer, and the scrap factors are slightly increased in the production process. This results in the following inventory optimization potentials:

▶ **Reducing the lead time**
By reducing the production lead times, you can reduce buffer stocks and increase your ability to deliver.

▶ **Reducing the number of setup changes**
Production plans with optimized setups result in higher output figures, which releases capacities that can be utilized for other requirements.

▶ **Increasing production flexibility and transparency**
An increased transparency of the production process enables you to react faster and with more flexibility to exceptional situations without compromising important sales orders.

▶ **Reducing buffer stocks**
You can reduce your buffer stocks by implementing a better coordination across all production levels, thereby eliminating long wait times for orders at higher production levels and reducing the overall lead time.

▶ **Reducing the number of product variants**
The reduction of the number of product variants enables an improved utilization of production capacities because you can produce bigger lots. The

production transparency increases, because you can focus on a smaller number of products.

1.3.3 Comprehensive Optimization Measures

You can also take comprehensive measures that affect the entire company and therefore include both the demand and the supply side:

▶ **Integrating inventory management into the company strategy and organization**
To fully utilize existing inventory potentials, you must implement clear inventory responsibilities in your company. You can achieve this by implementing a centralized inventory managent process, for example. It is essential that clearly defined areas of responsibility exist and that the inventory management process plays a major role in the strategic plannings of your company.

▶ **Integrating cross-system processes**
In complex system landscapes, you can utilize inventory optimization potentials by integrating cross-system processes to increase transparency and flexibility. For example, if your inventory is distributed to several different systems, you should use a central inventory system to make clear statements about your ability to deliver and the delivery reliability at any given time.

▶ **Increasing the transparency in the supply chain**
A global supply-chain transparency, for example, a tracking-and-tracing system, keeps you informed at any time on the current whereabouts and condition of your inventories. For example, SAP's Supply Chain Event Manager (SCEM) enables you to make real-time status requests to determine whether your goods are currently caught in a traffic jam and consequently won't be delivered on time, or if you have to send a substitute delivery via an alternative route to your customer.

▶ **Coordinated objectives for all organizational areas**
Each individual organizational area in a company often follows its own financial goals and objectives, regardless of how this impacts integrational aspects to other areas within the same company. Each area tries to ensure its own security, instead of ensuring the safety of the company as a whole. For example, the sales and distribution department seeks to achieve its goals (high customer satisfaction and high revenues, which can both be achieved by a high delivery capability), whereas the production department tries to keep the production costs as low as possible, which is

reflected in an equal utilization of resources and the production of large quantities of as few different products as possible. The purchasing department, in turn, tries to purchase the quantities to be procured in big lots to keep the prices as low as possible.

The coordination of individual objectives for these company areas usually results in a higher inventory sensitivity and an improved understanding of business processes across the entire company. It is also important to make the each of the many different inventory producers in the company bear the consequences of inventory shortages or surpluses. Each producer of inventory should feel the consequences of his or her own actions so that a certain sensitivity regarding inventory-related decisions can be established in the company. For this purpose, you would normally have to implement a reporting process that is geared towards inventory management and reflects the objectives of your company. Moreover, it is essential that all company areas clearly define consistent objectives that support intelligent inventory management processes across the entire company.

There's no doubt about it—inventory is important. But too much of it is counterproductive. Yet, what is the best way to manage inventories? This chapter provides a brief overview of the five instruments that you can use to manage and optimize your inventory—demand planning, material requirements planning (MRP), service level and safety stocks, lot sizes, and production.

2 Factors Influencing Inventory

Today's supply chain networks can cross both organizational and geographical boundaries. This forces companies to control what cannot be controlled. The future of Supply Chain Management (SCM) depends primarily on the ability to quickly react to supply and demand changes and important events in the supply chain on a global basis. The faster a supply chain network can adapt to such events, the higher the added value and the more likely it is to influence the inventory. Inventory optimization is the key to keeping the profitability of a company at a constant level and to increasing the company's competitiveness.

2.1 Five Instruments

Supply chain planning is influenced by a number of factors that cannot be forecast with absolute certainty. For example, when forecasting customer requirements, there is generally an uncertainty regarding the quantity and the exact selling date. In addition, disturbances and fluctuations in production cause deviations in the planned replenishment lead time. For this reason, safety stocks are used to secure the supply chain against uncertain influences and the optimization potentials described in Chapter 1, *Why Inventory is Necessary.*

Colgate Palmolive was able to increase its forecast accuracy up to 98%, to reduce its inventory by 13%, and to improve its cash flow by 13% by using mySAP Supply Chain Management (mySAP SCM). Similarly, a manufacturer of handheld computers, who had implemented a new SCM solution, managed to reduce the planning cycles by 50%, to increase the inventory turnover from six to ten times, and to reduce the delivery stocks by 32%. In that case, however, an entire range of processes had to be improved, namely the demand and requirements forecasts, inventory management, production planning, and order processing. All these changes were based on the goal of increasing the company's competitiveness and on shortening the delivery times. In the highly competitive handheld market, factors such as price, availability, and on-time delivery have a direct influence on a company's growth and profitability.

A research carried out by Gartner Group recently predicted that 90% of today's leading enterprises that have no SCM strategy will lose their preferred vendor status in the future.

In the following sections, we'll take a closer look at the instruments that enable us to optimize our inventories.

2.1.1   Demand Planning

The first instrument we'll consider is demand planning. Demand planning and forecasting are inevitable elements in logistics and the comprehensive planning process for the entire company. They are used to create rough realistic and consistent production plans based on the potential sales volume and the available budget. A good demand planning leads to a reliable characteristics-based forecasting, which, in turn, is the basis for all subsequent processes. The results derived from demand planning determine the production and financial resources. The annual plan and the regular revision of the target plans largely depend on the level of accuracy of sales forecasts and on an efficient production planning.

When planning future sales and production, the planner should not only rely on forecasts. Instead, she must include her knowledge of future market trends, planned advertising campaigns, and changes to specific product groups in the planning.

If the forecast sales volumes are smaller than the customer demand, the previously produced stocks will be completely reduced; furthermore, there will be a need to resort to the safety stock. If the delta between the forecast of sales and the actual customer demand is too big, it can cause stockouts. Customers are lost if they turn permanently to the competition. In addition to a loss of sales, a loss of image for the company and market shares can also result.

If demand planning is higher than the actual customer demand, surplus inventories can result, which may have to be scrapped or written off. This leads to a lower profit margin and a reduced profitability.

Ultimately, it is the accuracy of the forecast that determines the volume of the safety stock. If the forecast deviates substantially from the actual demand values, the safety stock is correspondingly high or low respectively. Finally, the planner determines the primary requirements on the basis of the production quantities and forwards the data to material requirements planning. Chapter 4, *Demand Planning and Forecasting*, provides further detailed information on using demand planning as an instrument for optimizing the inventory.

2.1.2 Material Requirements Planning (MRP)

The second instrument, material requirements planning (MRP), is used to create and manage the production programs for finished as well as unfinished products. For this purpose, customer orders and forecasts are needed. Moreover, all other components of the entire product structure are planned—down to the lowest level. This is done on the basis of the secondary requirements, which must be identified by MRP.

Frequently, specific finished products, sub-assemblies, or raw materials must be produced or procured in advance to ensure short delivery times when customer sales orders come in. This advance planning, which at first is not based on any sales order, is based on the planned independent requirements that are offset against incoming customer sales orders at a later stage. This type of planning triggers the procurement of raw materials and the production of sub-assemblies or final products that will be stored in the warehouse.

MRP monitors inventories and determines the material that will be needed at a specific quantity on a certain date. In addition, MRP automatically generates the procurement proposals necessary for this process. In MRP, a nct requirements calculation is automatically carried out in which the available warehouse stock or the planned stock receipts from purchasing or production are compared with the primary requirements. For a material shortage— if the available inventory is smaller than the required quantity—the system automatically generates a procurement proposal. Then, MRP initiates make-or-buy decisions. If dates or quantities change, the planned orders must be automatically adjusted in the MRP process. MRP must be able to quickly adjust procurement and production to meet new requirement situations. Choosing the right lot sizes is another task handled by MRP.

MRP is the interface between demand planning in sales and distribution and production planning in production. If demand planning is too high, MRP has to compensate for the discrepancy by selecting the best safety stock level, the correct range calculations, the best delivery rhythm, and optimal lot sizes so that the optimal quantity can be produced at minimum production costs.

This means that MRP is an important adjustment screw for optimizing inventory, because it must find the optimum between the different inventory goals of sales and distribution (high service level = high inventories) and production (short lead times = low inventories).

MRP's influence on the operational result of a company can be expressed as a direct, an indirect, and a non-quantifiable success potential:

The *directly quantifiable potential* results from the portion of material costs in sales or in the prime costs. This cost pool can be influenced by choosing the optimal lot size, or the level of the optimal safety stock.

An *indirectly quantifiable potential* represents, for example, the creation of supplier relationships, the reduction of overall procurement costs, or the inclusion of inventories in the financial report.

The *non-quantifiable success potential* becomes manifest in the way the company is viewed by its customers on the basis of a high ability to deliver and delivery reliability.

Chapter 5, *Material Requirements Planning*, provides further details on the MRP strategies and parameters you can use to optimize your inventory.

2.1.3   Service Level and Safety Stocks

The decision of a company to provide a comprehensive service level is a strategic one. It must be geared towards other objectives such as cost minimization and capacity utilization. This means that compromises must be found and priorities set. To achieve a high service level, you may have to increase your warehouse stocks so that you can satisfy the demand with finished products from your stocks. Moreover, production must be able to start processing an order when it is first released, while distribution must be able to deliver on time. However, keeping warehouse stocks generates stockholding costs and therefore counteracts the objective of minimizing cost.

The decision to provide a high service level always requires a definition of subgoals that the company wants to pursue. Reliability can be ensured by creating intermediate storage facilities and final product storage facilities. In addition, buffers that you include in production planning ensure that the capacities can produce the right product at the right time in accordance with the planning. This, however, causes longer wait times and larger storage quantities, which is why you must use the service level value that causes customers to accept higher prices and long-term commitments against the actual costs. Unfortunately, not many companies do that.

If, on the other hand, the company pursues its goal of providing a high delivery flexibility and speed, it must organize its business processes in such a way that the planning lead times are as short as possible, especially regarding order acceptance, planning, and production. In that case, the machine utilization buffers are kept small in to shorten the order-processing timeframe and to guarantee a fast delivery and shorter turnaround times for the customer. Here, the cost risk is rooted in the downtime costs which, for example, occur when required materials are not delivered on time. Moreover, the company must bear additional costs that can hardly be measured when machine failures or disruptions result in delayed productions and deliveries so that confirmed delivery dates cannot be adhered to.

The costs generated by an increase of the service level must be considered on the basis of profitability aspects. When comparing the costs with the revenues, which have been generated by the service level, the services must far outweigh the costs; otherwise, the business objective of profit maximization and the long-term existence of the company would be at risk. Contrary to the objective of cost optimization, however, the service level orientation enables the company to better respond to market requirements, which, after all, is the basis for a complete success. Depending on the focus of a company, the direction towards a service level increase requires a different orientation and processing of the business processes. In this context, striving for speed and flexibility is as important as concentrating on the readiness to deliver, as well as the delivery time and reliability.

An organization can achieve a readiness to deliver of 99% within a maximum of 48 hours only if it permanently maps peak demands in its inventories; however, since those peaks often occur only sporadically, high inventories must be maintained throughout the entire year. Consequently, the company faces increased direct and indirect costs such as high depreciations and accumulated depreciations for short product lifecycles.

So, what is the optimal service level that satisfies your customers and compensates for the costs? How can the service level be measured and which processes support an optimal service level? These and other questions are addressed in great detail in Chapter 6, *Service Level and Safety Stocks*.

2.1.4 Lot Sizes

One of the primary goals of MRP is the economic supply of external customers and internal customers, that is, production. Here, MRP must optimize the material, order processing, and stockholding costs. Material costs depend on the order quantities and can be determined on the basis of the net landed costs. The order-processing costs depend on the specific operations. They can be described as proportional staff and material costs for procurement, receiving inspection, invoice verification, and data processing. Stockholding costs depend on stockkeeping and can be determined on the basis of the delivered price, the interest rate for stockkeeping, and the inventory cost rate. As a result of the order calculation, you obtain the optimal or cost-effective lot size as a production requirement, which represents the initial value for purchasing and production.

For example, if you want to increase your delivery flexibility, you must produce smaller lots, which, in turn, entails a reduced capacity utilization due to longer machine downtimes that are caused by a higher number of set-up processes. At the same time, the set-up and unit costs go up, as well as the procurement costs in purchasing. Moreover, smaller lots reduce the costs and procurement costs in purchasing. They also reduce the procurement quantities, which results in smaller discounts and rebates; whereas the cost pool for the procurement process remains unchanged and acts as a cost driver due to the shorter replenishment cycles.

Chapter 7, *Lot Sizes*, describes how you can influence your inventories by selecting the right lot-sizing procedures.

2.1.5 Production

The logistics of production is a central functional area within the entire supply chain. The largest portion of the entire added value of a manufacturing company is generated within production logistics. All upstream processes, such as procurement, but also all the downstream processes, like distribution, are linked to production. Products are produced and refined within production. The value creation within production logistics is what makes money. The essential goals of production are therefore short product lead times, low inventories, on-time deliveries, and a high degree of machine utilization and customer satisfaction.

Success factors that lead to a high degree of customer satisfaction and therefore a long-term relationship with a customer are therefore short delivery times and a high delivery reliability. Short delivery times can be achieved by short product lead times, high delivery reliability, low scrap rates, and a high degree of capacity utilization. But, short product lead times and a high degree of capacity utilization are contradictory objectives. The optimization of these goals is the focus of production planning and control. Production planning consists of all the essential planning tasks, such as the creation of master data, work scheduling, and the creation of a production program, as well as capacity leveling. Basically, production planning comprises all work that occurs prior to the actual production start. The production program determines the type and quantity of items to be produced. This applies to final products, semifinished products and subassemblies. The program is also used to define the most favorable production lots and procurement quantities. The production dates (planned dates) and the order sequence are defined in capacity scheduling.

Production control monitors and controls the actual production process. The task of production control is to ensure the supply of production with material components and raw materials, as well as the adherence to production dates. Changes at short notice also entail changes to the short-term production program. The changes to the production program lead to changes on the supply side: Orders must be canceled. Suppliers are asked to deliver later or earlier. Suddenly the lot sizes in procurement are no longer optimal. Rush deliveries must be triggered if a production standstill is imminent, because of an insufficient material supply. Not only does this increase the procurement costs, but the costs in production also increase as inefficient machine setup changes become necessary.

Inventory is supposed to avoid such firefighting and to balance those short-term changes. This means that the inventory level must be appropriate so that, on the one hand, stock surpluses are avoided, and on the other hand, process disturbances can be compensated.

To identify optimization potentials in production, the entire production process must be considered as a whole, both from the standpoint of production and costs. The following section summarizes the potential areas for optimization in production:

▶ **Shortening of product lead times**
  This leads to an increase in machine capacity, a reduction of inventories, shorter delivery times, and a higher customer satisfaction. Liquidity

increases due to the shorter delivery times because customers pay earlier. Because individual orders no longer occupy machines as long as they used to due to the shorter product lead times, a higher number of orders can be processed in production. This leads to increased revenues in a demand-driven market.

▶ **Improving unit costs**
A reduction of the unit costs can be achieved by a high degree of machine capacity utilization. A set-up optimization and a finite planning lead to a reduction of set-up costs and an optimization of the production lots. This increases the capacity utilization. In general, it also increases the variable unit costs; however, it also increases the marginal revenues as the fixed costs remain unchanged.

Chapter 8 describes the influences of *Production* on the inventory in greater detail and introduces options for using SAP in this context.

2.2 Controlling by Inventory Monitoring

Because the supply chain is very complex, all aspects of the supply chain that we have described so far only become clear by using the right controlling instruments. But many companies will find the "standard key figures" inappropriate. These figures often cannot be used for the organization or the objectives pursued in SCM, or they are simply not the right means of control.

One of the most common serious mistakes is the isolated use of logistics key figures. For example, if a company measures the professionalism of inventory management based only on the inventory turnover or range, the resulting picture will be blurred. Transport costs must also be considered; otherwise, management will see only the low inventories without noticing that the transport costs have risen and this negative effect will outweigh the benefits of the positive inventory effects.

You can only take the right action if various key figures are combined intelligently into key figure systems. Therefore, the key figures must be consistently defined and implemented across the entire company. Today, an appropriate key figure system enables a company to proactively identify and counteract problems. The description of a holistic key figure system would exceed the scope of this book; however, Chapter 9, *Inventory Controlling*, describes the most important key figures and their relevance to real-life production processes.

Before you can optimize your inventories, you must accurately ana-lyze them. This chapter describes how you can implement proven methods to segment your inventories so you can analyze their most important aspects.

3   Inventory Analysis

In the previous chapter, the instruments and potentials available to optimize and reduce inventory were described. Keeping this in mind, you should ensure that you take specific actions to optimize your inventory and that you implement these actions consistently. But, to determine which actions are the right ones for your company, you must first carry out a detailed analysis of your inventories. You can then use the results of the analysis as a basis for defining the appropriate inventory optimization measures. From hereon, a theme that runs throughout this book will be the basic analysis principles described in this chapter.

Note that you should try to avoid making the following mistake, which is unfortunately all too frequently made in many companies: Pressure exerted by top management to reduce the inventory can generally only lead to a short-term success. For medium-term success, the inventories usually return to the previous level that existed before the decreed inventory reduction. To ensure medium and long-term success, you should continuously use these analysis tools, and you should also use them as a basis for controlling your supply-chain processes.

The *ABC analysis* can be used as an inventory analysis instrument. It is a data classification tool. For inventory analyses, these classifications can represent material consumptions, goods movements, and material stocks. The materi-als are roughly divided into three classes (A, B, and C).

Then a detailed analysis can be carried out using an *XYZ analysis*. The XYZ analysis is a classic secondary analysis that is based on the ABC analysis. The XYZ analysis is used to analyze the weighting of individual units according to their consumption pattern. This means that a consumption fluctuation key figure is determined for each unit. Depending on how regularly a unit is con-sumed, it is assigned to one of the three classes, X, Y, or Z.

The combination of ABC and XYZ analyses represents the *ABC-XYZ matrix*. In that matrix, you can combine the results of the two analyses and thereby obtain important information on your materials and inventories that enables you to define appropriate measures for optimizing your inventory.

This chapter will describe the basic instruments of the ABC and XYZ analyses in more detail. Chapter 9, *Inventory Controlling*, provides a more detailed description of the available inventory analysis options.

3.1 Inventory Analysis Options

3.1.1 ABC Analysis

The ABC analysis is an organizational procedure that can be used to classify large data quantities. The data can represent material or processes. It is roughly divided into three classes (A, B, and C).

Pros and Cons of the ABC Analysis

The advantages of the ABC analysis are as follows:

▶ **Ease of use**
The ABC analysis can be easily used. Usually, the data already exists, and most IT systems provide standard ABC analyses. The separation into three classes can be carried out using the simplest calculating procedures.

▶ **Use of methods does not depend on analyzed objects**
You can use the ABC analysis not only for analyzing materials, but also for customer and vendor data. Moreover, you can examine individual process steps and cash flows using the ABC analysis.

▶ **Clear graphical presentation of the results**
The graphical presentation of the ABC analysis enables you to obtain a quick and clear overview of the analyzed data. You will be able to identify trends faster using a graphical presentation than you could using a tabular display.

There are also some disadvantages about the ABC analysis, which you shouldn't neglect when using it for inventory analysis purposes:

▶ **Very rough classification**
The separation into three classes (A, B, C) is very rough. Therefore, you should go into further detail after the first rough analysis and perhaps extend the separation to four or more classes. This may not always be nec-

essary. But it is advisable for a further subdivision of the C class (the Z class in the XYZ analysis), because that class typically contains particularly large data quantities.

▶ **Provision of consistent data**
One of the pitfalls in the ABC analysis is the provision of consistent data. This data is essential to determine the significance of an ABC analysis. If your data is consistent, the ABC analysis can help you obtain a lot of information on your product and customer structures; however, if the data is not consistent, the ABC analysis can be very confusing. You should therefore pay specific attention to the quality of your data. Note that even SAP does not provide some important consistency checks, which means that you have to check the consistency of your data by yourself.

Classification Into A, B, and C

The classification into the A, B, and C classes and their typical value and quantity percentages can be illustrated using the Lorenz curve (see Figure 3.1).

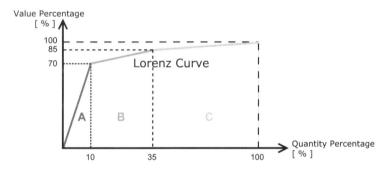

Figure 3.1 Classification into A, B, and C Classes Based on the Lorenz Curve

The quantity portions of materials in *Class A* are usually approximately 10%, while the value portion represents approximately 70%. This means that those materials are the most important ones and have the biggest potential for optimization. The quantity portion of materials in *Class B* is 25%, whereas *Class C* contains 65% of the materials. Thus, C materials occur most often. However, the value of 15% only is the smallest one. They mainly involve automatic processes in order to keep the costs as low as possible.

A general problem that occurs when performing the ABC and XYZ analyses is the definition of the borders between the individual classes. Basically, neither the number of classes (A, B, C) nor the class boundaries (A = 10%, B = 20%, C = 70%) are fixed values. The definition of class boundaries for specific critical value portions is therefore a subjective decision and can vary depending on the purpose of use. Although SAP does suggest some standard boundaries, you can also use your individual ones (see Figure 3.6 on page 61).

For example, in the retail and wholesale trading industries, the Lorenz curve is relatively flat, whereas for technical products, for instance in the manufacturing industry, it is rather steep.

The stronger the upward bend of the Lorenz curve, the more useful it is to treat its individual parts separately. Still, the separation into three classes has become widely accepted both in theory and daily work.

The ABC analysis is supposed to enable you to focus on the essential processes in the supply chain. Its goal is to separate the essential from the nonessential.

The focus of the activities is to be directed to the most profitable area (A parts), while the costs in the other areas are to be reduced by the simplification of processes (for example, by implementing a usage control).

Although the ABC analysis has been known for a long time and can be easily used, it is still being ignored in many business areas. But the ABC analysis is a universally usable method of classifying objects. Table 3.1 lists some of the possible objects.

Object	Analysis Goal	Classification Criteria
Customer	Analysis of the customer sales distribution	Customer sales in relation to the overall sales within a period
Customer	Analysis of distribution costs per USD of customer sales	Distribution costs per customer in relation to customer sales
Vendor	Analysis of monetary procurement volumes per vendor	Vendor procurement volume in relation to the entire procurement volume within a period
Finished products	Analysis of capital tie-up caused by inventories in relation to the annual revenue	Average value of inventory in relation to the annual revenue per item
Semifinished products	Analysis of the distribution of the usage value per period per semifinished product	Usage value per period of the semifinished product in relation to all usage values per period

Table 3.1 Possible Objects for an ABC Analysis

The selection of the appropriate classification criterion is a significant factor for the ABC analysis. If you choose the right classification criterion for your problem, the analysis result enables you to make the right decisions. If you choose the wrong criterion, the result won't be satisfactory.

The ABC analysis is used predominantly in materials management and in the sales and distribution department of a company. Here it is used to classify material types and products to be procured and used, as well as to classify and prioritize customers.

Typically, a small number of materials tends to represent a large portion of the overall value; however, you should note that the actual relationships between quantities and values can differ, depending on the actual organization.

The following typical classification has been generally established:

▸ **A materials**
Materials of the most valuable class represent 5–10% of the total number and account for approximately 70–80% of the entire usage value per period. These are high-quality materials, which have a high value, and therefore must be handled with more care by planners than other lower quality materials.

The prioritized handling of A materials is often reflected in the use of exact, program-driven requirements planning procedures, an exact inventory maintenance and control, an intensive market observation, and the closing of master contracts with particularly efficient vendors. The cost structures must be controlled precisely and the determination of procurement proposals should be carried out based on well defined lot-sizing processes.

Due to the high value of A materials, it is critical that you are always automatically informed in realtime about exceptional situations in the process and that you are optimally supported in the search for a solution. The logistics information system in mySAP ERP contains a static monitoring system. In SAP APO, the Alert Monitor (see Figure 3.2) alerts you as soon as an exception message occurs.

▸ **B materials**
Class B contains all types of materials that represent 15–20% of the total number and 15–20% of the entire usage value per period. For these average materials it makes sense to implement a differentiated procedure. This means that you must decide separately on the planning and analysis meth-

ods that you want to use for each material group and even for each individual material within the B class. For this reason, it can be useful to further subdivide the class of B materials into B1 and B2 materials.

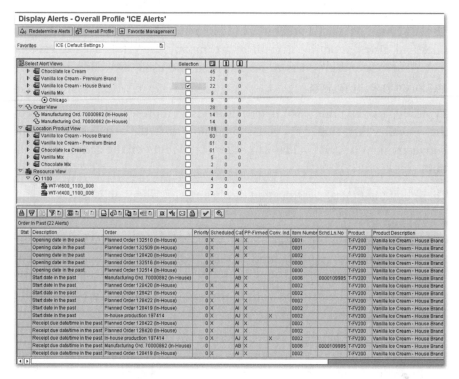

Figure 3.2 Alert Monitor in SAP APO

▶ **C materials**

C materials contain material types that represent 70–80% of the total number and the remaining 5–10% of the entire usage value per period. C materials are therefore of a low value, and their handling is intended to simplify work processes and reduce costs.

C materials eat up your yield return. The process costs are disproportionally high. They tie up capacities and cause approximately 60% of all procurement processes. Here, you should consider other strategies like single sourcing or even outsourcing.

C materials should be driven in an automated way through the supply chain without any manual effort, because the small value portion should not be inflated by additional manual activities. C materials can generally be planned using fixed or periodic lot sizes. You should avoid doing a time-consuming inventory analysis if at all possible. However, C materials can have a substantial influence on the production costs, for example, if a C part is missing, which would obstruct the downstream production process. This can lead to production downtimes or delays for the B and A materials.

For C materials it can also make sense to further subdivide the items into C1 and C2 materials.

Table 3.2 provides an overview of the different way in which A and C materials are managed.

	A material	C material
Procurement market research	Global sourcing	E-procurement
Value analysis	Mandatory	Not necessary
Requirements planning	Deterministic	Stochastic
Inventory-taking	Permanently	Once a year
Safety stock	Small	Large
Order cycle	High—JiT	Larger cycles

Table 3.2 A and C Materials Require Different Strategies

The costs involved in a professional *procurement market research* are worthwhile only for high-quality A materials. For C materials, it is preferable to implement automated and lean procurement processes, such as E-procurement.

An exact *value analysis* is mandatory for A materials due to their high value portion, whereas such an analysis is not necessary for C materials.

For A materials, *material requirements planning* (MRP) should be deterministic while you can use stochastic methods for C materials.

Usually, *inventory taking* is carried out permanently for A materials. For C materials, the annual inventory taking at the end of a fiscal year is sufficient.

Safety stocks should be as small as possible for A materials, since those materials have a high value, which means that even small stocks would generate a high inventory value. For C parts also, the safety stocks shouldn't be too high, but they can contain more buffers than the A material stocks because the value of C materials is lower.

A materials should be regularly procured in short *order cycles*. C materials can be procured weekly or monthly in fixed lot sizes.

3.1.2 XYZ Analysis

The ABC analysis is a primary analysis. It can be used as a basis for follow-up or secondary analyses such as the segmentation or the XYZ analysis. The XYZ analysis enables you to perform the next step of the inventory analysis. The following typical classification has been generally established:

▶ **X materials**
X materials are characterized by a constant, non-changing usage over time. The requirements fluctuate only slightly around a constant level so that the future demand can basically be forecast quite well. Unfortunately, experience has shown that even the forecast for X products can be poor. With X products, it's important to recognize fluctuations straightaway so you can respond quickly and appropriately. For this reason, you should install an outlier correction process, for example, in demand planning (see Figure 3.3, top).

▶ **Y materials**
The usage of these materials is neither constant nor sporadic. With Y materials, you can often observe trends, for example, that the usage increases or decreases for awhile, or that it is characterized by seasonal fluctuations. For these materials, it's harder to obtain an accurate forecast (see Figure 3.3, center).

▶ **Z materials**
These materials are not used regularly. The usage can strongly fluctuate or occur sporadically. In these cases, you can often observe periods with no consumption at all. The creation of a forecast is extremely demanding and very difficult. It is useful to further subdivide the Z materials into Z1 and Z2 materials, the latter being used even less regularly than the Z1 materials. This enables you to trigger detailed counteractive measures for particularly critical materials (see Figure 3.3, bottom).

The quality of the access fluctuations can also be determined using a fluctuation coefficient. This coefficient represents the deviation of the access pattern in the current period from that in the previous period. If the fluctuation coefficient increases, the forecast accuracy decreases. X materials have a fluctuation coefficient of < 0.1; Y materials are located between 0.1 and 0.25; and Z materials are > 0.25 (see also Figure 3.4).

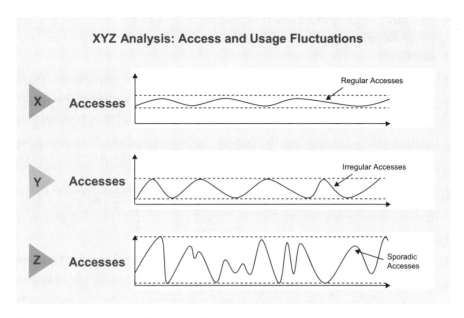

Figure 3.3 XYZ Analysis with Access and Usage Fluctuations for Materials (Source: FIR)

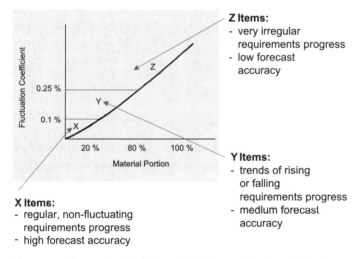

Z Items:
- very irregular
  requirements progress
- low forecast
  accuracy

Y Items:
- trends of rising
  or falling
  requirements progress
- medium forecast
  accuracy

X Items:
- regular, non-fluctuating
  requirements progress
- high forecast accuracy

Figure 3.4 Fluctuation Coefficient in Relation to the Material Portion in an XYZ Analysis

3.2   ABC Analysis With SAP

In the SAP environment, you can use the ABC analysis in different departments of your company.

▶ You can use the purchasing information system in *purchasing*. Using the ABC analysis, you can classify vendors with regard to the **Invoice amount** key figure.

▶ You can use the S&D information system in *sales and distribution*: Using the ABC analysis, you can classify sales organizations regarding the incoming orders key figure, and materials according to the **Revenue** key figure.

▶ In *production*, you can use the production information system. Using the ABC analysis, you can classify work centers with regard to the **Scrap quantity** key figure.

▶ For your *plant maintenance*, you can use the plant maintenance information system. Using the ABC analysis, you can classify object classes with regard to the **Breakdown duration** key figure.

▶ To analyze your inventory you should use the *inventory controlling* module in SAP: Using the ABC analysis, you can classify materials, material groups, storage locations, and even entire plants. For example, you can run comparisons of material movements per storage location or of outgoing quantities at finished goods level per plant. By default, the SAP system provides a wide range of key figures for ABC and XYZ analyses, such as *usage values*, *stock receipts values*, *safety stocks*, *average inventory levels*, and the *number of material movements*. Key figures like the usage or consumption can be measured in terms of quantities (e.g., kg, units, and so on) or value units (e.g., USD).

3.2.1 Outlining the Analysis Process

The following sections will outline an ABC analysis of the inventory controlling component of mySAP ERP. Later in the chapter, we'll do the same with an XYZ analysis. The ABC analysis is performed based on the following steps:

1. Determining the analysis goal
2. Defining the area to be analyzed
3. Calculating the data basis
4. Selecting the analysis basis as a subset of the data basis
5. Defining the ABC strategy and ABC class boundaries
6. Defining the priorities and assignment to the classes

3.2.2 Determining the Analysis Goal

First, we need to define the questions that you want answered and determine in which areas of the supply chain you expect the biggest potential for optimization. In the following example, we'll first conduct an ABC analysis for the consumption quantity and then we'll do a quantity flow analysis for the individual storage locations in plant 1200.

In the mySAP ERP menu, select **Logistics · Logistics Controlling · Inventory Controlling · Standard Analyses · Plant**.

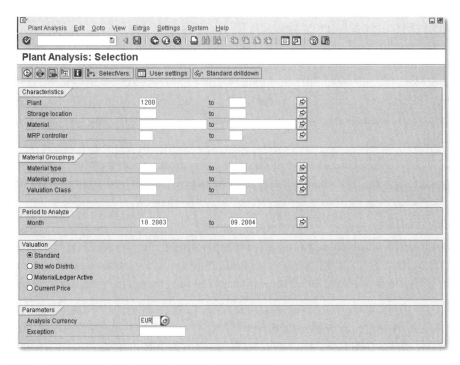

Figure 3.5 Selecting the ABC Analysis in mySAP ERP

3.2.3 Defining the Area to be Analyzed

Then select the objects to be analyzed (materials, customers, ...) and the corresponding timeframe (year, month, ...) that you want to use at the beginning of the analysis. You can extend the analysis at a later stage in iterative steps.

Figure 3.5 illustrates the selection of an ABC plant analysis in the inventory controlling area of mySAP ERP.

In the upper section, you can see the **Characteristics** field group where you can select the objects on which you want to run an ABC analysis. Enter 1200 for the plant. You can also restrict the selection to specific storage locations or exclude specific storage locations from the selection, for example, consignment storage locations.

The **Material Groupings** field group enables you to further restrict the selection, for example, according to material types (e.g., only finished products) or material groups.

The timeframe for the ABC analysis can be entered in the **Period to Analyze** field. For seasonal items, you should enter at least one entire year. If you want to analyze the material consumption only within the season, then you can enter only the period of one season. The longer the period you select, the more significant the trend you identify. For products with a very short product lifecycle (e.g., mobile phones), you should select the product lifecycle period. It is extremely important that you choose the right data basis for the analysis.

Moreover, you can use the **Valuation** field group to determine how the inventory is to be evaluated. Select the **Standard** entry if you want to refer to the standard price that is stored in the material master.

The determination of the inventory value is essential for the ABC analysis, because the value is used as a basis for separating the materials into A, B, and C materials. For this purpose, you should determine a separate value for each item in the data basis, for example: annual requirements in units x cost price per unit.

The next step is carried out automatically in mySAP ERP on the basis of the prices stored in the material master. Figure 3.6 shows that Material T-B1000 is standard-price-controlled. Go to the material master and select **Logistics · Production · Master Data · Material Master · Material · Change · Immediately**. Then go to the **Costing 2** view (**Price control = S**). The current **standard price** is set to 315 Euro and 98 cents.

Figure 3.7 shows the subsequent screen. It shows that Material T-B1000 is specified with a goods receipt value of 31,598.00 Euro. This means that the received quantity of 100 PCs was valuated with the standard price of 315.98 Euro from the material master.

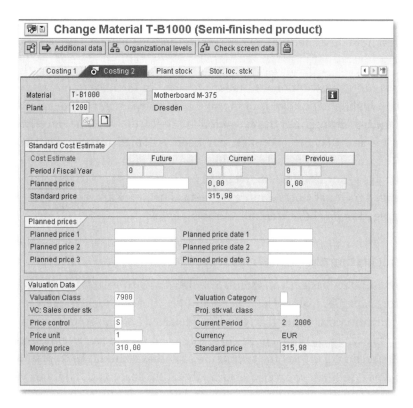

Figure 3.6 Prices Are Automatically Taken from the Material Master in mySAP ERP

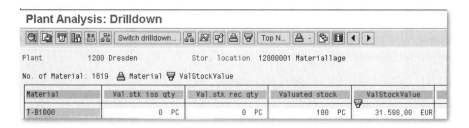

Figure 3.7 Key Figure Values are Calculated on the Basis of Quantities and Prices

The only remaining parameter you can still define is the **Analysis Currency**. If you specify an analysis currency, all key figure values are converted into the specified currency and therefore calculated in a standard format. The specification of an analysis currency can entail longer runtimes. For this reason, you should specify an analysis currency only if you're sure that the system will output different currencies and you want the results to be displayed in only one currency. The currency translation is based on the currency type for the exchange rate that is valid on the system date. The currency type is either stored in the user settings or can be specified in Customizing.

You can also specify a defined *exception* in the parameters using the early warning system. The exceptional situations defined in the **Exception** parameter are then highlighted in color in the standard analyses. A prerequisite is that the standard analysis and the exception are based on the same information structure and that the exception has been activated for the standard analyses. The use of different colors enables you to easily navigate within the standard analysis. For example, if exceptions occur at the materials level (for instance with a material stock of more than 1m USD), they are displayed at a higher aggregation level (for example at the plant level).

3.2.4 Calculating the Data Basis

Make sure your data basis is consistent. The data basis consists of all characteristics (for example, material numbers) and key figures, such as the consumption quantity and value that you have selected for the ABC analysis. Take your time when carrying out the first ABC analysis and pay attention to quality. The recurring efforts for staging the data basis should be kept at a minimum level so that you can perform the ABC analysis continuously. Another important factor is the cleansing of data. Many ERP systems often contain unused materials that are included in data selections, which actually shouldn't be the case. It also happens that materials are selected because they still have a small stock value but have already been marked for deletion.

You should therefore pay particular attention to the following aspects when selecting and cleansing your data:

▶ Scrap materials that show no goods movement

▶ Delete materials from the data basis that have been marked for deletion

▶ Complement your data with missing prices, units of measure, and so on

▶ Scrap materials with negative values

You should first examine your data basis and then decide on the key figures that you want to analyze in the ABC analysis. If you choose a wide data basis, you can narrow it down step by step and evaluate it according to specific values. In our example, the plant analysis result first displays the **value stock receipts** and **value stock issues**, as well as the **total usage** key figures that have been previously set in the standard selection profile, as shown in Figure 3.8.

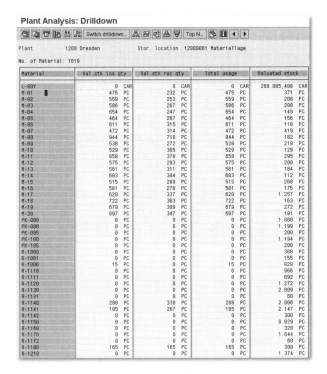

Figure 3.8 Basic List for an ABC Analysis with Key Figures: Value Stock Issues, Value Stock Receipts, and Total Usage

Figure 3.9 shows the definition of key figures on which you want to base your ABC analysis in mySAP ERP. Once you have selected the data basis using a set of key figures, you can follow the menu path **Goto · Select key figures** to make your selection.

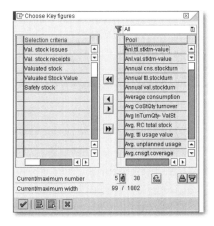

Figure 3.9 Selecting Key Figures for an ABC Analysis

The system displays all available key figures of your data basis (**Pool**), as well as the key figures you actually selected by using the arrow buttons (**Selection criteria**). For our ABC analysis, we'll select the key figures **Valuated stock** and **Valuated Stock Value**.

Next, we'll obtain the analysis based on the selected key figures. Then you can classify the data at the key figures level to examine the data basis prior to the actual ABC classification and to define the ABC boundaries (see Figure 3.10). To do that, you should highlight the **key figure** you want to classify and then click on the **Sort** button.

Plant Analysis: Drilldown

Switch drilldown... | Top N... | ◄ ▶

Plant   1200 Dresden   Stor. location 12000001 Materiallage

No. of Material: 1619 ☞ ValStockValue

Material	Val.stk iss qty		Val.stk rec qty		Valuated stock		ValStockValue		Safety Stck	
Total	50.156,270	***	46.431,000	***	72317645605,279	***	7459575.321,30	EUR	93.010,000	***
40-200C	0	PC	0	PC	5.887.613.468	PC	601.225.798,92	EUR	0	PC
L-40C	0	CAR	0	CAR	1.708.389,296	CAR	413.208.686,62	EUR	0	CAR
80-200C	0	PC	0	PC	3.576.010.875	PC	393.779.825,86	EUR	0	PC
60-200C	0	PC	0	PC	3.155.304.011	PC	347.452.984,72	EUR	0	PC
60-200F	0	PC	0	PC	3.154.752.563	PC	347.392.189,93	EUR	0	PC
80-200F	0	PC	0	PC	2.629.977.981	PC	289.605.420,74	EUR	0	PC
L-80C	1,430	CAR	1.430	CAR	1.042.006,024	CAR	287.298.631,26	EUR	0	CAR
40-200F	0	PC	0	PC	2.629.956.965	PC	268.563.702,55	EUR	0	PC
L-60C	1,840	CAR	1.840	CAR	921.834,990	CAR	229.012.643,12	EUR	0	CAR
L-60F	0	CAR	0	CAR	915.544,480	CAR	208.016.474,20	EUR	0	CAR
L-80F	0	CAR	0	CAR	762.441,400	CAR	192.144.608,75	EUR	0	CAR
L-40F	0	CAR	0	CAR	762.919,400	CAR	188.817.986,44	EUR	0	CAR
40-210	0	PC	0	PC	5.246.085.413	PC	173.074.965,64	EUR	0	PC
60-200Y	0	PC	0	PC	1.424.852.276	PC	144.064.277,32	EUR	0	PC
L-40Y	0	CAR	0	CAR	488.406,656	CAR	129.500.157,38	EUR	0	CAR
L-40R	0	CAR	0	CAR	469.829,026	CAR	124.598.608,72	EUR	0	CAR
60-200R	0	PC	0	PC	1.190.748.610	PC	120.234.988,24	EUR	0	PC
YY-250	0	M	0	M	211903.542,150	M	118.759.812,04	EUR	0	M
80-200R	0	PC	0	PC	1.139.566.950	PC	115.218.867,90	EUR	0	PC
L-60R	0	CAR	0	CAR	427.278,824	CAR	108.686.177,88	EUR	0	CAR
YY-260	0	PC	0	PC	9.627.206.437	PC	105.984.448,14	EUR	0	PC
80-210	0	PC	0	PC	3.311.797.311	PC	93.344.251,01	EUR	0	PC
L-60Y	0	CAR	0	CAR	309.138,240	CAR	72.073.803,63	EUR	0	CAR
L-80R	0	CAR	0	CAR	247.366,992	CAR	69.671.847,26	EUR	0	CAR
L-80Y	0	CAR	0	CAR	268.085,408	CAR	67.168.479,04	EUR	0	CAR
YY-240	0	KG	0	KG	7.636.420,586	KG	42.923.423,01	EUR	0	KG
YY-230	0	PC	0	PC	5.453.252.102	PC	30.559.500,41	EUR	0	PC
YY-220	0	PC	0	PC	5.453.252.102	PC	30.559.500,41	EUR	0	PC
YY-270	0	PC	0	PC	4.812.093.227	PC	26.968.997,00	EUR	0	PC
YY-210	0	KG	0	KG	4.816.223,247	KG	22.158.101,91	EUR	0	KG
60-210	0	PC	0	PC	3.055.498.226	PC	17.123.731,76	EUR	0	PC
40-200Y	0	PC	0	PC	1.360.947.622	PC	13.742.083,45	EUR	0	PC
40-200R	0	PC	0	PC	1.309.800.795	PC	13.225.637,27	EUR	0	PC
80-200Y	0	PC	0	PC	1.234.536.329	PC	12.482.129,85	EUR	0	PC
XX-200	0	M	0	M	973466.441,560	M	9.759.389,08	EUR	0	M
T-ASD30	0	PC	0	PC	10.000	PC	7.772.300,00	EUR	0	PC
T-ASD29	0	PC	0	PC	10.000	PC	7.772.300,00	EUR	0	PC

Figure 3.10 The Dataset Can Be Sorted According to Selected Key Figures

3.2.5 Defining the ABC Strategy

Once you have defined the data basis and the key figures for the ABC analysis, you must select a strategy. To do that, you must once again select a key figure and then click on **Edit · ABC Analysis**. The system displays the screen in which you can select the ABC strategy, as shown in Figure 3.11.

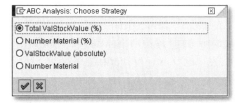

Figure 3.11 Selecting the ABC Strategy

After selecting the strategy, you must select the ABC strategy parameters:

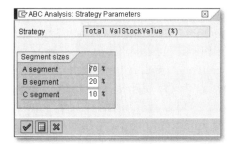

Figure 3.12 Selecting the ABC Strategy Parameters

In Figures 3.11 and 3.12, you can see the analysis strategy and the class boundaries we defined in mySAP ERP for our example. We decided to use the standard strategy, **Total ValStockValue (%)** and the standard class boundaries: **A = 70**%, **B = 20**%, and **C = 10**%.

Prior to the actual analysis in the ABC analysis, you must define the analysis strategy, as described above. To do that, mySAP ERP provides the following four strategies:

Total Key Figure (%)

The total of the characteristic values (materials) assigned to the A, B, or C segment represents a specific percentage of the total value of the key figure (in the above example, that's the **total valuated stock value**).

An example: You enter 70% for the A segment, 20% for the B segment, and 10% for the C segment. These values have proven useful in actual practice; however, you can also use slightly modified values if you have already run the ABC analysis on the same data basis several times and concluded that the modified settings are more appropriate for your data basis.

The system creates an internal list that is sorted by the key figure values in descending order. The A segment is assigned all values that represent 70% of the total key figure value. The B segment is assigned the values representing 20%, and the C segment is assigned the values that represent 10% of the total key figure value.

Number of Characteristic Values (%)

The number of characteristic values (the number of materials in the above example) that are assigned to the A, B, and C segments is provided as a percentage of the total number.

An example: You enter 10% for the A segment, 30% for the B segment, and 60% for the C segment. The system creates an internal list that is sorted by the key figure values in descending order. The A segment is assigned 10% of the total number of characteristic values with the highest key figure value, the B segment is assigned the following 30%, while the C segment is assigned 60% of the characteristic values with the lowest key figure value.

Key Figure (absolute)

The boundaries between the A and B and between the B and C segments must be defined.

An example: You enter the value 500,000 to mark the boundary between the A and B segments, while 150,000 represents the boundary between the B and C segments. The A segment is then assigned all characteristic values whose key figure value is higher than 500,000. All characteristic values whose key figure value is between 150,000 and 500,000 are assigned to the B segment. And finally, all characteristic values whose key figure value is lower than 150,000 are assigned to the C segment.

You should opt for this strategy only if you know your data basis very well and if you have previously performed several ABC analyses for the same data basis. This strategy helps you tune up your ABC analysis and perform detailed analyses.

Number of Characteristic Values

The number of characteristic values must be defined for the A and B segments. All other characteristic values are assigned to the C segment.

An example: You enter 20 as the value for the A segment, and 30 for the B segment. As a result of the ABC analysis, the system creates an internal list that is sorted by the key figure values in descending order. The first 20 characteristic values in the list are assigned to the A segment, the next 30 values are assigned to the B segment, and the remaining values are assigned to the C segment.

You should choose this strategy only if you know your data basis very well and if you have previously performed several ABC analyses for the same data basis. This strategy can also be used for fine-tuning your ABC analysis. It is particularly useful when you want to quickly identify the top 20 characteristic values and when you want to accelerate the ABC analysis when dealing with large data quantities.

3.2.6 Defining Class Limits

After selecting the strategy, you must define the class limits. Note that the SAP system provides only one suggestion. You can define the final class limits in accordance with your requirements, and even define more than three of them; however, the three limits have proven useful in actual practice.

Alternatively, Figure 3.13 shows the definition of six individual classes.

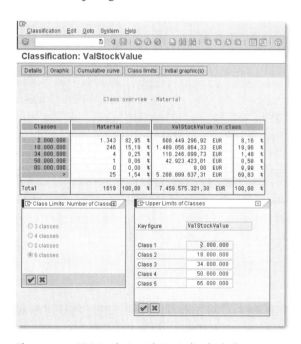

Figure 3.13 ABC Analysis with Six Individual Class Limits

Six class limits are useful only if you want to perform a very detailed ABC analysis and to further subdivide the standard A, B, and C classes. A real-life example would be the more detailed separation of C materials. A large quantity of C materials, for example, can be subdivided into C1 materials (low value) and C2 materials (very low value).

But let us now return to the ABC analysis with the three standard class limits.

3.2.7 Assigning Classes

The SAP system defines the ranking of the values (for example, rank No. 1 is the highest annual requirement in USD) and sorts the materials in the subsequent ABC analysis correspondingly. Here, it is useful to calculate aggregated values with regard to the assignments to ABC limits. The system calculates the rank or the material as a percentage of the total value. Then, it calculates the aggregated percentage of the total value.

The respective materials are automatically assigned by the system to the previously defined classes. The result you obtain is an ABC classification. The identified classification criterion for each material (A, B, or C) can be automatically stored in the material master data. If you don't use this function, you must manually enter the newly determined ABC identifiers in the material master.

Figure 3.14 displays the result of an ABC analysis in mySAP ERP, which you can select via the following path: **Edit · Segmentation**.

ABC Analysis: ValStockValue

| Details | Graphic | Cumulative curve | New Strategy | Initial graphic(s) |

Overview of segments - Material

Segments	Material		ValStockValue in segment	
A segment	26	1,61 %	5.251.823.060,32 EUR	70,40 %
B segment	212	13,09 %	1.464.912.964,06 EUR	19,64 %
C segment	1.381	85,30 %	742.839.296,92 EUR	9,96 %
Total	1619	100,00 %	7.459.575.321,30 EUR	100,00 %

Figure 3.14 Overview of an ABC Analysis Result

The figure shows the class limits with their absolute values, the percentages, and aggregated values. In the above example, 0.85% (26 materials) represents 70.40% of the total valuated stock value. By double-clicking on the respective class, you can prompt the system to display the individual materials, including their values in greater detail (see Figure 3.15).

ABC Analysis: ValStockValue

| Graphic | Initial graphic(s) |

Total list

ABC ind.	Material	ValStockValue	
A	40-200C	601.225.798,92	EUR
A	L-40C	413.208.686,62	EUR
A	80-200C	393.779.825,86	EUR
A	60-200C	347.452.984,72	EUR
A	60-200F	347.392.189,93	EUR
A	80-200F	289.605.420,74	EUR
A	L-80C	287.298.631,26	EUR
A	40-200F	268.563.702,55	EUR
A	L-60C	229.012.643,12	EUR
A	L-60F	208.016.474,20	EUR
A	L-80F	192.144.608,75	EUR
A	L-40F	188.817.986,44	EUR
A	40-210	173.074.965,64	EUR
A	60-200Y	144.064.277,32	EUR
A	L-40Y	129.500.157,38	EUR
A	L-40R	124.598.608,72	EUR
A	60-200R	120.234.988,24	EUR
A	YY-250	118.759.812,04	EUR
A	80-200R	115.218.867,90	EUR
A	L-60R	108.686.177,88	EUR
A	YY-260	105.984.448,14	EUR
A	80-210	93.344.251,01	EUR
A	L-60Y	72.073.803,63	EUR
A	L-80R	69.671.847,26	EUR
A	L-80Y	67.168.479,04	EUR
A	YY-240	42.923.423,01	EUR
B	YY-220	30.559.500,41	EUR
B	YY-230	30.559.500,41	EUR
B	YY-270	26.968.997,00	EUR
B	YY-210	22.158.101,91	EUR
B	60-210	17.123.731,76	EUR
B	40-200Y	13.742.083,45	EUR
B	40-200R	13.225.637,27	EUR
B	80-200Y	12.482.129,85	EUR
B	XX-200	9.759.389,08	EUR
B	T-ASD01	7.772.300,00	EUR
B	T-ASD02	7.772.300,00	EUR
B	T-ASD03	7.772.300,00	EUR
B	T-ASD04	7.772.300,00	EUR

Figure 3.15 Detailed View of an ABC Analysis Result

3.2.8 Evaluating an ABC Analysis

You can display the ABC analysis results as a totals curve or as a three-dimensional graphic.

Totals Curve

The totals curve can be displayed for absolute values or percentages. It provides information on the relative concentration of materials. The abscissa represents the number of materials (or the percentage of the number of materials respectively), while the ordinate displays the aggregated consumption values or requirements values (or percentages of those values respectively).

The totals curve provides information of the following type: X (%) materials combine into Y (%) of the aggregated key figure value. By looking at the curve, you can tell to what degree the total consumption value or the total requirements value is concentrated on a small number of materials.

To call a totals curve, select **Edit · Totals Curve (abs.)** or **Totals Curve (%)** respectively.

3D Graphic

The 3D graphic (see Figure 3.16) enables you to evaluate and show the analysis results in a presentation to upper management.

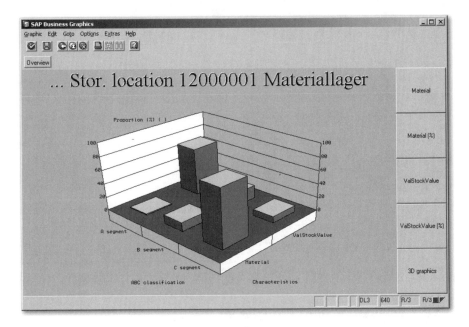

Figure 3.16 Graphical Evaluation of an ABC Analysis

You can also download the results of the ABC analysis in Excel for a graphical presentation.

3.2.9 Performing an ABC Segmentation

You can combine different ABC analyses to clarify relationships between the key figures and to target potential problem areas. To do that, you can either create complex tables in Excel or use the segmentation function in mySAP ERP.

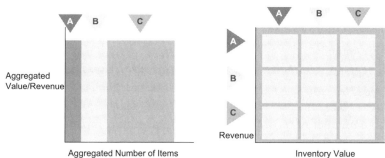

Figure 3.17 An ABC Matrix with Revenue and Inventory Value

The illustration on the left in Figure 3.17 shows the possible combination from the ABC analysis to the revenue and from the ABC analysis to the inventory value. Such segmentation generates nine new possible analysis combinations (AA to CC). This enables you to identify the materials that generate most of the total revenue and those materials that don't contribute much to the total revenue, including the inventory values for the materials.

The mySAP ERP system provides segmentations for the following organizational areas:

▶ **Purchasing**
You can segment materials into classes according to the key figures, *Number of order items* and *Order value*. This filters out materials that have a relatively low order value and a high number of order items. Materials that can be found in the higher classes with regard to those two key figures are not critical.

▶ **Sales and Distribution**
You can segment customers into classes according to the key figures, *Number of orders* and *Revenue*. This helps you to identify customers with a relatively low revenue, but a high number of orders.

▶ **Inventory Controlling**
You can segment materials into classes according to the key figures, *Average inventory value at goods receipt* and *Range of coverage of average inventory at goods receipt*. For example, this way you can see materials that are assigned to the higher classes with regard to the two key figures.

▶ **Production**
You can segment work centers into classes according to the key figures, *Available capacity* and *Required capacity*. This segmentation enables you to

identify work centers that have a high capacity requirement, but little capacity available. Work centers that can be found in the higher classes with regard to those two key figures are not critical.

▶ **Plant Maintenance**
You can segment maintenance planner groups into classes according to the key figures, *Number of recorded notifications* and *Number of completed notifications*. This enables you to identify maintenance planner groups with a high number of recorded, but a low number of completed notifications.

The following example establishes a relationship between the key figures, **Total usage**, and **Valuated stock value** in order to check which materials with a low valuated stock value also show a low total usage value so that we can streamline the materials (see Figure 3.18).

You can display the result of the segmentation as a 3D graphic by clicking on the **Graphic** button (see Figure 3.19). It becomes immediately clear in our example that we have a strong need for streamlining our materials because a large portion of materials has neither a high valuated stock value nor a high total usage value.

Dual Classification: Total usage/ValStockValue

| Details | Graphic | Class limits | Initial graphic(s) |

Overview of segments - Material

Total usage	ValStockValue						Total
	2000000	18000000	34000000	50000000	66000000	>	
150	1.305	246	4	1	0	25	1.581
300	3	0	0	0	0	0	3
450	0	0	0	0	0	0	0
600	11	0	0	0	0	0	11
750	9	0	0	0	0	0	9
>	15	0	0	0	0	0	15
Total	1.343	246	4	1	0	25	1.619

Figure 3.18 Segmentation in the ABC Analysis According to Total Usage and Valuated Stock Value

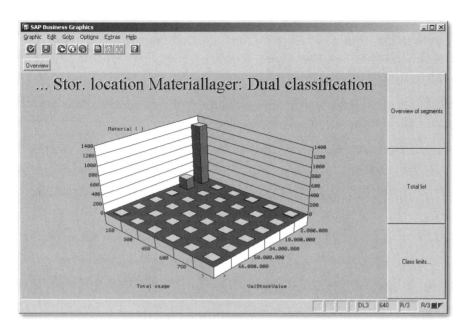

Figure 3.19 Example as a 3D Graphic—a Large Portion Shows Neither a High Consumption Value Nor a High Consumption Quantity

3.2.10   Case Scenario: ABC Analysis for Warehouse Optimization

The result of the ABC analysis alone does not help you to identify the potentials. You have to run an additional analysis to determine the origin of the problems and to develop possible solutions.

In the following sections, we'll describe a sample scenario to demonstrate how you can misinterpret the ABC analysis. You will see how important it is to choose the right object for analysis if you are to obtain valid results.

In the example, we first analyzed the **Business volume value** key figure; however, based on that value, we initiated the wrong activities. Later, we ran another ABC analysis, but this time, on the basis of the **Access frequency** key figure. This key figure proved to be the right approach as the resulting activities led to a successful outcome.

Here are the details of our example: The warehouse management of a device manufacturer was supposed to be reorganized. The initial problem was that, due to a strong growth, the company had to include an increasing number of goods into its range of products so that a growing number of materials had to be stored and removed from stock. Since stock keeping was completely disorganized, the paths in the warehouse became increasingly longer, which

77

reduced the overall efficiency. For this reason, the warehouse management had to be maximized by an optimal distribution of the materials to the available storage locations. The optimization process was carried out based on an ABC analysis.

First, a material list was generated from the SAP system, including the sales quantities and the business volume value.

Then the list was sorted according to the sales values, and ABC identifiers were assigned (see Table 3.3). This resulted in an ABC classification of the materials in the picking area according to the business volume value in the month of May.

Material number	Material description	Access frequency	Price in USD	Business volume value	Aggregated business volume value	ABC identifier
M-500	Machine 1500	850	75	63 750	34.43	A
M-100	Machine 1100	120	500	60 000	66.83	A
M-400	Machine 1400	75	400	30 000	83.03	A
M-200	Machine 1200	250	75	18 750	93.16	B
S-09	Lubricant	2 200	3	6 600	96.72	C
S-10	Screws	4 400	0.5	2 200	97.91	C
M-300	Machine 1300	50	40	2 000	98.99	C
M-600	Machine 1600	75	25	1 875	100.00	C

Table 3.3 ABC Analysis for a Warehouse Optimization According to the Business Volume Value

This analysis enabled a reorganization of the warehouse so that the A materials were stored near the entry, while the B and C materials were placed further to the back. But, this decision soon proved to be a costly mistake, because the access frequency of the C materials was much higher, so that filling an order (i.e., storing or picking goods) took even longer. External help was consulted and a new analysis was carried out, but this time, it was based on the *Access frequency* criterion. Lastly, the cost savings that the company had hoped for did in fact materialize (see Table 3.4).

Material number	Material description	Access frequency	Price in USD	Business volume value	Aggregated sales quantity	ABC identi-fier
S-10	Screws	4 400	0.5	2 200	54.86284289	A
S-09	Lubricant	2 200	3	6 600	82.29426434	A
M-500	Machine 1500	850	75	63 750	92.89276808	B
M-200	Machine 1200	250	75	18 750	96.00997506	B
M-100	Machine 1100	120	500	60 000	97.50623441	C
M-400	Machine 1400	75	400	30 000	98.44139651	C
M-600	Machine 1600	75	25	1 875	99.3765586	C
M-300	Machine 1300	50	40	2 000	100	C

Table 3.4 ABC Analysis for a Warehouse Optimization According to Access Frequency

The case scenario shows us that errors can occur even with one-dimensional criteria. It can become even more complex if you have to examine multidimensional criteria. For example, vendors are not only evaluated on the purchase volume, but also on the quality, delivery reliability, delivery periods, and replaceability. This requires a detailed understanding and examination of the issue and the necessary classification criteria.

3.2.11 Case Scenario: ABC Quantity Flow Analysis

In mySAP ERP, you can use the ABC analysis to analyze the quantity flows of individual storage locations in the following manner: The quantity flow analysis provides information on the quantity flows that must be processed in and between the individual storage locations, and it indicates whether the assignment of materials or staff to the storage location must be optimized. You can access the quantity flow analysis in the menu by selecting **Logistics · Logistics Controlling · Inventory Controlling · Standard Analyses · Quantity Flow**. The system then selects the selection screen shown in Figure 3.20.

As analysis **characteristics**, you must select the storage locations (the warehouse numbers in this example) that you want to evaluate in the quantity flow analysis. You can also select all storage locations for a placement storage type or for a material. Note that you must specify the **analysis period**. Optionally, you can specify the **parameter** for exception messages, similar to the ABC analysis.

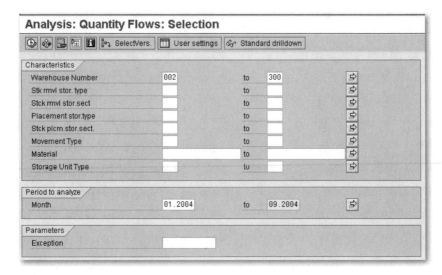

Figure 3.20 Selecting the Quantity Flow Analysis in mySAP ERP

Analysis: Quantity Flows: Basic List

No. of Warehouse No.: 5

Warehouse No.	Moved weight	Moved quantity	No. mvmts	No. real df	Real diff. quantity	Tm.
Total	243.735,600 KG	6.572 PC	72	0	0 PC	
010	87.027,800 KG	2.892 PC	11	0	0 PC	
012	21.108,800 KG	1.270 PC	41	0	0 PC	
024	33.880 KG	121 PC	6	0	0 PC	
025	41.160 KG	147 PC	6	0	0 PC	
300	60.559 KG	2.142 PC	8	0	0 PC	

Figure 3.21 Result of a Quantity Flow Analysis in mySAP ERP

Figure 3.21 displays the result of a quantity flow analysis. The system provides a tabular overview of all storage locations and the key figures you required, such as **Moved quantity** and **Number of movements**.

You can use the menu item **Goto · Portfolio Matrix** to display the tabular result as a portfolio matrix (see Figure 3.22).

The portfolio matrix shown in Figure 3.22 contrasts the key figures **Moved quantity** (bottom coordinate) and **Number of movements** (left-hand coordinate). For example, you can immediately see that the storage location 010 (far right) works much more efficiently than storage location 012 (top) which processes less amount with a lot more movements. To find out why this occurs, we would have to perform another more detailed analysis. For example, the next step could be an ABC analysis for both storage locations.

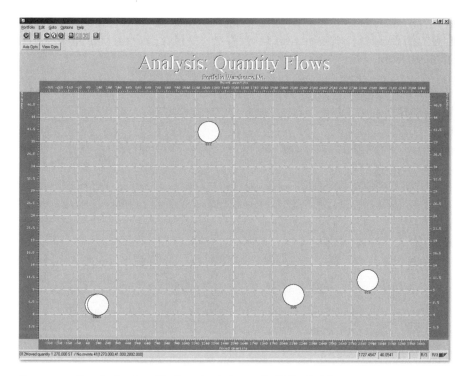

Figure 3.22 Result of a Quantity Flow Analysis as a Portfolio Matrix

3.3 XYZ Analysis With SAP

As stated earlier, the XYZ analysis is a classic secondary analysis that is based on the ABC analysis. It is a method for weighting the parts according to their consumption pattern. This means that a consumption fluctuation key figure is determined for each unit. This results in the necessity of a safety stock. The goals of the XYZ analysis are as follows:

▶ Identifying items that can be planned well and have a high value portion

▶ reducing the warehouse stock, especially for AX items

▶ Reducing inventory and process costs by increasing individual planning costs for AX items and by significantly reducing these costs for CZ items

▶ Supporting the forecast selection

3.3.1 Running Analyses in mySAP ERP

The standard version of mySAP ERP does not contain the XYZ analysis, but you can easily enrich the data from mySAP ERP in Microsoft Excel to perform an XYZ analysis. This process is described in the following sections. Figure 3.23 shows an XYZ analysis in mySAP ERP based on the sample material analysis from plant 1200.

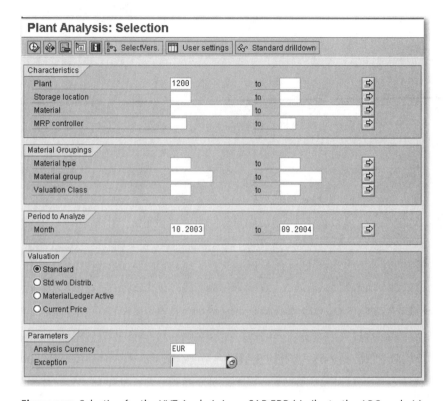

Figure 3.23 Selection for the XYZ Analysis in mySAP ERP (similar to the ABC analysis)

During the selection process, you must define the **analysis objects** and the **analysis period**, as well as the **analysis area** and **analysis strategy**. The process itself is similar to the ABC analysis process described in Section 3.2.

As you can see in Figure 3.24, the result you obtain consists of data for the basic list in the XYZ analysis, including the number of material movements.

The material movements must now be examined along a time stream. To do that, you must create a time series for each material, which contains the number of material movements per material. Select **Goto · Time Series** from the menu. The system displays an overview of time series, as shown in Figure 3.25.

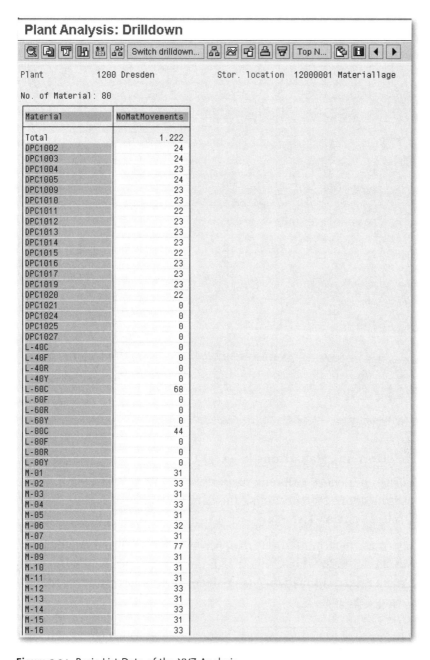

Figure 3.24 Basic List Data of the XYZ Analysis

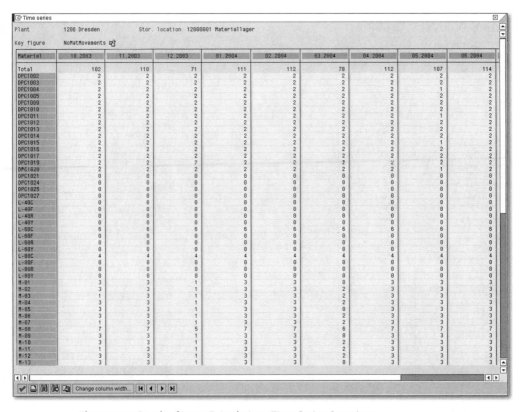

Figure 3.25 Result of an XYZ Analysis as Time Series Overview

3.3.2 Performing Valuations in Excel

Up to this point, mySAP ERP fully supports your XYZ analysis. But now you must load the above table including the data basis into Microsoft Excel. To do that, select **System · List · Save**.

Then, you must determine the variation coefficient in Excel. For this purpose, you should insert three columns. In the first column, you must calculate the standard deviation of the material movements across all periods. Use the following formula:

$$\tilde{s} = \sqrt{\tilde{s}^2} = \sqrt{\frac{1}{n}\sum_{i=1}^{n}(x_i - \bar{x})^2}$$

Use the following formula to determine the average value of the period values in the second column:

$$\overline{x} = \frac{1}{n} \sum_{i=1}^{n} x_i$$

Use the following formula to calculate the variation coefficient in the third column:

$$V = \frac{\tilde{s}}{\overline{x}} = \frac{\sqrt{\dfrac{1}{n} \left(\sum\limits_{i=1}^{n} x_i - \overline{x} \right)^2}}{\dfrac{1}{n} \sum\limits_{i=1}^{n} x_i}$$

Microsoft Excel then displays a table similar to the one shown in Figure 3.26.

Material	Standard deviation	Average value	Coefficient	Oct 03	Nov 03	Dec-03	Jan 04	Feb 04	Mar 04
L-80C	1.154700538	4.4	26.24319405	4	4	4	4	4	4
L-80F	0	0	#DIV/0!	0	0	0	0	0	0
L-80R	0	0	#DIV/0!	0	0	0	0	0	0
L-80Y	0	0	#DIV/0!	0	0	0	0	0	0
M-01	0.9962492	3.1	32.13707097	3	3	1	3	3	0
M-02	0.621581561	3.3	18.83580488	3	3	1	3	3	2
M-03	0.792961461	3.1	25.57940197	1	3	1	3	3	2
M-04	0.621581561	3.3	18.83580488	3	3	1	3	3	2
M-05	0.9962492	3.1	32.13707097	3	3	1	3	3	0
M-06	0.651338947	3.2	20.35434209	3	3	1	3	3	2
M-07	0.792961461	3.1	25.57940197	1	3	1	3	3	2
M-08	1.240112409	7.7	16.10535596	7	7	5	7	7	6
M-09	0.9962492	3.1	32.13707097	3	3	1	3	3	0
M-10	0.792961461	3.1	25.57940197	3	3	1	3	3	2
M-11	0.792961461	3.1	25.57940197	1	3	1	3	3	2
M-12	0.621581561	3.3	18.83580488	3	3	1	3	3	2
M-13	0.9962492	3.1	32.13707097	3	3	1	3	3	0
M-14	0.621581561	3.3	18.83580488	3	3	1	3	3	2
M-15	0.792961461	3.1	25.57940197	1	3	1	3	3	2
M-16	0.621581561	3.3	18.83580488	3	3	1	3	3	2
M-17	0.9962492	3.1	32.13707097	3	3	1	3	3	0
M-18	0.621581561	3.3	18.83580488	3	3	1	3	3	2
M-19	0.792961461	3.1	25.57940197	1	3	1	3	3	0
M-20	0.9962492	3.3	30.189697	3	3	1	3	3	2
M-21	0.621581561	3.3	18.83580488	3	3	1	3	3	0
M-22	0.621581561	3.1	20.0510181	3	3	1	3	3	2
M-23	0.792961461	3.1	25.57940197	1	3	1	3	3	2
M-24	0.9962492	3.1	32.13707097	3	3	1	3	3	0
M-25	0.9962492	3.1	32.13707097	1	3	1	3	3	0

Figure 3.26 Result of an XYZ Analysis with Standard Deviation, Average Value, and Variation Coefficient

To obtain a graphical overview, you can also load the time series overview in Excel and then prepare it as shown in Figure 3.27.

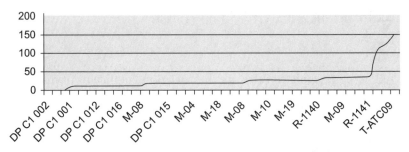

Figure 3.27 Result of an XYZ Analysis in Excel, Prepared as a Graphic

The enhancements in Excel and the calculations of the variation coefficient can also be determined in the Logistics Information System (LIS) in mySAP ERP. A key factor for the XYZ analysis is the analysis period. Selecting a longer period can reduce fluctuations.

An example: Table 3.5 shows the result of the XYZ classification when you select **Week** as your period.

Material	Week 1	Week 2	Week 3	Week 4	Week 5	Week 6	Week 7	Week 8	Average value	Standard deviation	Coefficient	XYZ
L-80c	15	20	25	30	20	15	15	20	20	5.34	26.72	X
L-80d	10	2	4	25	1	23	33	2	12.5	12.63	101.10	Z
L-80e	20	30	15	30	15	35	5	10	20	10.69	53.45	Y

Table 3.5 XYZ Classification with Week Period

Table 3.6 shows the same XYZ classification for the **Month** period.

Material	Month 1	Month 2	Average value	Standard deviation	Coefficient	XYZ
L-80c	90	70	80	14.14	17.67	x
L-80d	41	59	50	12.72	25.45	x
L-80e	95	65	80	21.21	26.51	x

Table 3.6 XYZ Classification with Month Period

3.4 Combining ABC and XYZ Analyses

The combination of ABC and XYZ analyses represents the third step in a detailed inventory analysis. Figure 3.28 once again illustrates the entire process: Step 1 depicts the ABC analysis; Step 2 depicts the XYZ analysis; and Step 3 depicts the creation of an ABC-XYZ matrix.

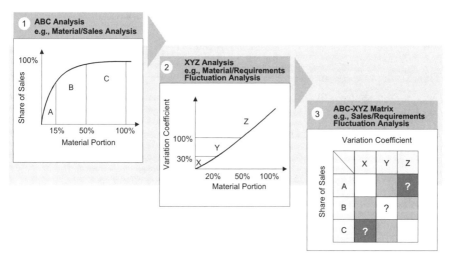

Figure 3.28 Three Steps Towards an ABC-XYZ Matrix (Source: FIR)

SAP SI developed meanwhile an mySAP ERP based Tool, where you can perform the ABC-XYZ Matrix within SAP ERP and on the bases history values which are stored in SAP.

3.4.1 Optimization Using the ABC-XYZ Matrix

The combined analyses results in a matrix that contains nine different values. This enables you to implement a specific inventory optimization process for each value. Experience has shown that this process can uncover substantial optimization potentials.

Deriving Optimization Potentials

The ABC-XYZ matrix enables you to derive actions to optimize your inventory. For example, you can clearly see that AX materials have a high potential for rationalization, whereas CZ materials only show a low economization potential. This means that CZ materials should be planned to be fully automated, thereby not wasting any of your planners' valuable time. However, if your planners do expend time on these materials, there is a potential for optimizing the process at this point.

Basically, the optimization potential (O) is higher for A and B materials and the control overhead (C) is higher for Y and Z materials (see Figure 3.29).

	A	B	C
X	o High value portion Constant requirements High forecast value	o Medium value portion Constant requirements High forecast value	Low value portion Constant requirements High forecast value
Y	o c High value portion Fluctuating requirements Medium forecast value	Medium value portion Fluctuating requirements Medium forecast value	Low value portion Fluctuating requirements Medium forecast value
Z	c High value portion Irregular requirements Low forecast value	c Medium value portion Irregular requirements Low forecast value	Low value portion Irregular requirements Low forecast value

{ **O**ptimization Potential ⇧   **C**ontrol Overhead ⇧ }

Figure 3.29 Optimization Potentials Derived from the ABC-XYZ Matrix

You can also derive actions to optimize your inventory on the basis of the ABC-XYZ matrix (see Figure 3.30).

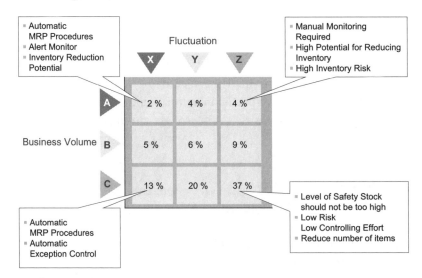

Figure 3.30 Inventory Optimization Actions Derived from the ABC-XYZ Matrix

The planning process for AX materials should be automated as much as possible. It is vital that the planner receive information on variances and exceptional situations as soon as these fluctuations occur. The planner should focus on AZ materials and plan them manually, because Z materials cannot be automated due to their fluctuating consumption values. AZ materials show a substantial potential for reducing the inventory.

An Example from the Trading Industry

Another real-life example from the trading sector, as shown in Figure 3.31, illustrates the process of deriving actions based on the relationship between the storage volume and the procurement costs. In the case of high procurement costs (A) and materials with a high storage volume (X), the storage range should be small (< 30 days) so that the capital tie-up can be kept as low as possible and the storage space used is minimal. For materials with low procurement costs (C) and a low storage space requirement (Z), the storage range can be < 120 days.

The ABC and XYZ analyses are among the most important instruments used in inventory analysis and should be used on a regular basis. Throughout this book, we'll frequently refer to the ABC analyses.

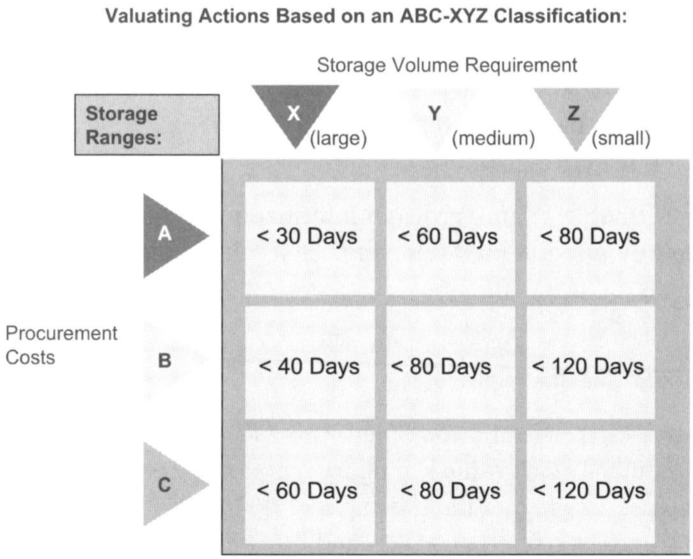

Valuating Actions Based on an ABC-XYZ Classification:

Storage Volume Requirement

Storage Ranges:	X (large)	Y (medium)	Z (small)
A	< 30 Days	< 60 Days	< 80 Days
B	< 40 Days	< 80 Days	< 120 Days
C	< 60 Days	< 80 Days	< 120 Days

Procurement Costs

Figure 3.31 Storage Ranges for the Trading Sector, Derived from the ABC-XYZ Matrix (Example)

3.4.2 An ABC-XYZ Matrix With SAP

To create an ABC-XYZ matrix, you must first carry out the same steps as described in Section 3.2 for the ABC analysis and in Section 3.3 for the XYZ analysis. Once you have created the data basis, you must select the relevant key figures as described earlier in this chapter. For our example, we have chosen the following key figures: **valuated stock value** and **variation coefficient**, as shown in Figure 3.32. The **variation coefficient** key figure takes into account the fluctuations of material movements and has already been realized and valuated in mySAP ERP for our example.

Analysis: Quantity Flows: Basic List

No. of Material: 1619

Material	Variationskoeff.	ValStockValue	
Summ	1.221	11.792.467,39	EUR
M-08	77	690.253,41	EUR
L-60C	68	446,25	EUR
L-80C	44	384,21	EUR
M-20	33	402.726,58	EUR
M-18	33	664.455,88	EUR
M-16	33	487.168,52	EUR
M-14	33	384.119,23	EUR
M-12	33	293.998,93	EUR
M-04	33	431.378.37	EUR

Figure 3.32 Result of an ABC-XYZ Matrix in mySAP ERP (Basic List)

The **valuated stock value** key figure provides information on the classification of the materials. A high value represents an A material, while a low value represents a C material.

The **variation coefficient** key figure provides information on the consistency of the material consumption. A high value represents an X material, while a low value represents a Z material.

You can summarize both key figures in an ABC-XYZ matrix via the menu item **Edit · Segmentation** (see Figure 3.33).

Figure 3.33 displays the result of a combined ABC-XYZ analysis as an ABC-XYZ matrix. The **valuated stock value** key figure represents the ABC classification. C materials are assigned to the class up to 1,000 USD, B materials to the class ranging from 1,000 to 20,000 USD, and A materials are assigned to the class higher than 20,000 USD.

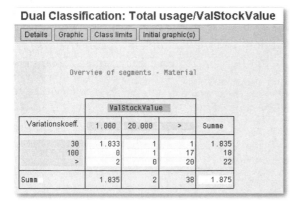

Dual Classification: Total usage/ValStockValue

| Details | Graphic | Class limits | Initial graphic(s) |

Overview of segments - Material

Variationskoeff.	ValStockValue			
	1.000	20.000	>	Summe
30	1.833	1	1	1.835
100	0	1	17	18
>	2	0	20	22
Summ	1.835	2	38	1.875

Figure 3.33 Result of an ABC-XYZ Matrix in mySAP ERP (Overview)

The **variation coefficient** key figure represents the XYZ classification. In this case, the material movements have already been realized with a variation coefficient in mySAP ERP and have been valuated accordingly. X materials are assigned to the class with a variation coefficient of up to 30. The class, which has a variation coefficient that lies between 30 and 100, contains the Y materials. The class, which has a variation coefficient that is higher than 100, contains the Z materials.

You can identify the individual material numbers by double-clicking on the corresponding segments. The AX materials shown in Figure 3.34 are located at a place where there is the highest inventory optimization potential, because the consumption and the value are highest.

ABC Analysis: ValStockValue

| Graphic | Initial graphic(s) |

Total list

Segment	Material	Variationskoeff.	ValStockValue
3/3	M-01	31	257.513,97
3/3	M-03	31	371.524,02
3/3	M-05	31	132.843,22
3/3	M-07	31	267.823,10
3/3	M-09	31	418.136,96
3/3	M-10	31	432.774,89
3/3	M-11	31	571.933,60
3/3	M-13	31	301.201,40
3/3	M-15	31	366.010,54
3/3	M-17	31	570.494,47

Figure 3.34 The Highest Inventory Optimization Potential Exists for AX Materials

The AZ materials represent another segment. The MRP controller should pay particular attention to this group because it includes materials with a high value and an irregular consumption. You should implement a smart monitoring system that automatically notifies the material requirements planning (MRP) controller of exceptional situations.

"An economist is an expert who will know tomorrow why the things he predicted yesterday didn't happen today." This is how Winston Churchill described the core competency of a planner. To a certain extent, this quotation also applies to logisticians, even though he probably didn't have them in mind at the time. This chapter describes how you can efficiently optimize your inventory by implementing the right demand planning.

4 Demand Planning and Forecasting

Demand planning tries to estimate quantities that will be required in the future. For this purpose, demand planners use their own knowledge to estimate the demand for selected products manually. In addition, they use mathematical tools, which are referred to as statistical forecast techniques that enable them to automatically predict future sales figures, particularly for large data and product quantities. Without the support of these tools, the individual demand planner wouldn't be able to process all the necessary quantities of data.

Currently, many companies still use common tools like Microsoft Access or Microsoft Excel, although there are integrated tools available that enable you to carry out the demand planning process much more efficiently. Successful companies use tools that use forecast techniques, which are aimed at specific markets, products, and goals.

4.1 The Influence of Demand Planning on Inventories

A comparison of the forecast result with actual sold quantities can result in three possible situations.

Forecast Smaller Than Requirements

In this case, sales and distribution estimated smaller quantities than could actually be sold. This leads to *stockouts*, that is, situations whereby the warehouse is empty and new sales orders cannot be filled, because the entire quantity of the product has been sold out. Usually customers are annoyed when this occurs, particularly if it happens repeatedly, resulting in their attempt to procure the product somewhere else. This often means that those customers are lost to the competition. So, not only does your company lose revenue due to the low forecast, but it also loses customers.

Period 3 in Figure 4.1 shows the inventory development if the forecast is smaller than the actual requirements. The previously produced warehouse stock is completely consumed, making it necessary to fall back on the safety stock. If the delta is too big, it can cause stockouts.

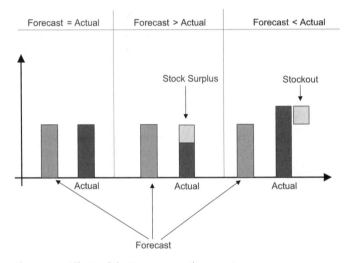

Figure 4.1 Effects of the Forecast on the Inventory

Forecast Meets Requirements

In real life, this situation almost never occurs. A forecast accuracy of 100% is very rare in demand planning, because it is highly unlikely that nothing needs to be optimized and everything has been optimally planned.

Period 1 in Figure 4.1 shows the inventory development if the forecast is an exact prediction of the actual requirements. In this case, the previously produced warehouse stock is consumed completely and no delta is left.

Forecast Bigger Than Requirements

In this case, the planners have overestimated the demand. The finished products (or assemblies) have been produced to stock, but are not sold as planned. The warehouse remains filled and the stocks are not consumed.

Production has produced a surplus of stocks and used valuable resources for the wrong products. The stocks, which haven't been sold, decrease the company's profits because they are tied-up capital.

Period 2 in Figure 4.1 shows the inventory development if the forecast is bigger than the actual requirements. The previously produced warehouse stock is not consumed completely. Some stock remains in the warehouse and parts of it may even have to be scrapped.

Optimizing Demand Planning

Figure 4.1 illustrates what happens if the forecast accuracy can be improved. In period 2, surplus stocks are reduced, while in period 3, stockouts are reduced. This means that an improved forecast accuracy has a direct influence on the inventory and therefore results in an optimization.

Additional Influencing Factors

An inaccurate demand planning affects all processes in the company's supply chain.

▶ **Influences on distribution**
  ▹ Decrease of the service level due to stockouts
  ▹ Loss of sales due to non-deliveries, resulting in a loss of customers to the competition
  ▹ Extension of the sales order lead time if non-availability of an order contributes to the stagnancy of production and procurement, which cannot be triggered until a sales order comes in

▶ **Influences on logistics**
  ▹ Increased capital tie-up due to high inventory levels
  ▹ Increase of the scrap rate due to limited shelf life of products
  ▹ Increased capital tie-up (storage resources) due to increased requirement of storage capacities

▶ **Influences on production**
  ▹ Increased utilization of resources if production exceeds actual requirements
  ▹ Reduced availability of resources and flexibility in production if additional stockout orders must be processed

> ▶ Increased capital tie-up if surplus production causes higher capacity requirements

> ▶ Increased lead times in production due to excessive use of capacities and constant exception control during stockout order processing

▶ **Influences on procurement**

> ▶ The procurement reliability of vendors decreases due to constant rush orders disturbing the production process

> ▶ Procurement costs increase, because the increased production costs of the vendors (due to rush orders) are forwarded in the long run

> ▶ Raw material stocks increase, because the finished products are changed due to the nonexistent requirements

4.2   The Bullwhip Effect

In addition to the company's internal influences on the inventory, we must also consider the external influences across the entire supply chain. It is exactly at this point that the bullwhip effect comes into play. The bullwhip effect was first described by Forrester in 1961 (1997, pp. 546–558), and it demonstrates the effects of uncertainties within a cross-company supply chain. Let's look at an example from the consumer goods industry to better understand this effect. Figure 4.2 illustrates the sales of diapers.

Figure 4.2 The Bullwhip Effect

Example of a Bullwhip Effect

The consumption of diapers by the babies is relatively constant; however, parents buy the diapers irregularly, because they want to take advantage of price differences and stock up on diapers. The retailers and the wholesale traders do the same with larger quantities. So, despite the constant consumption of diapers, the producer of the diapers and the vendors receive a sudden large-scale order. The safety stocks increase step by step and at each step there's a different need for security. In this way, the demand increases across the entire supply chain. Often, the quantity variations reach values of up to 50 to 70%. Consequently, the individual levels in the supply chain hold too much stock. The individual ordering behavior leads to the creation of safety stocks, because the second level only knows the consumption of the previous level and cannot use the actual consumption values for the planning process.

Causes of the Bullwhip Effect

The three major causes of the bullwhip effect can be found in the following areas:

▸ Safety-conscious attitude

▸ Non-harmonized order quantities and processes

▸ Low forecast accuracies

If the forecast accuracy is low, the safety stock requirement increases because uncertainties and planning variances must be compensated with increased stocks to ensure the ability to deliver.

4.3   Optimization Potentials for the Forecast

A *forecast* is always a statement about future events that is based on past observations. Usually, a forecast is predicated on the belief that future data behaves like past data; however, it's very rare that a past trend will repeat itself in exactly the same way. Therefore, based on experience, we can speak the following truth about forecasts:

There's one thing common to all forecasts: They are usually wrong!

The individual forecast methods and the models they are based on differ primarily in the degree of their wrongness. Each planning step that is based on data taken from the demand planning process contains a degree of uncertainty. The difference between the forecast quantity and the actual figures affects the service level of the entire supply chain. Since the service level can usually never reach 100%, safety stocks represent an appropriate instrument for increasing the service level and reaching a certain degree. The level of safety stock is closely linked to the forecast, because it is calculated using the forecast error.

Therefore, it is important that you try to reduce the number of forecast errors to zero, which would be the ideal state. Of course, that's not possible, as we have already demonstrated. Nevertheless, we'd like to introduce some optimization potentials in the following sections that enable you to generate better forecasts.

4.3.1 Analyzing Market Influences

At the beginning of each forecast process, you should always perform an exact analysis of the market situation. The following questions will help you to do just that:

▸ How dynamic is the market?

▸ At what speed do changes occur?

▸ Am I participating in a buyer-driven or seller-driven market?

▸ Am I acting in a local or global market?

▸ How many competitors exist?

▸ Are there any legal regulations for a market that I have to consider?

Market Dynamics

In a *rapidly changing market*, you must carry out the demand planning process more often and in small intervals. Your forecast should include the market changes as soon as they occur. If the product lifecycle periods of your products are short, you must constantly verify your forecasts and adjust them to new products. For this reason, the forecast horizon should also be short.

If you want to introduce new, innovative products to the market, you must activate the lifecycle and promotion plannings. Here, you must ensure that the demand for your established products will decrease.

In a strongly growing market with a fierce competition, you must use slightly higher forecasts to prevent you from losing any sales and market shares due to stockouts.

In a market with a high rate of inflation, excess productions are deliberately taken into account to ensure that the capital is tied up in the warehouse rather than with the bank. The reason for this is that a high inflation rate can decrease the capital value much faster if it is in the bank account instead of in the warehouse.

Increased import tariffs can also affect the demand. Therefore, it is important that the planner have access to such information immediately from the sales and distribution or marketing departments, so that the forecast can be adjusted in real time.

To improve your forecast and increase the forecast accuracy, you must continuously observe your sales market so that you can immediately respond to the influences described above. If the market grows while the market shares remain unchanged, you must simply multiply your forecast by the market growth value. If market shares change due to aggressive price dumping by the competition, or due to the entry of new players to the market, it is very difficult to estimate the influences. But it is important that you use a forecasting tool that provides the transparency and flexibility required in order to quickly adapt to changing influences.

The Marketplace

If you carry out a forecast for a product in a locally known market, your planner will certainly be able to provide better figures than in a more distant, unknown market. At home you're more familiar with the demand and competition, you can refer to a longer history, and sometimes you even know your own customers personally. The conditions can be much different in another country, where orders are placed either by partners or sales offices; hoardings or non-calculable changes in the order date are not unusual; and often, the workdays and opening hours in shops are different. You must take all of this into account if you want to forecast the requirements in a different country.

The more distant the market, the lower the forecast accuracy (see Table 4.1).

	Local Market	Distant Market
Average error rate 30-day forecast	12%	22%
Average error rate 90-day forecast	38%	45%

Table 4.1 Average Error Rate on Local and Distant Markets

For a 30-day forecast, the average forecast error rate is 12%, in this case, for a customer from the consumer goods industry. The error rate increases to approximately 22% at a global level for the same forecast period. The same phenomenon occurs for long-term forecasts (i.e., over 90 days).

On the one hand, you should determine different levels regarding the target forecast accuracy; on the other hand, you should take into account continuity and experience as influencing factors when doing a forecast for a foreign country.

Competitors

The competitive situation in the market and the market dynamics can suddenly change the requirement situation of traditionally stable products. Consequently, you should observe and analyze market influences with the utmost precision. A new competitor can have a substantial influence on the demand for your products and you must be able to respond quickly to this new player. It is essential that you can estimate how much influence these changes will have on the demand for your products. A forecast method won't detect these changes until they become historical data changes. So, the best thing to do is for you to record the changes immediately and stabilize the requirement quantities forecast upwards or downwards (by adjusting the alpha, beta, and gamma factors), or reduce the forecast for the area in which the new competitor enters the market. In this arena, it is the planner's experience that determines the outcome.

4.3.2 Analyzing Product Influences

Once you have analyzed the market situation, you must examine the product influences on your forecast and consider the following questions:

- How frequently are new products introduced to the market?
- How long has the product been on the market?
- At what stage of their lifecycle are my products?
- Are there any seasonal requirements?
- Should I sell standard products or products with many variants?

Product Lifecycle

You should analyze the lifecycle of your products. The lifecycle of a product is usually divided into the following stages: introduction, growth, maturity, saturation, and discontinuation (see Figure 4.3).

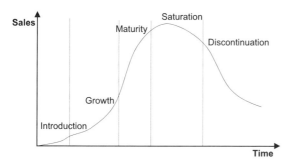

Figure 4.3 Lifecycle of a Product and Its Different Stages

In the *growth stage* of the product, the demand grows stronger than it does in the *introduction stage*. This means that the forecast model of the first stage no longer fits. Because the speed of the demand changes, the speed of the forecast method must change accordingly.

The same applies to the next stage when the product leaves the maturity stage and enters the *saturation stage*. If demand planning does not take this stage into account, its requirements' forecasts will be too high and the increase of its stocks will be inexorable. This change of the stages also requires the adjustment or even replacement of the forecast model. Products at the saturation stage have a long history and are the demand planner's favorites, because there's usually always a demand for them and specific influences can be easily calculated.

Product lifecycles are becoming increasingly shorter in many areas. This represents another major challenge for the forecast accuracy at the introduction stage, as the following example will demonstrate.

A manufacturer of sporting goods sells sporting equipment and textiles that are subject to strong seasonal demands. Most of the products have very short lifecycles that run between two and six months, which is due to a high product renewal rate. For example, a new range of products usually consists of 40 to 60% of new products. There are four new product ranges per year. In addition, new products are difficult to forecast due to the lack of historical data. In this example, qualitative forecast methods have an advantage.

New products often include analogisms, that is, you search for products that have as many characteristics as possible in common with the new product, and the history of those analogous products can be used as a basis for forecasting the new product. Yet you can never be sure that your new forecast is really accurate, and again, it is important that you realize this as soon as possible (transparency) so you can respond to the new situation quickly and with flexibility. Without the appropriate tools that do the "manual" work for the planner, you cannot take action at the right time.

Cannibalization

The cannibalization of products is a phenomenon that's closely linked to the product lifecycle. It describes the mutual influence that two or more products have on each other. The demand for a new product (at the introduction or growth stage) can affect the demand for existing products, which are at the saturation or discontinuation stages.

For example, if a coffee maker is introduced in a new color, the demand or the existing model will probably weaken. In fact, the market for coffee makers has not grown, because a new product color has been introduced. The same situation applies to a promotion action. Promotions are supposed to specifically advertise certain products, for example, chocolate ice cream. At the same time, the demand for vanilla ice cream decreases because the customers are influenced by the advertising campaign. In other words, the vanilla ice cream is cannibalized by the chocolate ice cream.

You can counteract this problem by implementing *phase-in* and *phase-out mechanisms*. In a phase-in/phase-out modeling process, the result of the statistical forecast is multiplied by a time-dependent factor. The result of this process is the final forecast. The time-dependent factor is stored in a phase-in or phase-out profile. In phase-in profiles (for the coffee maker in the new color), the factor increases over time, whereas it decreases in phase-out profiles (for the coffee maker in the old color). This interdependency or cannibalization must be taken into account in demand planning.

Lifecycle Planning Using SAP APO

Lifecycle planning in SAP Advanced Planner and Optimizer (SAP APO) comprises two functions—like modeling and phase-in/phase-out modeling. Both functions enable a forecast at details and aggregate levels; however, they can also be used for other characteristics. For example, if you introduce an existing product at a different location, you can use *like profiles* to base your calculations on historical data from the current locations. You can then use a phase-in profile to reduce the forecast to the introductory period.

Lifecycle planning is linked to the univariate forecast, the causal analysis, and the composite forecast.

Like Modeling

At the beginning of a forecast creation for new characteristic values combinations, it is unlikely that historical data, which could be used as a basis for the forecast, exists. You can copy data from a different characteristic values combination using the realignment function, but that would result in an unnecessary increase of the quantity of redundant data in the system. In a like modeling process, one characteristic value is replaced by another value or values. This results in a new combination for which historical data does exist. Based on this data, the team can then create a forecast.

The following example describes the introduction of a new ice cream flavor—almond—with the product number, T-FV300. For this new flavor, there is no historical sales data available that could be used as a basis for the creation of a new forecast. For this reason, the historical data (sales history) for the vanilla and chocolate flavors is to be used to simulate historical data for the new flavor. You can do this by using the like profile.

In SAP APO, you can maintain the like profile in the following menu: **SAP APO Menu · Demand Planning · Environment · Life Cycle Planning**.

The system displays the input screen shown in Figure 4.4. Specify a **Planning Area** and a **Characteristic**, and assign a **Like Profile** number and a **Description** to the like profile.

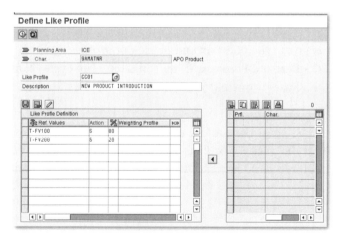

Figure 4.4 Maintaining a Like Profile in SAP APO

In the **Reference Values** column, you should enter materials that are to be referred to for forecasting the new product, T-FV300. In the above example, the forecast for the new product, T-FV300, is based at 80% on the historical data of the T-FV100 product, and at 20% on the historical values of the T-FV200 product. Finally, the like profile must be assigned to the new product, T-FV300.

Therefore, SAP APO enables you to base your forecast on one or more similar products.

Phase-in-/Phase-out Modeling

The demand for an object in its introduction and discontinuation phases usually differs from the demand in the product's maturity phase. At the beginning, the demand rises with every period, whereas it decreases towards the end of the lifecycle. A statistical forecast that's based on the situation in the maturity phase cannot predict such a behavior. In a phase-in/phase-out modeling process, the result of the statistical forecast is multiplied by a time-dependent factor. The result of this process is the final forecast. The time-dependent factor is stored in a phase-in or phase-out profile. In phase-in profiles, the factor increases over time, while it gets smaller in phase-out profiles.

In our forecast example, we now want to take into account the lifecycle curve for the new almond ice cream product. For this purpose, we have chosen a time series that's supposed to map the product lifecycle influences. The time series must be assigned to the new ice cream flavor. After that, the forecast is multiplied by the time series in the respective periods so that the influences of the lifecycle can be integrated into the forecast.

In SAP APO, you can maintain the phase-in and phase-out profiles in the following menu: **SAP APO · Demand Planning · Environment · Life Cycle Planning**. Then click on the **Phase-in/out** button. The system displays the input screen shown in Figure 4.5.

Select a **planning area**, assign a **name** and a **description** to the time series, and define the period for the phase-in or phase-out by entering the **start** and **end dates**. Select the required period by choosing the respective **period identifier**.

In our ice cream scenario, we have defined a phase-in period of 10 weeks, in which the sales figures increase by 10% per period until they reach a value of 100% above the basic value in week 10. Phase-in time series are entered in ascending order; phase-out time series are entered in descending order.

Similar to the phase-out and like profiles, the phase-in profile must be assigned to a material (see Figure 4.6).

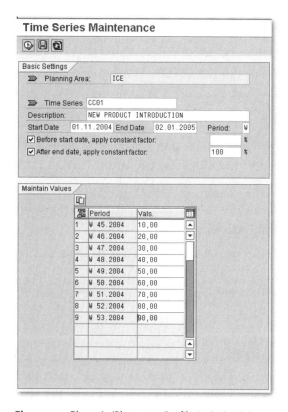

Figure 4.5 Phase-in/Phase-out Profile in SAP APO

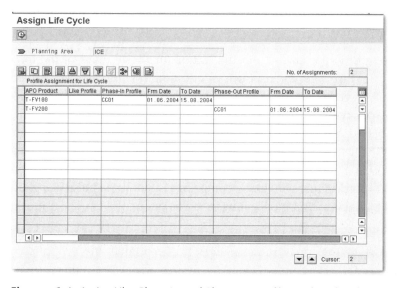

Figure 4.6 Assigning Like, Phase-in, and Phase-out Profiles to the Lifecycle

Therefore, when you introduce a new product or discontinue an existing one, you should be cognizant that the demands differ substantially from those in the maturity phase. Using the phase-in/phase-out modeling function in SAP APO enables you to take this differentiation into account; however, you should note that you couldn't map a real lifecycle using the phase-in profile. Because real-life requirements are often highly complex, you cannot simply meet them via a simple time series. Nevertheless, you can at least create a facsimile of real-life requirements by using that function. Additionally, you can also map the lifecycle directly in the forecast method, as illustrated in the example shown in Figure 4.6.

4.3.3 Creating a Consistent Data Basis

The most important basis for selecting the right forecast method and for increasing the forecast accuracy is the historical data. Without this data, statistical methods won't work. Consequently, you must ensure that your forecast is based on a consistent data basis.

Historical Consumption (Actual Data)

When optimizing your forecast, note that you must change or adjust your forecast models for different phases. Just because a forecast model has been chosen and optimized once doesn't mean that it is the optimal forecast. General conditions such as the volume of demand or the product lifecycle phase can change and necessitate a new selection process for the right forecast method.

One of the most important influencing factors for the accuracy of the forecast is the sales history of the products in question. If a product has been on the market for a very long time and if the historical sales figures are archived, an automatic forecast method could refer to comprehensive sales figures that may have been achieved in a distant past. And yet, we cannot say unequivocally that the quality of the forecast increases with the quantity of historical data. There are many influencing factors. One of the reasons that accounts for the poor forecast quality in many companies is that those influencing factors are often ignored. But we'll get back to that later.

In general, historical data is very important because it enables you to identify trends and alterations, as well as changes in the product lifecycle phases. Let's look at another example. A manufacturer of sporting equipment who sells a multitude of fashionable products has difficulty forecasting demands for the different style and color combinations. The degree of uncertainty that exists for products, which strongly depend on trends or are entirely new, is substantially higher than that for traditional branded products such as a Levi's 501 jeans or a Coke whose forecasts are based on large data quantities with a long history.

Data Quality Requirements

If you want to create different forecasts, the underlying data should be taken from different sources and be statistically independent. Therefore, you must pay special attention to the quality of the underlying data. For each forecast project and each attempt at increasing the forecast accuracy, you must first analyze the historical data and probably also correct it.

Example: If certain customers of yours require a specific product every year during the month of March, they will order the product at exactly that time every year, provided it can be delivered at short notice. If the product is available, it will be delivered and invoiced in March. The requirement, the actual sales, and the invoiced quantity occur at the same time.

If the customer requirement cannot be delivered until April due to a shortage, this means that the requirement occurred in March, but the actual consumption occurred in April. If the actual consumption is then used as a basis for a forecast, without considering the delivery bottlenecks, your forecast will predict a requirement for this customer and product in April, although the actual requirement will occur again in March.

Therefore, it should be our goal *to make the time of requirement available* to the forecast so that the actual demand can be determined. To do that, you can choose between the following two approaches:

▶ The first approach tries to calculate a virtual demand series that's based on the actual sales figures and on the information on sold-out products. The forecasts can then be calculated based on the new demand series. According to Wagner (2000) this approach provides useful results if the number of sellouts is small.

▶ Alternatively, you can use complex statistical methods that consider the sales figures observed as a censored sample. For this approach, it is necessary to know the stockholding methods for the considered products.

Another aspect that you should consider to ensure a consistent data basis is the *confirmation behavior during delivery*. For a consumption-driven forecast, in particular, the forecast is determined on the basis of actual consumption data. The actual consumption results from the goods issues from the warehouse at the time of delivery. Normally, the goods issues should be posted in the system at the time of the actual delivery on the basis of the material withdrawal document; however, in some companies, goods issues are not posted on a regular basis.

Figure 4.7 shows the difference between a regular and an irregular confirmation discipline. The upper image illustrates the consumption progress for a regular confirmation behavior, while the lower image displays the consumption for an irregular confirmation behavior. The red line represents the possible forecast result if the forecast had been carried out on November 30, 2004. The different confirmation behaviors would cause the system to calculate a completely different forecast.

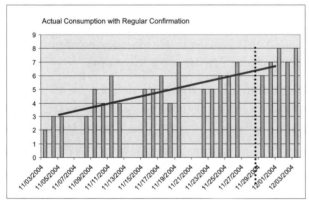

Possible forecast on 11/30/2004 with regular confirmation discipline

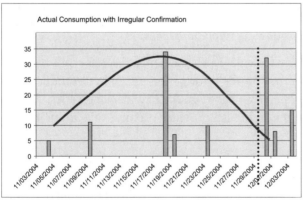

Possible forecast on 11/30/2004 with irregular confirmation discipline

Figure 4.7 Possible Forecast Based on a Regular and Irregular Confirmation Discipline

The preceding examples clearly show that the historical data is subject to various requirements that you have to take into account:

▸ You should use only forecast-relevant data records as a basis for the historical data and exclude all remaining data from the forecast.

▸ Exceptional processes such as returns must also be considered separately. Those processes should be stored in a separate key figure. Returns would increase the consumption value that's actually relevant to the forecast, because they have to be added to the customer requirements to be met. As a matter of fact, the requirement did exist even though you weren't able to satisfy it due to poor product quality.

▸ It is necessary to restrict the timing of the periods exactly and regularly. For this purpose, you should use the correct document date (customer's preferred date/delivery date/purchase order date). The original date preferred by the customer best represents the actual requirement date.

▸ You must also ensure that the data is consistently determined for all periods to avoid gaps in your data history (confirmation discipline).

Correcting the Historical Data Basis

To create forecasts with a high degree of accuracy, you must remove *influences resulting from one-time actions* from the actual data. Typically, those corrections are not done in the original key figure, but in the **Corrected History** key figure.

Figure 4.8 (page 110) shows the original history on the left, which contains one-time effects. On the right-hand side of the figure, you can see the history that has been corrected by yourself. It no longer contains the one-time effects and therefore represents a better basis for your forecast.

In the forecast profile, you can define whether you want to base the forecast on original actual data or on corrected actual data.

To define the data basis in such a way that it supports your demand planning process optimally, you should at least use the following key figures in planning the demand:

▸ **Key figure "Enter Historical Data"**
The key figure for historical values can be entered in the univariate forecast profile in the **Read Historical Data** group field (see Figure 4.9, page 111). You can access the forecast profile via the following menu path: **SAP APO · Demand Planning · Environment · Maintain Forecast Profiles**.

The key figure used to enter historical data (sometime it is also referred to as order history) is the key figure whose actual data is used to calculate the forecast.

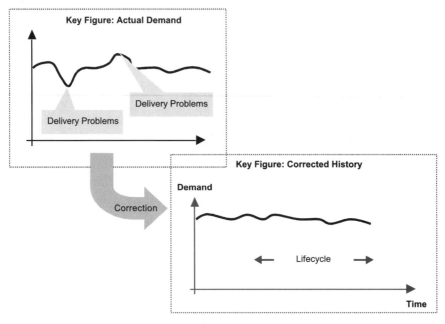

Figure 4.8 Real History (upper left) and Corrected History (bottom right) (Source: SAP)

▶ **Key figure "Original History"**
The original history is usually almost identical to the **Enter Historical Data** key figure. The system corrects the historical data values that you entered according to the phase-in and phase-out profiles, provided you use those proiles in your forecast. The result is referred to as the original history. The original history is displayed in the interactive demand planning if you have previously included an actual data row for the Enter Historical Data key figure in the planning book.

▶ **Key figure "Corrected History"**
This is the key figure that stores the history, which has either been corrected automatically by the system or manually by the user. If you set the **Corrected forecast from planning version** flag, the system uses the corrected history as a basis for the forecast instead of the historical data key figure (**Enter Historical Data**) in the univariate profile. This way you can use the planner's know-how to adjust the history without affecting the original history.

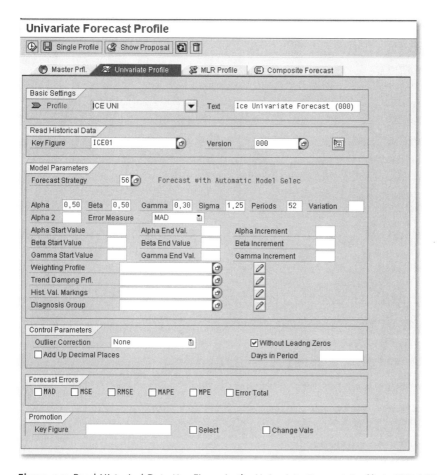

Figure 4.9 Read Historical Data Key Figure in the Univariate Forecast Profile in SAP APO

▶ **Key figure "Baseline Forecast (original forecast)"**
The baseline forecast describes the key figure that stores the results of the original forecast. Furthermore, if a phase-in or phase-out profile exists, that profile is applied to the original forecast. You must enter the key figure of the original forecast as a **forecast key figure** in the **master profile**. You can maintain the forecast profile via the following menu path: **SAP APO · Demand Planning · Environment · Maintain Forecast Profile**.

▶ **Key figure "Corrected Forecast"**
This is the key figure that stores the forecast, which has either been corrected automatically by the system or manually by the user. This way you can use the planner's know-how to adjust the forecast determined by the system without affecting the original forecast.

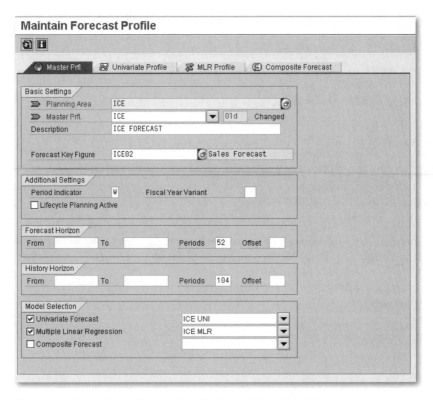

Figure 4.10 Forecast Key Figure in the Master Profile in SAP APO

▶ **Key figure "Promotion"**
The system stores a promotion as an absolute figure in the **Promotion** key figure. If you define your promotion as a percentage value, the system converts the percentage into an absolute value prior to saving it. This key figure enables you to differentiate between the baseline and promotion forecasts. Ideally, you should also differentiate between promotional sales and regular sales by using a flag in the customer sales order, or by using different types of customer sales orders so that you can calculate a forecast accuracy for promotion forecasts.

▶ **Key figures for other events**
To purge your forecast from exceptional influences, you can store the exceptional influences in separate key figures. You can use two key figures for this purpose. You can use one of the key figures for regular events such as trade shows or public holidays. This enables you to monitor and measure the forecasts separately for the events. The other key figure that you can use is the **Promotion** key figure. You could also use an additional key

figure for irregularly occurring events, for example, for sales that are caused by exceptionally hot weather, or by a one-time event such as the FIFA Soccer World Cup 2006.

Correcting the Work Days

When preparing your forecast, you must also understand that identical time periods can contain a different number of workdays or different days of sale.

By correcting the work days you can account for a varying number of work-days per month. In SAP APO, you base your forecast on an average number of work days per forecast period. You can enter that number in the **Days in Period** field in the Univariate Forecast Profile (see Figure 4.9). You can main-tain the forecast profile via the following menu path: **SAP APO · Demand Planning · Environment · Maintain Forecast Profile**.

In the example shown in Figure 4.11, the forecast period is called **Month** and the assumed number of work days in the period is **20**.

Past			
	M1	M2	M3
Original Act.	1900	2100	2300
Days	19	21	23
Corr.	2000	2000	2000

Forecast			
	M4	M5	M6
Non-corr.	2000	2000	2000
Days	22	20	18
Corr.	2200	2000	1800

➡ Specify average number of work days (e.g., 20) in forecast profile

Figure 4.11 Correcting the Past Work Days (left) in the Forecast (right)

You can carry out the forecast as follows:

1. Correct the historical data according to the following formula:

$$Corrected\ history = (\frac{original\ history}{actual\ workdays}) \times average\ number\ of\ workdays$$

In Figure 4.11, the result of the corrected history is shown in the **Corr.** fields in the **Past** table.

2. Calculate the forecast on the basis of the corrected historical data and enter the result in the **Non-corr.** fields in the **Forecast** table. The system adjusts this first "uncorrected" forecast result according to the following formula:

$$Corrected\ forecast = (\frac{uncorrected\ forecast}{average\ number\ of\ workdays}) \times actual\ number\ of\ workdays$$

The result is shown in the bottom line of the right-hand table in Figure 4.11. The number of work days in the period is determined by the factory calendar in the planning area. The result of the correction of plan data is stored in the **Corrected Forecast** key figure.

Correcting Outliers

To obtain a consistent data basis, you must also correct outliers in your historical data. Even though this is difficult when dealing with large data quantities, the planner must quickly react to outliers, evaluate forecast errors, and identify trends and exceptional influences. A modern forecasting system can help you meet all those requirements. SAP APO supports you in quickly and efficiently monitoring and evaluating large data quantities by using standard and user-specific alerts. This is very useful for correcting outliers.

There are several options available to handle outliers. On the one hand, the developer can use a tolerance lane, which is not determined until after the model has been adjusted. All values outside that range can then be corrected, for example, to the calculated average value of historical data or to the forecast value of the corresponding period. On the other hand, you can use percentage deviations to correct outliers. For this purpose, you must first correct all forecast values whose difference to the historical value exceeds or falls short of a certain percentage. But, you must not mistake outliers for extreme values, which can be part of a seasonal component.

To respond to outliers, the forecasting function in SAP APO determines a tolerance lane. Each observed value outside of the calculated tolerance lane is automatically corrected. SAP APO provides two methods of outlier correction:

Ex-post method
In this method, the system uses the ex-post forecast to determine a tolerance lane. If an historical value falls outside that range, the system considers it to be an outlier and corrects it. This is done in such a way that the historical

value corresponds to the ex-post forecast value determined for the respective period. Section 4.7.1 contains more detailed information on ex-post forecasts.

Median method

The system uses the median method to determine the ex-post forecast values for the basic value, trend value, and seasonal index. It can therefore calculate an expected value for each historical period.

The width of the tolerance lane for the automatic outlier correction is defined by the *sigma factor*. This factor determines the permitted standard deviations. The smaller the sigma factor, the lower the tolerance and the higher the number of outliers determined and corrected. The default value is 1.25. If you want to set a different factor, you should use a value between 0.6 and 2, as recommended by SAP.

Once the outlier correction has been performed, the ex-post forecast is calculated once again, but it is now based on the corrected values.

Time Series Patterns

Choosing the right forecast method is another essential aspect to obtain a high degree of forecast accuracy. Therefore, you must identify the time series patterns of your products. When considering a time series, you should examine the causes of the movements and treat the movement itself as a component that depends on the calendar time. The benefit of this approach is that you don't have to take into account the many influences that affect the time series. Instead, you can split up a time series into the following different components:

▶ **Trend component**
The trend describes the long-term direction of the time series, for example it can be increasing arithmetically, decreasing arithmetically, increasing quadratically, and increasing decliningly.

▶ **Cyclical component**
This component describes the medium-term development, for example, for economic cycles. If only a few months or years are considered, the cyclical component can hardly be distinguished from the trend component. It is therefore not examined separately, but is integrated in the trend component.

▶ **Sesonal component**
The seasonal component records regularly recurring, short-term, and seasonal movements. Not only does this component depend on specific types of products such as winter clothing, but also on the weather or on specific public holidays such as Christmas, for example.

▶ **Random or rest component**
All short-term influences that occur irregularly are assigned to the random or rest component.

The easiest method you can use to identify the individual components in a time series is a graphical display. To obtain a graphical display, you should click on the **Graphic** button in the interactive planning.

4.3.4 Defining the Optimal Forecast Horizon

To react flexibly to your customers' requirements, you need to implement short lead times and a short forecast horizon, as well as a high forecast frequency.

Flexibility by Short Forecast Horizons

Long *lead times* have a negative effect on the forecast accuracy and the company's ability to react. Rush orders cannot be filled on short notice, because production is not flexible enough due to the long lead times. Shortening the production lead times, on the other hand, increases the flexibility and leads to an increased planning accuracy.

Moreover, long lead times require long *forecast horizons*. The forecast horizon is the period for which the forecast is carried out. It often happens that the replenishment lead time for individual critical components determines the forecast horizon. The longer the forecast horizon, the bigger the forecast error. The shorter he lead time, the longer a planner can wait to include a higher number of sales orders and to collect information that can be integrated in the forecast. The longer the demand planner can wait before publishing the forecast and the shorter the forecast horizon, the more accurate the forecasts.

In addition, the degree of *flexibility* and the ability to respond to demand changes increase if the forecast frequency corresponds to the short forecast horizons. This means that you can carry out a forecast for a horizon of three to six months, whereas you are forecasting the current month in weekly periods. Sales and distribution should also be able to enter current sales figures into the forecasting tool on a weekly basis. In this way, you can ensure that you'll be able to respond to market fluctuations very quickly.

Whereas in the past negotiations between customers and suppliers used to focus only on the price, today the object of the negotiations is often the time factor. The *delivery time* therefore becomes a competitive factor and represents an essential decision criterion for the customer when selecting the products. You should not underestimate the influence of the overall order lead time in global competition. Consequently, companies must provide their customers with incentives for early orders, which, in fact, simulates a prolongation of the wait time for the customers. In this way, you can reduce expensive safety stocks and replace them with a higher degree of flexibility and an improved forecast accuracy.

Defining the Forecast Horizon in SAP APO

In SAP APO, you can use the planning buckets profile to make the following definitions:

▶ Define the periods you want to use in your planning

▶ Define the number of periods of each period type you want to use

▶ Define the sequence in which you want to display the periods in the planning table

Planning can occur based on monthly, weekly, or (in combination with fiscal year variants) on specifically defined periods. You can create several planning buckets profiles and planning horizons for a planning book. The planning buckets profile is assigned to the data view within the planning book. For example, you can create three different data views for three different users, basing each view on a different planning buckets profile. The marketing department plans in terms of months; sales and distribution plans in terms of months and weeks; and logistics plans in terms of weeks and days.

The timeframe shown in the example in Figure 4.12 comprises three months. The first two months are displayed in terms of weeks. The first week is displayed in terms of days.

This subdivision enables you to better control the forecast in the short-term horizon than in the medium and long-term horizons.

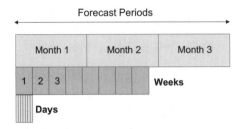

Figure 4.12 Optimal Display of Forecast Periods

4.3.5 Considering Promotions

Marketing instruments such as actions and promotions are used to increase the sales figures on a short-term basis. They are often prepared well in advance, planned in cooperation with customers, and then carried out as planned. The quantities required for promotional goods can vary. Sales promotions strongly increase the short-term demand, which sets higher requirements to transportation and warehouse logistics. Specific displays are also often required. All this requires a high degree of flexibility across the entire supply chain. Usually customers are integrated in the process at a very early stage and provided with all the relevant information. For example, for price reductions, the retail businesses purchase the promotional goods in excess of the actual requirement so as to benefit as much as possible from the lower cost prices (forward buying, see Figure 4.13). The retailers' demand on the manufacturer's side will be lower than the actual end consumer demand when the sales promotion is finished.

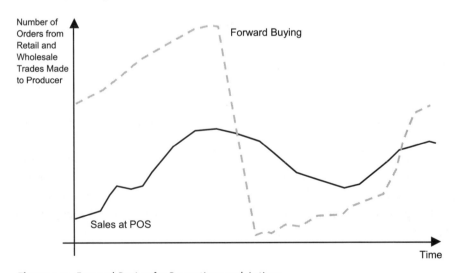

Figure 4.13 Forward Buying for Promotions and Actions

With a sales promotion, the vendor unexpectedly receives several larger orders over a short period of time. These orders are not reflected in the vendor's historical data. The company's sales forecast will have a poor quality with regard to the promotion period of its customer if the company is not integrated in the promotion planning process at an early stage.

The demand planning process must distinguish promotional measures and other special events from other forecast activities. Promotions are planned either as one-time events (for example, when a new product is introduced), or as recurring events (for example, quarterly advertising campaigns). Other examples of promotions include trade shows, trade discounts and commissions, high-visibility sales, promotional actions including gift certificates, raffles or magazine supplements, competitive activities, market research, economic upswings and downturns, as well as large natural phenomena. Prior to introducing the promotional campaign, you should therefore try to estimate the promotional quantities as accurately as possible so that you have the right quantities in stock and at the point of sales (POS).

Segmenting Promotions

First you must analyze how precisely you can forecast the demand for your promotion. Here, it is essential to know if it is a recurring action (for example a trade show), or the introduction of a new product. Some new introductions merely involve the introduction of a new variant. If that is the case, you can base your forecast on historical consumption values of existing variants. But, for an entirely new product line or range of products, generating a forecast will be much harder. You can use a matrix to support your analysis efforts (see Figure 4.14).

The promotion matrix illustrates the product policy on the vertical axis and the market dynamics on the horizontal axis. The product policy tells you whether the product in question is a replacement product or a new product, whether a new product will extend the range of products, and whether a product variant or a new product is planned. The market dynamics subdivide the seasonal cycle into *No Season*, a *Medium Season* over a period of six to 12 months, and a *Short Season* of three to six months. For the introduction of a replacement product that doesn't depend on any season, the promotion is easily predictable. When a new product is introduced in the short-season area, it will be very difficult to forecast the promotion.

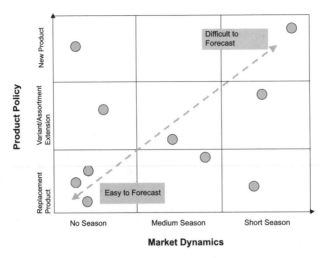

Figure 4.14 Promotion Matrix for the Introduction of a New Product

You can create a similar matrix for promotions related to events (trade shows, Christmas, and so on), as shown in the example in Figure 4.15.

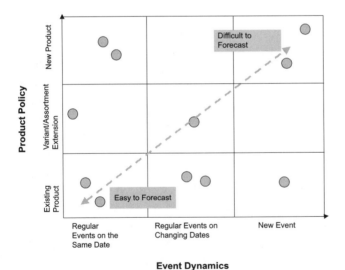

Figure 4.15 Promotion Matrix for Events

In this matrix, you can see that the product policy on the vertical axis can be subdivided into the promotion of an existing product, an extension of the range of products, and the promotion of a new product. The event dynamics distinguishes between events that occur regularly at the same time (e.g., Christmas) and those that occur regularly but at different times (e.g., trade shows). In addition, it identifies events that occur for the first time and for which there are no historical values available (e.g., the FIFA Soccer World Cup 2006).

The segmentations described above provide information on the forecast quality that you can expect for the promotion. This is also important for possible target definitions for sales and distribution, since those definitions can differ depending on the event or on the product policy.

In those cases where the promotion forecast is difficult, you should build forecast teams. First, you should collect different forecasts from the marketing, sales and distribution, and demand planning teams. Then, all team members involved can synchronize the figures in a consensus-based forecast. Big differences in the different forecasts mean increased uncertainties for the promotion. You should therefore assign the ordered promotion quantities to the distribution areas and organizations as late as possible. If the different forecasts correspond with each other to a large extent, you can make those assignments at an earlier stage.

Forecast Horizon for Promotions

The forecast horizon is very important in promotion planning. The promotion must be well prepared. This involves the production of the promotion quantities prior to the promotion start. Moreover, it must be verified that the quantities are actually available at the point of sales when the promotion starts. During the promotion period, which can last several weeks, the actual consumption data must be included in the promotion planning in real time. This means that short forecast horizons are required. You can start each promotion planning by using monthly periods; but when the promotion starts, you should switch to weekly or even daily horizons so that you can include the actual consumption values.

Allocations with Scarce Supplies

When planning promotions you must pay special attention to hoardings from the foreign distribution offices. They often order a multitude of the product quantities they actually require to obtain at least a part of the scarce supply. This increases the forecast for the planned promotion dramatically, which is unrealistic, because it means that remaining stocks must be sold at a lower profit margin or even be scrapped. To avoid this situation, you should allocate promotion quantities to the distributors on the basis of the historical accuracy of the forecast. If a distribution organization or area creates a particularly accurate forecast, it should be rewarded with the quantity it has ordered, since it is very likely that the organization or area will actually sell all products.

Cannibalization in Promotions

Cannibalization effects can also be observed in promotion planning. It can happen that one and the same promotion affects the sales of some products positively and other products negatively. The mutual influence of the demand for similar products is referred to as *cannibalization*.

For example, a 5% discount on 32 oz. bottles of a peach shampoo can cause a sales increase of 30,000 units (in the figure on top), whereas the sales of 8.5 oz. bottles decreases by 3,000 units and that of 17 oz. bottles by 5,000 units (in the figure at the bottom). This situation is illustrated in Figure 4.16.

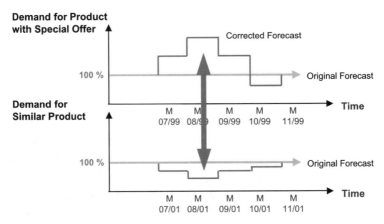

Figure 4.16 Example of Cannibalization (Source: SAP)

In an SAP system, you must define the members of a cannibalization group and assign them a factor. The factor determines the amount by which the sales of the relevant product are influenced. To do so, select **SAP APO · Demand Planning · Planning · Settings · Maintain Cannibalization Group**. The system then displays the input screen shown in Figure 4.17.

Enter a **name** and a **description** for the cannibalization group and select the **materials** that you want to allocate to the cannibalization group. Enter a positive or negative figure for each material in the **Factor** column, depending on whether the sales of the product are positively or negatively influenced by the promotion.

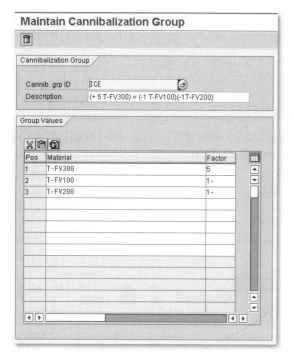

Figure 4.17 Maintaining the Cannibalization Group in SAP APO

Separating the Promotion Data Basis

A prerequisite for using promotions in demand planning is the separate specification of promotion quantities and sales from the promotion. These quantities must be available to the demand planner at any time. If they aren't, a high degree of uncertainty will prevail even when you carry out regular promotions, because you won't be able to distinguish between consumption figures that result from normal sales and those resulting from promotional sales. In mySAP ERP and SAP APO, the separate specification is part of the standard functionality and can be easily configured.

An important requirement of a promotion forecast is that it must be separated from both the baseline forecast and the historical data. The benefits of this separation are the following:

▶ You can compare the forecast without promotions with the forecast with promotions.

▶ You can correct the historical sales data in such a way that you can exclude historical promotions and therefore obtain historical data without promotional data for the baseline forecast.

▶ The process of creating baseline forecasts and the promotion planning process can be handled separately. For example, sales and distribution could create an initial forecast while marketing is responsible for the promotion planning.

To differentiate the forecast sales quantities from the promotional sales quantities, you must create at least two key figures in demand planning administration: the **baseline forecast**, which includes the normal demand planning, and the **promotion forecast**, including the key figure for the promotion.

The Promotion Planning Process

The following steps describe the complete implementation of the promotion planning process.

1. The demand planner creates a baseline forecast by using mass processing.

2. The demand planner verifies the forecast results in interactive demand planning.

3. The required promotions are created in promotion planning: For example, all promotions such as the marketing calendars that are filled with actions, industry-specific promotions, and knowledge on the exit of a competitor are assigned to the **Sales** key figure. Promotion planning can be called via the interactive demand planning.

4. In interactive planning, the demand planner views the effects of all planned promotions on the forecasted overall demand and implements final corrections in the demand plan.

5. The demand plan, which represents the final result of the baseline forecast, promotion plan, and final corrections, is released for supply network planning.

6. The constrained supply network-planning plan, which takes restrictions into account, is returned to demand planning.

7. The forecast accuracy is checked against actual data.

Promotion Planning in SAP APO

In SAP APO, you can proceed as follows to create promotions: Select **SAP APO · Demand Planning · Planning · Promotion · Promotion Planning** from the menu. Then click on the **Create Promotion** button. The system displays the input screen shown in Figure 4.18.

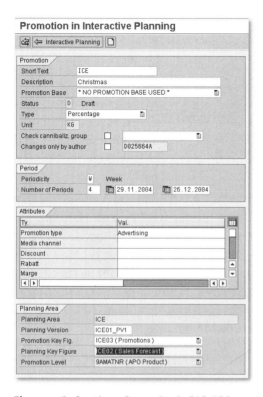

Figure 4.18 Creating a Promotion in SAP APO

Here you must enter general information such as the name of the promotion (in the **Short Text** field) and a description (**Description** field), as well as the following information:

- The **promotion type**—here you can either enter absolute figures (pieces, kilograms) or percentages of the baseline figures.
- Whether a **cannibalization group** is to be used, and if so, which one
- Whether only the **author** can make changes to the promotion
- The name of the **promotion base**, provided you want to use one
- The **status** of the promotion (first **In process**) and the **quantity unit** used in the promotion (you can only display but not enter that).
- The **periodicity** in the **Period section** (e.g., day or week)
- The **number of periods** of the promotion and either the **start date** or the **end date**
- The **in-depot periods** and **buy-in periods** for a further detailing of the period information Here you should base your assumptions on the fact

that the in-depot periods begin with the promotion start and are immediately followed by the buy-in periods. Then you can also calculate the number of in-store periods and their respective start dates. You can use those period types to map individual phases if the entire impact of the promotion is not yet to be expected.

▶ A freely defineable attribute in the **Attributes** section. The Promotion type of attribute is used as a filter for selection and analysis purposes. The **Media channel** attribute type could contain the attributes **TV**, **radio**, and **Internet**.

Once you have created the promotion, you must enter the planning data for the promotion. To do that, go to the **Interactive Demand Planning** (via **Demand Planning · Planning – Interactive Demand Planning**), and click on the **Promotion Planning** button. Then you can select the promotion you have previously created (ICE in our example) and enter the planning data either as absolute figures or as percentages. Figure 4.18 shows the entry of planning data for the promotion via the following menu: **SAP APO · Demand Planning · Planning · Interactive Demand Planning**.

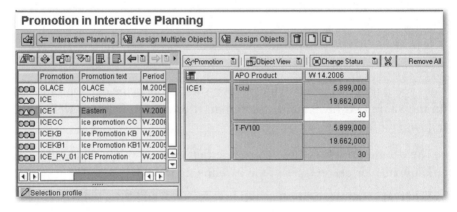

Figure 4.19 Planning Data for the Promotion in SAP APO

The left-hand part of the figure shows the selected promotion, ICECC, with a green traffic light that indicates the release of the promotion for planning purposes. The selected promotion, ICE1, has a yellow traffic light that indicates the customer does not give the release of the promotion until now. The right-hand part of the screen displays the planning data for the promotion that has been entered as a percentage increase for the following three months.

Once you have entered the planning data, you can adjust the status of the promotion. For this purpose, several default values are available. The initial status is **In process**. The statuses **Offered to customers** and **Confirmed by customers** are only to provide information. You can use them as selection criteria. The statuses are displayed with a yellow traffic light in the selection area for promotions. If a partner rejects a project in the context of an apparent collaboration, the status changes to **Rejected by customer**, and the traffic light switches to red.

The two statuses **Planned, in future** and **Active, in current periods** indicate that the promotion is included in the interactive-planning process. If you set one of those statuses, the traffic light in the promotion selection area changes to green.

When you return to the **Interactive Demand Planning** view, the system displays your planned promotion quantities (see Figure 4.20). In our example, the promotion quantities have been planned as monthly quantities, whereas the demand planning is based on weekly periods. The monthly quantities are thus distributed to the individual weeks on the basis of the number of work days. At this point, SAP APO provides a flexible integration function for the promotion and demand plannings.

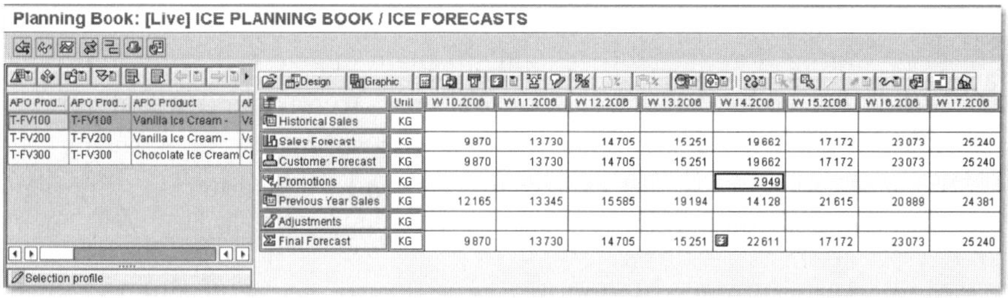

Figure 4.20 Integrated Promotion and Demand Plannings in SAP APO

4.3.6 Defining Forecast Responsibilities

To obtain an optimally created forecast, you need a clear separation of responsibilities. In this context, you must find answers to questions like the following:

▶ Who is responsible for the forecast?

▶ Who must be involved in the forecasting process?

- ▶ Do the sales and distribution and production departments cooperate optimally?
- ▶ Do the defined goals support a high forecast accuracy?
- ▶ Is the forecasting process clear and is it known within the company?

You should determine your planning and forecasting figures within a clearly defined monthly or weekly period. Involve all-important organizational areas in the forecasting process, for example, by setting up meetings across different units within your organization. The use of a binding schedule helps you establish a planning discipline in which everyone knows of and is committed to performing his or her tasks. Common reconciliation rounds (i.e., meetings in which the forecasting results are discussed and released, and which involve all organizations within the company, for example, sales, marketing, production, etc.) can be used to ensure that the promotion is understood and supported by everyone who is involved in it.

A structured planning process helps you avoid encountering the problem whereby there's only one organizational unit that is responsible for demand planning so that the final planning will be accepted across the entire company. This will enable you to establish a forecast that is binding for everyone.

An exact schedule establishes transparency and therefore motivates people to undertake responsibilities for subtasks within the entire process. The best-practices approach requires that demand planning be centrally controlled and monitored in the company. Decentral units are involved and are part of the process, but central demand planning is responsible for ensuring that everyone adheres to the process definitions, and for maintaining the planning discipline, especially with regard to the defined schedule.

For the practical implementation of this approach, it is advisable to replace the decentrally distributed Excel sheets in the company with a standardized, central software solution. As long as the planning is created using offline solutions, individual planning figures will continue to deviate from each other. In addition, you cannot implement any uniform forecast monitoring mechanisms if you continue to use offline solutions.

Forecast Levels (Aggregation/Disaggregation)

It's often difficult to predict certain developments on the basis of individual products or product variants, because either the data basis is too small, or it's virtually impossible to draw conclusions based on one product that would have company-wide ramifications. For this reason, you must use the different levels of aggregation to define at which level you want to create a forecast for a specific product. For example, by aggregating individual materials into product groups, you can create a data basis that provides sufficient information, which helps you to make specific developments visible. You can also carry out the forecasting process based on the level of material numbers or product groups.

Aggregation describes a process in which planning data is generated at a summarizing level either by totaling or copying key figure values, or by creating average values at an underlying details level. Contrary to that, the *Disaggregation* process involves the creation of planning data at a detailed level by distributing key figure values.

An aggregation process can be used to balance irregular fluctuations, which means that the forecast accuracy is always higher at an aggregate level than at a detailed level. For example, the forecast accuracy for one year is higher at the level of months and of product groups than at the product level. This also means that you can pretend to have a high forecast accuracy, even though it is rather poor at the details level.

If the degree of aggregation is too high, some information is no longer available or even lost. For example, if the aggregation occurs at the level of a strategic business area, which contains product groups with positive and negative trends, these groups can cancel out each other. This can be critical for production planning, because it can cause a heavy workload for one machine while the utilization of another machine decreases simultaneously. You should therefore define the degree of aggregation exactly instead of leaving it up to the planner's discretion. In addition, the degree of aggregation should be fixed for at least one year so that comparisons during the course of the year don't lose their meaning.

Automatic aggregations and disaggregations can support central and decentral plannings. For this purpose, you must carry out top-down and bottom-up plannings in complex planning hierarchies. This means that it is up to your company to decide whether the demand-planning process should be carried out centrally or decentrally. You can also combine the two. For example, central planning can collect data from your sales organizations and create a central forecast. This forecast can then be transferred to the sales organizations to perform plausibility checks and short-term adjustments. The adjustments of the sales organizations could occur decentrally. This entire process can be supported by an automatic aggregation and disaggregation.

Sales Goals and Bonuses Based on Forecast Accuracy

Another factor that influences the forecast accuracy is an incentive system for sales employees, who are usually involved in the demand planning process. Sales employees are supposed to predict the demand of their customers and regions. In most companies, variable salary components are linked to sales goals. If those goals are exceeded, the bonus increases; if the sales goals are not achieved, it is reduced. This means that a sales employee will always try to keep the goal as low as possible during the planning and budgeting processes.

Note that this behavior can result in an underestimation of the actual demand when planning the budget at the organizational level. The result usually involves a plan that overshoots its goal in the subsequent year.

It's not only the incentives of sales employees that cause a constant under-budgeting; often it is a too conservative attitude of the company management that is also to be blamed. The opinion that high budgets cause high fixed costs is still commonly held. Companies usually try to avoid building up capacities (machines and staff) that aren't utilized if business slows down.

Moreover, you often identify areas within companies that tend to create overplannings or underplannings, depending on their individual interests. As described above, sales and distribution tends to produce underplannings due to the incentive system for the sales employees.

In production, it is similar. The production goals are aimed primarily at the utilization of existing capacities. In case of an underplanning, capacities are scarce right from the beginning so that additional orders can be fulfilled only with a high degree of extra effort. The finance and controlling areas also try to restrict their goals as this reduces the working capital.

Contrary to that, marketing tries to increase the plannings because usually a certain percentage of the planned sales is used for marketing and advertising campaigns.

In logistics (distribution), it is important to guarantee a service level as high as possible to the customer and thereby ensure customer satisfaction. You can achieve this by ensuring that you have a high level of surplus stocks (safety stocks).

All those different views and opinions cause substantial problems in the logistics area. In the event of an underplanning, the production capacities are insufficient. This leads to short-notice changes, as important rush orders must be prioritized. Planning is incorrect and safety stocks are created at an early stage. The ability to deliver and the forecast accuracy are reduced, and consequently, the trust in the planner wanes. This results in lost sales and therefore, lost revenues.

A change in the incentive system would represent a solution to this problem. Incentives shouldn't be based on the achievement or non-achievement of sales goals, but rather on the accuracy of the forecast. Large deviations should be penalized, while the adherence to the planning should be rewarded. As a result, the plannings would be more realistic. Figure 4.21 shows a pointed curve, which demonstrates that a large deviation causes a bonus reduction. The full bonus is paid only if the deviation between the forecast and the actual achievement is plus or minus 20%. A bonus of 120% is paid if the deviation does not exceed plus or minus 10%. This is just some food for thought. The ideal incentive system must be developed individually in each company.

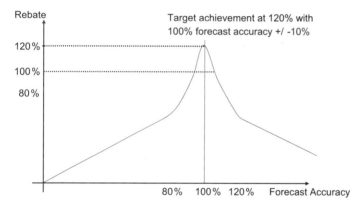

Figure 4.21 Bonus System Based on the Forecast Accuracy

Another aspect of an incentive system are the key figures, such as the service level and ranges of coverage. This is especially relevant for demand planners, because demand planning has a major influence on those figures.

In addition, products should also be evaluated according to their profitability. Products with a high profit margin should be overplanned to avoid lost sales. On the other hand, products that have a low profit margin should be underplanned to avoid surplus stocks that eat up the margin entirely.

4.4 Selecting the Forecast Method

"There are three kinds of lies: lies, damned lies, and statistics."
(Benjamin Disraeli)

We can deduce from this quote that Benjamin Disraeli's experience with statistics was not very pleasant. Yet statistics are nothing more than a method of collecting, analyzing, and presenting data. For a demand planner who uses statistical forecast methods, it is very important to understand these mathematical methods and to know what they can be used for. For this reason, in the following sections, we'll provide you with a brief description of the forecast methods in such a way that you'll understand them even if you're not a friend of mathematics. Those of you who are interested in the formulas can find them in the Appendix. In addition to the brief description of the forecast methods, we'll also explain how you can use them and provide some examples.

4.4.1 Different Forecast Methods

Basically, you can distinguish between qualitative and quantitative forecast methods.

Qualitative Forecast Methods

Qualitative forecast methods are based on experience, knowledge, and instinct. They are mainly used if no quantitative data is available. Examples of qualitative methods include the Delphi technique, expert surveys, and the scenario technique.

The Delphi method is predominantly used for long-term developments, the acquisition of capital goods, or for long-term forecasts. In these areas, qualitative methods have an advantage over quantitative methods. The Delphi method process is as follows:

1. Selection of the forecast problem
2. Selection of staff for processing the problem
3. Individual interviews with the participants
4. Collecting the information
5. Anonymous evaluation of participants' answers
6. Written comment by experts on their own judgement as compared to that of the group

7. Distribution of (anonymous) results and comments

8. Repetition from Step 3, forecast after three complete rounds with homogeneous answers from all participants

Quantitative Forecast Methods

Of greater importance to demand planning are the quantitative methods. These are based on mathematical procedures, which include, for example, trends, time series analyses, the indicator forecast, and the exponential smoothing method.

Quantitative forecast methods have been developed for forecasting business-relevant situations and for economic purposes (such as unemployment figures) since the 1950s. Their use in software modules enables the creation of forecasts for many different items within just a few seconds.

To optimize the forecasts and to provide optimal support for the demand planner, you should always use statistical forecast methods. The following sections provide a brief overview of the different methods, which represent the core of an optimized forecast. Unfortunately, most companies still use either no statistical methods or the wrong ones. Demand planners should therefore not only know the different models, but also be able to decide which model should be used for which specific situation.

A detailed analysis of the use and of the pros and cons of available methods is essential prior to selecting a forecast model. Figure 4.22 shows a possible effect of different forecast methods, which have all been used for the same material and based on the same set of historical data.

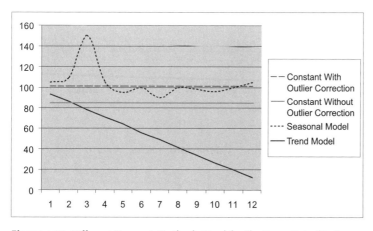

Figure 4.22 Different Forecast Methods Used for the Same Set of Data

The figure shows a simulation of the following four different forecast models for the same historical data of a specific material:

- Constant model with outlier correction
- Constant model without outlier correction
- Seasonal model
- Trend model

Although they are based on exactly the same historical data, the forecasts show clear differences. It is therefore apparent that choosing the right model can determine the success of your forecast.

The demand-planning module in SAP APO contains many statistical forecast methods and can be complemented with additional customized forecast models without any problem. Each of the methods tries to integrate historical key figures of a product into the forecast for future figures. There are two different methods that are based on different foundations: the time series analysis and causal models.

Time Series Analysis (Univariate Models)

The *time series analysis* is based on the assumption that the demand follows a specific pattern. For this reason, a forecast method is supposed to provide an estimate for that pattern by using historical observations. The forecasts can then be calculated based on that estimated pattern. The advantage of those methods is that they require only historical observations of the demand.

Univariate forecasts can be divided into the following types of time series pattern:

- **Constant progression**
  The demand deviates only slightly from a stable average value.

- **Trend-like pattern**
  The demand decreases or increases continuously over a longer period of time, with occasional fluctuations.

- **Season-like pattern**
  Periodically recurring requirement peak and slacks deviate substantially from a stable average value.

- **Seasonal trend pattern**
  Periodically recurring requirement peaks and slacks with a constantly increasing or decreasing average value.

▶ **Sporadic pattern**
  Irregular demand

▶ **No change compared to the previous year**
  No forecast is carried out; the system uses the actual data from the previous year.

These time series models cover almost all possible developments that are known in real-life business.

In a *constant pattern*, the observed values fluctuate around a fixed value, whereas a *trend-like pattern* or *seasonal trend pattern* is assumed to be based on a linear trend that rises or falls over the period of several years. In addition, the time series model with constant pattern can be regarded as a special case of the trend-like pattern in which the gradient of the trend line equals zero.

The *season-like pattern* is typical of everyday business where a season often corresponds to a calendar year. The degree of seasonal fluctuations frequently represents a multiplication of the trend level. An example of this is the pre-Christmas business, which often causes December sales to increase by 20% compared to the long-term trend.

The *sporadic pattern*, on the other hand, is not very typical. It is characterized by the fact that only a few periods show values greater than zero.

Causal Models

The second statistical forecasting method is referred to as *causal models*. Causal models are based on the assumption that the demand is determined by several known factors. For example, the demand for ice cream depends on the temperature on a specific day. Therefore, the temperature is a so-called main indicator of the demand for ice cream. If enough observations regarding the demand and the temperature are available, the underlying model can be estimated. Because historical sales figures and a time series with indicators are required to estimate the parameters in causal models, the required data quantity is substantially bigger than in a time series analysis. Simple time series models can generate better forecasts than complex causal models if stochastic fluctuations are interpreted as "structures" and thus a systematic error creeps into the model. For this reason, you must pay special attention to the analysis and, if necessary, the correction of the data basis when using causal models. But basically, we can say that causal models provide a more accurate forecast than time series models if a sufficient amount of historical data exists and the models are correctly used.

Naive Methods

The so-called *naive methods* do not consider the historical data and calculate the forecast based on a basic value and a trend value.

Composite Forecast Methods

Another method available is the *composite forecast*. This is actually not another separate method, but rather a combination of the methods described above, for instance, of time series and causal models. Modern forecasting tools such as SAP APO enable you to create several forecasts simultaneously and to determine a composite forecast from the individual ones. Given this background, you can establish average values for example, but also select different weighting factors (e.g., 20% time series analysis and 80% causal model). For more detailed information on composite forecasts, see Section 4.4.1.

4.4.2   Procedure Model for the Selection

The life of the demand planner would be much easier if a specific forecast method turned out to be the optimal method and all other methods could simply be abandoned. Unfortunately, that's not the case. This conclusion made by Gilchrist (1976) has held true until this very day. In addition, Emde (1977) rightfully states that many publications try to describe certain forecast methods as being especially useful and better than other methods. In many cases, the authors don't even describe the theoretical and practical prerequisites that must be met, so that it makes sense to use the methods. But, if we accept that there is no single forecast method that is optimal for all situations and that a criterion can have a positive effect in one situation and a negative effect in another situation, it makes sense to analyze and evaluate the various forecast methods in the hopes of finding the optimal procedure model to resolve a specific problem.

When using statistical methods, there is one typical question that arises over and over again: How can it be that a software application creates better forecasts that a human planner with years of experience? The simple answer is that mathematical methods are not biased. Empirical studies (see also Makridakis, Wheelwright 1997) have shown that human prejudices are the main reason why statistical methods often generate better results. But, you could also argue that information on specific events or changes such as promotions, customer feedback on new products and the like, can entail significant changes to the demand patterns. Such changes are not considered in standard time series. Consequently, it is necessary to combine the benefits of both worlds. The integration of statistical and subjective forecasts only makes sense if the factors for a subjective estimate are not yet part of the statistical forecast. Otherwise, you would have double counts and overestimate the demand.

To help you select the right forecast model for your products, we'd like to introduce you to a generic procedure model. In this procedure, you must perform the following steps and substeps, some of which are optional. The procedure model focuses on the selection of only one method in the following sections. If you want to carry it out directly after the introduction, you can skip the subsequent sections and go directly to Section 4.6. There, you'll find the steps that immediately follow the method selection.

Step 1: Data Analysis

First, you must examine the key factors that influence your product inventories. The resulting data basis can then be used in Step 2 to determine which model selection procedure should be used for the forecast.

▶ **Step 1.1: Analyzing the product lifecycle**
First, you must analyze the lifecycle of your products and determine the product lifecycle phase that your product is currently in, if that is possible. You should know whether your product is currently in the growth phase, or in the saturation phase, because this can affect the forecast. This is particularly the case when the lifecycles of your products are rather short.

▶ **Step 1.2: Analyzing the causal factors**
Then, you must analyze if causal factors (such as the temperature, price changes, and so on) affect the demand for your products and, if so, determine the effects of those factors. Create separate time series for the individual factors and maintain their influence on the historical data.

▶ **Step 1.3: Analyzing the influence of promotions, events, and actions on your history**
In this step, you must analyze the influence of past actions and promotions on existing actual data. At this time, you must create separate time series for regular and irregular promotions so that you can examine the influence of actions and promotions separately. Determine the influence of the promotions and save them in separate key figures.

▶ **Step 1.4: Cleansing the historical data**
Based on the results of your analyses in Steps 1.2 and 1.3, you should cleanse your historical data. When doing so, you should not use the time series for the original history, but generate a new, separate time series using the *Corrected History* key figure, and change the history there.

▶ **Step 1.5: Identifying and correcting outliers**
Once you have corrected your historical data, you should correct your outliers. If possible, this should be done in an automated way. Analyze the outliers and eliminate them from the history. You can do that manually, or use the outlier correction function in SAP APO. Although this step is part of the historical data correction, it should be regarded as the final step of the correction phase.

Step 2: Selecting the Selection Model

The data has been determined in Step 1. In the next step, you must select the model based on which you want to create the forecast. For this purpose, the following two procedures are available: the manual and the automatic model selection.

Manual Model Selection
Let's first look at the detailed individual steps involved in a manual model selection:

▶ **Step 2.1: Analysis regarding trend and season**
At the beginning of the model selection, you must determine whether your products are subject to trend-related or seasonal influences, and determine for each individual product whether the demand is trend or season-dependent. For the right selection of the forecast method, it is critical that you identify the time series pattern because certain forecast methods can be used only for season-dependent product, whereas other methods can be used for only constant time series. You should use graphical analysis tools for the trend and season analysis to better understand the historical development of the demand.

▶ **Step 2.2: Determining predecessors and follow-up products**
In the next step, you want to determine whether old products exist that are similar to the new ones, and if so, whether the sales figures of those old products match your estimates for the new ones. If such products do exist, you should assign the historical data of the old products to the new ones. When doing this, you should also include the results of the product lifecycle analysis performed in Step 1.1.

▶ **Step 2.3: Performing an XYZ analysis**
The next step in the model selection process involves an XYZ analysis to examine the sales behavior of your products. If possible, you should base your analysis on the corrected historical data.

▶ **Step 2.4: Creating the product segmentation matrix**
Then you must create a matrix to map the product segmentation. Based on the historical data and the analysis results we have so far, you can subdivide your products in a portfolio matrix according to products with stable sales and products with unstable sales. In addition, you can separate the historical data of your products according to their degree of completeness. Consequently, you'll obtain a product segmentation matrix (see Figure 4.23).

▶ **Step 2.5: Assigning the forecast methods to the products**
Based on the data that is available to you up to this point, you can make a preliminary assignment of the forecast methods to the products. To do that, you must compare the product segmentation matrix with the matrix of the forecast techniques (see Figure 4.24).

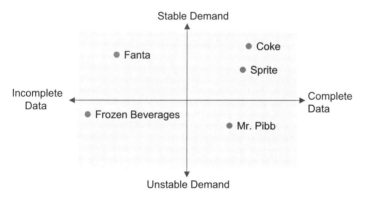

Figure 4.23 Sample Product Segmentation

Here you can see that forecast methods have been assigned to the product segmentation made in Figure 4.23. For products with an unstable sales behavior and a short or incomplete history, the *Moving Average* method, a *Manual forecast*, the *Bass model*, or a *Composite forecast* would be the most appropriate solutions. The use of a *Forecast Team* instead of an individual planner would also be conceivable.

For products with a stable sales behavior and a short or incomplete history, you should use the *1st or 2nd Order Exponential Smoothing* methods, the *Winters* method, or the *Box-Jenkins* method.

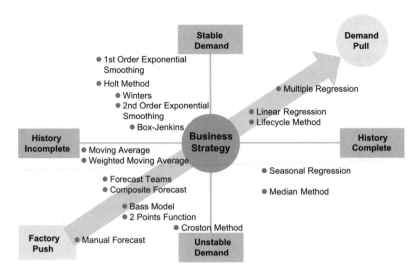

Figure 4.24 Portfolio of Forecast Techniques

For products with a stable sales behavior and a complete history, the most appropriate methods are the *Multiple Regression* and *Lifecycle Method*.

The individual forecast methods are described in the following sections. In this context, we distinguish between the following four criteria, as shown in Figure 4.24:

▶ Stable demand and incomplete history

▶ Unstable demand and incomplete history

▶ Stable demand and complete history

▶ Unstable demand and complete history

In daily work, you cannot always clearly assign each product to a specific segment. Therefore, the manner in which forecast methods are distinguished here can vary, depending on the individual situation. For that reason, it is very likely that, for example, the Box-Jenkins method may provide a better result for a product with an unstable demand and a complete history than would the median method. However, you should use the schema provided here as an initial basis when selecting the forecast methods and then try to identify the optimal method step by step. In other words, you should consider this procedure model as a method that you can use to select the best forecast model for each product.

Automatic Model Selection

Unlike the manual model selection, the automatic model selection uses a mathematical method to select the forecast model.

If you use the automatic model selection, you must determine which criteria to use in order to select the most appropriate time series model. Several options are available to help you find a solution. On the one hand, you can implement a strategy in which all possible models are calculated, that is, adjusted to the available data, and then use a time series model for the forecast, which provides the best forecast quality. Consequently, iterations occur in the model selection and adjustment phases. Although this solution is acceptable, its performance is poor because it processes all possible options completely and then decides on which forecast method to use.

The second option that describes the forecasting process uses several significance tests that support and facilitate the decision to select a specific model. The easiest solution consists of carrying out a trend and a seasonal test; however, there are some problems associated with this approach. On the one hand, random fluctuations can lead to a successful result of the seasonal test in the initialization phase and thereby promote a seasonal model although the time series shows a constant pattern, for example. The reason for this can be found in the higher number of parameters that are always available for adjusting the seasonal model as opposed to the constant model. A higher number of variables definitely facilitates the adjustment. Conversely, a trend test that is based on the linear regression method cannot identify an exponential trend, for instance. This means that the test selects the constant model, although the values it provides are not as good as the ones provided by a time series model with a linear trend-like pattern. Contrary to the first option, the execution of several tests is much faster and therefore better suited for the automatic model selection. But, the tests are not that easy to implement because the developer has to deal with the described problems and may have to take into account the number of parameters for the model adjustment when performing the significance tests.

A prerequisite for a successful automatic model selection is a high quality level of the historical data. Therefore, it is definitely worthwhile for you to perform Steps 1.1 through 1.5, even if you want to use the automatic model selection. To obtain results that approximate those of the manual selection, you must carry out these steps per product.

Moreover, the automatic model selection should use product-specific forecast and history horizons. For products with different seasonal periods, for example, you must take into account the difference in the automatic model selection. If, however, you use a forecast profile, the same number of historical periods is used for all products. This ensures that the automatic model selection cannot reach the quality level of a product-specific model selection.

SAP APO contains two automatic model selection strategies. What both strategies have in common is that the system automatically carries out the forecast on the basis of a constant pattern, when no regular pattern can be identified with regard to the trend or seasonal components.

The *automatic model selection procedure 1* tests historical values with regard to constant, linear trend-like, season-like, and seasonal trend developments. The seasonal test is performed based on the autocorrelation coefficient, while the regression analysis is used as the basis for the trend test. After that, the system uses the time series model for the forecast which, based on the results of the significance tests, seems to be the most appropriate model.

For example, if both the seasonal and the trend test are completed successfully, this procedure will select a seasonal trend model.

The automatic model selection procedure 1 is used in the forecasting strategies 50 through 55 (see also Table 4.2 on page 139).

A seasonal test is carried out in forecasting strategies 50, 51, 53, and 54:

1. Any trend-related influences on the historical time series that may exist are removed.

2. An autocorrelation coefficient is calculated.

3. A significance test is performed on the coefficient.

A trend test is carried out in forecasting strategies 50, 52, 53, and 55:

1. Any seasonal influences on the historical time series that may exist are removed.

2. A validation parameter is calculated according to the above formula.

3. The system verifies whether the historical data shows a trend-like pattern by checking the data against a value that depends on the number of periods.

Based on the seasonal and trend tests performed, the system identifies the most appropriate forecast method. It chooses from the constant model, trend model, seasonal model, and the seasonal trend model. Please note that at least two complete seasonal cycles must be available as historical data so that a seasonal test can be performed. You should always provide at least two seasonal cycles and three periods as historical data.

We recommend that you carry out procedure 1 without outlier correction. If you don't follow these recommendations, you won't be able to compare the results with those of other procedures, because it can happen in procedure 1 that the outlier correction is carried out using a different procedure than the final forecast since the characteristics of the time series can change once the outlier correction is completed. Also note that the trend test depends on the number of periods as well. The trend test uses a history that is adjusted by the season and that history can strongly depend on the number of seasonal periods. If you want to test only the trend, then you should set the number of periods per season to 1. If the number of periods per season that you specify is greater than or equal to the number of existing historical values, you virtually terminate the trend test.

The **Periods per Season** value in the forecast profile plays a very important role. For example, if your historical data contains a season that consists of seven periods and you enter a value of three periods per season, the seasonal test will probably be negative. Unlike trend and constant models, seasonal models are not verified. You can make the corresponding setting in the forecast profile (see Figure 4.25). To do that, select **SAP APO · Demand Planning · Planning · Interactive Demand Planning** from the menu, click on the **Run Forecast** button, and select the **Parameters** tab.

| ❋ Profile | ♟ Model | ▦ Horizons | ▪ Parameters | ᠓ Forecast Errors | ᠋ Settings |

Control Parameters					
Periods per Season	52	Error Measure	MAD	▤	➡
Length Variation					
Alpha Start Value	0,10	Alpha End Value	0,50	Alpha Increment	0,10
Beta Start Value	0,10	Beta End Value	0,50	Beta Increment	0,10
Gamma Start Value	0,10	Gamma End Value	0,50	Gamma Increment	0,10

Parameters Determined By the System					
Alpha	0,50	Beta	0,50	Gamma	0,30

Figure 4.25 Settings in the Forecast Profile for the Automatic Model Selection in SAP APO

Table 4.2 provides an overview of the strategies that employ the automatic model selection 1.

Automatic Model Selection 1 – Forecast Strategy	Positive Trend	Positive Season	Selected Model
50 – Automatic selection 1	No	No	10 – Constant
	Yes	No	20 – Trend

Table 4.2 Overview of Strategies Using Automatic Model Selection 1

Automatic Model Selection 1 – Forecast Strategy	Positive Trend	Positive Season	Selected Model
	No	Yes	30 – Season
	Yes	Yes	40 – Seasonal trend
51 – Test for trend	Yes	N/A	20 – Trend
	No		10 – Constant
52 – Test for season	N/A	Yes	30 – Season
		No	10 – Constant
53 – Test for trend and season	No	No	10 – Constant
	Yes	No	20 – Trend
	No	Yes	30 – Season
	Yes	Yes	40 – Seasonal trend
54 – Seasonal model plus test for trend	No	Yes	30 – Season
	Yes		40 – Seasonal trend
55 – Trend model plus test for season	Yes	Yes	40 – Seasonal trend
		No	20 – Trend

Table 4.2 Overview of Strategies Using Automatic Model Selection 1 (cont.)

The automatic model selection procedure 1 therefore does not take into account any forecasts for sporadic requirements (Croston method), external forecasts, and regression procedures.

The disadvantages of the automatic model selection procedure 1 clearly beg the question: "Can this procedure provide an optimized selection process for the best forecasting method?"

Automatic Model Selection Procedure 2

The automatic model selection procedure 2 performs various tests to determine the model to be used (constant model, trend model, seasonal model, and so on). The system then varies the corresponding forecast parameters (alpha, beta, and gamma) in the intervals and with the increments that you have previously specified in the forecast profile.

The procedure starts with the following initial values: alpha = 0.1, beta = 0.1, and gamma = 0.1. It uses the constant model, trend model, seasonal model, and the seasonal trend model, and then varies the individual parameters by increments of 0.1 until they reach a value of 0.5. You can also set the increment values manually. By default, the system then selects a model and parameter combination with the smallest mean absolute deviation (MAD). You can also specify which error is to be minimized in the forecast profile. Moreover, you can use a customer-specific error level. But, this does not mean that the system identifies the procedure or parameters where the error value is smallest. On the one hand, not all forecasting methods are tested; on the other hand, the system does not examine all parameter combinations down to the finite increments. For example, a constant model with alpha = 0.14 may have a smaller MAD value than the result of a forecast calculation using automatic procedure 2, which didn't even test that parameter.

In procedure 2, you must also ensure that you provide at least two seasonal cycles and three periods as historical data. Furthermore, you must understand that if you use the outlier correction function, you cannot compare these results with those obtained in the individual procedures, because the procedures used for the outlier correction and the final forecast can differ.

The model selection procedure 2 is used only in forecast strategy 56.

Table 4.3 provides an overview of the strategies that use the automatic model selection 2.

Automatic Model Selection 2 – Forecast Strategy	Test for Sporadic Data	Seasonal Test	Trend test
Croston model	X		
Trend model			X
Seasonal model		X	
Seasonal trend model		A	A
Linear regression		O	X
Seasonal linear regression		A	A
X – The model will be used if the test is positive. A – The model will be used if all tests are positive. O – The model will be used if this test is negative.			

Table 4.3 Strategies of the Automatic Model Selection 2

Since SAP's Supply Chain Management (SCM) Version 4.1, the Croston method, the linear regression, and the seasonal linear regression are also included in the automatic model selection 2. In addition, a trend test, a seasonal test, and a white noise test are included in that procedure. If the trend test is negative, no models or parameters (beta = 0) are tested that are assigned to a trend. If the seasonal test is negative, no models or parameters (gamma = 0) are tested that are assigned to a season. Whenever white noise is detected, the constant model will be used.

Drawbacks of Automatic Model Selection

The optimization of the smoothing factors is closely linked with the automatic model selection. That optimization process is carried out in the basic function module by using the grid search and increments of 0.01.

Based on the grid search, this strategy automatically selects the model with the smallest smoothed mean absolute error. But, you should note that very rarely does it happen that the system identifies the model with the smallest mean absolute deviation (MAD), one of the reasons being that not all possible model and parameter combinations are used. Moreover, the linear regression procedure is also not used here. Another problem with that selection procedure is that the mean absolute deviation should not be used as a criterion for comparisons.

The trend test, which is based on the regression analysis, for example, only recognizes linear trends. But, if a time series represents an exponential trend, the significance test will fail and reject a trend-like model. Consequently, the trend test proposes a constant model, although it usually forecasts data of an inferior quality than would be present in a time series model with a trend-like pattern.

The same situation can happen in a seasonal test, which is based on the autorelation coefficient. For example, if a time series shows several random fluctuations in the initialization phase, the time series may pass the significance test although the fluctuations are part of the random component, not of the seasonal component.

For the automatic model selection procedures, you must define the timeframe on which you want to base your calculations. The system examines all available statistical forecast procedures and parameter combinations, and selects a combination that provides the best forecast accuracy. Therefore, it provides a list of the forecast methods and corresponding parameters for each item to be analyzed. Afterwards, the planner must determine whether the model is appropriate for his or her needs. The planner can use the provided set of statistical methods as a black box.

According to Wagner (2000), the automatic model selection procedures described here have the following disadvantages:

▶ The time series is often too short when a demand planning process is introduced.

▶ The criterion used for evaluation purposes is often one of the forecast accuracy criteria previously described. However, those values do not provide any information on the robustness of the model results.

▶ Three periods of the demand series are required for the selection procedure:

  ▷ In the first period, the model components are initialized.

  ▷ In the second period of the time series, the parameter values are optimized.

  ▷ The optimized parameters are used to obtain forecasts for the third period. Those forecasts are also evaluated based on the forecast accuracy. This degree of accuracy is then used as a selection criterion for the most appropriate forecast model.

  ▷ The definition of the length of the individual periods has a significant influence on the model selection result. Most often, the user cannot change these settings, as it is even impossible to view them in the software.

For this reason, the best use of the automatic model selection is to use it specifically to help you find the right method. Experienced users should not use the automatic model selection as a mere black box.

Ultimately, however, we recommend that you don't use the two automatic model selection procedures provided in SAP APO in your daily operations. But, you can use these procedures for testing purposes, especially if you want to learn which forecast method you can use before you start the actual selection procedure, or if you need some initial help for optimizing the smoothing parameters.

In accordance with this procedure model, the following sections now describe the individual forecast methods in further detail. We have deliberately omitted the formulas, because you can find them in the respective literature. Instead we'll focus on the logic of the forecast methods and their areas of application.

4.5 Details of the Individual Forecast Methods

When selecting a forecast strategy, you must consider the stability of the demand and the completeness of the historical data on which the forecast will be based. The following sections describe the most appropriate forecast methods to be used for different cases.

4.5.1 Unstable Demand and Incomplete History

Manual Forecast

Definition: This forecasting strategy, which is also referred to as a manual or naive forecast, enables you to specify the basic value, trend value, trend dampening profile, and seasonal indices manually in the interactive demand planning. Figure 4.26 illustrates a typical manual forecast (without trend dampening) in the graph on the left. The graph on the right shows a trend dampening of 5% for the same forecast.

Usage: These models can be used for products that have no historical data; however, you must be able to predict the trend value with as much accuracy as possible if you want to be successful. The forecast is not calculated on the basis of historical values, but on a basic value to be specified, and on a trend value. You should not use the model with mass data, because the maintenance effort would be too high (i.e., you would have to enter different basic values and trend values for each individual product).

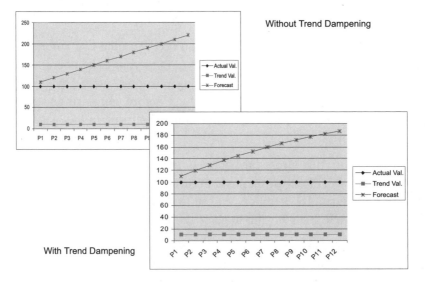

Figure 4.26 Naive Forecast With (Lower Right) and Without (Upper Left) Trend Dampening

Moving Average Model

Definition: This strategy calculates the average of the time series values within an historical timeframe. The moving average model is used to exclude irregularities in the time series pattern. Since all historical data is equally weighted with the factor *1/n*, it takes precisely *n* periods for the forecast to adapt to a possible level change. The accuracy of the forecast increases with the length of the time series, and the less likely it is that random deviations will affect the forecast.

Usage: The simple moving average model is used for products with a stable demand, which is for time series that don't show a trend-like or season-like pattern. Therefore, the moving average model excludes random irregularities in the time series pattern.

If the demand level changes on a regular basis, this method doesn't provide any useful results. In addition, the information obtained in historical observations is lost in this procedure.

Weighted Moving Average Model

Definition: The weighted moving average model is similar to the simple moving average model with the only difference being that each historical value is weighted with the factor specified in the weighting group in the univariate forecast profile. When determining the average value, this model enables you to put a higher weight on younger historical data instead of older data. You can use this option if there is a stronger correlation between younger data and future requirements than older data and future requirements. This means that a faster adaptation to level changes is possible.

Usage: The accuracy of this model largely depends on the weighting factors you choose. If the time series pattern changes, you must adapt the weighting factors accordingly; however, it remains questionable whether the forecast methods can actually map a changing environment. The increasing level of competition requires that the methods be up-to-date, flexible, and customer- and future-oriented. But those criteria are not considered in the methods described so far as those methods only update historical values for future purposes. Ensuring that methods are up-to-date is a problem that is inherent in many quantitative procedures. For example, when you determine an average value, the forecast value for the month of June cannot be calculated until the end of May, when the actual values are available. Even the second-order exponential smoothing method lags behind the periods, which can easily be calculated using $2(1-\alpha)/\alpha$.

Composite Forecast Methods

Definition: The forecast methods described so far can be combined. For example, you can combine several different forecast methods on the basis of a constant or time-dependent weighting procedure (see Figure 4.27).

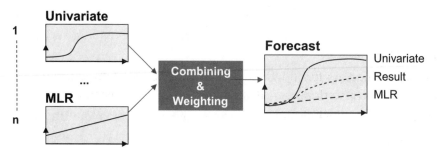

Figure 4.27 Composite Forecast Method

By combining forecasts, you can use the strengths of different methods simultaneously (e.g., you can use the trend and seasonal models based on short-term temperature influences).

Usage: We have learned through experience that composite forecasts, which are based on different mathematical estimation procedures, have an advantage over individual forecasts. In a composite forecast procedure, you can determine either the simple average or a weighted average of all forecasts involved.

The planners generate subjective forecasts based on their knowledge of the relevant data, such as historical figures, causal factors, and so on. Then they are confronted with forecasts that have been calculated using statistical methods. At that stage, the planners can improve their first estimates. It is not initially defined to what degree the two forecast models are integrated into the final forecast. This procedure often produces more accurate results than a simple evaluation without the help of statistical methods. Furthermore, the advantage of this procedure is that the planner has full control of everything.

You can obtain a more objective result by combining the two values using previously defined weighting schema. Even if you choose an equal distribution of the weightings, you will be able to obtain better results.

We should add that many companies have adopted the habit of manually adjusting statistical forecasts to integrate the specific personal knowledge of the planner. Nevertheless, this process of improvement must be structured accordingly, that is, the adaptation must be based on previously defined signals (e.g., promotions, the weather, and so on).

For all these methods, the assessment of experts is critical; however, this may result in your facing the problem of dealing with too many experts who have reached different conclusions.

Bass Model

Definition: The Bass function is a forecast method that can be carried out irrespective of historical data. It describes the market penetration on the basis of two consumer groups:

▶ **Innovators**
 The buying behavior does not depend on other consumers.

▶ **Imitators**
 The buying probability increases commensurate with the level of satisfaction.

Figure 4.28 illustrates the two consumer groups to the right (imitators) and left (innovators) of the basic value.

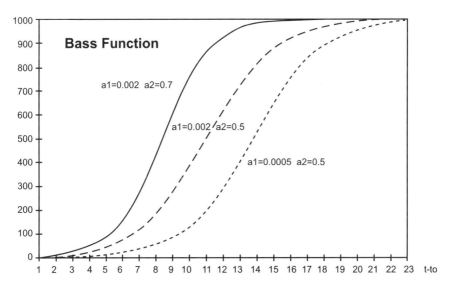

Figure 4.28 Consumer Groups in the Bass Model
(Implementation in SAP APO Using External Forecast)

The innovation and imitation coefficients must be known. They differ by industry and product, as shown in Figure 4.29.

Product / Technology	Innovation Coefficient	Imitation Coefficient
Color TV	0.005	0.84
Air Conditioner	0.010	0.42
Tumble Drier	0.017	0.36
Mobile Phones	0.004	1.76
Steam Iron	0.029	0.33
McDonald's Fast Food	0.018	0.54

Figure 4.29 Bass Coefficients for Different Product Types (Source: Lilien, Rangaswamy, 1998, p. 195 ff.)

Usage: This forecast method is used in a large European telecommunications company to forecast the requirements of telephone mainlines and could be implemented into SAP APO in the context of a project. If you don't know the imitation and innovation coefficients, you can estimate them based on the historical data, and then verify them via an ex-post forecast.

Two-Points Function

Definition: The two-points method uses two fixed future sales values to determine a continuous demand pattern based on the natural logarithm. Here, the forecast does not include the historical data. For example, if you know the sales figures for the years 2000 and 2006 (the latter having been determined by market research or by an independent analyst), you can use these two fixed points to carry out a forecast. The fixed points can also represent both past and future values. In addition, you must define the degree of market saturation (e.g., 2%) and the shape of the curve (concave or convex). Once you have defined the two points and the shape of the curve, the system generates a forecast as the one shown in Figure 4.30.

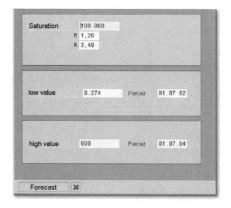

Figure 4.30 Two-Points-Model as Displayed in SAP APO

Usage: This individual forecast method is also contained in SAP APO. It is generally used to introduce new products, or to simulate targets defined by marketing or corporate management.

4.5.2 Stable Demand and Incomplete History

Constant Model of First-Order Exponential Smoothing

Definition: The consistent enhancement of the weighted moving average model takes us to the exponential smoothing model. The first-order exponential smoothing is based on the following principles:

▸ The older the time series values, the less important they become for the calculation of the forecast.

▸ The present forecast error is taken into account in subsequent forecasts.

From the preceding two considerations, we can derive the exponential smoothing constant model. A simple transformation produces the basic formula for exponential smoothing.

To determine the forecast value, the system uses the preceding forecast value, the last historical value, and the "alpha" smoothing factor. This smoothing factor weights the more recent historical values more than the less recent ones so they have a greater influence on the forecast.

How quickly the forecast reacts to a change in the time series pattern depends on the smoothing factor. If you choose 0 for alpha, the new average will be equal to the old one. In this case, the basic value calculated previously remains; that is, the forecast does not react to current data. If you choose 1 for the alpha value, the new average will equal the last value in the time series.

The following two methods are available to determine the smoothing factor: the use of experience and a selection by the forecast error.

The suggested values you can find in commonly used literature (e.g., Tempelmeier 2003) usually lie between 0.1 and 0.3. You should choose a low factor if the random component has a great influence on the time series. The selection by forecast errors involves simulations using different factors to calculate forecast errors. The factor that produces the smallest forecast error will be selected.

The example shown in Figure 4.31 illustrates the effects of the alpha value on the historical values.

You can see that a low alpha value compensates coincidences, whereas a high alpha value weights the periods differently so that present coincidences can have a greater influence.

The smoothing principle:

▸ Weighting of the current value: α β γ parameters

▸ Weighting of the previous value: (1 – parameter)

Smoothing Principle:

- Weighting of the current value: Parameters α β γ

- Weighting of the previous value: (1-Parameter)

Sample Weightings (in %):

Parameter	Current Period	Past Period 1	Past Period 2	Past Period 3
0.1	10	9	8	7
0.3	30	21	15	10
0.5	50	25	13	6
0.7	70	21	6	2

Figure 4.31 Alpha Values of Exponential Smoothing

Table 4.4 provides a brief overview of the effects of the alpha factor.

Criterion	Alpha = Large	Alpha = Small
Past	low	high
New values	high	low
Smoothing	low	high
Adjustment	fast	slow

Table 4.4 Effects of the Alpha Factor on Different Criteria

A large alpha factor puts less importance on the less recent past than on the most recent past. It has a minor influence on the forecast smoothing, but reacts quickly to requirement adjustments.

In SAP APO, you can automatically adapt the alpha factor in each historical period corresponding to the mean absolute deviation (MAD) and the error total (ET).

Usage: This model avoids a loss of information in the event of a decrease in demand, because it allocates different weightings to all observed data and includes those weightings in the forecast. Therefore, the importance of historical data decreases exponentially the older it gets. The more recent historical data, on the other hand, has a greater influence on the forecast. Consequently, the forecast values can more easily adapt to possible changes in the demand pattern and can relatively easily react to changes in the time series.

This means you can change the weighting of the historical data by changing a single parameter. The bigger the alpha value, the greater the influence of the latest historical value of the demand time series on the forecast value. However, the exponential smoothing method should be used to create a short-term demand forecast only if the observed values fluctuate around an average value that is constant over time. You should therefore use the constant model of first-order exponential smoothing for time series that neither shows a trend-like pattern or any seasonal fluctuations.

By adapting the alpha factor, you can automatically use a known forecast error from the previous month to optimize the new forecast. This allows you to use an automatic error feedback function in your forecast, which helps you to achieve better results than you would in a first-order exponential smoothing process without adapting the alpha factor. The exponential smoothing with trend correction is a modification of this method, which can take into account an existing trend.

Contrary to the linear regression and moving average methods, you can estimate and optimize one or more smoothing factors—depending on the algorithm—in the exponential smoothing models in order to obtain more accurate forecast results.

The optimized estimation of the smoothing factors automatically entails an optimization of the forecast values. Makridakis (1998, p. 172 f.) states that an optimization of the smoothing factors requires the same statistical key figures as the assessment of the forecast quality. Apart from that, when selecting the optimization variables, the interests of the user play a major role. If the user focuses on relative forecast errors and information, the smoothing factors are estimated optimally when the mean absolute error percentage is minimal. Conversely, the user can also focus on absolute errors. In that case, the most appropriate optimization variables are the mean quadratic and the mean absolute errors.

So far, we've based the descriptions of our models on a linear trend. In everyday business, however, this is not realistic, because the historical values usually show a saturation effect after a certain period of time. You can counteract this phenomenon by using a dampening factor to diminish the future trend. For example, if you assume that the growth rate of a company's revenue decreases by 10% every year due to the competitive situation in the market, the trend value of each future period is dampened by 0.9.

Trend Models and Seasonal Models of First-Order Exponential Smoothing

Definition: The following formula is used in forecast strategies 20, 21, 30, 31, 40, and 41, as well as in forecast strategies 50 through 56 in which a trend model, a seasonal model, or a seasonal trend model is determined. The calculation takes into account both trend and season-dependent changes. The basic value (alpha), trend value (beta), and seasonal index (gamma) are calculated on the basis of the initial period. Figure 4.32 illustrates the difference between the three values.

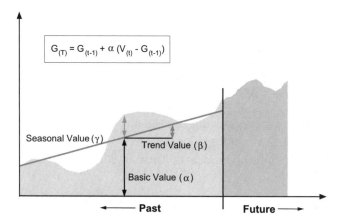

$$G_{(T)} = G_{(t-1)} + \alpha (V_{(t)} - G_{(t-1)})$$

Seasonal Value (γ)

Trend Value (β)

Basic Value (α)

Past ← | → Future

Figure 4.32 Exponental Smoothing with Trend-Season Index

Usage: You should use the trend, seasonal, or seasonal trend model of first-order exponential smoothing for time series with a trend-like pattern or seasonal fluctuations.

Models of Second-Order Exponential Smoothing

Definition: The method can be extended for trend models and multiplicative seasonal models. In that case, a second-order exponential smoothing is used. This means that the same smoothing process is used once again for the time series of the forecast values (i.e., for the average values that have been calculated in the first-order exponential smoothing procedure). As a result, you obtain second-order exponentially smoothed average values, which are average values of the first-order average values.

The second-order exponential smoothing procedure is used in forecast strategies 22 and 23; it is based on a linear trend and consists of two equations. The first equation is almost identical to the equation of the first-order exponential smoothing, with the exception of the bracketed indices. In the second equation, the values calculated in the first equation are used as initial values and smoothed a second time.

Usage: If a time series shows a trend-like change of the average value across several periods, the forecast values calculated in the first-order exponential smoothing process always lag one or more periods behind the actual values. The second-order exponential smoothing method can then be used to achieve a faster adaptation of the forecast to the actual pattern of the consumption values.

The Holt Procedure

Definition: As early as 1957, Holt criticized that the first and second-order smoothing processes were not flexible enough because they only used one smoothing parameter (alpha). So he proposed a model, which today is referred to as the Holt procedure, in which both terms of the model – level a and the trend component b – are smoothed using different parameters α and β.

Usage: Gardner (1980) compared the exponential smoothing models with each other based on empirical time series and came to the conclusion that the Holt procedure provided better forecasts in many cases. This is not surprising because the additional parameter has a greater ability to influence the forecast values, even though it carries with it some problems regarding its determination.

The Winters Procedure

Definition: Winters introduced the seasonal model of exponential smoothing, which is based on the Holt procedure. The Winters procedure is an efficient tool for predicting seasonal patterns, as it smoothes the forecasts for the three parameters, a (for the axis section), b (for the gradient), and c (for the seasonal factors). Winters assumes a linear trend that is linked by multiplication with the season. The basic value is smoothed using the smoothing factor; the trend value is smoothed with the gradient factor; and the seasonal index is smoothed with the seasonal factor.

Usage: The demand for products is often subject to seasonal patterns, but this fact is often not considered in forecast methods, and if it is included, then it is only done so on a manual basis. Ponder, for example, the manager of a shoe shop who needs a sales forecast for the coming two weeks in terms of daily periods. Because the sales figures are higher on Saturdays than they are on Mondays, the shoe manager must take into account in his calculation the weekly "season." According to Wagner (2000), a reliable forecast of the seasonal coefficients requires the consideration of at least two cycles of the demand time series. This means that contrary to the previous two models, the seasonal models require a higher quantity of data to initialize the parameters.

According to Tempelmeier, another disadvantage is that each seasonal factor is not updated until a complete seasonal cycle has ended. This means that substantial changes in the seasonal patterns are identified and translated into new seasonal factor values at a very late point in time.

A disadvantage of the model is the relatively late change of the seasonal indices, because an observed value can be used only to adjust one seasonal index, although the entire seasonal pattern may have changed. Thus the Winters model cannot completely identify the time series structure when structural interruptions occur. Structural interruptions describe an abrupt change of the time series values due to changes of the causal foundations. Such structural interruptions can be caused by winning or losing major customers, the opening or closing of a subsidiary, the introduction or abandonment of a product variant, and so on.

Moreover, it is difficult to determine the three smoothing parameters. Due to the many combinations of the seasonal factor and seasonal cycle, it is almost impossible to perform simple tests in the context of forecast simulations. However, Winters provides many examples that show that the forecast error function has a flat progress when it is close to the optimal parameters so that a rough optimization can already provide good results. For a more accurate determination, you can use non-linear optimization methods and gradient methods. Those methods, however, don't provide any global optimum, just suboptimums that lie in the area of the default parameters a, b, and c.

4.5.3 Unstable Demand and Complete History

Seasonal Linear Regression

Definition: The seasonal linear regression can be used as an alternative for forecast strategies 30 and 31, which provide high basic values if the seasonal index equals 0 or almost 0.

As shown in Figure 4.33, the linear regression is a line that runs through a scatterplot, whereby the total of quadratic distances between the line and the historical values is minimal.

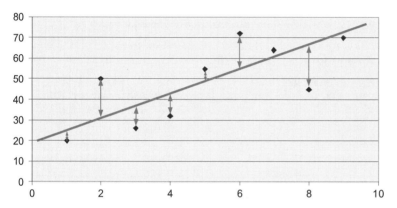

Figure 4.33 The Linear Regression—a Line That Runs Through a Scatterplot of Historical Values

The system calculates the seasonal linear regression as follows:

1. **Determination of seasonal factors on the basis of historical values**
   Figure 4.34 illustrates the first step of the seasonal linear regression. The most appropriate seasonal index is determined by the seasonal history.

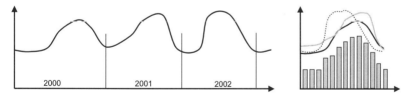

Figure 4.34 Step 1: Calculating the Seasonal Index for the Past

2. **Deseasonalization of historical values**
   The second step corrects the actual data on the basis of the seasonal indices calculated in Step 1 and converts them into a linear curve (see Figure 4.35).

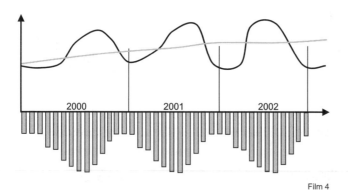

Film 4

Figure 4.35 Step 2: Correcting the Historical Data Using the Seasonal Index

3. Determination of forecast values using linear regression

In the third step, the linear regression is carried out for the non-seasonal historical values from Step 2. Figure 4.36 shows a forecast for 2003.

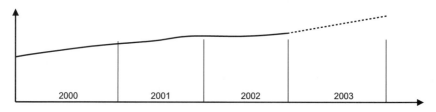

Figure 4.36 Step 3: Performing a Linear Regression Based on the Linear History

4. Seasonalization of forecast values

In the fourth step, the seasonal indices are applied to the results of the linear regression method; this results again in seasonal forecast results, as shown in Figure 4.37.

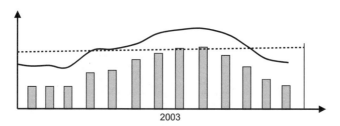

Figure 4.37 Step 4: Multiplying the Seasonal Index by the Linear Result

Usage: You should not use the linear regression method if your historical data shows a distinct trend-like pattern.

The Croston Method

Definition: The Croston method is a univariate forecasting strategy for products with an irregular or sporadic demand. A time series is sporadic if it contains periods without any demand and if the distribution of the demand does not depend on the amount of time that has passed since the last occurrence of the demand. This demand pattern is typical for spare parts, but it can also occur if the subdivision of your periods is too detailed (for example, daily periods).

In that case, the use of statistical forecast methods would produce big errors. An additional subjective forecast would not improve the quality, because periods without a demand usually occur randomly and therefore cannot be predicted. Moreover, a sporadic demand occurs primarily for large quantities of inferior parts for which planners can only carry out low-cost forecasts, which shouldn't prove to be too time-consuming.

There are efficient methods available for an automatic forecast of sporadic demands. Those methods try to seperately forecast the two components, *Occurrence of a period with positive demand* and *Demand quantity*.

The Croston method comprises two steps. First, it uses the average requirement level to determine estimated values by applying the exponential smoothing procedure. Second, it calculates the average amount of time that passes between the demands.

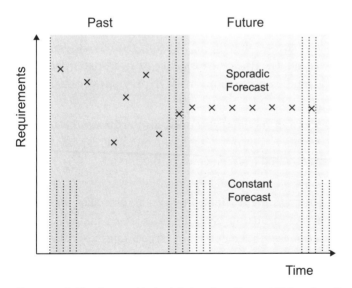

Figure 4.38 The Croston Method Determines Forecast Values for a Sporadic Demand

Figure 4.38 shows the sporadic historical values on the left, and the sporadic forecast on the right. The forecast values do not occur in every period, but are also determined sporadically.

Usage: With inventory management systems, the exponential smoothing method is frequently used for forecasting the requirements. For sporadic requirements, the use of this method almost always results in inadequate stocks. For this reason, you should use the Croston method if the requirements occur sporadically. If we look at the demand for spare parts as an example, we see that spare parts are usually ordered in large quantities to replenish the warehouse. Traditional forecasting models have great difficulties with those zero periods (i.e., periods with a zero demand). Another advantage of the Croston method is that, in addition to the requirements level, it also takes into account the intervals between demands, in other words, the average duration.

Box-Jenkins Method/ARIMA

Definition: The autoregressive-integrated moving-average (ARIMA) model uses dependent demands as a basis and makes no assumptions on the underlying demand pattern. Instead, it generates a function based on different components, which best approximates the observed data. This function can be found by iteratively processing the following three steps:

1. **Model selection**
   You can select an appropriate ARIMA model by comparing the autocorrelation of the theoretical distribution with the autocorrelation of the observations. The autocorrelation describes the existence of a correlation between the current demand and the observations made in previous periods.

2. **Parameter estimation**
   As is the case in regression models, you must also estimate the forecast parameter in ARIMA models. For this reason, the method searches for values that minimize the squared average error of the model.

3. **Model verification**
   If the error is random and independent, you can assume that the model is reliable. As you can probably imagine, the Box-Jenkins method requires a lot of experience and the entry of a large amount of data by the planner. Furthermore, according to Wagner (2000), the selection of the model should be based on at least 50 observations of the demand. For this reason, ARIMA models are used for only very important products and medium-term forecasts.

Median Method

Definition: This empirical method that is used in strategy 36 determines the median of the basic and trend parameters and of the seasonal index, if needed.

This method requires historical data of at least three preceding seasons. If the number of periods in a season is 1, the seasonal index is set to 1. A seasonal effect does not exist. For products that don't have any seasonal pattern, the system requires three periods to determine the trend parameter and the basic value. No initialization is required.

Because this method automatically excludes the influence of outliers, no outlier correction is necessary. The outlier correction function is not available in the context of the median method.

The system determines the difference between the first and second values of the historical data, then, between the second and third values, and so on, until it reaches the end of the data series, and then generates a forecast, as shown in Figure 4.39.

Subsequently, it sorts the values, for example, in ascending order. Finally, the system selects the value that is located exactly in the middle of this list. This value is referred to as the median value (see Figure 4.40).

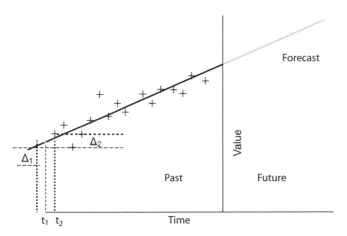

Figure 4.39 Forecast Based on the Median Method

The method proceeds as follows to determine the trend parameter, the seasonal indices, and the basic value. It creates groups of data for the first period in the cycle, as well as for the second, third, and so on, as shown in Figure 4.41.

t_1	0.3		t_2	0.1
t_2	0.1		t_1	0.3
t_3	20.6	Sorting	t_4	0.4
t_4	0.4	➡	t_n	Δ_n
...			...	
t_{n-1}	Δ_{n-1}		t_{n-1}	Δ_{n-1}
t_n	Δ_n		t_3	20.6

Figure 4.40 Selecting the Median Value in the Context of the Median Method

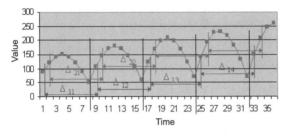

Figure 4.41 Defining Data Groups to Determine the Trend Parameter T in the Median Method

The values from the first period of each cycle are used to determine the trend parameter T. The seasonal index for that period is set to 1. The seasonal indices for the other groups can then be calculated as follows: The differences Δ are divided by the trend parameter and multiplied by the number of periods of one season. This produces as many estimates of the "i th" seasonal index (1st index, cd-index, rd-index, 4th index, ..., 99th index, etc.) as there are groups minus 1 (the first group was used to determine the trend parameter). The median value of each group represents the seasonal index for that group.

Usage: As with every forecast model, the median method cannot be used for all types of historical data. You should try to avoid the following situations: Time series that represent step functions and time series with several data points that have the same value.

4.5.4   Stable Demand and Complete History

Multilinear Regression (Causal Models)

Definition: If some factors can be identified that have a significant influence on the demand pattern, it is advisable to use causal models. The regression analysis is the standard method used for estimating the parameter values in the causal model. Normally, linear relationships that exist between the dependent variable (e.g., the demand) and the main factors (e.g., variables that are independent of each other, such as the temperature, expenditures for promotions, and so on) are considered. If several independent influencing factors exist, the model is called a multiple regression model.

The multiple linear regression procedure uses the method of the smallest squares to estimate the model parameters. This procedure minimizes the total of the squared difference between the actual and the forecasted demand that is determined by the model. Whereas the exponential smoothing procedure can take into account all historical values, the regression method is applied to a restricted set of data. The disadvantage of such a method is the loss of information, as is the case with the moving average method. Furthermore, the weight of all values considered is 1, which is why the model cannot react flexibly to changes in the demand pattern.

Usage: Because the liner regression models require a significantly higher quantity of data, you should use them only for medium and long-term forecasts or for important products. The accuracy and plausibility of the historical data are vital factors here.

The example shown in Figure 4.42 illustrates the use of the multiple linear regression for the consumption of beer, assuming that the owner of a beer garden observes the demand and the temperature over time.

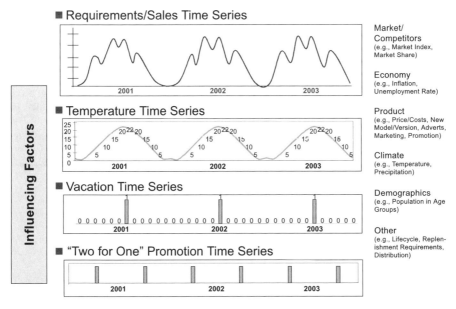

Figure 4.42 MLR Influencing Factors for Beer Consumption

The uppermost time series describes the beer consumption observed. The next time series shows the temperature pattern, while the third time series illustrates the vacation time pattern. The time series at the bottom represents the sales values for those periods in which a special promotion ("two for one") was carried out.

As long as the owner of the beer garden is aware of the factors influencing the demand for beer, he or she won't be surprised by changes in the consumer behavior, for example, if summer is exceptionally hot or cold.

The MLR forecast enables you to answer the following typical questions:

▶ How can we achieve a sales of x units?

▶ Which is the most cost-efficient solution?

▶ How will the market react if we (or one of our competitors) change the price?

▶ How successful were the past advertising campaigns?

▶ How strongly does the demand depend on the climate (for example, for ice cream and drinks)?

▶ To what extent does the economic cycle affect our sales?

▶ What are the factors that determine the long-term development of our sales?

Requirements: The demand planner must identify and quantify the most important independent variables, and model the causal relationship. The data must meet the following requirements:

▶ Actual data must exist for all variables.

▶ Comparisons with the competition are often required, but it is difficult to obtain actual data from competitors.

▶ The forecast quality depends on the forecasts for independent variables.

The logical challenges for the MLR include the following:

▶ Which variables affect the sales?

▶ How do the variables affect the sales?

▶ Modeling outliers, trend, and season

The following statistical problems must be considered:

▶ Correlation

▶ Autocorrelation

The advantages of the causal analysis are as follows:

▶ Complete modeling freedom

▶ Disintegration of the overall problem into small, individual problems that are easier to estimate

▶ "What if?" simulations are possible

▶ Chances and risks are more transparent

Evaluation: Several adaptation values are available for evaluating the quality of the MLR forecast. We'll restrict ourselves to the most important values at this point: the R square. The R square is automatically calculated during the forecasting process. Its value is always between 0 and 1. The following intervals can be used for enhancing the forecast quality:

▶ R square = 1: The MLR model describes the demand pattern perfectly.

▶ R square = 0: The MLR model does not describe the demand pattern.

▶ R square > 0.75: The MLR model describes the demand pattern adequately.

Lifecycle Forecast

Definition: The demand for an object in its introduction and discontinuation phases usually differs from the demand in the product's maturity phase. At the beginning, the demand rises with every period, whereas it decreases towards the end of the lifecycle. Figure 4.43 illustrates the demand behavior during the product lifecycle.

A statistical forecast that is based on the situation in the maturity and saturation phases cannot predict such a behavior. The most commonly used statistical forecast methods require a larger number of historical observations. In many innovative business areas, the lifecycle of certain products is less than one year. But in many industries, it lasts several years. Consequently, the knowledge of the entire lifecycle is necessary to obtain useful results.

Two main procedures—lifecycle management and the phase model—are commonly known in everyday business. They both analyze the lifecycle of products and generate appropriate models. You can find detailed descriptions of those methods in Wagner (2000).

In the following sections, we'll describe the lifecycle function, which has already been used in SAP APO for a customer-specific project. The forecast can be carried out both depending on and independent of historical data.

167

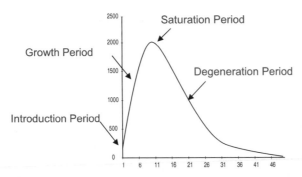

Figure 4.43 The Development of Products Usually Follows a Lifecycle

The method does not take into account any seasonal effects. It is controlled by three parameters (A, B, C) that determine the position and shape of the forecast curve. A fourth parameter, the T0 value, represents the beginning of the lifecycle.

If the forecast uses historical data, the A, B, and C parameters are determined based on a regression analysis of the historical values. The parameters are then used to carry out an ex-post forecast that is placed with a minimum degree of errors into the scatterplot of historical values. This forecast curve is then extended into the future. Figure 4.44 shows the three parameters.

If parameters A, B, and C are not known, they must be defined manually. For example, the parameters for a new product can be taken from an old, similar product. The forecast is then created on the basis of those three parameters.

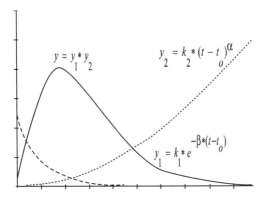

Figure 4.44 Lifecycle Function Forecast (Implementation in SAP APO Using an External Forecast)—Multiplying a Power Function by a Subsiding E-Function

Usage: To successfully use the models, the advanced planning and scheduling system (APS) must be able to create a model "library." Such a database stores the lifecycles and phase models for all product groups considered. Generally, only one lifecycle exists for the entire product group, and the data record is updated at each end of a lifecycle. SAP APO is able to do that. The great advantage of this method is that you can carry out a forecast with and without the use of historical data, and also, that you can determine the lifecycle on the basis of historical data by using the regression analysis; for example, this model is used with SAP APO in a large German telecommunications company.

Summary

Table 4.4 provides an overview of all forecast models that are available in SAP APO and mySAP ERP:

Models	Methods	Strategies	No.	SAP APO	mySAP ERP
Univariate forecast	Constant	Constant model	10	X	X
		First-order exponential smoothing	11	X	X
		Constant model with automatic alpha adaptation and first-order exponential smoothing	12	X	X
		Moving average	13	X	X
		Weighted moving average	14	X	X
	Trend	Forecast using the trend model	20	X	X
		First-order exponential smoothing	21	X	X
		Second-order exponential smoothing	22	X	X
		Constant model with automatic alpha adaptation and second-order exponential smoothing	23	X	X
	Seasonal	Forecast using the seasonal model	30	X	X
		Winters method	31	X	X
		Seasonal linear regression	35	X	

Table 4.5 All Forecast Models Available in SAP APO and mySAP ERP

Models	Methods	Strategies	No.	SAP APO	mySAP ERP
	Seasonal trend	Forecast using the seasonal trend model	40	X	X
		First-order exponential smoothing	41	X	X
	Automatic model selection 1	Test for constant, trend, seasonal, seasonal trend	50	X	X
		Trend test	51	X	X
		Seasonal test	52	X	X
		Trend test and seasonal test	53	X	X
	Automatic model selection 2	"Full parameter test"	56	X	
	Manual model selection	Seasonal model and trend test	54	X	X
		Trend model and seasonal test	55	X	X
	Actual data of previous period	Transfer historical data	60	X	X
	Manual forecast	Manual forecast	70	X	
	Sporadic	Croston method	80	X	
	Linear regression	Simple linear regression	94	X	
Causal forecast		Multilinear regression (MLR)		X	
Composite forecast	Composite forecast methods	Combination of univariate and MLR possible		X	
External forecast	External forecast models	Lifecycle function, two-points function, Bass function, …		X	

Table 4.5 All Forecast Models Available in SAP APO and mySAP ERP (cont.)

4.6 Running a Forecast

Now that you have carried out some market and product analyses (see Section 4.3) and selected a forecast method (see Section 4.4), you still have to determine some basic parameters for your forecast before you can carry out the actual forecast.

4.6.1 Configuring the Settings

Here, we'll also continue introducing the procedure model from Section 4.4.2 to demonstrate step by step the settings that you must make prior to carrying out the forecast.

Step 1: Optimizing the Parameters

Most forecast models must be optimally set with additional parameters. This involves the optimization of smoothing factors and the carrying out of a trend and seasonal significance test. The estimation of the required parameters represents the core task if you want to create an accurate forecast.

To optimally determine the parameters, a rolling approach is advantageous. Several tests enable you to carry out a manual parameter optimization (alpha, beta, gamma, delta) and thereby obtain the optimal settings. You should update the parameters on a regular basis (for example, every year).

For example, you could perform an automatic model selection as your starting point because that procedure tries to optimize the smoothing parameter in increments of 0.01. Then, you would have to refine or completely change the result in a manual parameter optimization process. The automatic model selection process could be useful here.

But, ultimately, you must optimize the individual parameters manually. Therefore, it is important that you know the meaning of each parameter. In the following sections, we'll introduce the four most important parameters and how they influence the forecast.

Step 1.1: Determining the alpha factor
The system uses the alpha factor to smooth the basic value. If you do not specify an alpha factor, the system uses an alpha factor of 0.2.

	Influence of a Large Alpha Value	Influence of a Small Alpha Value
Consideration of historical values	weak	strong
Consideration of most recent values	strong	weak
Smoothing of the time series	weak	strong
Adaptations to level changes	fast	slow

Table 4.6 Influences of the Alpha Value

Table 4.6 shows the possible influence of the alpha value. A small alpha value results in a stronger weighting of historical values than a large alpha value. Therefore, the most recent historical values are less important if the alpha value is small. A small alpha value smoothes the time series more significantly than a large alpha value. Adaptations to level changes occur more slowly if the alpha value is small.

Step 1.2: Determining the beta factor
The system uses the beta factor to smooth the trend value. If you don't specify a beta factor, the system uses a beta factor of 0.1. Therefore, a small beta value smoothes the trend value more significantly than a large beta value. Adaptations to trend changes occur more slowly if the beta value is small.

Step 1.3: Determining the gamma factor
The system uses the gamma factor to smooth the seasonal index. If you don't specify a gamma factor, the system uses a gamma factor of 0.3. Therefore, a small gamma value smoothes the seasonal index more significantly than a large gamma value. Changes in the seasonal behavior are reflected more slowly if the gamma value is small.

Step 1.4: Determining the delta factor
The system uses the delta factor to smooth the mean absolute deviation (MAD) and the error total. If you do not specify a delta factor, the system uses a delta factor of 0.3.

Step 2: Composite Forecast
Step 2.1: Deciding on a composite forecast
Experience has shown that the composite forecast, which is based on various mathematical estimation methods, often has an advantage over individual forecasts. You should decide whether you want to use a composite forecast during the forecast selection process, instead of depending on the market and product analyses.

Step 2.2: Parties involved in the composite forecast process
Once you have decided to use the composite forecast, you must define the parties that you want to be involved in the process. For example, do you want your demand planner to be joined by the S&D department, or do you want marketing to be involved when introducing new products? You should clearly determine which areas and how many people from the respective areas you want to involve.

Step 2.3: Weighting the composite forecast

When using the composite forecast, you can determine the forecasts either based on the simple average value of all forecasts involved or as a weighted average value. The example in Table 4.7 shows a possible weighting of the composite forecast.

Involved Party	Forecast Method	Weighting	Unit	August	September	October
Marketing	MLR	0.2	Units of 6	12,000	34,000	43,000
Sales and distribution	Manual	0.4	Units of 6	20,000	40,000	60,000
Central planning	Median method	0.4	Units of 6	9,000	25,000	45,000
Total forecast	–	1	Units of 6	14,000	32,800	50,600

Table 4.7 Composite Forecast with Different Weightings

You must determine the weight that you want to put on each involved area, and you should continuously verify the weightings. If you discover that the forecast accuracy of one of the involved parties is significantly higher than that of the others, you should assign a higher weight to that party.

Step 3: Forecast Periods

Step 3.1: Defining the forecast frequency

First, you must define the forecast frequency per product or product group. In other words, you need to determine how often you want to forecast the products? Usually the sales and distribution department has a great influence on the forecast frequency, because that area is responsible for estimating the sales figures. And it depends on the specific customer relationships to determine how often the forecast should be carried out. Moreover, the product lead times should also be included in this process, the reason being that the length of the lead times plays an integral role here, especially when trying to establish whether production can react to weekly forecasts.

Step 3.2: Defining the forecast horizon

Next, you must define the forecast horizon: How many periods (e.g., months) in advance do you want to create the planning figures? Do you want to create your demand planning for the next three, six, or even 24 months? Here, you should also take into account the lead times of your products, the production flexibility, the replenishment lead times for your material components, and the preferred delivery times of your customers. In addition, sales and distribution should provide you with information regarding how early your customers place their purchase orders and make plannings themselves.

Step 3.3: Defining the forecast periods

After that you must define the forecast periods: Up to which month do you need the forecast results on a daily, weekly, or monthly basis? In a long-term horizon, you should use monthly or quarterly periods so that you don't compromise the performance of the forecast tool unnecessarily. In a short-term horizon, it is often useful to base the forecast on weekly periods, provided your company can process weekly figures at short notice.

Step 3.4: Defining the historical periods

You should define the number of historical periods that you want the forecast to be based on for each product. For seasonal influences, you must specify the number of periods that a season should comprise. You can make this definition also for each product, if necessary.

Step 3.5: Defining the aggregation level

You must specify the level of aggregation to define which products you want to forecast at the product level and which products you want to forecast at the product group level. For this purpose, you have to consider the level at which the transfer of requirements to production should occur and at which level sales and distribution should issue planning figures. Note that the degree of forecast accuracy is higher at the aggregated level, but that it is a greater challenge for production to obtain the figures at the aggregated level.

Step 4: Promotions and Events

Step 4.1: Creating a promotion Matrix

First you must create a promotion matrix, as described in Section 4.3.5. This will provide you with a good overview of the types of promotions and events and their forecasting potential.

Step 4.2: Analyzing historical promotions and events

To create a consistent data basis for forecasting promotions and events, you must first divide previous events (actions, promotions, trade shows, ...) into regular and irregular events. Regular events must be planned on a regular basis, whereas the influence of one-time events must be corrected in the data basis. To do so, you must create different key figures for the different events, as described in Step 1, and then create different time series from the historical data, if possible. If you can no longer separate the influence of the different events, you should at least generate a new time series for past promotions and events.

Step 4.3: Period adjustment

When analyzing historical data, you should ensure that the previous events will occur in the same period in the future. If necessary, you should create a key figure for the corrected history of event consumptions and adjust the periods.

Step 4.4: Consistent data basis for promotions and events

You should store the historical sales figures for regular and irregular events in separate key figures. If you want, you can also store the historical regular events in several separate key figures to obtain a more exact history. If you do that, you should use the key figures described in Section 4.3.3 for the original and corrected histories.

Step 4.5: Carrying out forecasts for promotions and events

You should carry out separate forecasts for past regular events (one for the Christmas period, one for the February trade show, one for the summer events, and so on), and add those forecasts to the baseline forecast.

Step 4.6: History for promotions and events

Store the events in separate key figures so that you can differentiate between the baseline forecast and the forecast for the individual events at any time. This provides a degree of transparency that enables you to interfere with and correct the forecast whenever you want, for example, if an event occurs in a different period or not at all.

4.6.2 Running a Forecast in SAP APO

The Demand Planning Desktop

Since the previous chapter already described the most important settings required for carrying out the forecast, we'll now describe the basic process of a forecast using SAP APO.

First, you must analyze and describe the time series that are stored in Info-Cubes, which represent multidimensional databases. Data can be accessed easily in these InfoCubes, and you can load it from mySAP ERP or other ERP systems into APO via an update rule. Then, you can prepare and analyze the data using Business Explorer Analyzer (BEx Analyzer). In this way, you can use the data when selecting the most appropriate forecast method.

The demand planning function in SAP APO supports top-down, middle-out, and bottom-up planning. The top-down planning describes a planning process at a high level. Middle-out planning is a planning done at medium level, while the bottom-up planning refers to the details level. For example, you can plan the demand for an entire region, for individual divisions within the region, or for individual products of each division within the region.

The desktop in interactive demand planning is the tool that enables you to directly view and edit planning data. Figure 4.45 shows the desktop. To access it, select **SAP APO · Demand Planning · Planning · Interactive Demand Planning** from the menu.

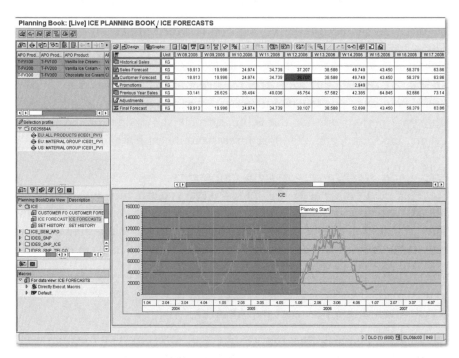

Figure 4.45 Interactive Demand Planning in SAP APO

The desktop consists of two major components—the selection area and the work area. The selection area, which is also referred to as the selector, is the most important tool for searching, sorting, and organizing information. It is located in the left-hand area of the screen.

In the top left-hand area, you can see the shuffler, which is the pane in which you select the planned InfoObjects (e.g., materials, locations, customers, or promotions). You can also use the shuffler to store frequently used selections by their selection IDs.

The selection profile is located directly underneath the shuffler. It displays the selection IDs that the planner is currently using. The selection profile enables you to quickly access frequently used selections.

In the data views area below, you can select your planning books and data views. This makes it easy for you to flexibly design the work area on the right. The planner can assign different key figures in several planning books and then use these key figures to carry out separate plannings in the work area.

The bottom part of the selection area displays the macros that are enabled for all the data views in this planning book, as well as for the current data view. Macros are algorithms that support the planner in the demand planning process.

The work area is used for display and planning purposes. It is located in the right-hand area of the screen. It consists of a table (also referred to as a grid) and a graphic. The table displays the selected planning book. All key figures of the table can be defined freely and flexibly.

Different data views in a planning area enable you to view the same data from different points of view. The normal tabular or graphical display of your data helps you to compare key figures, run macros, and manually change data.

But you can also view the forecast figures per customer-product combination, as shown in Figure 4.46. To do that, select the **Customer Details (all)** button from the **header data section** in the interactive demand planning.

You can assign planning books and data views to specific users. Moreover, you can define whether a user should be able to access other planning books and data views.

In addition to the data views created by your company, you can use one or more of the following standard SAP views for your work:

▶ Interactive demand planning

▶ Promotion planning

▶ Multiple linear regression (MLR) forecast view

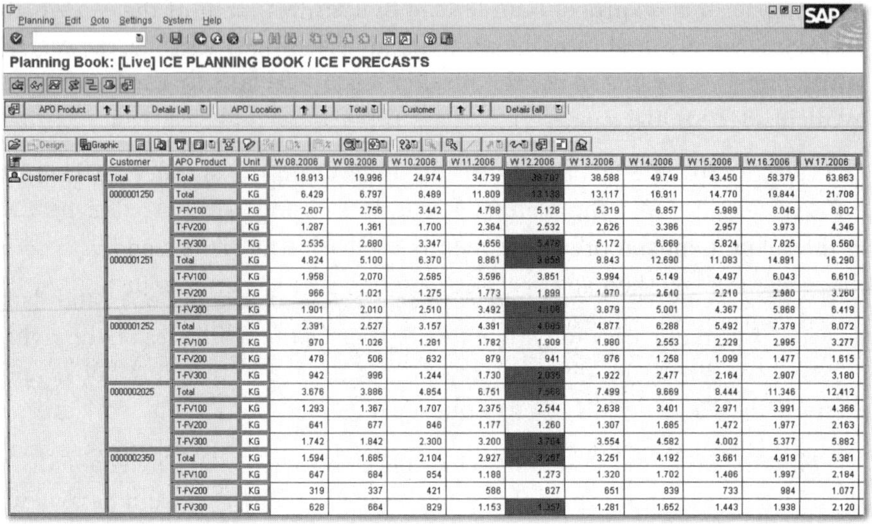

Figure 4.46 Forecast View: Customer-Product Combination

In the planning book, you can define the standard views that should be available to the demand planner.

Based on the graphic and the key figures mentioned above, the forecast is then started and a time series model that is most appropriate for the historical data is selected.

In the following example, we'll do a forecast for a specific ice cream flavor. As you can see in Figure 4.46, three ice cream products have been selected for the forecast. The historical demand is shown in the Historical Demand row.

Running the Forecast

Click on the **Forecast** button in the interactive demand planning tool to start the forecast process. Typically, the forecast profile is automatically proposed by the system and used in the forecast. This step is performed in the background and is therefore transparent to the user so that he or she doesn't need to select a profile for each forecast. However, you can also assign the forecast profile manually. In SAP APO, you can carry out the planning both interactively and in the background. Normally, you perform a planning run in the background by using the mass processing for several products function and then correct the figures on the demand planning desktop. You can also work in interactive demand planning to check different forecast models.

The model selection process is followed by an adjustment of the models to the data. The adjustment process is divided into several areas. In the model initialization phase, the second-order exponential smoothing method is used to calculate the initial values with regard to the trend and basic values. These values can, for example, result from the regression line that runs through the points of the initialization period.

In the subsequent smoothing phase, the basic value and the trend value are changed and smoothed after each forecasting step to better adjust the forecasted values to the observed values and therefore to minimize the forecast error. In this way, an ex-post forecast with the increment of 1 is carried out from one period to the next, up to the end of the time series.

With an automatic model selection, you might be able to calculate several forecast models and adapt them to the observed values before you use a specific model for your forecast. In this case, iterations of the forecast models may occur in the forecasting process.

The adaptation of the model to historical values must be carried out to ensure that the user can produce a forecast with as much accuracy as possible. The second-order exponential smoothing process requires the basic and trend values of the most recent historical period for performing the forecast. Based on those values, the exponential smoothing method calculates the future values, whereby the most recent historical values obtain a greater weight due to the use of the smoothing factors, α and β.

The adaptation phase is essential for the comparison of several time series models and forecast methods, because it is often only the forecasted values from the adaptation phase that are involved in the analysis of the forecast accuracy. But, since every one-step forecast is followed by an adjustment of the model parameters to the observed values, the significance of the forecast accuracy measures is reduced. The forecast accuracy measures become more important if the values of a multiple-step ex-post forecast are used to calculate the forecast accuracy, because the model parameters are not changed in an ex-post forecast.

In our example, we used the total profile ICE for the ice-cream scenario. You can use the forecast profile to dictate which forecast profile should be selected, how long the forecast horizon should be, and which forecast errors should be calculated, for example. In our example, there is only one profile available, namely the univariate ICE profile, which means that we'll carry out a univariate forecast.

Figure 4.47 displays the types of forecast models available in SAP APO. To access this list, select the **Model** tab in the forecast view.

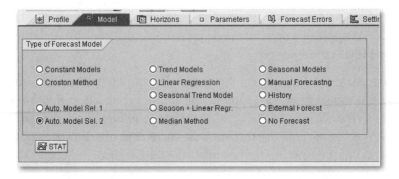

Figure 4.47 Forecast Models in SAP APO

The screen shows the forecast method assigned in the ICE forecast profile; in this case, it is the automatic model selection 2. Here you can also select another forecast model, for example, if you want to perform a simulation. If the forecast errors are still too big, you can select a different method to optimize your forecast. You can use the **External Forecast** radio button to integrate customer-specific forecasts.

Forecast Analysis

After the forecast has been completed, the next step is to run a forecast analysis. To provide a detailed picture of this step, we'll manually go through each of the individual stages of analysis. Of course, in practice, these stages are executed automatically. The user only receives relevant messages in exceptional situations. In these cases, SAP APO automatically alerts the user and suggests appropriate follow-up actions.

The manual forecast analysis starts with an analysis of the forecast result in the forecast view in SAP APO. The **forecast view** shown in Figure 4.48 is the result of our forecast for ice cream in SAP APO.

The sales figures calculated by the system using the univariate forecast are shown in the **Sales Forecast** row. You can adjust the forecast here if necessary. In the **Corrected History** row, SAP APO corrects the original history based on specific influences, such as outlier correction, correction of work days, phase-in/phase-out profiles, and like profiles. In other words, these corrections do not have to be done manually, which makes the planner's job much easier.

	W 08.2006	W 09.2006	W 10.2006	W 11.2006	W 12.2006	W 13.2006	W 14.2006	W 15.2006	W
Sales Forecast	14664	14664	14664	14664	14664	14664	14664	14664	
Historical Sales									
Corrected History									
Ex-Post Forecst									
Corrected Forecast	14664	14664	14664	14664	14664	14664	14664	14664	
Seasonal	1,00	1,00	1,00	1,00	1,00	1,00	1,00	1,00	
Trend									
Basic Value	14664,15	14664,15	14664,15	14664,15	14664,15	14664,15	14664,15	14664,15	

Figure 4.48 Forecast View in SAP APO

Once the forecast results are output, you can analyze them using the various tabs in the lower part of the screen. If necessary, you can change the forecast profile, forecast model, planning horizon, forecast parameters, or forecast settings. Which forecast parameters you can set depends on the forecast model. You can use any of the forecast models.

To provide a clearer picture of the different forecast options and their analysis in SAP APO, the individual tabs are discussed in more detail below.

The **Horizons** tab shows the forecast settings for the forecast horizon, as shown in Figure 4.49.

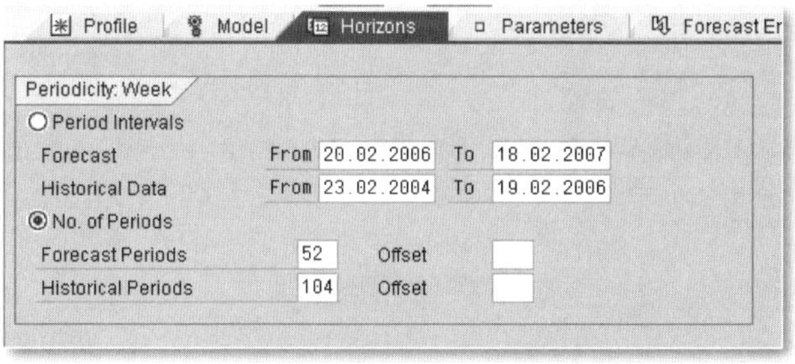

✴ Profile	🍴 Model	📧 Horizons	▢ Parameters	🗒 Forecast Er

Periodicity: Week				
⚪ Period Intervals				
Forecast	From 20.02.2006	To	18.02.2007	
Historical Data	From 23.02.2004	To	19.02.2006	
⦿ No. of Periods				
Forecast Periods	52	Offset		
Historical Periods	104	Offset		

Figure 4.49 Forecast Analysis: Forecast Horizon

Here you can enter the period for which your historical data is to be analyzed, as well as the period for which the forecast is to be run. You can check whether the correct period is selected and change it as required. The forecast for our ice cream scenario is to be executed for the period from February 20, 2006 to February 18, 2007, that is, a period of 52 weeks. The forecast is to go back 104 weeks into the past and take historical data into account. This historical period was selected because the full seasonal cycle of the ice cream in this scenario is one year.

In addition, you can specify **offset** periods if the forecast will not be executed for the period following the current period.

You can configure the other forecast parameters for the ice cream forecast on the **Parameters** tab on the next input screen (see Figure 4.50).

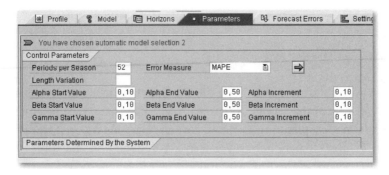

Figure 4.50 Forecast Analysis: Forecast Parameters

Here you can enter the length of the season for seasonal items. A seasonal length of one year is maintained here for our ice cream. In addition, an error measure is set for the season selection. MAPE has been selected here as the **error measure** for the forecast analysis. The alpha, beta, and gamma parameters calculated by you or by the system—in case of automatic model selection—are also shown.

The **forecast errors** calculated by SAP APO for the ice cream are shown in Figure 4.51.

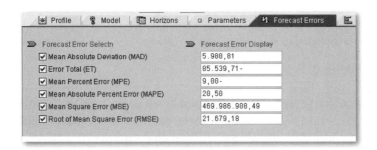

Figure 4.51 Forecast Analysis: Forecast Errors

By simply selecting the relevant errors, you can determine which forecast errors the system should calculate in order to analyze the forecast. If you want additional errors to be calculated, you can use the relevant macros provided in interactive demand planning. The forecast error allows you to identify whether the quality of your forecast is sufficient. For more detailed information about the various forecast errors, see Section 4.7.2.

Additional forecast settings for the ice cream example are shown in the **Settings** tab in Figure 4.52.

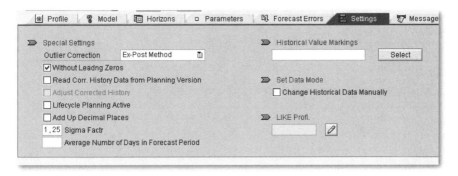

Figure 4.52 Forecast Analysis: Forecast Settings

Here you can make various settings for your forecast. In the ice cream forecast, outlier correction is not activated, because this was already done before the forecast model was selected. This means that our data has already been adjusted. Because one of the three ice cream flavors will be marketed for the first time, replacing an old flavor that has been withdrawn, we will use lifecycle planning here, and therefore have activated this option.

Next, messages appear for the forecast in the **Messages** tab in the message monitor.

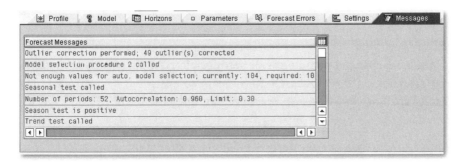

Figure 4.53 Forecast Analysis: Forecast Messages

Here you can see, for example, that a seasonal test has been conducted during automatic model selection for our ice cream. The system has detected white noise and executed an ex-post forecast, resulting in the system having selected a constant model. Lifecycle planning and the phase-in/phase-out profiles are then taken into account.

Finally, you should choose **Back** to return to interactive planning. Figure 4.54 shows that the forecast values have been copied.

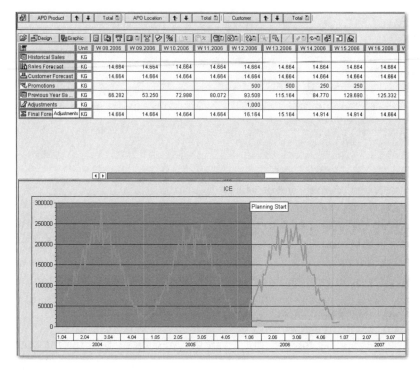

Figure 4.54 Forecast Result in Interactive Demand Planning

Forecast Comparison

If you have changed parameters or settings after the forecast is completed, you can click on the **Forecast** button again to execute a new forecast. The results are not copied into the active planning version until you save the forecast.

You can then compare the results of the two simulation runs in a forecast comparison. You should use this function to compare planning versions, forecast versions, forecast parameters, and forecast errors. Figure 4.55 shows that the results have deteriorated with each forecast. Our first forecast using model 22 produced the best results. To navigate to that screen, select the menu option **SAP APO · Demand Planning · Planning · Interactive Demand Planning** and press the **Forecast Comparison** button.

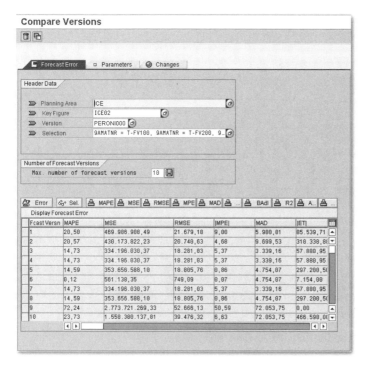

Figure 4.55 Forecast Comparison, Forecast Error Tab

As shown in Figure 4.56, the forecast comparison comprises three tabs:

▶ **Forecast Error**
This tab shows the various estimated error values calculated by the system as part of the forecast. You can sort the different versions according to the required error measure. When you have calculated the forecast settings that provide the best possible results, you can generate a forecast profile from these settings (this is only possible with a univariate forecast).

▶ **Parameters**
This tab shows the parameters used by the individual versions for the univariate forecast (this does not apply to MLR), as well as possible lifecycle profiles that are used along with the selection (this does not apply if aggregated lifecycle planning is used).

▶ **Changes**
This tab displays more general information, such as the version (planning version or forecast version), the planner who created the version, the date and time of the forecast, the profile used, and the profile type (univariate, MLR, or composite).

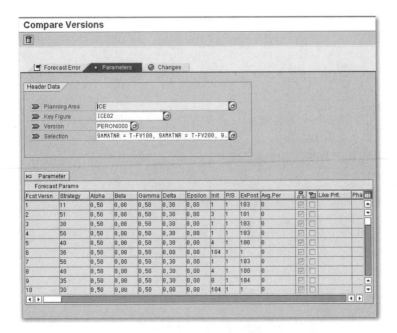

Figure 4.56 Forecast Comparison, Parameters Tab

In the **Version** field, you can specify whether you want to display data belonging to other planning versions and selections. In our example, the system displays only the data of the most recent forecast, that is, the data of the current forecast version. Alternatively, you can also display all forecast versions (up to the maximum number of entries) for a planning version and selection.

4.7   Forecast Accuracy and Alert Functions

The selection of the correct forecast method plays an integral role in forecasting. Therefore, you need to know how to determine the optimal forecast method to meet your requirements. You should note how striking it is that the criteria developed in relevant literature for evaluating forecasts analyzes the forecast errors almost exclusively by using measured values, which compare the ex-post forecast values with the actual observed values.

4.7.1   Ex-Post Forecast

We recommend that you perform an ex-post forecast to check the accuracy of the forecast.

Definition: An ex-post forecast is a forecast that is run in past periods for which a history with actual sales data also exists. It calculates forecast accuracy measurements by comparing the differences between the actual values and the ex-post values. You use an ex-post forecast to obtain information about the different forecast errors.

Figure 4.57 shows two period blocks in the past: the initialization period, which is used as the history for the ex-post forecast and must be sufficiently long, and the ex-post period, during which a forecast is generated.

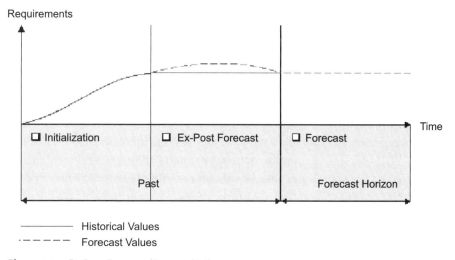

Figure 4.57 Ex-Post Forecast (Source: SAP)

Usage: An ex-post forecast is automatically run as follows if sufficient historical data is available.

The historical values are divided into two groups:

▸ The first group, containing the older values, is used for initialization.

▸ The second group, containing the more recent groups, is when the ex-post forecast is run.

The basic value, trend value, seasonal index, and mean absolute deviation (MAD) are modified in each ex-post period. These values are used to calculate forecasts for the future.

The system calculates the error total in the ex-post horizon. The error total is the total of the differences between the actual (historical) values and the planned values (in this example, the values in the ex-post forecast).

An ex-post forecast provides a sound basis for evaluating the quality of the forecast, because it allows you to compare the forecast with the actual data before the next forecast interval. An ex-post forecast is also very important for analyzing historical data and for selecting a suitable forecast procedure.

You should run an ex-post forecast and analyze the forecast errors to assess the quality of your forecast. We will discuss forecast errors in the next sections.

4.7.2 An Overview of Forecast Errors

Forecast errors can be calculated automatically. First, several forecasts are generated (using different parameters) for this purpose, based on historical data. The forecast errors are then calculated and the model with the fewest forecast errors is selected. In a second step, the parameters of the selected forecast model are optimized. Forecasts are generated with different parameters and the forecast errors are compared. Unfortunately, many companies don't have forecast tools that can generate several forecasts and then select the optimal forecast. Generally, demand planners still use Excel for demand planning, so it's simply not feasible to compare forecasts for different products, or to consider deviations in forecast errors when selecting a forecast procedure.

This chapter displays a selection of forecast errors and provides a brief description of their significance and potential uses. This will enable you to select appropriate forecast errors for your products and use them in your company.

Forecast errors are divided into two groups of alert types in SAP APO:

- ▶ Alerts for the univariate forecast
  - ▶ Error total (ET)
  - ▶ Mean absolute deviation (MAD)
  - ▶ Mean square error (MSE)
  - ▶ Root of the mean square error (RMSE)
  - ▶ Mean absolute percent error (MAPE)
  - ▶ Mean percent error (MPE)
  - ▶ Absolute percent error (APE)
  - ▶ Adjusted absolute percent error (APE-A)

- ▸ Median absolute percent error (MdAPE)
- ▸ Median relative absolute error (MdRAE)
- ▸ Geometric mean relative absolute error (GMRAE)
- ▸ Relative absolute error (RAE)
- ▸ Alerts for the MLR forecast
  - ▸ R square
  - ▸ Adjusted R square
  - ▸ Durbin-h
  - ▸ Durbin-Watson
  - ▸ t-Test
  - ▸ Mean elasticity

4.7.3   Univariate Forecast Errors

The forecast errors of the univariate forecast procedure can be classified as follows:

- ▸ Percentage errors
- ▸ Relative errors
- ▸ Mean values
- ▸ Other errors

First, you will learn how to calculate percentage errors and relative errors. Next, you will be introduced to the methods for summarizing individual values (mean, median, and geometric mean). Finally, some additional, standard errors will be described.

Error Total

The deviations between the forecast value and the actual observed value in each period are added together to calculate the error total.

Error total = $\Sigma\,|(C_t - F_t)|$

Legend: C_t = consumption; F_t = forecast

Table 4.8 shows the error total for our example above.

Actual Value	Forecast	Absolute Deviation	Error Total
120	110	10	
140	160	20	
			30

Table 4.8 Calculation of Error Total

Mean Absolute Deviation (MAD)

The MAD is the average absolute error:

$MAD = \frac{1}{n} \Sigma (C_t - F_t)$

Legend: C_t = consumption; F_t = forecast, n= number of periods

Positive and negative deviations do not outweigh each other. The smaller the value, the better the forecast in a given period. A large value may signify a small percentage deviation when dealing with a large volume. Therefore, volume should always be taken into account as well (see percentage errors).

By adding the differences between the forecast value and the actual value, positive and negative deviations are given equal weighting.

Table 4.9 shows the MAD error for our example.

Actual Value	Forecast	Absolute Deviation	MAD
120	110	10	
140	160	20	
			15

Table 4.9 Calculation of MAD

Mean Square Error (MSE)

The MSE is the square of the sum of the deviations across all periods, divided by the number of periods.

$MSE = \frac{1}{n} \Sigma (C_t - F_t)^2$

Legend: C_t = consumption; F_t = forecast, n = number of periods

Table 4.10 shows the MSE error for our example.

Actual Value	Forecast	Absolute Deviation	MSE
120	110	10	
140	160	20	
			250

Table 4.10 Calculation of MSE

Outliers in the individual periods have a significant effect on the MSE. The deviations within one period have a more significant effect on the result than the deviations in two periods divided by two. The current literature advises against using this key figure.

Root of the Mean Square Error (RMSE)

RMSE is the root of the mean square error (MSE).

$$RMSE = \sqrt{\tfrac{1}{n}}\ \Sigma\, (C_t - F_t)^2$$

Legend: C_t = consumption; F_t = forecast, n = number of periods

The RMSE was used very frequently in the past. More recently, however, it has been overtaken by other error calculations (see above). The current literature advises against using the RMSE to compare forecast models, because few outliers have a significant effect on the RMSE.

Table 4.11 shows the RMSE error for our example.

Actual Value	Forecast	Absolute Deviation	RMSE
120	110	10	
140	160	20	
			15.81

Table 4.11 Calculation of RMSE

Absolute Percent Error (APE)

The absolute percent error (APE) indicates the degree to which the forecasts deviate from the actual values. The APE is calculated as a percentage. Positive and negative deviations do not outweigh each other, because the absolute error is always used.

$$APE = (C_t - F_t) / C_t * 100$$

Legend: C_t = consumption; F_t = forecast

The APE is used very frequently, because it is easily understood and interpreted; however, the APE has two distinct disadvantages. The first disadvantage is that APE favors forecasts with values that are too low. In other words, it penalizes forecast values that are higher than the actual value to a greater degree than values that are lower than the actual value. This behavior is considered to be an asymmetrical error. The lower limit is 100% (forecast = 0), while there is no upper limit, that is, an error of more than 100% is possible. In reality, this means that the forecast accuracy is greater if the forecast is conservative. But, this could result in a loss of sales because planners who use this error to measure the forecast accuracy will tend to create forecasts with values that are too low.

The second disadvantage of APE is that, if the actual values are zero or close to zero, the error becomes very large or cannot be calculated (division by zero).

Still another disadvantage posed by the APE is the possibility of varying calculations. Since the APE is a percentage error, the actual value may be in the denominator, as shown in the formula above; however, it may also be in the numerator and the forecast value in the denominator. If the actual value is in the denominator, the APE favors forecast values that are too low, as we already mentioned. If, on the other hand, the forecast value is in the denominator, the APE favors forecast values that are too high. Table 4.12 shows an APE calculation.

Actual Value	Forecast	APE with Forecast Value in the Denominator	APE with Actual Value in the Denominator
120	100	20	16.67
140	160	12.50	14.29

Table 4.12 Calculation of APE

If you use this error in your company, you should pay particular attention to the calculation method, because the same figures may be represented in different ways with this error.

Due to its asymmetrical behavior, the APE should not be used if large values are predicted.

Adjusted Absolute Percent Error (APE-A)

The adjusted APE was developed to counteract the disadvantages of the APE.

$$APE\text{-}A = (C_t - F_t) / ((C_t + F_t)/n)$$

Legend: C_t = consumption; F_t = forecast

The difference between the APE-A and the APE is that the average of the actual value plus the forecast value is used as the denominator, rather than just the actual value. Consequently, the APE-A produces comparable results, regardless of whether the forecast value exceeds the actual value, or the actual value exceeds the forecast value. It also returns a result if the actual value is equal to zero.

The APE-A is always between 0 and 2. Other values are not accepted. In contrast to the example shown above, the APE-A would calculate the errors shown in Table 4.13 below.

Actual Value	Forecast	APE-A
120	100	0.18
140	160	0.13

Table 4.13 Calculation of APEA-A

General rule: the smaller the value, the better the forecast with the APE-A.

Mean Absolute Percent Error (MAPE)

The MAPE calculates the arithmetic mean of the percentage errors across several periods, based on the APE. First, the APE or APE-A is calculated for each period and the mean value of these errors is then calculated.

$$MAPE = \Sigma((C_t - F_t) / C_t * 100)/n$$

Legend: C_t = consumption; F_t = forecast, n = number of periods

Table 4.14 shows the MAPE error for our example.

Actual Value	Forecast	APE	MAPE
120	100	16.67	
140	160	14.29	
			15.48

Table 4.14 Calculation of MAPE

The advantage of the MAPE is that it provides a meaningful error value for a time series, because it calculates a mean value from all the errors in the individual periods; however, the disadvantage is that it does not allow you to draw any conclusions regarding effects on inventories. The MAPE cannot tell you whether a forecast is good or bad from the point of view of inventory management. The individual periods would have to be examined for this purpose. This drawback applies to all forecast errors that calculate a mean value across several periods.

When interpreting the MAPE result, you must ask yourself the following questions:

▸ **For which products was a forecast created with the MAPE?**
The MAPE comprises the forecast results of various products. You should analyze precisely which products are included in the MAPE. Often, the products are very diverse, so it doesn't make sense to calculate an overall forecast error.

▸ **Which periods are included in the MAPE?**
The monthly MAPE may be lower than the weekly MAPE.

▸ **What is your current MAPE?**
The development of the MAPE must be taken into account over time. This is often a much better indicator of forecast accuracy than a situation-specific MAPE.

Median Absolute Percent Error (MdAPE)

The median value is the middle value in a list of figures sorted in ascending order. With an even number of values, you take one of the two values in the middle of the sequence. If the two values differ, which is rare, you take the arithmetic mean of the two values.

Example of an even number of values:
*10, 11, 15, **20**, **21**, 25, 30, 40 → Median = 20.5*

Example of an odd number of values:
*10, 11, 15, 20, **21**, 25, 30, 40, 100 → Median = 21*

The APE for each period is calculated first and the median is calculated using the logic explained above.

The advantage of the median over the arithmetic mean is that it is robust against outliers, that is, against numbers that deviate significantly from the norm. In this regard, MdAPE is preferable to MAPE.

The MdAPE is best suited to the selection of forecast models where sufficient data is available.

Relative Absolute Error (RAE)

With relative errors, two alternative forecasts are always compared with each other. The RAE formula is therefore as follows:

$RAE = (Ct - Ft) / (Ct - Prw)$

Legend: Ct = consumption; Ft = forecast, Prw = alternative forecast

Table 4.15 shows the RAE error for our example.

Actual Value	Forecast 1	Forecast 2	RAE
120	117	100	0.15
140	160	142	10

Table 4.15 Calculation of RAE

As you can see, the RAE is very large if the absolute error of the alternative forecast is very small. This error favors the alternative forecast.

Because the RAE (like the APE and the APE-A) must be calculated for each period, only these periods can be compared with one another individually. A cumulation therefore results in an incorrect interpretation with the RAE.

Median Relative Absolute Error (MdRAE)

The MdRAE is the median of the RAE. It is well suited to those forecast models where only a small amount of data is available (unlike the MdAPE). It is also robust against outliers.

Geometric Mean Relative Absolute Error (GMRAE)

The geometric mean of the RAE is used to summarize relative errors with marginal outliers.

The GMRAE summarizes the RAE for a time series. For example, it could provide you with a value for a period of 12 months. The GMRAE should be used if the parameters of a selected forecast model are to be optimized. The GMRAE is calculated as follows:

$GMRAE = (RAE_1, RAE_2, ..., RAE_n)^{1/n}$

Tracking Signal

If you want the forecast procedure to have a certain range of tolerance with regard to the error, you can use the tracking signal to define this range. In this case, normal distribution of deviation is assumed. Therefore, if you wanted to allow the forecast model to have a tolerance range of 95% of the mean value, you would use a standard deviation of approximately +/– 1.6.

The tracking signal is calculated as follows:

$$Tracking\ signal = |Error\ total/MAD|$$

Table 4.16 shows the MAD error for our example.

Actual Value	Forecast	Absolute Deviation	Error Total	MAD	Tracking Signal
120	110	10			
140	160	20			
			30	15	2

Table 4.16 Tracking Signal Calculation

In our example, the forecast model must be reconfigured if the deviation signal is outside the permitted range of +/– 1.6.

The tracking signal is not, strictly speaking, a forecast error. Rather, it is used to define a range of tolerance for an error, which is useful when you're creating a forecast.

Theil Coefficient

Nondimensional measures enable you to compare the forecast errors of different time series. If you divide the measures by the arithmetic mean, you can then interpret these as percentage errors.

The Theil coefficient is not, strictly speaking, a forecast error. Rather, it helps the user to compare different forecasts.

Summary of Univariate Errors

The current literature (see Marakidis; Armstrong, Collopy) recommends the following error measures for univariate forecasts:

▶ The median relative absolute error (MdRAE) for selecting forecast models if only a small amount of historical data is available

▶ The median absolute percentage error (MdAPE) if a sufficient amount of historical data is available

▶ The geometric mean relative absolute error (GMRAE) if the parameters of a selected forecast model are to be optimized

4.7.4   Causal Forecast Errors (MLR)

With multiple linear regression (MLR), you evaluate the effects of various causal factors on the forecast. Several different functions are provided for this purpose. The system generates an alert if the statistical result of the calculation exceeds or falls short of the defined upper/lower limit.

R Square

With MLR, the R square indicates how well a certain combination of X variables (the drivers or independent variables of the model) explains the variation in Y (dependent variable).

The R square lies within the value range of 0 to 1. A value of 0 signifies that the multiple linear regression model cannot explain the variation in Y. A value of 1 means that the model is a perfect fit. A value of 0.9 or higher indicates an acceptable model.

R square is also known as the coefficient of determination or the measure of goodness of fit.

If you use this measure to compare two models, you must ensure that the same dependent variable is used.

Adjusted R Square

In a multiple linear regression model, the adjusted R square measures the percentage variation in the dependent variables that is accounted for by the explanatory independent variables. Contrary to R square, the adjusted R square incorporates the degree of freedom associated with the sums of the squares. Although the residual sum of squares may decrease or remain the same when new explanatory variables are added, this is not necessarily the case with the residual variance. Adjusted R square is therefore considered to be a more accurate measure of goodness of fit than R square.

You should note the following points regarding adjusted R square:

▶ If the adjusted R square is significantly lower than R square, this usually means that one or more explanatory variables are missing. Without these variables, the variation in the dependent variables cannot be fully measured.

▶ If you use this measure to compare two models, you must ensure that the same dependent variable is used.

Durbin-h

The Durbin-h statistic checks to ensure that there is autocorrelation in time series where independent variables are shifted by one or more periods.

If Durbin-h is 1.96 or higher, it is very likely that autocorrelation exists. The Durbin-h test is suitable for large samples, that is, samples of 100 or more time series values.

Autocorrelation occurs if the error variables of a regression model are not independent, that is, if the values in the historical periods in the forecast model influence the values in the current periods. Time series with a marked seasonal or cyclical pattern are often highly correlated. A high degree of correlation means that multiple linear regression (MLR) is not suitable as a forecast method if you're using the usual method of the smallest squares for the available data.

Durbin-Watson

Durbin-Watson is a measure used to test for first-order autocorrelation in time series in which independent variables are not shifted.

The Durbin-Watson statistic lies within a value range of 0 to 4. A value of 2 or close to 2 indicates that no first-order autocorrelation exists. The acceptable range is 1.50 to 2.50.

In cases with consistently small error differences, the Durbin-Watson is low (< 1.50), which indicates positive autocorrelation. Positive autocorrelation is very common. In cases with consistently large error differences, the Durbin-Watson is high (> 2.50), which indicates negative autocorrelation. Negative autocorrelation is rare.

In time series with shifted variables, the Durbin-Watson statistic is not reliable, because it tends towards a value of 2.0.

t-Test

The t-test, which is also referred to as the t-statistic, indicates whether an independent variable correlates with the dependent variable. By checking if the independent variable contributes to the explanation of the dependent variable, the t-test determines whether the independent variable should remain part of the model.

The t-test does not provide any information on the significance of the size and influence of an explanatory variable.

The significance of a t-test of approximately 4.6 is not higher than that of a t-test of 2.4. It simply means that the independent variables linked with the t-test are significant in that they explain the deviation in the dependent variable. The size of this relationship is measured by the coefficient of the independent variable, including its unit of measurement.

The reference value for a t-test is +/−2.0. This value is used to determine whether an independent variable significantly correlates with the dependent variable at a confidence level of 95%. Empirical tests have shown, however, that a t-test of +/−1.4 or higher is structurally significant at a confidence level of 90%. For this reason, SAP recommends that you keep explanatory variables in the model if the t-test is +/−1.4 or higher.

Mean Elasticity

The elasticity measures the effect on the dependent variable caused by a change of 1% to the explanatory variable. The elasticity is calculated as a percentage change of Y (dependent variable), divided by the percentage change of X (explanatory or independent variable). Elasticities often differ if they are measured at different points of the regression. The mean elasticity represents the average value of the elasticities measured at different points.

Elasticities are useful because they aren't specified in any unit. Therefore, they provide a simpler way of interpreting and describing the effects of causal variables, for example, in upper management.

A high elasticity means that the dependent variable reacts sensitively to change in the explanatory variable.

Other errors can be flexibly determined by using macros.

4.7.5 Forecast Errors in SAP APO

Table 4.17 provides an overview of the forecast errors described above. It also indicates which errors are supported in SAP APO.

Forecast Error	Description	Formula	Univariate/ Causal	SAP APO Standard	SAP APO Macro
Error total	Error total	$\Sigma \mid (C_t - F_t) \mid$	Univariate error	X	
MAD	Mean absolute error	$1/_n \Sigma (C_t - F_t)$	Univariate error	X	
MSE	Mean square error	$1/_n \Sigma (C_t - F_t)^2$	Univariate error	X	
RMSE	Root of mean square error	$\sqrt{1/_n} \Sigma (C_t - F_t)^2$	Univariate error	X	
APE	Absolute percent error	$(C_t - F_t) / V_t * 100$	Univariate error		X
APE-A	Absolute percent error (adjusted)	$(C_t - F_t) / ((C_t + F_t)/n)$	Univariate error		X
MAPE	Mean absolute percent error	$\Sigma ((C_t - F_t) / C_t * 100)/n$	Univariate error	X	
MdAPE	Median absolute percent error	Median of MAPE	Univariate error		X
RAE	Relative absolute error	$(C_t - F_t) / (C_t - P_{rw})$	Univariate error		X
MdRAE	Median relative absolute error	Median of RAE	Univariate error		X
GMRAE	Geometric mean absolute error	$(RAE1, RAE2, ..., RAEn)^{1/n}$	Univariate error		X
Tracking signal		$\mid$Error total/MAD$\mid$	Support for univariate errors	X	
Theil coefficient			Support for univariate errors	X	
R square			Causal error	X	

Table 4.17 Forecast Errors in SAP APO

Forecast Error	Description	Formula	Univariate/ Causal	SAP APO Standard	SAP APO Macro
Adjusted R square			Causal error	X	
Durbin-h			Causal error	X	
Durbin-Watson			Causal error	X	
t-Test			Causal error	X	
Mean elasticity			Causal error	X	

Table 4.17 Forecast Errors in SAP APO (cont.)

4.7.6 Comparability of Forecast Errors

When calculating the forecast errors, you must ensure that you can compare the basic data. Because many companies have difficulties with comparing data, the value of the forecast error is influenced by the following parameters:

▶ The data basis

▶ The forecast periods

▶ The aggregation level of the forecast

▶ The time between two forecasts, or between the forecast values and the actual values

Comparable Data Basis

You must be able to evaluate the databases used for the forecasts that are to be compared, or for the forecast values and the actual values. For example, if the forecast does not contain any deliveries that are free of charge, you must not include these deliveries in the actual quantity because the forecast does not contain them.

Comparable Forecast Periods

Table 4.18 shows an example of forecast errors in different forecast periods. As you can see, the forecast error for the monthly basis is 0%, which means that an exact forecast was produced for the monthly level, whereas an incorrect forecast was generated for the individual weekly periods.

			Forecast Error	
	Actual	Forecast	Week	Month
Week 45	25	0	100%	0%
Week 46	25	50	100%	
Week 47	25	50	100%	
Week 48	25	0	100%	

Table 4.18 Forecast Errors in Different Periods

Comparable Aggregation Levels

Forecast errors can also occur at different aggregation levels.

Table 4.19 shows that no forecast error exists at the product group level, while for each forecast at the product level a forecast error of 100% has been determined.

			Forecast Error	
	Actual	Forecast	Product	Product Group
Product 1	50	100	100%	0%
Product 2	100	50	100%	

Table 4.19 Forecast Errors at Different Aggregation Levels

Comparable Points in Time

Different points in time at which forecasts are carried out can also cause forecast errors.

	Actual	Forecast Version 1 Week 40	Forecast Error	Forecast Version 2 Week 41	Forecast Error
Week 45	25	0	100%	25	0%
Week 46	25	50	100%	25	0%
Week 47	25	50	100%	50	100%

Table 4.20 Forecast Errors at Different Points in Time

	Actual	Forecast Version 1 Week 40	Forecast Error	Forecast Version 2 Week 41	Forecast Error
Week 48	25	0	100%	0	100%
Total	100	100	100%	100	50%

Table 4.20 Forecast Errors at Different Points in Time (cont.)

Table 4.20 shows that the average forecast error (total) was 100% for forecast version 1 in week 40. When forecast version 2 was carried out in week 41, the forecast error had decreased to 50%. We can infer that because the second forecast was carried out one week later, there was a significant improvement of the forecast.

Consequently, in order to use forecast errors in your daily work, you must ensure that you can compare forecasts with one other, and that they are determined at a level that is useful for your specific demand planning.

4.7.7 Forecast Accuracy

You can use the forecast errors described above to support the forecast selection process and to optimize the parameters of a model. The lower the degree of error, the better the forecast method selected.

Basically, the forecast accuracy is the reverse of the forecast error with the only restriction being that values between 1% and 100% are possible.

The forecast accuracy is the reverse of the absolute percent error (APE):

Forecast accuracy % = 1 – APE

If APE > 1, the forecast accuracy would be negative; however, because we want to obtain only values between 1 and 100%, that is not how we want to determine forecast accuracy. For this reason, the exact formula is as follows:

Forecast accuracy % = maximum of (1 – APE; 0)
(= if APE > 1, the forecast accuracy = 0%)

The APE cannot be calculated when the actual value is equal to zero (division by zero). In those rare instances, the forecast accuracy is equal to zero.

The forecast accuracy method is frequently used in everyday work, because it is easy to understand and calculate. No complex mathematical formulas are required here. This method indicates how good or bad the forecast is when compared with the actual sales figures. The smaller the deviation between planned and actual figures, the higher the forecast accuracy.

Actual Value	Forecast	APE	Forecast Accuracy
120	100	16.67	83.33
140	160	14.29	85.71

Table 4.21 Calcuation of Forecast Accuracy

Table 4.21 shows that the forecast accuracy is always the reverse of the APE. The total of both is 100%.

The forecast accuracy is an important measure to verify the demand planning based on actual values. The calculation of the forecast accuracy described here is a commonly and frequently applied method.

4.7.8 Alert Monitor

In *demand planning*, you can measure the forecast accuracy based on different forecast error calculation methods. The system stores several forecasts for a certain period and compares the forecasts with the actual values. If deviations occur, the system generates an alert.

In SAP APO, you can automate how forecast errors are interpreted. This is particularly useful when you have to create a forecast for many products. A system will generate an alert when the selected forecast method doesn't provide any reliable values. Then, the planner can individually define the threshold values and limits regarding the tolerance range of the forecast error. The SAP APO Alert Monitor enables you to monitor the quality of your forecast during the planning process and to determine whether your plan can be carried out smoothly. For this purpose, you must define alert profiles for the applications that you want to use. These alert profiles store information for those situations when the system notifies you of a problem, that is, it generates an *alert*.

It's not always possible for all planners involved to actively monitor the alerts in the Alert Monitor. However, you can use notification functions to ensure that each planner is notified of alerts in his or her respective area of responsibility.

In demand planning, the Alert Monitor distinguishes from among the following alert groups:

Forecast alerts: The system generates these alerts if the historical data, which the forecast is based on, is incorrectly described by the selected forecast models. For example, you assume that the demand rises constantly, but over time you discover that the demand is dependent on the season.

To navigate to the forecast alert maintenance shown in Figure 4.58, select **SAP APO · Supply Chain Monitoring · Alert Monitor**.

In the upper part of the screen, you can see the maintenance of the **Overall Profile** and the **Period** for which you want SAP APO to generate alerts. The center of the screen displays separate tabs that enable you to maintain the alerts for the individual SAP APO modules. You can maintain the forecast alerts in the **Forecast** tab. The above example shows that threshold values are maintained for the forecast errors, MAD, error total, and MAPE. If the threshold values are exceeded, for example, if the MAD value determined by the system is higher than 10%, the system generates notifications, warnings, or error messages.

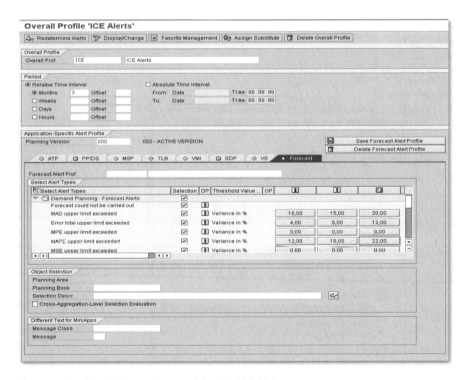

Figure 4.58 Alert Monitor—Forecast View in SAP APO

Macro-dependent alerts: These alerts refer to customer-specific problems, for example, if a requirements forecast exceeds or falls short of a customer-specific key figure. You can also assign customized status messages to individual macro steps and have these messages displayed like alerts in the Alert Monitor. Figure 4.59 shows an example of this type of macro alert.

This macro calculates the difference between the forecasts of the current week and the previous week and generates an alert, if the difference is bigger than 20%. *Forecast* and *Previous forecast* are two key figures (two rows) in the planning table.

The company XYZ produces the basic product ABC that shows a stable demand over time. For this reason, the forecasts for the current and previous weeks shouldn't differ too much, because under normal circumstances no sudden changes are expected. If the forecast for period 3 in the current week is 100 and if it was 60 for the same period in the previous week, this represents an exception of which the demand planner must be notified. The macro shown in Figure 4.59 records such exceptions, triggers an alert, and highlights the relevant row in the color red. The planner can then take the necessary action.

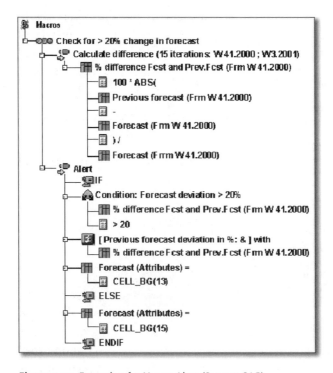

Figure 4.59 Example of a Macro Alert (Source: SAP)

The purpose of material requirements planning (MRP) is to ensure that an enterprise always has the required amounts and types of materials at the right time. This chapter shows that there are more efficient ways of material requirements planning than just maintaining a full warehouse.

5   Material Requirements Planning

Material requirements planning (MRP) comprises all activities necessary to optimally provide an enterprise with the required amounts and types of materials at the right time. In MRP, the word "optimally" can be equated with finding a balance to resolve the main conflict of materials management, which is maintaining a high service level without tying up a lot of capital and incurring high material costs.

To achieve this optimization, material requirements planning must create numerous internal and external interfaces. *Internal interfaces* are interfaces to purchasing, distribution, storage, engineering, quality management, work scheduling, production planning, and shop floor control. *External interfaces* are interfaces to customers and suppliers.

Therefore, material requirements planning includes the following basic steps:

- ▶ Gross and net requirements calculation, including meeting the material requirements across all production levels
- ▶ Determining the economic lot size for internal and external orders
- ▶ Differentiated specification of inventory strategies (for example, safety stocks) for ensuring the service level
- ▶ Management of delivery and release modalities

Using these basic steps, material requirements planning must solve the conflict mentioned earlier. In this chapter, we explain in detail how to promote inventory optimization. In this regard, we will explain the gross and net requirements calculation, as well as the management of delivery and release modalities. Chapter 6, *Service Level and Safety Stocks*, discusses specific inventory strategies for ensuring your desired service level. Chapter 7, *Lot Sizes*, discusses how to determine dynamic and economic lot sizes.

5.1 MRP Strategies

To perform these basic steps, MRP implements these three functions: **requirements calculation, accumulation of balances, and order calculation**. The requirements calculation generates the gross requirements, the accumulated balances generate the net requirements, and the order calculation generates the economic lot size.

5.1.1 Requirements Calculation

The requirements calculation generates the gross requirements. In practice, they are determined in two ways: through program-oriented (deterministic) demand determination and through consumption-oriented (forecast-based) demand determination.

Program-oriented (deterministic) demand determination
The program-oriented method is an exact process of demand determination that is based on the production schedule. In the production schedule, the primary or market demand is planned in the form of warehouse or sales orders. Using the bill of materials (BOM) explosion, if you multiply the primary demand by the demand per product unit, you get the secondary demand. This process is called low-level coding, because the individual BOM levels are planned from top to bottom.

Consumption-oriented (forecast-based) demand determination
The consumption-oriented method is a statistical procedure used to extrapolate the past consumption to the future. This procedure is based on time series of the past material requirements. By analyzing the time series, it is possible to determine typical consumption sequences for every material. These can run horizontally, show trends, run seasonally, or run irregularly. For more information about this analysis method, see Chapter 4, *Demand Planning and Forecasting*.

The applicability of the demand determination process depends on the specific export control class. For more information about export control classes, see Chapter 3, *Inventory Analysis*.

The following sections discuss the methods of program- and consumption-oriented material requirements planning as well as their implementation in SAP in more detail.

5.1.2   Balance Accumulation

Based on the gross requirements determined from the requirements calculation, you can now calculate the net requirements in consideration of the available inventory. For this purpose, the reorder points, safety stocks, and, in specific MRP strategies, the service level, are considered. More information about *Service Levels and Safety Stocks* can be found in Chapter 6.

5.1.3   Order Calculation

The order calculation applies the determined net requirements to the lot size settings of the materials. The result of the order calculation is the optimal or cost-effective order quantity that, as a production requirement, represents the initial value for purchasing; and as a planned order, represents the initial value for production. See Chapter 7 to learn more about the available *Lot Sizes* and how to implement them.

5.2   Impact of Material Requirements Planning on Inventory

As described above, the purpose of the requirements calculation is to determine required quantities and delivery dates for finished products.

Selection of Production Type

In the customer-independent *make-to-stock type of production*, the requirements are first forecast as planned independent requirements. All materials necessary for production are planned. This generates orders for the suppliers and production orders in production. Inbound sales orders are then calculated against these planned independent requirements, orders, and production orders. If the planned independent requirements are too optimistic, there might be stock surplus quantities. If there are more inbound sales orders than planned independent requirements, there might be stockout situations, that is, supply bottlenecks. Therefore, forecast accuracy is very important in make-to-stock production.

Usually, *sales-order-related production* generates purchase orders and production orders only after the sales order has been received. This can cause problems such as long delivery times or missed promised delivery dates due to supply or production bottlenecks. This results in delayed deliveries and customer cancellations.

While make-to-stock production focuses on accurate planning and ensured availability, sales-order-related production focuses on minimizing production costs and lead times. If production time is rather long in relation to delivery time, finished products or specific assemblies should be prefabricated before sales orders come in to minimize order lead times and to extend the ability to deliver.

Selecting the MRP strategy

The MRP strategies for specific products represent the economically sensible procedures for planning and manufacturing or procuring a product. By applying these strategies, you can decide whether production should be generated by sales orders (make-to-order) or by warehouse orders (make-to-stock). If you select the right MRP strategy, you can avoid both overstock and substock situations and optimize your inventories.

▶ With make-to-stock production, you create the production schedule based on *sales forecasts*. Therefore, the quality and accuracy of these forecasts is very important. Planning bassed on inaccurate forecasts can lead to stock-outs or overstocks.

▶ With make-to-order production, you create your production schedule based on sales orders. In this case, the product often comprises complex and multi-level production structures. Therefore, MRP must be able to ensure *coordination between the production, procurement, and sales departments*. If there is no such cross-department view, frictional losses at the interfaces can result. For example, if a supplier indicates that their delivery of raw materials will arrive two days later than planned, production should be notified quickly so that it can reschedule the production order.

▶ You can also *move the stocking level down to the assembly level* so that only the final assembly is generated by the incoming sales order. In this case, all other assemblies would be prefabricated to reduce the order lead times. Inventories, particularly safety stocks, could then be lowered to the more favorable stocking level so that inventory values can be reduced.

▶ If a specific assembly has very long replenishment lead times, the material requirements planning for this specific assembly can be performed earlier than for the rest of the finished product. This helps reduce order lead times and shorten delivery times.

mySAP ERP provides a wide range of MRP strategies that offer several possibilities for make-to-order production and make-to-stock production. In addition, you can also combine MRP strategies. For example, you can select the *planning with final assembly* strategy for a finished product and use the *planning at assembly level* strategy for an important assembly in the BOM of that finished product.

The following sections discuss the strategies for make-to-stock production, the strategies for subassembly planning as well as make-to-order production, and, finally, the strategies for consumption-oriented MRP.

Selecting Consumption Parameters

Please not that there will always be a delta between planned independent requirements and actual sales orders, because planning is a forecast of the future, and therefore it is never completely accurate. Using consumption parameters, however, you can minimize this delta and compensate by using a delta from another period. If no consumption parameters are maintained in the material master, the mySAP ERP system uses the default values from the planning group. To optimize your inventories, you should maintain these consumption parameters as product-specifically as possible and not use default settings. This applies to all of the following strategies.

5.3   Strategies for Make-to-Stock Production in mySAP ERP

The planning strategies discussed in this section address the planning of the procurement (production or purchase) of components by planning the finished products. Select a make-to-stock strategy if:

▶ The materials are not assigned to any specific sales order

▶ You perform a forecast for the materials, or

▶ The costs need to be monitored at the material level

Make-to-stock production should be used whenever you want to produce inventory irrespective of any orders and to be able to immediately provide customers with goods from that inventory at a later stage. The delivery times requested by the customers are shorter than the order lead times in your enterprise. Make-to-stock strategies help you to provide your customers with goods from your inventory as quickly as possible, and this, in turn, supports a very tight customer-supplier relationship. Returns that passed the quality assurance process as well as other unplanned goods receipts can be used for other sales orders. However, this does not imply that your ware-house stocks need to be excessively high. You can avoid this by taking the following steps:

1. Create a *production plan* in advance (while planning the production sched-ule) to forecast your inventory. During this process, you can decide whether sales orders that exceed your plan should influence production. For this purpose, make a forecast and make sure that the forecast is as accurate as possible. You can automate the planning phase by transferring the forecast results directly to program planning.

2. Make sure sales orders are available at an early stage (for example, via scheduling agreements) and are processed as quickly as possible. Informa-tion about incoming *sales orders* should be transferred in real time to pro-duction, purchasing, and logistics.

3. In a make-to-stock production environment, it can be favorable to *smooth out and anonymize requirement fluctuations for production*. Make-to-stock strategies are usually combined with a lot-size key or rounding value. For example, you can produce the entire quantity for the whole month or for full pallets in one go.

If you use the *planning without final assembly* and *planning with planning material* strategies, you can procure components based on your planning and generate a final assembly based on sales orders. You therefore reduce the inventory values and still remain flexible with regard to delivery times.

Make-to-stock strategies usually comprise six phases. Table 5.1 lists these phases and shows which strategies they apply to. Later we will take a closer look at each of the make-to-stock strategies, which are identified here by number.

		MRP Strategy					
	Phase	40	30	10	11	52	63
1	Forecast	Yes	Yes	Yes	Yes	Yes	Yes
2	Program planning (creating planned independent requirements)	Yes	No	Yes	Yes	Yes	Yes
3	Procurement before sales	Yes	No	Yes	Yes	Yes	Yes
4	Sales order	Yes	Yes	Yes	Yes	Yes	Yes

Table 5.1 Make-to-Stock Production MRP Strategies in mySAP ERP

		MRP Strategy					
	Phase	40	30	10	11	52	63
5	Procurement after sales	No	Yes	No	No	Yes	Yes
6	Goods issue for delivery and reduction of planned independent requirements	Yes	Yes	Yes	Yes	Yes	Yes

Table 5.1 Make-to-Stock Production MRP Strategies in mySAP ERP (cont.)

5.3.1 Planning with Final Assembly (40)

Areas of Use

This strategy is probably the most popular make-to-stock strategy. *Planning with final assembly* is advisable when you can forecast the production quantities for the finished products.

Planned independent requirements are offset against the incoming sales orders to adapt the production plan to the current requirement situation. Therefore, the most important advantage of this planning strategy is that it allows you to quickly react to customer requirements. Smoothing the production plan is less significant.

Prerequisites

To use the *planning with final assembly (40)* strategy, you must maintain the master data of your finished product. To do this, open the material master in the SAP menu via **Logistics · Production · Master data · Material master · Material · Change · Maintain immediately**. In the **Change Material** screen, do the following (see also Figure 5.1):

▶ On the **MRP 3** tab, in the **Strategy group** field, enter the number 40 to specify the strategy.

▶ Enter the consumption parameters (**Consumption mode, Bwd consumption per., Fwd consumption per.**) to enable the consumption of primary requirements by incoming sales orders.

▶ Specify the **Item category group** on the sales organization data screen of Sales (**sales org. 2** view) (see Figure 5.2). Using the item category group, you can determine if the sales order item is to be offset against the planned independent requirements. For this purpose, from the **MRP 3** tab, select the **sales org. 2** tab.

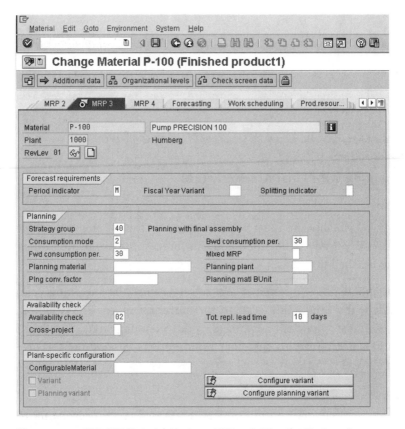

Figure 5.1 mySAP ERP Material Master—MRP 3: Setting the Strategy Group

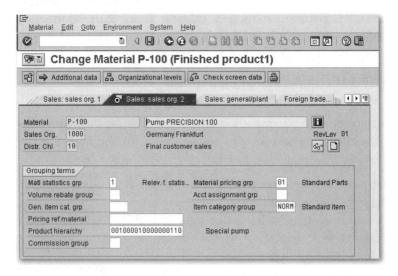

Figure 5.2 mySAP ERP Material Master—Sales Org. 2: Specifying the Item Category Group

Process

Figure 5.3 shows the process of the *planning with final assembly (40)* MRP strategy.

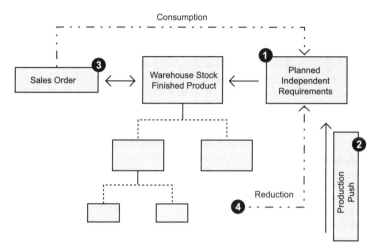

Figure 5.3 Process of the "Planning with Final Assembly (40)" MRP Strategy (Source: SAP)

This process includes the following steps:

1. **Planned independent requirements are entered**
   The planned independent requirements are entered at the finished product level. This generates the procurement and production of the required assemblies and components before the sales order is received. It is possible to use information from the sales forecast, from the Sales Information System, or from other tools for planning production quantities.

2. **Sales order is received**
   As soon as the sales order is received, it is offset against the planned independent requirements. This enables a comparison of planned and actual customer requirements.

3. **Availability check is performed**
   During sales order processing, an exact availability check is performed according to the Available-to-Promise (ATP) logic. The system checks if a sufficient quantity of planned independent requirements was planned to cover the sales order.

4. **Order is transferred to production**
   Requirements from the sales orders are transferred to production and can result in changes to procurement if the requirements from the sales

orders exceed the planned independent requirement quantities. If there is an insufficient amount of components(the sales order quantities exceed the planned independent requirements), the sales orders cannot be confirmed. Therefore, the system automatically adapts the production plan. Planned independent requirement quantities that are not fully used increase the warehouse stock of the finished products.

If despite your planning the requirements are still higher than the inventories and the demand is not fully met, you should take the following steps:

Check all sales orders that could not be confirmed, by using the backlog functionality in the Sales and Distribution (SD) module under **Sales · Environment · Backorder · Rescheduling · Execute**. If you execute the report in test mode (in the **Simulation** field, simply enter "X") you will obtain a log listing all sales orders that were not confirmed. Using this list, the sales and production departments can decide what to do next.

Another possibility would be to postpone the order (or some of its schedule lines). You could also increase production, if that is still possible.

5.3.2 Production by Lot Size (30)

Areas of Use

This strategy is recommended for enterprises that produce for large customers and also want to use the possibility to handle smaller requirements by selling from stock. The *production by lot size* strategy merges several sales orders for the same material and produces a single lot for these sales orders during requirements planning. This results in one production order for all received sales orders. When creating lots, you can use lot-size optimization and rounding procedures if you want to have leftover quantity that can be sold from stock. This strategy is used, for example, by automotive suppliers who sell their spare parts from stock.

Prerequisites

As described for strategy 40, with this strategy you need to maintain the master data for the finished product. In the SAP menu, navigate to the **MRP 3** tab via **Logistics · Production · Master data · Material master · Material · Change · Maintain immediately**.

▶ On the **MRP 3** tab, in the **Strategy group** field, enter the number 30.

▶ In the **Availability check** field, enter a value of 01 to perform an availability check with a replenishment lead time (see Figure 5.4).

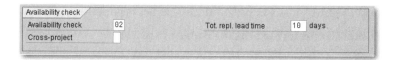

Figure 5.4 mySAP ERP Material Master—MRP 3: Setting the Availability Check

▶ Specify the **Item category group** on the sales organization data screen of Sales (**sales org. 2** view). Using the item category group, you can determine whether the sales order item is to be offset against the planned independent requirements. To do this, go to the **MRP 3** tab and select the **sales org. 2** tab.

Process

Figure 5.6 illustrates the process of the *production by lot size (30)* MRP strategy.

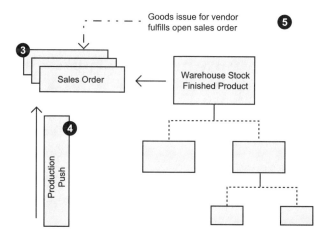

Figure 5.5 Process of the "Production by Lot Size (30)" MRP Strategy (Source: SAP)

This process includes the following steps:

1. **Sales order situation is determined**
   Procurement is exclusively based on sales orders. There is no planning for the finished product. This means that you usually need to know the sales order situation in advance with regard to replenishment lead times of the components and the production time.

Therefore, this strategy is sometimes combined with scheduling agreements. Alternatively, the necessary components can be procured via the **single-item planning of components**, for example, using strategy 70, via **KANBAN components**, or via **consumption-based components**.

2. **Availability check is performed during order processing**
During sales order processing, an accurate availability check is performed according to the ATP logic.

3. **Customer requirements are combined into a lot**
Depending on the deadline, this strategy merges several customer requirements into a lot using lot-size optimization or rounding procedures. In this process, the lot size depends on various production aspects, such as pallet size or production optimization, for example.

4. **Leftover stock is used**
The leftover stock from previous procurement processes can be used for other sales orders. This is particularly advisable for enterprises that mainly produce goods for large customers and additionally want to use the possibility to handle smaller requirements by selling from stock.

5. **Sales order items are offset**
Planned independent requirements are not offset against sales and warehouse orders. The schedule lines or sales order items, however, are offset against the delivery, because they are updated by them accordingly. The sales order requirements are reduced by the withdrawals posted to the sales order.

6. **Warehouse orders are reduced**
The warehouse orders are immediately reduced by selling directly from stock.

5.3.3 Net Requirements Planning (10)

Areas of Use

This planning strategy is particularly useful for mass production environments and is often combined with repetitive manufacturing. You should select this strategy if production is to be controlled via a production plan (program planning) and if sales orders do not directly affect production. One of the most important characteristics of this planning strategy is that it enables you to smooth the production program.

Here is an example: Strategy 10 is implemented by consumer goods manufacturers because, for example, the demand for ice cream can be planned in large quantities, while a single order may not affect production. In addition, the strategy is used for products with seasonal demand where production needs to be smoothed.

Prerequisites

As with strategy 40, with this strategy you need to maintain the master data for the finished product. In the SAP menu, navigate to the **MRP 3** tab via **Logistics · Production · Master data · Material master · Material · Change · Maintain immediately**.

▶ On the **MRP 3** tab, in the **Strategy group** field, enter the number 10.

▶ In the **Availability check** field, enter a value of 02 to perform an availability check without a replenishment lead time.

▶ Enter the **Item category group** on the sales organization data screen of Sales (**sales org. 2** tab). Using the item category group, you can determine if the sales order item is to be offset against the planned independent requirements. To do this, go to the **MRP 3** tab and select the **sales org. 2** tab.

Process

Figure 5.6 illustrates the process of the *net requirements planning (10)* MRP strategy.

This process includes the following steps:

1. **Procurement is planned according to forecast**
   Procurement quantities can be planned relatively effectively using planned independent requirements. It is possible to use information from the sales forecast, from the Sales Information System, or from other tools for planning production quantities. This means that production and procurement of the required components are generated before sales orders are received.

2. **Production is smoothed**
   Procurement is solely determined by the planned independent requirements. This enables a smoothing of production, that is, you can create a smoothed production plan that cannot be affected by irregular sales orders.

3. **Availability check is performed**
   During sales order processing, an accurate availability check is performed according to the ATP logic.

4. **Sales orders do not increase the production plan**
   Sales orders can be displayed for information; they do not increase the production plan. With this strategy, stock is used for sales.

5. **Planned and actual requirements are compared**
   The planned independent requirements are reduced during the goods issue for delivery. This enables a comparison of planned and actual customer requirements.

6. **Leftover stock is used**
   Planned independent requirements that have not been reduced increase the warehouse stock of the finished product, and therefore procurement is reduced or does not happen at all during the next period due to the stock level comparison.

7. **Consumption horizon is maintained**
   If you want material withdrawals for additionally planned sales orders to reduce planned independent requirements in the future, an appropriate consumption horizon must be maintained.

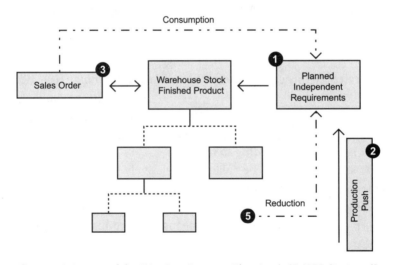

Figure 5.6 Process of the "Net Requirements Planning (10)" MRP Strategy (Source: SAP)

5.3.4 Gross Requirements Planning (11)

Areas of Use

The *gross requirements planning* make-to-stock strategy is particularly useful in mass production environments and is often combined with repetitive manufacturing. This strategy is advisable when production must take place irrespective of whether inventory exists or not. Enterprises in the steel or cement industry implement this strategy because they cannot interrupt production. A furnace or a cement factory must continue production even if this means that they produce for stock.

This strategy is also often implemented when there is a material requirements planning system in a legacy system that must be integrated with a mySAP ERP system serving as a production execution system. The legacy system calculates a specific production plan that must be executed regardless of the inventory situation in mySAP ERP.

Prerequisites

As described for strategy 40, with this strategy you need to maintain the master data for the finished product. In the SAP menu, navigate to the **MRP 3** tab via **Logistics · Production · Master data · Material master · Material · Change · Maintain immediately** and take the following steps:

- ▶ On the **MRP 3** tab, in the **Strategy group** field, enter the number 11.

- ▶ On the **MRP 3** tab, set the **Mixed MRP** option to 2 (see Figure 5.7).

- ▶ On the **MRP 3** tab, in the **Availability check** field, enter a value of 02 to perform an availability check without a replenishment lead time.

- ▶ Specify the **Item category group** on the sales organization data screen of Sales (**sales org. 2** tab). Using the item category group, you can determine if the sales order item is to be offset against the planned independent requirements. To do this, go to the **MRP 3** tab and select the **sales org. 2** tab.

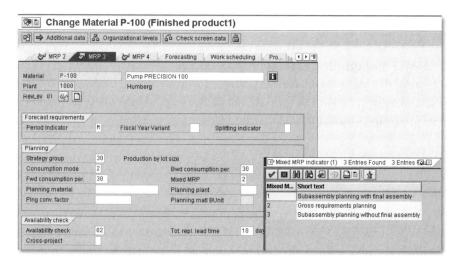

Figure 5.7 mySAP ERP Material Master—MRP 3: Setting the Mixed MRP Option

Process

This planning strategy is similar to the *net requirements planning* strategy *(10)*. However, there are differences, which are listed in Table 5.2.

Strategy	10	11
The inventory is considered	Yes	No
Reduction of the planned independent requirements takes place during ...	... the goods issue for delivery.	... the goods receipt for a production or a purchase order.

Table 5.2 Differences Between the "Net Requirements Planning (10)" and "Gross Requirements Planning (11)" Strategies

In addition, *gross* and *net requirements planning* have the following steps in common:

1. **Plan is made based on primary requirements**
   The production quantities can be planned relatively accurately using planned independent requirements. It is possible to use information from the Sales Information System, from flexible planning, or from other tools for planning production quantities. This means that the production and procurement of the required components is generated before the sales order phase.

2. **Production is not affected**
   Single sales orders that are received irregularly do not affect production.

3. **Availability check is performed**
   During sales order processing, an accurate availability check is performed according to the ATP logic.

4. **Lot-size optimization procedure is performed**
   During the planning phase, you can perform lot-size optimization so that you can always plan appropriate lot sizes using lot size or rounding keys in program planning or during the planning process.

5.3.5 Planning Without Final Assembly (52)

Areas of Use

This strategy enables you to procure components based on planned independent requirements. The production of the finished product, however, is based on actual sales orders. This planning strategy enables you to quickly react to customer requests even if the finished product has a long total lead time. You can avoid the value creation process of the last production stage until you receive a sales order. This will reduce the inventory costs because you only need to have the lower levels (i.e., previous production stages) on stock.

Prerequisites

Again, with this strategy it is important to maintain the master data for the finished product. In the SAP menu, navigate to the **MRP 3** tab via **Logistics · Production · Master data · Material master · Material · Change · Maintain immediately** and do the following:

▸ On the **MRP 3** tab, in the **Strategy group** field, enter the number

▸ On the **MRP 1** tab, specify the **Lot size** EX, because the lot-size optimization might otherwise be incompatible with the assignment logic. This, in turn, can lead to overplanning and wrong results in the availability check. You also need to make sure that no values are entered for **Rounding profile** and **Rounding value** (see Figure 5.8).

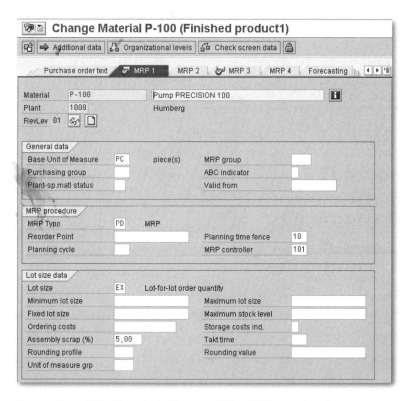

Figure 5.8 mySAP ERP Material Master—MRP 1: Setting the Lot Size

- On the **MRP 3** tab, in the **Availability check** field, enter a value of 02 to perform an availability check without a replenishment lead time.

- Specify the **Item category group** on the sales organization data screen of Sales (**sales org. 2** tab). Using the item category group, you can determine if the sales order item is to be offset against the planned independent requirements. To do this, in the **MRP 3** tab, select the **sales org. 2** tab.

- The finished product requires a BOM. Therefore, please note the following:

  - On the **MRP 1** tab, set the **MRP type** flag to **P*** (or **M***) to plan the components of material requirements planning.

  - On the **MRP 4** tab, set the **Individual/coll.** flag as the starting point for your master data setting to 2 (see Figure 5.9).

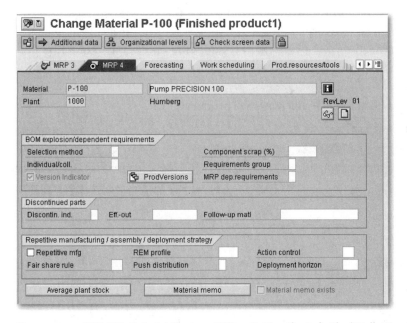

Figure 5.9 mySAP ERP Material Master—MRP 4: Setting the Individual/Collective Flag

Process

Figure 5.10 illustrates the process of the *planning without final assembly (52)* MRP strategy.

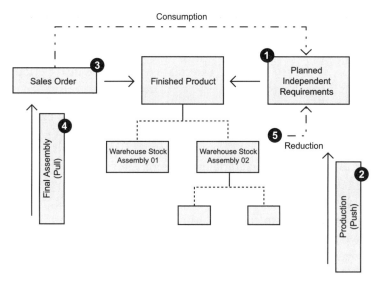

Figure 5.10 Process of the "Planning Without Final Assembly (52)" MRP Strategy (Source: SAP)

This process includes the following steps:

1. **Production quantities are planned and components are procured**
   The production quantities can be planned relatively accurately using the planned independent requirements for the finished product. You can use information from the sales forecast, from the Sales Information System, or from other tools for planning production quantities. Only the procurement of the components is generated by the sales order. The final assembly takes place after the sales order has been entered.

2. **Planned independent requirements are offset**
   The planned independent requirements are offset during the sales order phase. This enables a comparison of planned and actual customer requirements.

3. **Availability check is performed**
   An availability check is performed based on the planned independent requirements.

4. **Requirements are transferred to production**
   The requirements from sales orders are transferred to production and trigger production after the sales order phase, even if not enough components are planned. However, the sales orders cannot be confirmed if there are not enough components.

5. **Stock level comparison is performed**

   Planned independent requirements of finished products that have not been offset increase the warehouse stock of the components and cause procurement to be reduced or not to take place at all in the next period. This process is referred to as a stock level comparison.

6. **No overstocks existing**

   From a calculation point of view, this strategy is a make-to-stock strategy, in contrast to strategy 50, which is a make-to-order strategy. This means that the inventory of the final material is not connected to the individual sales orders. When creating a sales order, strategy 52 does not consider any inventory that exceeds the planned independent requirements (unplanned inventory due to customer returns or excess production, for example). Inventory for finished products should be handled via an exception process.

5.3.6   Planning with Planning Material (63)

Areas of Use

This strategy enables you to procure non-variable parts based on the planned independent requirements of a planning material. The production of the finished product, however, is based on actual sales orders. This planning strategy enables you to quickly react to customer requests even if the finished product has a long total lead time. You can suspend the value creation process until you receive a sales order.

This strategy has the same basic characteristics as the *planning without final assembly (52)* strategy. Additionally, more than one material can be offset against the planned independent requirements of a planning material.

The strategy enables you to plan the variants of a product. The term variant refers to "similar" parts. It is not used in the sense of variant configuration, which comprises a much higher number of variants. Using this strategy, you can, for example, easily exchange a component in all similar BOMs.

The *planning with planning material* strategy permits the planning of different sizes or packages for a product. It would be used, for example, if you wanted to sell a product in different package sizes or in packages with different labels.

All variants are set up with different material numbers. Additionally, a planning material is usually set up that only consists of the non-variable parts. Packaging material that forms the variants is therefore excluded. All variants are connected to the planning material using the correct conversion factors. The packaging materials (crates or cardboard boxes for the various sizes or labels) can be planned in a consumption-based way because they are relatively inexpensive.

Prerequisites

You should maintain the master data for the variant products and the planning material in different ways. A comparison is shown in Table 5.3.

Master Data	Variant Product	Planning Material
Strategy group (MRP 3 tab)	63	63
Item category group (Sales org. 2 tab)	e.g., NORM	e.g., NORM
Lot size (MRP 3 tab)	EX	EX
Consumption parameters, Consumption mode, Bwd consumption per., Fwd consumption per. (MRP 3 tab)	Does not need to be maintained; the values of the planning material will be used.	Must be maintained for the planned independent requirements to be found.
Planning material, Planning plant, and Plng conv. factor (MRP 3 tab)	Must be maintained	
MRP type (MRP 1 tab)	Set to P* or M* to plan the component in material requirements planning.	Set to P* or M* to plan the component in material requirements planning.
Individual/coll. flag (MRP 4 tab)	2	2
Bill of materials	Required, contains all parts	Required, contains the non-variable parts

Table 5.3 Maintaining the Master Data for the Variant Products and for the Planning Material

Process

The planning material can be sold in the same way as any other variant product. However, it is generally used as an "artificial" material that only contains the non-variable parts. The BOM of the variant products contains additional components that modify the product. These cannot be accurately planned using this strategy. Therefore, strategy 63 should only be used if one of the following prerequisites is met:

▸ The variant components are consumption-based.

▸ The variant components are planned independently using a planning strategy for components

▸ An overplanning or underplanning of variant components is acceptable

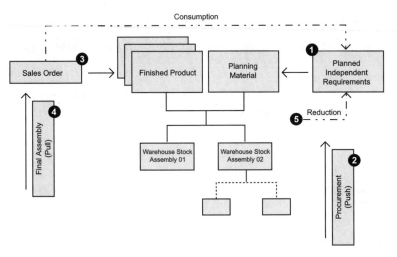

Figure 5.11 Process of the "Planning with Planning Material (63)" MRP Strategy (Source: SAP)

Other Implementations

The *planning with planning material (63)* strategy is often implemented when an enterprise wants to use a simple but effective method of *capacity planning*: The planned independent requirements for the planning material represent a given capacity situation. All variant materials require a similar capacity; when the order is entered, the existing capacity is mapped to the required capacity. You can easily check the capacity situation using the total requirements list.

Strategy 63 can also be implemented in an *overplanning and underplanning of components*: Assume the planning material contains the components A, B, and D, and the variant material contains the components A, B, and C. The planning material is planned with 100 pieces per month. Therefore, there are secondary requirements for 100 components per month. Because the planning material represents all variants, there is too much planned for component D, but too little planned for component C.

This situation is not problematic if you want to intentionally overplan component D, to obtain a higher warehouse stock for it, for example. In most cases, however, you would rather avoid this situation by implementing other methods or by not including the components C or D in the BOM of the planning material, for example. The variant parts can also be planned using the *planning at assembly level (70)* strategy or simply by using consumption-based variant parts.

5.4   Strategies for Planning Components in mySAP ERP

The planning strategies discussed in this section address the planning of the procurement (production or purchase) of components by planning the components themselves. They are particularly appropriate when *there are different finished products* (possibly with an irregular requirement pattern where planning is not possible). Plannings are then merged at the component level. At this level, the requirements can be consolidated and smoothed.

Using these strategies for planning components is also favorable if the *finished products are consumption-based*.

The overall goal of planning at the component level is to procure components to stock even without sales orders so that you can react to customer requirements as quickly as possible. Choose a strategy for planning components if: the components are not directly linked to specific sales orders or if costs should be monitored at the component (material) level and not at the order level.

Strategies for planning components can be used in both make-to-stock and make-to-order scenarios.

5.4.1   Planning at Assembly Level (70)

Areas of Use

This planning strategy is useful if you can make a safe forecast for specific assemblies rather than for a variety of finished products.

Prerequisites

As described for strategy 40, with this strategy you need to maintain the master data for the assembly. In the SAP menu, navigate to the **MRP 3** tab via

Logistics · Production · Master data · Material master · Material · Change · Maintain immediately.

- ▸ On the **MRP 3** tab, in the **Strategy group** field, enter the number 70.
- ▸ On the **MRP 3** tab, set the **Mixed MRP** flag to a value of 1.
- ▸ Specify the consumption parameters (**Consumption mode, Bwd consumption per., Fwd consumption per.**) to enable the consumption of primary requirements by incoming sales orders.
- ▸ If you implement this strategy in a make-to-stock environment, you must set the **Individual/coll.** flag on the **MRP 4** tab to a value of 2.

Process

Figure 5.12 illustrates the process of the *planning at assembly level (70)* MRP strategy.

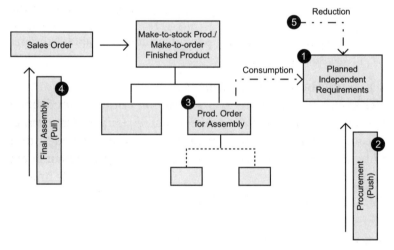

Figure 5.12 Process of the "Planning at Assembly Level (70)" MRP Strategy (Source: SAP)

This strategy is very similar to the *planning with final assembly (40)* strategy. It only varies in that planned independent requirements are offset against production order requirements and not against sales order requirements. Although all graphics in this documentation show this component one level beneath that of the finished product, it can show up at every BOM level.

The process for this strategy includes the following steps:

1. **Check inventory for assembly**
   Inventory is usually available for the assembly.

2. **Enter planned independent orders**
   In this strategy, planned independent requirements are also entered at the assembly level. The procurement planned using planned independent requirements is therefore triggered before the production order phase.

3. **Implement planned orders**
   The planned orders for the assembly or the components, respectively, are ready to be implemented.

4. **Smooth procurement**
   Additionally, you can smooth procurement according to the order requirements. In this strategy, however, being able to react to customer requirements in a more flexible way is of greater importance.

5. **Perform availability check**
   During production order processing, an accurate availability check is performed according to the ATP logic. Requirements from production orders are transferred to production and can cause changes to procurement after the sales order phase if the order quantities exceed the quantities of the planned independent requirements. However, the order quantities cannot be confirmed if there are not enough components. Therefore, the system automatically adapts the production plan.

6. **Offset planned independent requirements**
   The planned independent requirements are offset during the production phase. This enables a comparison of planned and actual order requirements. Planned independent requirements that have not been offset increase the warehouse stock of the component and cause procurement to be reduced or not to take place at all in the next period. This process is referred to as a stock level comparison.

5.4.2   Planning at Phantom Assembly Level (59)

Areas of Use

This strategy can be used for a number of components with the following characteristics: the components are always assembled to form specific finished products, they should be planned together, or they are not a "real" assembly, but only a "phantom" assembly.

Prerequisites

As described for strategy 40, with this strategy you need to maintain the master data for the phantom assembly. In the SAP menu, navigate to the

MRP 3 tab via **Logistics · Production · Master data · Material master · Material · Change · Maintain immediately**.

▶ On the **MRP 3** tab, in the **Strategy group** field, enter the number 59.

▶ On the **MRP 3** tab, set the **Mixed MRP** flag to a value of 1.

▶ Specify the consumption parameters (**Consumption mode, Bwd consumption per., Fwd consumption per.**) to enable the consumption of primary requirements by incoming sales orders.

▶ If you implement this strategy in a make-to-stock environment, you must set the **Individual/coll.** flag on the **MRP 4** tab to a value of 2.

▶ On the **MRP 2** tab, set the **Special procurement** field to 50 (phantom assembly) (see Figure 5.13).

▶ Additionally, on the **MRP 2** tab of the material master records for the phantom assembly components, you need to set the **Backflush** to 1.

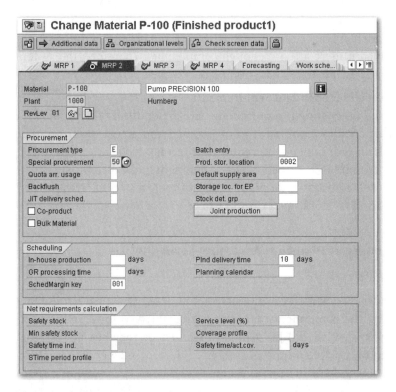

Figure 5.13 mySAP ERP Material Master—MRP 2: Setting the Special Procurement Key

The backflush is required because the components are planned with independent requirements that can only be orchestrated correctly if all reservations are reduced at the same time. This is only possible if the goods issue for the components is posted later than in the backflush. Additionally, all components of the phantom structure must be linked to the same process.

BOMs must be maintained for the finished products and for the phantom assemblies.

Process

Figure 5.14 illustrates the process of the *planning at phantom assembly level (59)* MRP strategy.

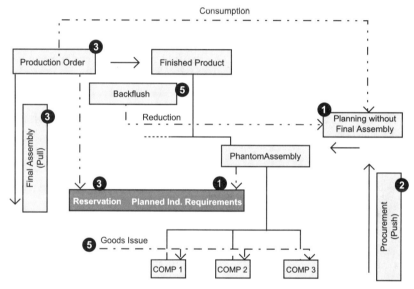

Figure 5.14 Process of the "Planning at Phantom Assembly Level (59)" MRP Strategy (Source: SAP)

This process includes the following steps:

1. **Plan planned independent requirements**
   Component requirements can be planned relatively easily. The procurement planned using planned independent requirements is triggered before the production order phase. The planned independent requirements are planned at the phantom assembly level. By means of a BOM explosion, component requirements are then determined that have been assigned to this phantom assembly.

2. **Smooth procurement**
   You can smooth procurement according to the order requirements. In this

strategy, however, being able to react to customer requirements in a more flexible way is of greater importance.

3. **Perform availability check**
During production order processing, an accurate availability check is performed according to the ATP logic. In the production order, it is possible to perform an availability check at the component level.

4. **Transfer requirements to production**
Requirements from production orders are transferred to production and can cause changes to procurement after the sales order phase if the order quantities exceed the quantities of the planned independent requirements.

5. **Offset planned independent requirements**
The planned independent requirements are offset during the production phase. This enables a comparison of planned and actual order requirements.

6. **Inventory for assembly does not exist**
In contrast to strategy 70, in strategy 59 there is no inventory for the assembly, due to its phantom character.

5.5 Strategies for Make-to-Order Production in mySAP ERP

The planning strategies described in this section are designed for the production of a material for a specific sales order. Finished products are not produced until a sales order is received. Therefore, make-to-order strategies always support a very tight customer-supplier relationship because the sales orders are tightly linked to production.

The same relationship exists between the sales order and production in a make-to-order environment. Make-to-order production can be implemented in a *production with variant configuration* or in an *assemble-to-order production*.

Choose a make-to-order strategy if the materials are clearly assigned to specific sales orders or if costs need to be monitored at the sales order level and not at the material level.

Unplanned goods receipts (like returns) usually cannot be used for other sales orders (even if they occur in the correct processing order), unless they are adapted to the customer's needs.

The planning strategies discussed in this section presume that you want to plan the procurement (production or purchase) of your components by planning the finished products. This means that there should be a relatively steady demand for your finished product.

5.5.1 Planning Without Final Assembly for Make-to-Order Production (50)

Areas of Use

This strategy is useful if a large part of the value creation process takes place during the final assembly.

This strategy and the *planning with planning material (60)* strategy are probably the strategies most often used in a make-to-order environment. Like all the other make-to-order strategies, strategy *50* should be implemented if the product is specifically produced for each customer and if it is not possible to change the inventory for different sales orders.

Prerequisites

As described for strategy 40, with this strategy you need to maintain the master data for the finished product. In the SAP menu, navigate to the **MRP 3** tab via **Logistics · Production · Master data · Material master · Material · Change · Maintain immediately**.

▸ On the **MRP 3** tab, in the **Strategy group** field, enter the number 50.

▸ Specify the consumption parameters (**Consumption mode**, **Bwd consumption per.**, **Fwd consumption per.**) to enable the consumption of primary requirements by incoming sales orders.

▸ Specify the **Item category group** on the sales organization data screen of Sales (**sales org. 2** tab). Using the item category group, you can determine if the sales order item is to be offset against the planned independent requirements. For this purpose, from the **MRP 3** view, select the **sales org. 2** tab.

The finished product requires a BOM. There is no major impact on the BOM components; however, you must maintain the following settings:

▸ On the **MRP 3** tab, set the **MRP type** field to **P*** (or **M***) to plan the components in material requirements planning.

▸ If you implement this strategy in a make-to-stock environment, you must set the **Individual/coll.** flag on the **MRP 4** tab to a value of 2.

Process

Figure 5.15 illustrates the process of the *planning without final assembly* MRP strategy, which includes the following steps:

1. **Plan production quantities**
   Production quantities can be planned effectively using a forecast.

2. **Plan procurement of components**
   The procurement of components is planned using the planned independent requirements entered at the finished product level. For these planned independent requirements, the system creates special planned orders at the finished product level. These orders do not become relevant to production until there is a sales order for the finished product. For the planned independent requirements that are created using this planning strategy, material requirements planning creates a separate planning segment. The planned orders cannot be implemented unless there is a sales order. The sales orders for this strategy are entered as make-to-order requirements and managed as individual segments in MRP.

3. **Produce or procure assemblies**
   Using this strategy, the assemblies are to be produced or procured before the sales order is entered. Production is performed up to the level before the final assembly. The assemblies and components necessary for producing the finished product remain in stock until the sales order is received.

4. **Trigger final assembly**
   The final assembly is triggered after a sales order has been entered.

5. **Check availability**
   An availability check is performed based on planned independent requirements. This means that unplanned inventory (like returns) is not considered for sales.

6. **Offset planned independent requirements**
   As soon as the sales order is received, the planned independent requirements are offset against the volume of the sales order.

7. **Create planned order**
   For the sales order quantity, a separate implementable planned order is created. If the planned order quantity is not completely used by the sales order, it remains in the system. If the sales order exceeds the planned independent requirements, the planned order quantity is increased.

8. **Warehouse stock reduces procurement**
   Planned independent requirements of finished product quantities that were not consumed increase the components warehouse stock and cause

procurement to be reduced or not to take place at all during the next period. This process is referred to as a stock level comparison.

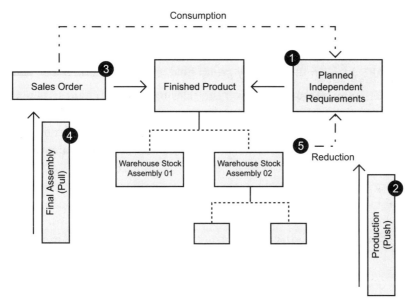

Figure 5.15 Process of the "Planning Without Final Assembly (50)" MRP Strategy (Source: SAP)

5.5.2 Make-to-Order Production (20)

Areas of Use

Make-to-order production is a process in which a product is specifically produced for one customer. This strategy is implemented if it is not necessary or not possible to plan the (higher-level) product. Program planning is not involved in this process, nor is there an assignment mechanism. Orders are taken as they are received. This strategy represents a production process in which every product is produced only once, although the same or similar production processes can reoccur over time. Every product is produced individually for a specific customer, so there is usually no stockholding.

For this strategy, you should be able to procure all required components within the replenishment lead time and to plan them at the component level, to use consumption-based or KANBAN-controlled components, or to receive the sales orders at a very early stage with regard to the replenishment lead time.

Prerequisites

As described for strategy 40, with this strategy you need to maintain the master data for the finished product. In the SAP menu, navigate to the **MRP 3** tab via **Logistics · Production · Master data · Material master · Material · Change · Maintain immediately**.

▸ On the **MRP 3** tab, in the **Strategy group** field, enter the number 20.

▸ Specify the **Item category group** on the sales organization data screen of Sales (**sales org. 2** tab). Using the item category group, you can determine if the sales order item is to be offset against the planned independent requirements. For this purpose, from the **MRP 3** tab, select the **sales org. 2** tab.

Process

Figure 5.16 shows the process of the *make-to-order production (20)* MRP strategy.

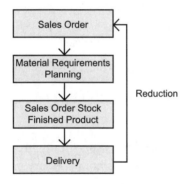

Figure 5.16 Process of the "Make-to-Order Production (20)" MRP Strategy (Source: SAP)

This process includes the following steps:

1. **Plan requirements**
   The sales orders are planned under the sales order number as requirements for production. The quantities produced for the individual sales orders cannot be changed. Every quantity is maintained specifically for the individual sales order. In requirements planning, a separate planning segment is created for make-to-order production.

2. **Single-segment planning (after sales order)**
   Starting from the sales order, the single-segment planning can be admitted into any level of the BOM structure. Therefore, assemblies and compo-

nents are then procured specifically for the sales order that generates the requirements and are managed for this sales order with regard to inventory.

3. **Manage costs specifically for sales order**
   The production and procurement costs are managed specifically for the sales order in a billing order or project at the sales order item level. This ensures a detailed analysis of planned and actual costs. It is also possible to use this production method for creating assembly orders. The assembly order initializes the automatic creation of a production order or a planned order and provides you with an exact forecast delivery schedule. The forecast delivery schedule is based on the availability and the production requirements of the relevant assemblies and components.

5.6 Consumption-Based Material Requirements Planning Using mySAP ERP

Within consumption-based MRP, the following MRP procedures are available: reorder point planning, forecast-based planning, and time-phased materials planning.

5.6.1 Reorder Point Planning

Areas of Use

This MRP procedure triggers procurement whenever the total amount of plant stock and fixed receipts falls below the so-called reorder point, that is, the reorder level, as shown in Figure 5.17.

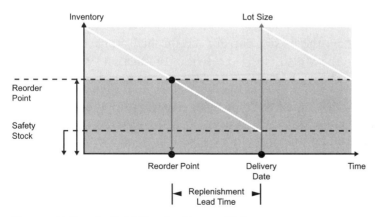

Figure 5.17 Reorder Point Planning (Source: SAP)

Prerequisites

The goal of the reorder level is to cover the anticipated average material requirements during the replenishment lead time.

The safety stock needs to cover the excess material consumption during the replenishment lead time as well as the additional requirements if delivery delays occur. The safety stock is therefore part of the reorder level.

For determining the *reorder level*, the following values are significant: the safety stock, the average consumption, and the replenishment lead time.

For determining the *safety stock*, the following values are significant: the previous consumption or future requirements, the on-time delivery performance of the supplier or production, respectively, the service level to achieve, and the deviation from the anticipated requirements or the forecast error.

With *manual reorder point planning*, you determine the reorder level and the safety stock in the material master yourself.

With *automatic reorder point planning*, the reorder level and safety stock are determined by the integrated forecast program. Using the previous material consumption values, the program determines the future requirements. Depending on the service level to be defined by the MRP controller and depending on the replenishment lead time of the material, the reorder level and the safety stock are then calculated and added to the respective material master. Because the forecast program is run at regular intervals, the reorder level and safety stock are adapted to the current consumption and delivery situation. This contributes to an inventory reduction.

Process

You should maintain the master data for the finished product. In the SAP menu, navigate to the **MRP 1** tab via **Logistics · Production · Master data · Material master · Material · Change · Maintain immediately**.

▶ On the **MRP 1** tab, in the **MRP type** field, enter an MRP type for reorder point planning.

▶ On the **MRP 1** tab, in the **Reorder point** field, enter a reorder level or have it calculated and entered automatically by the system.

▶ On the **MRP 2** tab, in the **Safety stock** field, enter a safety stock or have it calculated automatically by the system.

The **reorder point planning** process should include the following steps:

1. **Monitor the available warehouse stock**
   Continuous monitoring of the available warehouse stock in reorder point planning is performed by inventory management. For every material withdrawal, the system checks to see if the reorder level falls short. If so, an entry is created in the planning file for the next planning run. When material is returned, the system also checks to see if the available warehouse stock exceeds the reorder level again. If it does, another planning file entry is created so that the planning run can delete redundant procurement proposals. If planned goods receipts become redundant due to returns or similar circumstances, these goods receipts are proposed for cancellation by the planning run. In this case, the MRP controller needs to check with purchasing or production to see if the purchase order or the production order can be cancelled.

2. **Perform net requirements calculation**
   The net requirements are calculated. The available inventory at the plant level (including the safety stock) plus the fixed receipts (purchase orders, production orders, fixed purchase requisitions, etc.) are compared to the reorder level. If the total of the inventory and the receipts is smaller than the reorder level, there is a material shortage.

3. **Calculate procurement quantity**
   The procurement quantity is then calculated according to the lot-sizing procedure selected in the material master. For reorder point planning, the most favorable lot-sizing procedures are *fixed lot size* or *replenish to maximum stock level*. You can also use the periodic or the optimizing lot-sizing procedures for reorder point materials. In this case, you need to have the future requirements calculated based on the forecast. The forecast values are then interpreted as requirements.

4. **Schedule the procurement proposal**
   Finally, the procurement proposal is scheduled. This means that the date when the purchase order needs to be sent out or production needs to begin as well as the date when the supplier or production, respectively, is to deliver the requested quantity are calculated.

5.6.2 Forecast-Based Material Requirements Planning

Process

Forecast-based MRP is also based on material consumption. As with automatic reorder point planning, the integrated forecast program determines forecast values for the future requirements. In this case, however, these values form the requirement quantities for the planning process and become effective immediately as forecast requirements. Based on the forecast requirements, the net requirements calculation is then performed. This is carried out according to the MRP strategies discussed in Sections 5.1, 5.4, and 5.5. Chapter 4, *Demand Planning and Forecasting*, describes the best way to perform the forecast.

5.6.3 Time-Phased Materials Planning

Areas of Use

If a supplier always delivers a material on the same day of the week, you should plan the material requirements at the same interval, shifted by the delivery time.

Materials planned in this time-phased way are given a planning date. This is automatically reset when a material master is created, and then after every planning run. The planning date corresponds to the day when the material is planned for the next time and is calculated based on the planning cycle specified in the material master. To control this process and plan a material earlier, you can also define a planning date during the planning run. If the planning run is set for Monday, for example, you can perform this run on Saturday.

Time-phased materials planning can be performed in either a consumption-based or demand-driven manner:

▸ If you want to perform *consumption-based* time-phased materials planning, the requirements must be created via the forecast. In the consumption-based procedure, the net requirements calculation only considers the forecast requirements.

▸ If you want to perform *demand-driven* time-phased materials planning, all requirements that are relevant to the demand-driven MRP are considered in the net requirements calculation. In this procedure, the forecast requirements can also be taken into account.

Prerequisites

You must maintain the master data for the finished product. In the SAP menu, navigate to the **MRP 1** tab via **Logistics · Production · Master data · Material master · Material · Change · Maintain immediately**.

▸ On the **MRP 1** tab, in the **MRP type** field, enter an MRP type for time-phased materials planning and the planning cycle.

▸ On the **MRP 1** tab, in the **Lot size** field, enter a lot-sizing procedure.

▸ On the **MRP 2** tab, in the **Plnd delivery time** field, enter a planned delivery time.

Process

Figure 5.18 illustrates the time-phased materials planning process.

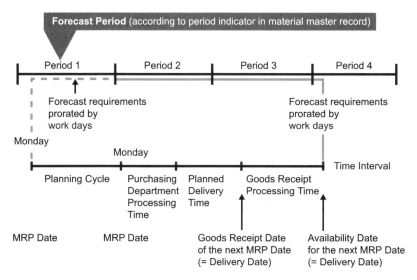

Figure 5.18 Time-Phased Materials Planning Process in SAP (Source: SAP)

This process includes the following steps:

1. **Trigger planning run**
   When the planning run is triggered, the mySAP ERP system checks the materials to be planned according to the planning date in the planning file. The planning date comes from the planning cycle.

2. **Calculate requirements**
   The requirements are then calculated. For this purpose, you first define a time interval. This is calculated from the time until the next MRP date

plus the delivery time. Therefore, the requirements are calculated using the following formula:

Forecast or other requirements for the interval (planning cycle + purchasing department processing time + planned delivery time + goods receipt processing time) + safety stock = requirement

The requirements of the periods that fall entirely into the respective interval are completely included in the calculation of the required quantity. The requirements of the periods that go beyond this interval are only partially included. The planned delivery time is given in calendar days, while the purchasing department processing time and the goods receipt processing time are given in working days.

3. **Calculate material shortage quantity**
   In the net requirements calculation, the mySAP ERP system reduces the requirements calculated for the time interval by the inventory and the fixed receipts. The remaining quantity is the material shortage quantity.

4. **Create new procurement proposal**
   Finally, a procurement proposal is created corresponding to the material shortage quantity at the exact lot size. If you selected a different lot-sizing procedure, the procurement proposal is based on the chosen lot-sizing procedure.

5.6.4 Range of Coverage Profile in Time-Phased Materials Planning

Areas of Use

Using a **range of coverage profile**, you can determine a requirements-oriented safety stock (dynamic safety stock). It is calculated based on the average daily requirements.

Prerequisites

You must maintain the master data for the finished product as in time-phased materials planning. In the SAP menu, navigate to the **MRP 2** tab via **Logistics · Production · Master data · Material master · Material · Change · Maintain immediately**.

On the **MRP 2** tab, in the **Coverage profile** field, enter a range of coverage profile.

Process

For example, say a material is planned every Tuesday and has a planned delivery time of two days. In the requirements calculation during the planning run, the system uses the interval between the MRP date and the availability date for the next MRP date. In this case, the interval goes from Tuesday until Thursday of the following week (eight working days).

Example data:

▶ Inventory data

  ▷ Requirement of the following eight days = 160 items

  ▷ Average daily requirement = 20 items

  ▷ Inventory = 0

  ▷ Receipts = 0

▶ Range of coverage profile

  ▷ Minimum range of coverage: three days (dynamic minimum safety stock: 60 items)

  ▷ Target range of coverage: five days (dynamic target safety stock: 100 items)

  ▷ Maximum range of coverage: 12 days (dynamic maximum safety stock: 240 items)

Result:

▶ Requirements calculation without a range of coverage profile and safety stock

  ▷ Without considering the dynamic safety stock, a procurement proposal of 160 items would be created.

▶ Requirements calculation specifying the range of coverage profile

  ▷ If the warehouse stock is null, the system adds another 100 items to the procurement proposal shown above, because the incoming quantity must last for another five days. This results in a procurement proposal of 260 items.

  ▷ If the warehouse stock is 200 items, the system creates a procurement proposal of 60 items, because the remaining 40 items would only last for two more days, and the inventory should last for at least three more days. If the minimum safety stock is not achieved, the system fills the inventory up to the target safety stock.

▶ If the warehouse stock amounts to 220 items, the system does not create a procurement proposal, because the remaining 60 items will last for another three days.

▶ If the warehouse stock amounts to 410 items, the system displays an exception message during the planning run that says there is an excess stock quantity; the inventory will last for more than twelve days (160 + 12 x 20 = 400). Additionally, the system reports that the inventory is 150 items too high. The target is an inventory of 260 items (*requirements + target safety stock*).

5.6.5 Time-Phased Materials Planning with Delivery Cycle

Areas of Use

To map more complex situations, you can define a delivery cycle in addition to the planning cycle. This lets you specify the days when the goods are delivered. You would always specify a delivery cycle when the delivery date (or goods receipt date) depends on the date of the purchase order. For example: You plan and order on Mondays and Tuesdays. If you order on a Monday, the goods will arrive on Wednesday; however, if you order on a Tuesday, the goods will not be delivered until Friday.

Prerequisites

You must maintain the master data for the finished product as in time-phased materials planning. In the SAP menu, navigate to the **MRP 2** tab via **Logistics · Production · Master data · Material master · Material · Change · Maintain immediately**.

On the **MRP 2** tab, in the **Planning calendar** field, enter a delivery cycle.

Process

Figure 5.19 illustrates the process of time-phased materials planning with a delivery cycle.

When the planning run is triggered, the system checks the materials to be planned based on the planning date in the planning file. The requirements calculation is performed irrespective of whether or not you indicated a delivery cycle.

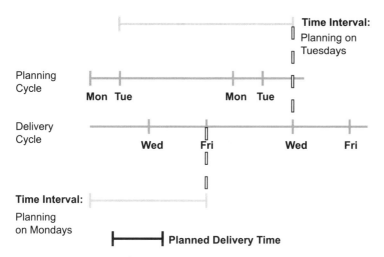

Figure 5.19 Process of Time-Phased Materials Planning With a Delivery Cycle (Source: SAP)

For its calculation, the system uses the *time interval* between the MRP date and the availability date for the next material requirements planning. It also considers that the supplier cannot deliver earlier than specified in the planned delivery time. Provided that there is no goods receipt processing time, this implies the following:

▸ If the MRP date is a Monday, the interval on which the invoice is based goes from Monday to Friday, because Friday is the goods receipt date of the next MRP date (Tuesday).

▸ If the MRP date is a Tuesday, the interval on which the invoice is based goes from Tuesday to Wednesday of the following week, because Wednesday is the goods receipt date of the next MRP date (Monday).

For this time interval, the material (*inventory + fixed receipts during this time interval*) must suffice. In the case of a material shortage, the system generates a new procurement proposal.

The system interprets the planned delivery time as minimum delivery time. This means that at least as many days need to pass between MRP (purchase order) and delivery as specified. In the example mentioned previously, the system recognizes that if the material requirements planning takes place on a Tuesday, the material is delivered on Friday and not on Wednesday. The purchasing department processing time is considered as well; *planned delivery time + purchasing department processing time* must be smaller than the period between the day of the next material requirements planning and the respective goods receipt date.

5.6.6 Time-Phased Materials Planning with Reorder Point Planning

Areas of Use

You can combine time-phased materials planning and reorder point planning. In this case, the material is not only planned on the planning date specified in the planning file, but also when the reorder level is not reached due to a goods issue, as shown in Figure 5.20.

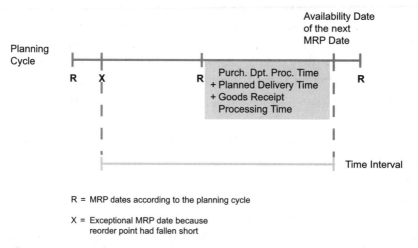

Figure 5.20 Time-Phased Materials Planning With Reorder Point Process (Source: SAP)

5.7 Requirements Strategies in SAP APO

The same MRP strategies are implemented in SAP APO as in mySAP ERP. The mySAP ERP planning strategies described above can easily be reproduced using the requirements strategies in SAP APO. Therefore, the requirements strategies do not need to be explained in detail.

In the standard version of SAP APO, four requirements strategies are delivered. If these are not sufficient, you can also define your own requirements strategies in SAP APO Customizing.

Prerequisites

In SAP APO, only sales orders that were created in mySAP ERP and then transferred to SAP APO or sales orders that were created using a BAPI are offset.

Functional Scope

In SAP APO, SAP delivers four standard requirements strategies:

▸ **Anonymous make-to-stock production (10)**
Select this strategy if sales orders do not affect production, as in mass productions. Single orders do not influence the produced quantity. Incoming orders are not offset against the forecast. The planned independent requirements are reduced as soon as the goods issue is posted in SAP R/3.

▸ **Planning with final assembly (20)**
Select this strategy if you can accurately predict the production quantities of the finished product. For the production quantities, this make-to-stock strategy considers actual sales orders as well as the forecast requirements. Incoming orders are offset against the forecast, and production quantities are the result of consolidated requirements. The advantage of this strategy is that it allows you to quickly react to customer demand.

Planning with final assembly is the standard case. Planned independent requirements are offset against sales orders. No special planning segment is used.

▸ **Planning without final assembly (30)**
Select this strategy if the final assembly represents the main value creation process. This means that the quantity of the sales order is fixed, and production takes place specifically for one customer. In this make-to-order strategy, only the components of a product are produced before a sales order is received. The sales order is offset against the forecast for the finished product, and at the same time generates production of the finished product.

Use this strategy for an "assemble-to-order" scenario. The planning of the finished product is not the deciding factor; rather, it's the planning of the components/assemblies that is most critical. One example is the assembly of PCs. Sales orders for assembled PCs are received; however, orders for PC components such as hard disks, CPUs, and graphics cards must be planned so that the components can be procured.

▸ **Planning product (40)**
In this scenario, you work with a dummy product to plan the requirements. Sales orders for the real product are offset against the planned independent requirements of the dummy product. Planning products are products that are primarily used for planning purposes. Under specific circumstances, they can also be produced or procured. A planning product is assigned one or more finished products that are produced or procured.

Planning products represent a combination of finished products. This means that products can be aggregated for planning purposes while the entire functionality related to products in SAP APO remains available.

Planning products are used in SAP APO in strategy 40 as well as in corresponding user-defined strategies. Planning products are implemented for planning purposes in SAP Demand Planning, Supply Network Planning (SNP), and Production Planning and Detailed Scheduling (PP/DS). They can be used to generate secondary requirements. Planned independent requirements for planning products are offset against sales orders for finished products.

If this requirements strategy, which is delivered in the standard version, does not meet your demands, you can also create your own requirements strategies in SAP APO Customizing.

Process

To specify the requirements strategies for a product in SAP APO, in the **SAP APO menu** under **Master data · Change product**, select the **Demand** tab (see Figure 5.21).

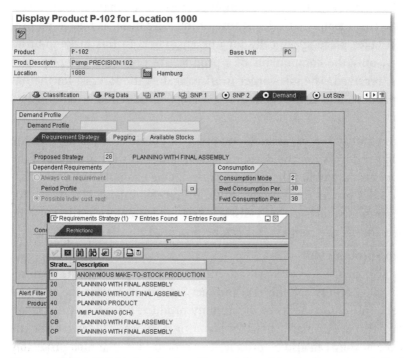

Figure 5.21 SAP APO Product Master—Demand: Specifying the Requirements Strategy

5.8 Potential for Optimization in Material Requirements Planning

5.8.1 Stockholding on Different BOM Levels

When implementing the demand-driven MRP strategies 52, 63, 50, and 60 or similar strategies for the finished product, specific questions arise with regard to the level at which the materials should be kept on stock. You can choose among the possibilities that are illustrated in Figure 5.22 and discussed in the paragraphs below.

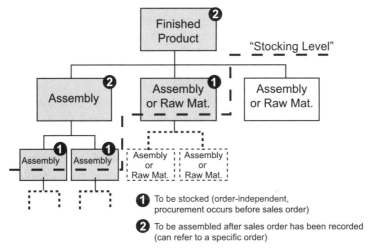

Figure 5.22 Provisioning at Different BOM Levels (Source: SAP)

Two Levels Below the Finished Product

This corresponds to the assembly on the left side in Figure 5.22. The assemblies of the second level should not be assembled until the sales order has been received, while the components of the assemblies should be kept in stock before the sales order is received. The assembly at the first level should also be assembled only after the sales order has been received. The component procurement before incoming sales orders should be performed based on planned independent requirements and should not be assigned to any specific sales order.

One Level Below the Finished Product

This corresponds to the assembly in the middle of Figure 5.22. The assembly should be assembled before sales orders are received and be kept in stock without being assigned to any specific sales order. Only when a sales order is received should the finished product be assembled.

This is probably the most common type of implementation for the strategies without final assembly (52, 63, 50, and 60).

No Stockholding of Components

This corresponds to the assembly/component on the right side in Figure 5.22. The components should not be assembled until a sales order is received, and they should not be kept on stock. When the finished product is assembled according to make-to-order production (in strategy 50 or 60), the component is assembled accordingly.

5.8.2   Optimize Master Data Parameters

Another potential for optimization is provided by the master data parameters in the material master. The demand-driven and consumption-based planning strategies in mySAP ERP and SAP APO use control parameters from the material master such as the safety stock, the reorder level, or the service level, for example. Unfortunately, this data is not always entered in mySAP ERP and SAP APO. Table 5.4 specifies which entries are **mandatory**, **optional**, and **not advisable**.

In all MRP strategies, the **safety stock** is an optional entry. The procedures can be used without specifying a safety stock. This means that you do not have to maintain safety stock in mySAP ERP and can still plan your materials in a consumption-based or demand-driven way. However, if you do not maintain safety stock in consumption-based planning (see Section 5.6), this might lead to incorrect economic results, because safety stocks are normally used. In general, you should know the planning strategies and their control parameters to be able to perform inventory optimization. In practice, it is often possible to find an enormous potential here that resulted from an incorrect implementation.

The **replenishment lead time** (RLT) includes the total time for in-house production or external procurement of a product. In the case of in-house production, the replenishment lead time should cover all BOM levels.

Control Parameter	MRP Parameter			
	Manual reorder point	Automatic reorder point	Forecast-based MRP	Demand-driven MRP
Safety stock	optional	optional	optional	optional
Reorder level	mandatory	mandatory	no entry	no entry
Replenishment lead time	optional	optional	mandatory	mandatory
Service level	no entry	mandatory	optional	optional

Table 5.4 MRP Control Parameters in mySAP ERP

In planning, the replenishment lead time is interpreted as follows (see also Figure 5.23):

▶ In *planning at component level*, the replenishment lead time is reduced to the in-house production time.

▶ In *planning at finished product level*, the replenishment lead time is the production time of the overall structure. In order to react quickly to customer demand, planned independent requirements are maintained at the level of the finished product, or the sales orders are entered well in advance.

Usually, the replenishment lead time is used in the availability check. However, if the in-house production time and the planned delivery time are maintained, they have a higher priority than the replenishment lead time when determining the component availability.

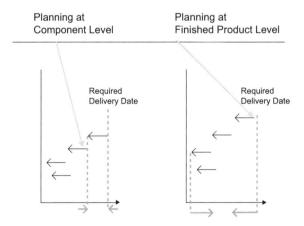

Figure 5.23 Definition of Replenishment Lead Time (RLT) in Planning at Component and Finished Product Levels

In practice, very often the RLT is not maintained, or it is determined only once for all master data. This has two disadvantages:

▸ First, the RLT changes on a regular basis. If the master data is not checked regularly and adjusted when necessary, the planning works with incorrect master data. Requirements dates and procurement proposals are created on the wrong dates. This can result in faulty lot-size calculations. Therefore, it is very important to update the master data, particularly the RLT.

▸ Second, it is important for material requirements planning to plan using replenishment lead times that are correct and stored per material. Here too is an enormous potential for inventory optimization.

The same possibilities as for the replenishment lead time also apply to the **reorder level** and the **service level**.

5.8.3 Selection of the Correct MRP Strategy

We have looked at numerous MRP strategies. We will now discuss how to select the correct strategy for your purposes. The following is an outline of several questions that you can use to help you determine your needs. The answers provided will help you in selecting the appropriate MRP strategy.

Which Planning Level Should You Use for Your Planning?

Finished product level:
▸ if you can recognize a stable sales behavior for the finished product (X or Y items according to an XYZ analysis).
▸ if the finished product has a high business volume value (A or B items according to an ABC analysis).

Assembly level:
▸ if you can recognize an instable sales behavior for the finished product (Y or Z items according to an XYZ analysis).
▸ if the finished product has a low material value (B or C items according to an ABC analysis).
▸ if you also sell assemblies to your customers.

Component level:
▸ if you can recognize an instable sales behavior for the finished product (Y or Z items according to an XYZ analysis).

- if the finished product has a low business volume value (B or C items according to an ABC analysis).

- if you can recognize an instable sales behavior for the assembly (Y or Z items according to an XYZ analysis).

- if the assembly has a low material value (B or C items according to an ABC analysis).

- if you can determine a stable sales behavior for the component (X or Y items according to an XYZ analysis).

- if the component has a high material value (A or B items according to an ABC analysis).

- if many finished products or assemblies require the same components, and the component requirements can therefore be aggregated and then prove to be stable.

Characteristic level:

- if you sell many variants of one product and can predict the values (characteristics) of the finished products rather than the individual product variants. A characterstic can be a color, a dimension, or a feature.

Which Production Strategy Should You Use?

Make-to-Stock: if you want to produce for stock before you receive a sales order, and then want to sell from stock. This is usually done when the order lead time exceeds the delivery time accepted by the customer.

Make-to-Order: if you do not want to produce your product until the sales order is received. In this case, longer delivery times are usually accepted by the customer.

Assemble-to-Order: if you do not produce or assemble the finished product until the sales order has been received, but already produce or procure the required assemblies and components beforehand. You therefore shorten your time to market by producing the assemblies using make-to-stock strategies, and then produce the finished product using a make-to-order strategy. Assemble-to-order is therefore a mixture of the two strategies mentioned above.

Which Procurement Strategy is Appropriate for Your Products?

Procurement depending on the requirements for finished products: If you generally procure your components depending on the requirements of the finished products, you should select a strategy for planning up to the level of the finished product. In this type of planning, the component requirements are automatically determined down to the lowest level depending on the requirements for finished products.

Procurement depending on the requirements for assemblies: The procurement of your components is partially dependent on the requirements of the assemblies. In this case, select a strategy that lets you use a planning strategy without final assembly. The component requirements are then determined depending on the requirements for assemblies. The components of the highest level are not procured until the sales order has been received.

Procurement before the sales order is received: The procurement of your components is independent of the requirements of the finished products. In this case, select a strategy that lets you use a planning for planning materials.

Which Department is Responsible?

Sales: In the sales department, you should ensure a good forecast quality so that the production department can really rely on the planned independent requirements and ensure timely and sufficient production. Additionally, you should work using appropriate service levels, and the sales department should also be responsible for the inventory. Generally you will plan at the level of the finished product in these scenarios.

Production: The production department should be measured using service levels. It should take over responsibility for inventory management. The production department would then also have the freedom to implement assembly or component planning strategies.

Influence of Inventory on Material Requirements Planning

Inventory should be considered: In this case, you should go for net requirements planning so that you can include your inventory in material requirements planning.

Inventory should not be considered: If you want to influence production so that changed requirements or newly incoming sales orders do not constantly force production to change, the inventory should not have any impact on the MRP strategy. Therefore, you should select gross requirements planning.

Safety stocks are an important element in safeguarding against uncertainties in planning. This chapter covers safety stocks and their influence on delivery service in detail.

6 Service Level and Safety Stocks

Sales departments often demand an optimal customer service level. Such a demand assumes that every incoming customer request will be fulfilled without delay. The service level must be 100%; however, actual operating practice must assume that the costs required to produce a 100% service level cannot be justified. The higher the service level that is sought:

▸ The lower the stockout costs

▸ The higher the storage costs for the larger amounts of stock

6.1 Safety Stock

If a warehouse were to be 100% ready to deliver a given material at all times, inevitable forecast errors would result in the storing of a considerable amount of safety stock, which would also be quite costly. The amount of safety stock depends on:

▸ The service level

▸ The replenishment lead time

▸ The forecast accuracy

To keep the amount of safety stock and therefore the storage costs as low as possible, most companies generally define a specific service level for each material. When formulated mathematically, this service level represents the probability that no stockout will occur during the replenishment lead time (RLT) of the material. If you select a relatively high service level, the system will calculate just as high a level of safety stock. If you select a low service level, the level of safety stock will also be low.

The replenishment lead time is the production time for materials produced in-house and the planned delivery time for materials procured externally. It involves the period between the start of the procurement process and the storage of the materials on site. The material requirements planning (MRP) controller defines the replenishment lead time. The longer the replenishment lead time, the higher the probability of stockouts. Therefore, with longer replenishment lead times, the amount of safety stock should be higher. Safety stock protects against various deviations, such as delivery date variances (when the replenishment lead time varies), requirement variances (when the forecast is inaccurate), delivery quantity variances (when the vendor does not deliver enough materials or the quality of the delivered materials is poor), and inventory variances (when inventory-taking recognizes a deviation between the plan and actual inventory). Figure 6.1 summarizes these deviations and shows the relationships among them.

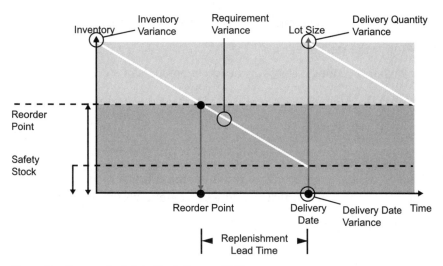

Figure 6.1 Reasons for Safety Stock (Source: SAP)

Figure 6.2 illustrates the relationship of the service level to the safety stock storage costs. The optimal service level is determined by the optimum of the stockout costs and the service costs, which, in this case, is the safety stock.

If we look at the optimal service level from the viewpoint of the enterprise, we see that it is determined by comparing the possible stockout costs with the cost of storing any safety stock, which is kept in addition to the actual requirements. Because the total stockout costs decrease as the service level increases and the costs of additional safety stock increase, the overall service level costs lead to a convex curve progression.

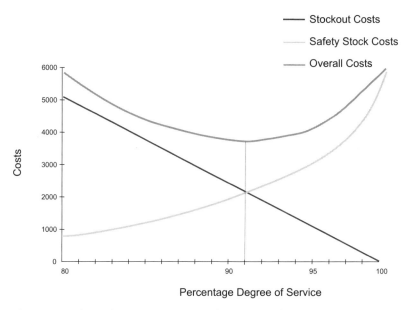

Figure 6.2 Relationship Between Costs and Service Level

If you chose a service level that is too high, you will end up with large stocks that tie up a great deal of capital and involve high storage costs. If the service level is too low, you must deal with high stockout costs for special circumstances such as overtime, additional shifts, and delay penalties. The last 5% of the service level makes up about 50% of inventory costs. You must carefully consider what each percentage point of service level is worth to you.

6.2   Service Level

6.2.1   Considerations and Goals

Supply chain management and service levels focus on the company's goals—speed, flexibility, integration, and direction—and how they can best meet customer requirements:

▸ *Speed* refers to the speed at which a company processes its customer orders or provides customers with goods from the warehouse. This process-oriented time management focuses on the time to customer: the time between the acceptance of a customer order and the complete and correct fulfillment of the order.

▸ *Flexibility* in this context means the ability of a company to modify existing products or to develop new products due to changes in customer requirements, and the ability of production to react to individual customer requirements within the existing production schedule.

All efforts within a company to improve the service level consist of an assortment of subgoals that are monitored and that must undergo a process of continuous improvement. In order for a company to meet the requirements of the service level it wishes to provide, it must focus on the following individual goals:

▶ Readiness to deliver

▶ Delivery time

▶ Delivery reliability

▶ Delivery quality

▶ Delivery flexibility

You have to first optimize the enterprise processes—processes such as those in planning, production, warehouse management, and order processing—if you want to pursue these goals. The following paragraphs cover these topics in more detail.

Readiness to Deliver

Readiness to deliver is the ability to satisfy a requirement on time. Readiness to deliver can be measured in different ways, depending on your focus:

If you want to measure readiness to deliver according to the number of units sold, use the following formula:

Service level = the number of quantities delivered on time / the total quantity of the demand

Table 6.1 contains additional formulas for the calculating the service level.

Criterion	Formula	Service
Stockout	Service level = the number of quantities delivered on time / the total quantity of the demand	Quantity service
Frequency of stockouts	Service level = the number of customer sales orders delivered on time / the total quantity of customer sales orders	Demand service
Frequency of stockouts	Service level = the number of order items delivered on time / the total quantity of order items	Demand service

Table 6.1 Options for Calculating the Service Level

Criterion	Formula	Service
Loss of sales	Service level = the value of the quantities delivered on time / the value of the total quantity of the demand	Sales quantity service
Stockout period	Service level = the number of periods (days) without stockouts / total number of periods	Period service

Table 6.1 Options for Calculating the Service Level (cont.)

Figure 6.3 illustrates the various results that can arise from different methods of calculating the service level.

Different methods of calculating the same key figure often lead to entirely different results!

Order 1 (Customer A)		
Item	Part No.	Quantity
1	1	250
.	.	.
.	.	.
10	10	250
Total (kg) 2,500		

Order 2 (Customer A)		
Item	Part No.	Quantity
1	1	250
.	.	.
.	.	.
10	10	250
Total (kg) 2,500		

Order 3 (Customer B)		
Item	Part No.	Quantity
1	11	1,500
.	.	.
.	.	.
20	30	
Total (kg) 5,000		

Different Calculations: (Assumption: total number of 100)		
DP (customer level)	:	50.0%
DP (order level)	:	66.7%
DP (quantity level)	:	85.0%
DP (items level)	:	97.5%
DP (product level)	:	99.0%

Figure 6.3 Options for Calculating the Service Level

You can see three customer orders in the upper boxes. Orders 1 and 2 are from the same customer (A), and each involves 10 order items with various materials. Order 3 is from customer B and involves 20 order items.

The total requirement for all customer orders is 10,000 kg. Only 8,500 kg can be satisfied because the first item of the last order cannot be fulfilled. A total of 100 materials was requested.

The readiness to deliver can now be measured at different levels, and each measurement produces different results:

▶ **Case 1: Readiness to deliver at the customer level = 50%**
The service level is calculated by determining the percentage of customers whose orders have been satisfied. All orders from customer A have been satisfied; all orders from customer B have not been satisfied completely.

▶ **Case 2: Readiness to deliver at the customer order level = 66.67%**
The service level is calculated by determining the percentage of customer orders that have been satisfied. Two out of three customer orders were completely fulfilled.

▶ **Case 3: Readiness to deliver at the quantity level = 85%**
The service level is calculated by determining the percentage of the quantity that could have been made available. Of the total of 10,000 kg, 8,500 kg was delivered.

▶ **Case 4: Readiness to deliver at the level of customer order items = 97.5%**
The service level is calculated by determining the percentage of customer order items that have been satisfied. Of the total of 40 items from the three orders, 39 items could be delivered.

▶ **Case 5: Readiness to deliver at the material level = 99%**
The service level is calculated by determining the percentage of the quantity that could have been made available. Of the 100 materials between the three orders, 99 materials could be delivered.

This example uses the different results to show that you must be precise in defining how the service level will be calculated in your company to ensure that you will have a uniform view of the service level.

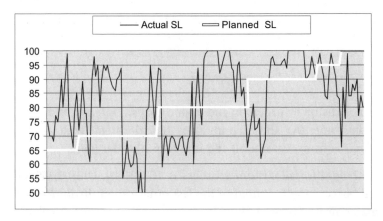

Figure 6.4 Analysis of Readiness to Deliver (Actual and Planned)

Figure 6.4 illustrates that a significant inventory potential lies in the readiness to deliver. This potential often remains unrecognized because the actual and planned service levels are not compared with each other.

In our example, you can see positive and negative differences between the actual and planned service levels. The positive differences are the deviations in which the actual service level is higher than the planned service level. The negative differences are the deviations in which the actual service level is lower than the target service level.

When the actual service level is higher than the planned service level, the actual service level is higher than required. This situation indicates the presence of too much safety stock. You should examine the safety stocks for these products very carefully. In general, you should be able to reduce stock here very easily.

If the actual service level is lower than the target service level, you might be losing sales or giving business to the competition because you cannot supply your customers on time. Here you need to examine the lead times in production, the replenishment lead times in procurement, and the safety stocks.

Delivery Reliability

Delivery reliability refers to the correlation between the confirmed date and the actual date of fulfilling the order (delivery date). The difference between the readiness to deliver and the delivery reliability depends on the date on which delivery to the customer actually occurs. The ability to deliver refers to the correleation between the delivery date desired by the customer and the confirmed order fulfillment date (delivery date). The service level reflects the correlation between the date desired by the customer and the actual date of fulfilling the order. The service level is therefore the comprehensive performance variable that unites the ability to deliver and delivery reliability.

The readiness to deliver is calculated on the ability to deliver—that is, whether or not the company can deliver on the date it promised to the customer, and which the customer has accepted. This date is called the confirmed delivery date. If a company adheres to the confirmed delivery date, it reaches 100% delivery reliability. Delivery reliability goes down when a company cannot adhere to the confirmed delivery date. The total delivery time is the amount of period from when the customer order is placed to when the delivery is made. Figure 6.5 illustrates these concepts.

You can calculate delivery reliability by taking the difference between the actual date the order was fulfilled and the confirmed delivery date. Please note that the confirmed delivery date can be changed in mySAP ERP. If changes have been made, you must consult the first confirmed date to calculate the delivery reliability. The difference between the actual delivery date and the delivery date desired by the customer is the customer request reliability. This reliability measures delivery reliability against the market; delivery reliability valuates the promise made to the customer.

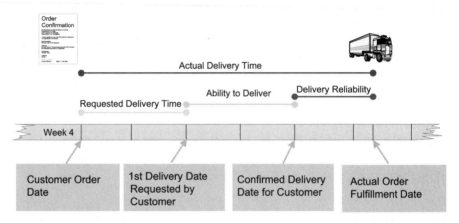

Figure 6.5 Delivery Time, Ability to Deliver, and Delivery Reliability (Source: SAP)

You should always consider delivery reliability in conjunction with customer request reliability. Otherwise, you run the risk of not being realistic when setting the confirmed delivery date to meet your targets. The risk of missing the delivery reliability required by the company's management is relatively low in the eyes of the customer when confirmed delivery dates are overly generous (i.e., deadlines are not rigid). As you will see, the difference between delivery reliability and customer request reliability can be considerable in day-to-day work.

You must distinguish between the ability to deliver and delivery reliability according to ABC classes in all cases. It does not make sense to try to reach the same service level for all products.

Delivery Time

The delivery time is the time from the issuance of an order up until goods receipt on the customer's side. It can be calculated according to the following formulas:

- *Average actual delivery time = order fulfillment date – date of incoming order*
- *Average desired delivery time = customer's desired date – date of incoming order*
- *Average confirmed delivery time = confirmed order fulfillment date – date of incoming order*

Your stocking strategy is an important element of delivery time that conforms to the market. There are generally two types of stocking strategies: make to order (MTO) and make to stock (MTS). With an MTS strategy, the delivery time is minimal because customers can be supplied directly from the warehouse. With an MTO strategy, due to the production process, the delivery time is often rather long. It is essentially determined by the production lead time and the replenishment lead time for material components.

Delivery Flexibility

Delivery flexibility refers to how easily and how quickly a company can react to the requirements of individual customers. Can products be configured freely? Can standard products be supplemented with small changes or additions? Can the services provided to the customer be expanded upon? The consumer goods industry does not have configurable products in the sense of variant production as is the case in the automobile sector. Nonetheless, food producers, in particular, must be able to respond to customer requirements with ease and flexibility. A customer might ask for special packaging, a special delivery time, a special price, or a specific period of time (e.g., summer) in which the demand for a specific product (e.g., swimwear) will be greater. Companies must be able to meet all such requirements in order to remain competitive. For example, the automobile industry must be able to produce equipment variants as required by individual customers.

In addition to individual customer requirements, special order requests are often made, such as for special order sizes or minimum quantities. Today, delivery flexibility is a major element of competitiveness. Of course, another question is whether or not the required flexibility is present in production. How easily can production perform setup changes, and how quickly can the number of personnel be adjusted upward or downward? Production flexibility influences delivery flexibility. Therefore, you should also consider optimizing the production process.

Delivery Quality

Delivery quality is a measurement of the number of completed orders without quality and quantity issues. Here it's a matter of establishing internal enterprise processes that ensure that customers can accept the type, quantity, delivery dates, and condition of products without complaints. Only by using this approach can companies develop medium and long-term customer satisfaction. Metrics for delivery quality can include the following:

▸ Portion of deliveries with complaints

▸ Portion of redeliveries

▸ Portion of deliveries with incorrect quantities

▸ Number of returns

▸ Number of complaints

Of course, product quality (determined by production) also influences delivery quality. Therefore, it's also important to focus on quality in production.

6.2.2 Service Level Optimization Potentials

Dissatisfied customers and suboptimal processes in order processing are usually caused by disruptions in internal value creation processes. External events might trigger the disruptions, but they often result in deficiencies within the company itself.

Companies have little or no control over acts of God. And they have just as little control over the dynamics of the market. However, some types of disruptions can be prevented or minimized, such as those that arise from order processing, rough-cut and detailed planning, procurement, production, company equipment, and the behavior of employees. Such deficiencies have a great influence on order processing in terms of service level. The following sections examine potential disruptions in planning and order processing, and those caused by inadequacies of the software solutions in use. They do not examine deficiencies that arise in production and the warehouse, or those due to human error in detail. Instead, they provide an overview of the various potential disruptions.

Disruptions in Order Processing

In addition to the process-oriented flow of order information through company departments, which is handled by both the technical and operational divisions of a company, order processing also has an administrative and organizational side. This side comes into play when an order is accepted. During this step, modifications can be made by sales employees or by a department especially created to do so.

If a company produces goods based on sales forecasts, sales figures can be a potential disruption. Because sales employees work hard to satisfy customer requirements on time, the availability of goods at the right time is particularly important to them. Therefore, planned sales figures are generally set higher than the quantities that the sales department can actually sell. But because no concrete orders from customers are yet present, the company plans and produces according to the estimated sales figures. The sales department can fulfill the customer demand, but the excess product must be stored in the warehouse until there is additional demand for it. Therefore, if you consider the complete internal supply chain, order processing is inefficient and not cost-optimized.

In MTO production, the initial hurdle in order processing is error-free order acceptance. Errors that occur in the interface between an employee in order acceptance and the order processing system can rarely be discovered in order processing. They become apparent only when the customer monitors the delivery. The order may be produced according to incorrect assumptions. During the bureaucratic orderingprocess, the order moves through many hands and responsibility for it changes frequently, which makes it easy for errors to occur. If paper documents with handwritten notes accompany the order through a company's various departments, this can be another source of errors.

If the order is accepted via conversation with the customer, the process must record the relevant data, information on the delivery date, and the status of orders that have already been completed. Here it's a disadvantage when the planning, executive, and warehouse departments have no electronic link to order acceptance. Delivery time specifications are generally given based only on standard lead times. Employees in order acceptance cannot view the planning system or the warehouse and cannot recognize if the setup times, maintenance work, or bottlenecks caused by order sequence will cause other delivery dates for the customer to appear or if the customer can be supplied more quickly due to free capacities in production.

Orders with start or end dates in the past represent another potential disruption that can be solved by downstream areas only with difficulty or not at all. Such orders are referred to as back orders. Filling these orders involves back-order rescheduling. If an order issued on short notice pushes other orders out of the way, it enjoys preferred handling over orders that should be filled because of forecasts, and therefore, it can jeopardize the delivery reliability of the other orders that should have had priority.

Disruptions in Planning

Interruptions in planning can be described as important deviations between the plan values expected by the MRP controller and the actual values that endanger achieving date reliability, stock, lead time, and utilization goals. The potential interruptions therefore endanger service level goals in MRP, cost goals related to stocks, and tracing the capacity load in production.

There are two deficiencies in planning today. The first is the limitation of having to rely on stochastic values that generally deviate from actual values. The second is the inability of current planning to take future bottlenecks and problems into consideration — issues that can arise from short-notice changes to orders or machines and personnel shortfalls. The planning systems require MRP controllers to enter values for the lead time or the capacity demands of an order, even though these values can be entered reliably only during follow-up planning — depending on the sequence of orders and machine utilization planning.

Also, the system works through the data in batch processes, so it does not enable planners to work with simulations in real time. Therefore, premature changes caused by new incoming orders or changes to existing orders often become part of new planning too late or are even ignored. Because planning anticipates additional short-term changes, it considers it unnecessary to design a new planning run when an early change is received. In hindsight, passive and expectant behavior of employees can lead to incorrect planning and short-term overloads of production capacity because optimal planning is impossible in the short term and the MRP controllers are busy dealing with current disruptions and keeping the damage to a minimum.

In addition to handling exceptions with short-term solutions and on-the-fly examinations of the problem, another area of potential optimization arises because routine tasks occupy the MRP controllers' time. The planner must schedule the suggested values and basic dates and respond to notification from the operative level about disruptions and delays in production. Because MRP controllers are the only connection between the planning and execution level, their time can quickly become a bottleneck during disruptions. In addition to the time spent on routine tasks and the management of short-term deviations, the multiplicity and complexity of the tasks that MRP controllers face make their work even more difficult. Through their work as interfaces between various departments, they become important sources of information. Because the responsibility for planning various processes lies with different people and because rough-cut, detailed planning and work planning in production are not directly coupled to each other, the MRP controllers also face an additional handicap—each area has a limited ability to see the big picture. Because planning occurs independently of the downstream production steps, MRP controllers cannot determine the direct effects of their planning on downstream areas of the supply chain.

Opportunities for optimization in MRP can also be seen in the difficulties that MRP controllers face in making optimal decisions. Their task involves having to choose between various extreme alternatives for action—by having to select a material. For example, a decision for a large lot size has the advantage of aiming long periods of operation for the machines and a high utilization of the capacity. But the high utilization of the capacity means that other orders are pushed aside. And producing small batches leads to equipment downtime for machines because of refitting and for employees: poor capacity utilization is the inevitable result.

Disruptions in Production

Additional disruptions also occur in production. Problems with materials or disruptions in production often occur in upstream areas or in the processing of specific business processes.

Delays in production often result from errors in MRP. When a product occupies a machine after the time allotted to it, other products must wait. The processing of those products is delayed and on-time processing is jeopardized. While the idle time lengthens for the waiting orders, an overload can occur on the bottleneck machine because production attempts to make up for the delay or incorrect planning with additional work. This can result in problems with quality, increased scrap, and defects in machines that lead to unscheduled repairs and therefore standstills in production.

Breakdowns that arise from materials can be traced back to errors in rough-cut planning and the resulting procurement procedures. Stockouts or incorrect deliveries can lead to production standstills in a company. An incorrect delivery is unusable for a company. If no one notices that a delivery does not meet specifications, quality problems in production can result. Internal reasons for disruptions can include the acceptance of orders whose start dates lie in the past and a late notification from planning to purchasing about the orders to be issued. Dealing with material resources in planning can also lead to internal disruptions in the materials area. Rigid regulation regarding the use of reserved materials, or being prohibited from using the safety stock can also lead to disruptions.

Disruptions in Master Data

Master data parameters in planning can also cause disruptions. For calculations, the planning runs use parameter settings that define specific handling of certain information, such as information regarding inventory levels, order rhythms, order processing, shipping options, or dealing with special cases. If the master data is not optimally selected, a large portion of the planning support that the system can offer is lost.

The currency of data is very important to planning and order processing in general throughout the company. Processing reliability depends on planning being current and executable, but this is possible only when previously dispatched orders do not contain any errors. Important information that other areas of the company are responsible for entering must be available at the right time for downstream areas. However, processing outside the system leads to additional unreliability that can affect downstream areas in the value chain.

Factors That Influence the Service Level

The potential disruptions noted above point to specific factors that influence the service level.

▶ A good requirements forecast is integral to accurately forecasting quantities and times; and because the forecasts are reliable, production and logistics can ensure that their planning is secure. Moreover, this improved sales planning increases the ability to deliver.

▶ For A items (items that account for a relatively high percentage of the overall revenue), employees are more responsive to requirement variances, and they keep a closer eye on these items in production and logistics. Therefore, you should use an ABC analysis to determine your service level.

▶ If the number of customers is rather small, you can plan logistics more simply and optimally. It's easier to deliver to a small number of customers than to a large number of customers. You should classify your customers according to an ABC analysis and define various service levels according to the analysis.

▶ If requirement variances rarely occur , and if they tend to be low, you can better and more seamlessly manufacture a product and deliver it to customers. The ability to deliver such items will be higher than the ability to deliver items that have more of a fluctuating demand. The same conclusions apply to short and lengthy transport routes.

▶ You can use options for substitution to improve the ability to deliver. By examining your inventories globally and checking incoming customer orders against availability, you can increase your ability to deliver. You can also increase your ability to deliver by suggesting alternate products to a customer when the product that the customer originally ordered is unavailable. Another way you can improve your ability to deliver is by checking production capacities in the event that a product is unavailable to determine if you can still manufacture the product on time.

6.2.3 Optimization with Order Processing in mySAP ERP

Order processing in mySAP ERP supports users by enabling them to observe, handle, and process orders collaboratively from the receipt of the order through its fulfillment in the post-sales phase, instead of passively directing orders through the individual functional areas in the company. The ability to view the status of an order from every department in the company, direct the order to competent staff, and intervene when necessary enables the company to process the order in a controlled manner throughout its lifecycle and to minimize uncertainties. As early as order creation in mySAP ERP, users find support with an incompletion log (see Figure 6.6) that indicates incomplete order data and helps users complete the missing data. To begin this procedure, use the SAP menu to select **Logistics · Sales and Distribution · Sales · Order · Change**, and then **Edit · Incompletion Log**.

You can also view and monitor the entire lifecycle of the order and its follow-up documents in mySAP using the document flow feature (see Figure 6.7). This feature enables you to find information on delivery notes, invoices, and payment conditions for a customer at any time. From the SAP menu, select **Logistics · Sales and Distribution · Sales · Order · Change**, and then **Environment · Display Document Flow**.

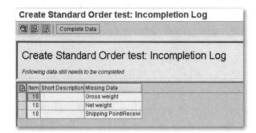

Figure 6.6 mySAP ERP: Incompletion Log in Order Processing

Document Flow

Document	Quantity	Unit	Ref. value	Currency	On	Status
▽ 🗋 ➡ Standard Order test 0000010787 / 10	52	PC	72.581,60	EUR	27.01.2005	Completed
▽ 🗋 Delivery 0080014177 / 10	52	PC			28.01.2005	Completed
🗋 WMS transfer order 0000004124 / 1	52	PC			28.01.2005	Completed
🗋 GD goods issue:delvy 4900033355 / 1	52	PC	47.848,67	EUR	28.01.2005	complete
▽ 🗋 Invoice (F2) 0090035273 / 10	52	PC	72.581,60	EUR	28.01.2005	Completed
🗋 Accounting document 0100000592 / 10	52	PC	72.581,60	EUR	28.01.2005	Cleared

Business partner 0000001033 Karsson High Tech Markt
Material M-17 TONER, CART, CLR, LW, BK

Figure 6.7 mySAP ERP: Document Flow in Sales and Distribution

You can also provide customers with the information they need in real time and therefore increase your service level.

Active management of the order cycle and tight integration of the order with planning and optimization tools not only improve your ability to find information, but also increase the flow of orders, which improves your ability to plan and fulfill customer orders. Customer satisfaction grows with reliabilty of the supply of information and delivery.

6.2.4 Optimization With Global ATP in SAP APO

Satisfying customer demand and the ability to forecast and specify reliable delivery dates is based on an availability check: Available-to-Promise (ATP).

ATP involves looking at inventory in near to real time and separating it into a non-reserved portion and a reserved portion. Inventory is determined from the stock that is currentlyavailable in the warehouse and the quantities planned in production. When a customer order reaches the system, it checks to see if the quantity ordered can be satisfied from the reserved stock. If it can be, the quantity is reserved for the customer. The traditional ATP method that is used in markets, where bottlenecks in procurement or capacities exist, handles customer requests on a first-come, first-served basis. It does not consider how profitable the order might be for the company, the status of the customer, and whether or not the order is based on a forecast. Therefore, using this ATP method, the company jeopardizes efficient order handling and customer service and can even trigger service penalties for the entire supply chain.

The goal of ATP, however, is to improve the ability of a company to fulfill its role in the supply chain and its ability to create reliable and accurate forecasts, even for changing requirements. ATP considers the status of the customer, limited capacities with materials or in production, and the supply of other goods in determining availability. ATP classifies and hierarchically arranges specific criteria such as the profitability of the order, the status of the customer, and a location in a given area. The reserved inventory quantities are then distributed according to previously defined rules (product allocation). When a customer asks about availability, the system examines these criteria. If applicable, the system gives the customer permission to access inventory according to specific rules. If an inquiry finds the desired goods in storage, the system allocates those goods. If the goods are not found, the system checks to see if a reservation is possible at an earlier date, if the same goods can be allocated from a different organizational class, or if other products can be offered to the customer.

The reliability of ATP depends on how precise the sales planning is in SAP Advanced Planner and Optimizer (SAP APO). Because reservations are not based on goods already present in the warehouse, but on goods still in the production planning process, some uncertainty remains concerning actual access to the warehouse at the agreed-upon time and if the customer can be supplied on time. Therefore, ATP requires optimization along the entire business process—from order acceptance to delivery to the customer. Product allocations based on promises that result from sales planning are reliable only when rough-cut planning is reliable, when the resulting procurement processes come in on time, and when production can manufacture goods on time. Inexact sales planning has a direct effect on service level. Better reliability produces greater customer satisfaction, and therefore fewer customers are lost, and the company increasesits market share. Deviations between a promised delivery and actual delivery cause just the opposite to happen: customers decide not to buy from the company and are lost to competitors or competing value chains.

Global ATP in SAP APO

The *Global ATP* feature in SAP APO uses a rule-based strategy to ensure that customers receive the deliveries promised to them. This feature carries out multistep component and capacity checks in real time and in a simulation mode so that it can balance supply and demand. The ATP checks can also increase performance by monitoring aggregated data stored in memory. Global ATP maintains the simultaneous, immediate access to production availability based on the supply chain so that you can ensure that you keep your delivery promises.

Global ATP uses several criteria to perform its tasks These criteria include the following:

▶ **Selection of alternate products**
  If a manufactured product or its components are unavailable, the system selects a substitute by using rule-based selection criteria.

▶ **Selection of alternate locations**
  If a product is unavailable at a certain location, Global ATP can check to see if the product is available at an alternate location. You can also integrate this logic with product substitution rules.

▶ **Product allocation**
  You can assign products or components in short supply to customers, markets, and orders. The ATP calculation will then consider these assignments (product allocations).

Global ATP consists of four major components:

▶ Basic methods

▶ Enhanced methods

▶ Rule-based ATP check

▶ Explanation and simulation

Basic Methods

The basic methods of ATP checks include an availability check against inventory and requirements, product allocation, and checks against preplanning. The basic methods for checking material availability include:

▶ A check against the ATP logic

▶ A check against product allocations

- A check against primary plan requirements
- All three checks are performed in sequence.

These methods enable you to carry out the following availability checks:

- Material availability check against inventory, planned stock receipts, and planned goods issues
- Material availability check against a production plan (according to material or plant)
- Material availability check against plan structures in consistent planning
- Product allocations
- Capacity check
- One-level correlation of confirmed quantities

Enhanced Methods

Enhanced ATP methods combine basic methods to check the availability of a requirements group. A requirements group might be, for example, all line items in a customer order or all materials in a bill of materials (BOM). In essence, the enhanced ATP methods consist of three options to select from in the event of a material shortage. You can select a similar, better, or poorer-quality product or material, procure the product from an alternate source, or increase your production.

The production process can be viewed as a multistep Bill of Materials (BOM) explosion and as a process for checking availability at a specific level. Here you use the ATP check, the enhanced planning methods, and scheduling methods in the production and detailed scheduling component, *SAP APO Production Planning and Detailed Scheduling (PP/DS)*. The enhanced methods include:

- Assembly order processing
- Material availability and product allocations
- Availability-driven product determination in the customer order
- Alternate items or discontinued material

All enhanced methods have a common characteristic in that multiple checks can be performed according to the procedure. For example, product determination keeps checking until the incoming order is completely satisfied.

Rule-Based Check

A rule-based ATP check refers back to the enhanced ATP methods. In SAP APO, rule-based ATP checks arestep-by-step availability checking processes controlled by rules, which you can define for your company. Depending on predefined parameters and based on the results of a specific step, the system decides whether or not to continue the availability check. A rule-based ATP check can include the following steps:

1. Is that product available at this location?

2. If it is not, is an alternate product available at this location?

3. If it is not, is the product available at another location?

4. If it is not, is an alternate product available at another location?

5. If it is not, should production be triggered to manufacture it?

A rule-based check represents another level of availability checking—beyond that of the enhanced methods. In broad terms, the selection of rules interweaves several enhanced methods. This means that the system performs a multistep check according to the product selection. In addition, the current solution also uses conditions to direct the progress of the checks. The decision to continue or end a check can be made on the basis of this procedure.

Global ATP enables you to search for available quantities in all possible locations and according to all selectable products in a multistep process. A rule-based ATP check in a global environment creates the foundation for decision support with the determination of realistic delivery dates. Integration of an enhanced ATP check and the explanation function in a complex business process guarantees greater transparency for the entire logistics chain—even in a heterogeneous system environment.

Explanation and Simulation

You can interpret the results of availability checks with the explanation and simulation function of Global ATP. The system delivers the results of the ATP checks as simple dialogs, material availability dates, and confirmed quantities. But it can also provide complex, multilevel dialogs. Such a dialog would result for rule-based availability checks combined with basic methods that consider various levels of an organization.

Dialogs are the core of the explanation and simulation function. The results of the availability check consist of the results of many individual steps. The order in which the steps are executed affects the results of a check. Therefore, to ensure execution of the correct sequence, the function leads you through the dialogs. At the lowest product level, you can navigate to individual checks. You can use the explanation and simulation function to simulate ATP checks based on one or more basic methods. You can also simulate rules-based ATP checks.

At Various Product Levels

You can execute a Global ATP check at the end product level. Checking customer requirements or preplanning requirements for the availability of end products is certainly the standard use for Global ATP checks; however, you can also use Global ATP to check at the component level for the availability of all the components that belong to the main product. Furthermore, you can implement these checks at multiple levels.

Flexible use of inventory types

The ATP functions must provide flexible usage options for different types of inventory, access, and requirements to manage the changing requirements of business events. During order processing, for example, a manufacturer of computer keyboards might want to check purchase requests, orders, safety stock, and available inventory, but not the quality inspection stock. At the point of delivery and picking, the manufacturer must consider all open orders and deliveries—but not purchase requests and orders.

Dynamic availability checks

SAP R/3 determines ATP quantities by checking the available stock in the warehouse or various planned stock receipts that have not yet been assinged to any goods issues before the requirements date. The availability check is dynamic, which means that the system assessing the current situation. If needed, the system modifies existing confirmation of the documents being checked when you trigger an ATP check. This ATP function is executed across the entire supply chain in multiple steps. Configurable settings enable unique combinations of data on inventory, goods receipts, and goods issues that each step in the ATP check should consider. As soon as the system checks the customer order, it displays three options for selection:

▶ The possible quantity on the required date

▶ A date for complete delivery

▶ Several dates for partial delivery as a delivery proposal

At Various Organizational Levels

Global ATP can check availability within a company at all levels of the organization (plant, warehouse location, and so on) that carry inventory. It can also check batch stocks.

Management of materials at various levels

Materials can be managed at several different organizational levels. Products can be stored at several storage locations or warehouses. Some products must be stored at a lot or batch level. The goal is to perform ATP checks for such products at the specific storage locations or for specific batches. The integrity of the ATP checks must be guaranteed in environments with a preponderance of mixed processing levels.

Checking lot and batch stocks

Global ATP provides a multilevel availability check to recognize stocks specific to a storage location or batch. An ATP check always begins at the lowest level. To ensure the integrity of the results from the lower levels, a check is also performed at the plant level. Global ATP also provides a selection option for where and at what time in the fulfillment process each location or batch is to be determined—either during order processing or later, during delivery processing. You therefore have the greatest possible flexibility when deciding if an ATP check should occur at the plant, storage location, or batch level.

Checking end products with forward and backward consumption

You can perform a forecast at the end product level and assemble the end products according to requirements. Alternatively, you can create the assembly yourself or procure them externally to support forecasts for the end products with a planning solution for warehouse production. With Global ATP, you can perform an ATP check at the end product level and select forward or backward consumption for each product. You can use either type of consumption during an ATP balance of requirements and forecasts. For this solution with Global ATP, neither stocks nor planned goods receipts are checked. Instead, only a check against the planned independent requirements (sales forecast) of the sales planning components is performed. The details on the ATP check are found at the level of the forecast period.

Controlling the Product Selection

In many industries, when a required product is not available, customers can accept an alternate product. In this case, the availability check can use defined, customer-specific rules to select alternate products.

ATP-driven product substitution

Your company likely has several alternate product offerings that it can use to satisfy a specific requirement. You might have to use an alternate, for example, if you want to support electronic products with expired shelf lives, substitution options desired by semiconductor manufacturers, various package sizes, or the campaign-dependent substitution of consumer goods. Such situations require ATP-driven product selection and substitution.

ATP-driven product variants

You can use Global ATP to define an ATP-driven sequence of product variants or packaging that the system takes into account during the availability check. If you want, you can execute this function as a one-time procedure up to the customer level. The system can perform the procedure automatically as part of order processing, or you can perform it manually.

Processing for Several Plants

Large companies often have various production and shipping operations that can deliver the same product to customers. When several plants exist, a representative must be able to quickly and easily find the location at which a given product is available and select the most appropriate operation.

With a Global ATP check, this procedure occurs as early as in the order processing stage. You can perform an ATP check for all possible plants or for only certain plants, then determine the optimal solution, navigate to the ATP details, and select the desired plant. You can also select additional options, such as complete or partial deliveries for each plant that you select.

Multiple Simultaneous Checks

Direct sellers of computers and consumer goods have such a large volume of customer orders to process that they must perform many checks simultaneously. The Global ATP logic ensures the integrity of the results of each individual check—even when multiple checks occur simultaneously. During order processing, for example, a material is blocked only during the ATP check. As soon as the check is over, the material is released for other ATP checks. Temporary reservations are made based on previous ATP runs. In this manner, the system deals with all events of the supply chain in which a specific material is involved.

In Materials Management

Global ATP functionality is completely integrated with materials management and with inventory management.

Integrating ATP with materials management
A superficial inventory analysis can easily provide misleading information about the amount of available goods . The products that seem available might well have been promised to certain customers. Accordingly, the system must be able to determine which units of the produced quantity are actually available. In other words, the ATP process must be integrated with goods movements to guarantee the integrity of the ATP check. It must also guarantee that if an unsatisfactory item has been received, this information is sent directly to production, or that a replacement item is sent as quickly as possible.

Dynamic ATP check based on the movement type
Global ATP performs a dynamic ATP check based on the movement type that is assigned to the inventory management process. The system also automatically transmits a missing part message to the responsible employee when a goods receipt from vendors or from production is recorded.

6.3   Replenishment Lead Time

6.3.1   Replenishment Lead Time in mySAP ERP

The replenishment lead time is the time needed to procure an item. It can be determined accurately only in hindsight. But because it must be estimated in advance for MRP, you generally work with an average replenishment lead time. The average replenishment lead time is calculated by adding the following values:

▶ Average time to generate an order

▶ Average delivery time

▶ Average goods receipt and goods inspection time

▶ Average staging time

mySAP ERP distinguishes between the replenishment lead time for goods produced in-house and for those procured externally. In the case of in-house production, the overall replenishment lead time from the viewpoint of **MRP 3** in the material master is used (see Figure 6.8). From the SAP menu, select **Logistics · Materials Management · Material Master · Material · Change · Immediately**, and then select the **MRP 3** tab.

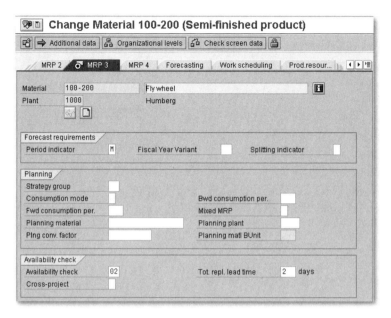

Figure 6.8 MRP 3 View in the mySAP ERP Material Master

In the case of in-house production, the overall replenishment lead time is the time required to make the product available again — after all levels of the BOM have been procured or produced. It is not calculated by the system; it is determined in this field as the sum of the in-house production times or planned delivery times of the longest production path.

You can maintain the planned delivery time and the in-house production time in the **MRP 2** tab of the material master (see Figure 6.9). From the SAP menu, select **Logistics · Materials Management · Material Master · Material · Change · Immediately**, and then select the **MRP 2** tab.

If you have various vendors for a material, you must enter an average value. The same applies if you order the material from a vendor that has varying delivery times. This value is necessary if the availability check is to consider the replenishment lead time for materials produced in house.

An availability check with replenishment lead time checks only within the replenishment lead time to see if sufficient incoming quantities and stocks are available to cover requirements. Outside of the replenishment lead time, the system assumes that the material will once again be available in a sufficient quantity. Therefore, it is usually necessary in this case to map the entire replenishment lead time of the product with all BOM levels as the replenishment lead time.

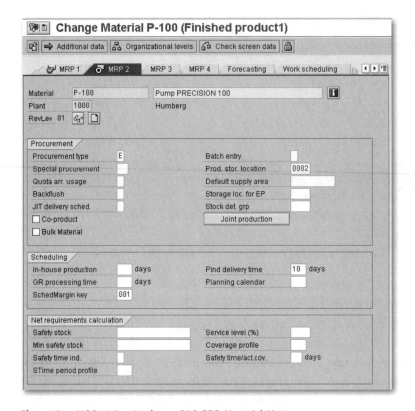

Figure 6.9 MRP 2 View in the mySAP ERP Material Master

If you perform an availability check with replenishment lead time, you have the following options for materials produced in house:

▸ The **Tot. repl. lead time** field is maintained. The time maintained in this field is used for the availability check.

▸ The **Tot. repl. lead time** field is not maintained. The system reads the in-house production time and, if available, the time needed to process a goods receipt, and interprets their sum as the replenishment lead time for the availability check.

For materials procured externally, there is no point to maintaining the **Tot. repl. lead time** field. For external procurement, the availability check with replenishment lead time is always interpreted as the sum of the processing time of procurement, the planned delivery time, and the time needed to process the goods receipt.

6.3.2 Optimization Potentials Related to RLT

The replenishment lead times (RLT) must be stored in master data manually and are valid until the next modification of the master data. Unfortunately, experience has shown, however, that the RLT is maintained only for a portion of all materials.

The RLT for materials that do have an RLT maintained is adjusted only very rarely. The system plans using the standard RLT from the material master and calculates the availability of materials. The standard RLT often does not correlate with the actual RLT, as a comparison of the actual and target RLT clearly shows.

A lack of correlation means that the material arrives too early and the company must therefore pay for storage, or that the material arrives too late, causing stockouts to occur. mySAP ERP does not consider the variance in the actual RLT. Information on current market developments or raw materials shortages are lost in such a situation. Ideally, the actual RLT should be determined automatically and adjusted automatically in the material master. Small add-ons for this purpose exist and have been implemented by some customers. The add-ons determine the actual RLT from the difference between the last order and the goods receipt. This value is then compared with the RLT maintained in the material master and changed if necessary. As an alternative, you can use the static delivery time for a comparison. In any case, note that the RLT from the material master is also used for vendor evaluation.

6.4 Forecast Quality

Customer demand is generally subject to random fluctuations that can be represented by probability distributions.

6.4.1 Normal Distribution

With normally distributed requirements quantities, the most probable value of the requirements quantities lies in the middle of the scale of all possible requirement requests. Because this value is part of the formulas used to determine requirements, only 50% of all requirement requests can be covered. In other words, only a service level of 50% is ensured.

Therefore, the primary task of safety stock is to cover requirement requests that go beyond the most probable value or to limit the risk of an inadequate service level. In light of the relationship noted above between safety stock and stockout costs, when you decide on the amount of safety stock, you must balance the effects on cost and revenue if you fail to deliver or if deliveries are disrupted with the costs of maintaining safety stock.

Accordingly, the service level can be interpreted as a one-sided, statistic security if you assume a normal Gaussean distribution (see Figure 6.10).

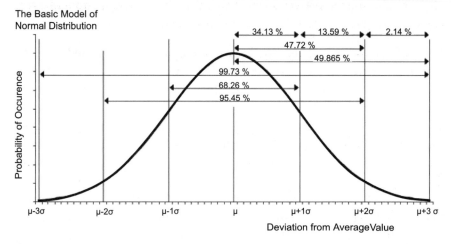

Figure 6.10 Gaussean Distribution

The basic idea of normal distribution is that the probability of the occurrence of a specific condition (characteristic property) increases the farther the condition is from the average value μ. The measure used here is the variance σ. The resulting normal probability curve describes this behavior.

The curve in Figure 6.10 describes the occurrence of all possible conditions, or 100% probability. In other words, in this scenario, you will always find stock.

The law discovered by the mathematician Gauss states that the probability of a characteristic property occurring between the average value (μ) and the average value plus a variance ($\mu+\sigma$) is exactly 34.13%. The probability that a charateristic property lies between μ and $\mu+2\sigma$ is 47.72%, while the probability that it lies between μ and $\mu+3\sigma$ is 49.865%. One half of the symmetrical curve is always exactly 50%. The probability that the characteristic property lies between $\mu-\sigma$ and $\mu+\sigma$ is 68.26%, and the probability of a result between $\mu-2\sigma$ and $\mu+2\sigma$ is 95.45%. The law applies regardless of the individual case under consideration. Normal distribution is a basic element of most warehouse management strategies.

6.4.2 Normal Distribution with Variances

You will not always encounter normal distribution in daily work. You are much more likely to encounter variances in normal distribution. If small quantities are ordered often, inventory "hovers" around an average value, which results in a smaller variance (see Figure 6.11). If orders come in less often, but each one involves a larger quantity, the deviations from the average value are greater, and the σ value is also greater.

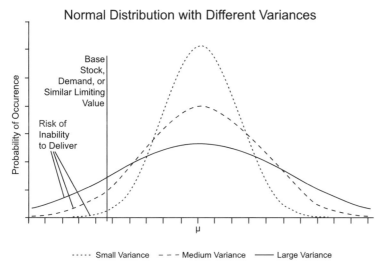

Figure 6.11 Normal Distribution with Variances: Small Variance (Large Amplitude), Medium Variance (Medium Amplitude), and Large Variance (Small Amplitude)

Risk of an inability to deliver
The law described above is useful in estimating *warehouse-related risks*. For example, if μ = 1,000 items, as a result, σ = 200. If the basic stock (BS) = 500 items, it is therefore 500 items under the average value. Stated in variances, the distance between the average value and the basic stock is 2.5 σ. Table 6.2 indicates that the probability of lying between μ and $\mu < 2.5 \sigma$ is 99.37903%. The probability of ending up with fewer than 500 items is therefore less than 1%.

Setting a risk-related strategy
If the probability of having to use basic stock should be a maximum of 5%, you can use Table 6.2 to find the 45% value that corresponds to 5% and

determine the corresponding σ value. For σ = 1.64, we find 94.94974%; for σ = 1.65, we find 95.05285%.

We can then estimate the σ value that corresponds to 95%, as σ= 1.645.

*500 + 1.645 σ = 500 + 1.645 σ * 200 = 829 items*

The approach is also used in quality management and process engineering. It provides relatively reliable statements about risks and probabilities.

Assuming that the forecast of future requirements is distributed normally with an average forecast error of 0, you can determine the security factor k (the z value) that guarantees the required service level. Table 6.2 lists the security factors that result for each service level based on normal distribution.

Service level	Security factor k
50.01%	0.0003
80.00%	0.8416
90.00%	1.2816
95.00%	1.6449
98.00%	2.0537
99.00%	2.3263
99.50%	2,5758
99.90%	3.0903
99.99%	3.7191

Table 6.2 Security Factors According to Service Level

6.5 Safety Stock

As noted, safety stock serves as a buffer. It absorbs fluctuations in demand and delivery quantities during replenishment lead time with a certain probability. The amount of safety stock depends on the accuracy of the demand forecast, the length of the replenishment lead time, and the required level of service.

Reorder Level

Along with safety stock, the *reorder level* is also recalculated for materials with automated harmonization. It is defined as the sum of the safety stock and the forecast requirements within the replenishment lead time (see Figure 6.12).

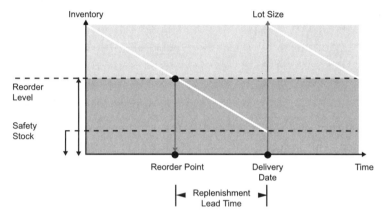

Figure 6.12 Reorder Level and Safety Stock in Relation to the Replenishment Lead Time

During goods issue, static availability is checked against the reorder level. By static availability, we are referring to the current availability, not the future availability. Static availability is the difference between the remaining stock and the reorder point. If the result is smaller than the reorder point, the material is earmarked for MRP. The next MRP run will then automatically generate a purchase order or a planned order for the material.

If the reorder level is too low, stockouts may occur, as illustrated on the left side of Figure 6.13. This means that certain orders cannot be satisfied. If the reorder level is too high, you will generally have surplus inventories, which you might not even realize under certain circumstances (see the right side of Figure 6.13).

Inventory Turnover

Inventory turnover is another factor that influences the amount of safety stock. The frequency of inventory turnover is an important key figure in warehouse management. You can calculate it by item, material group, material, type of storage, and so on.

Inventory turnover = goods issue / year (in quantity or value) / average inventory

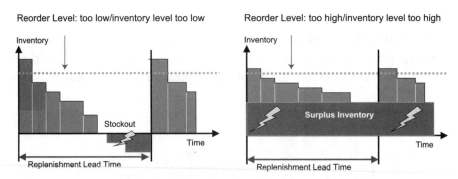

Figure 6.13 Influence of the Reorder Level: Stockouts on the Left and Surplus Inventories on the Right

If the inventory turnover is high, the items in the warehouse must be issued and replaced often. This indicates that on a regular basis, sales volumes are high. In this case, you must increase the amount of safety stock, because when there is a high rate of inventory turnover, the probability of a stockout increases.

Range of Coverage

The range of coverage or the overage time is another key figure that influences safety stock.

Period time = period stock / (average goods issue / number of periods)

Monthly range of coverage = average monthly inventory / monthly requirements

The range of coverage indicates the number of periods that the stock will most likely cover—when you consider current requirements.

If the stock will have as long a range of coverage as possible because the replenishment lead times are lengthy, the amount of safety stock must increase. If there is no default value, then a long range of coverage usually indicates a high level of safety stock because consumption is too low, which has resulted in a long range of coverage.

6.5.1 Standard Safety Stock Planning in mySAP ERP

mySAP ERP provides two types of buffers that can be scheduled to examine uncertainties in requirements trends:

- ▶ Quantity buffer
  - ▹ Safety stock

- ▹ Partially available safety stock
- ▹ Dynamic safety stock
- ▸ Time buffer
  - ▹ Requirements lead time
  - ▹ The following sections examine these two buffers in more detail.

Safety Stocks in mySAP ERP

Safety stock defines the quantity that is to satisfy unexpectedly high requirements in the coverage period. The purpose of having safety stock is to avoid the occurrence of stockouts.

With manual reorder point planning, you can enter a value in the material master record; however, this entered value is only for information purposes. With automatic reorder point planning and with stochastic MRP, the system automatically defines and adjusts the value within the context of the forecast.

When inventory turnover falls short—that is, when it falls below the reorder point—the system reserves the quantity for MRP by generating a planning file entry. The reorder point is significant only for reorder point planning. With manual reorder point planning, you enter the reorder point manually. With automatic reorder point planning, the system automatically defines the reorder point within the context of calculating the forecast.

If the material master record is recreated, you must manually enter the reorder point in the material master: **MRP 1** view, **MRP procedure** field group, **Reorder Point** field (see Figure 6.14). This must be done even if the system will later overwrite the entry. In this case, you can also perform MRP for a material if no forecast has been performed.

From the SAP menu, select **Logistics · Materials Management · Material Master · Material · Change · Immediately**, and then select the **MRP 1** tab.

The normal amount of safety stock depends on the service level specified in the material master record (**MRP 2** view), not on the accuracy of the forecast. The more accurate the forecast is, the smaller the amount of safety stock can be. Table 6.9 shows that customer requirements can be met at 50% without safety stock.

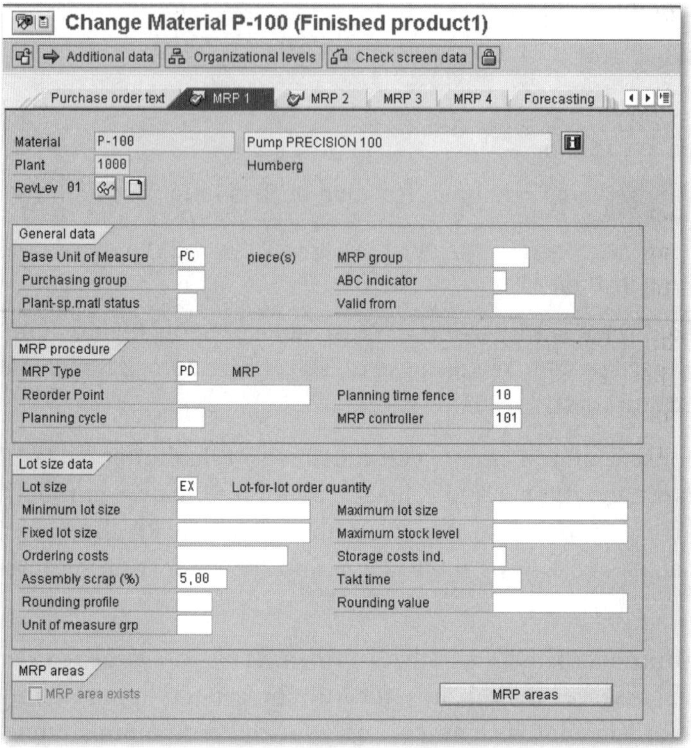

Figure 6.14 MRP 1 View in the mySAP ERP Material Master

Figure 6.31 shows that it's almost impossible to cover customer requirements at 100%. The safety factor describes the relationship between the accuracy of the forecast and the service level.

If the replenishment lead time is W times larger than the forecast period, the mean absolute deviation (MAD) is recalculated for this period. MAD is a key figure for the accuracy of the forecast (see Chapter 4, *Demand Planning and Forecasting*).

> $SS = r * \sqrt{W*MAD}$
> $W = delivery\ time\ in\ days\ /\ forecast\ period\ in\ days$
> $SS = safety\ stock$
> $R = safety\ factor$

For in-house production of the materials, the delivery time = *starting period + in-house production time + goods receipt processing time*. The entry for the delivery time is given in business days. The forecast period is read from the material master record and is also given in business days. For external production of the material, the delivery time = *goods receipt processing time +*

planned delivery time + goods receipt processing time. The delivery time is specified in calendar days. The forecast period is read from the material master record and is also provided in calendar days. Note that the calculation of safety stock can be affected by rounding operations.

You can enter the safety stock in the **MRP 2** view (**Net Requirements** field group, **Safety Stock** field). From the SAP menu, select **Logistics · Materials Management · Material Master · Material · Change · Immediately**, and then select the **MRP 2** tab.

You can enter a threshold for the safety stock. If the calculation of the safety stock returns a value lower than this threshold,, the safety stock is automatically set to the minimum level. You can enter the threshold for the safety stock in the material master record (**MRP 2** view), under the **Net Requirements** field group, in the **Min. Safety** field.

Dynamic Safety Stock

The statistical range of coverage calculation helps you define a requirements-oriented — in other words, a dynamic — level of safety stock. Here "statistical" means that instead of using actual requirements, the average daily requirements for a given period are calculated.

The dynamic safety stock (Figure 6.15) is recalculated for each MRP element in the planning run and is completely available for the MRP controller and can be used in MRP.

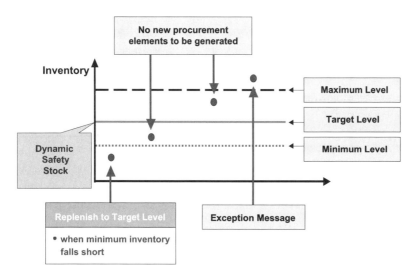

Figure 6.15 Dynamic Safety Stock (Source: SAP)

The planning run ensures that the available quantity does not fall below the minimum inventory level. Should that occur, it is replenished to at least the level of the target inventory level.

If the maximum inventory level is exceeded, the quantity is adjusted—as long as a fixed order suggestion is not involved. An exception message is issued for a fixed order suggestion.

The statistical range of coverage calculation typically refers to the concrete requirements of make to stock. 'Therefore, it can be used only for requirements that are listed in the requirements/stock list, the MRP list, or in the net or gross section. It cannot be used for requirements in other MRP sections, such as preplanning requirements, for example.

As shown in Figure 6.16, the range of coverage for dynamic safety stock is calculated on the basis of the average daily requirements and therefore automatically adjusts itself to changing requirements.

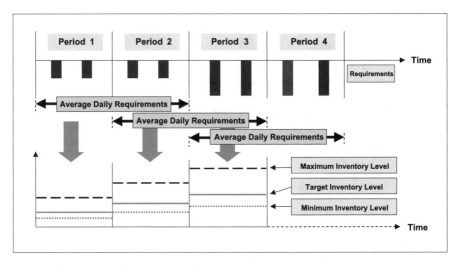

Figure 6.16 Dynamic Safety Stock and Range of Coverage Profile (Source: SAP)

The flow in mySAP ERP is as follows:

Step 1: Calculating the average daily requirements
The system calculates the average daily requirements based on the parameters set in the range of coverage profile.

You can set the parameters for calculating the average daily requirements in customizing: **SAP Implementation Guide · Logistics · Production · Require-**

ments **Planning**, and in the **Determine range of coverage** section (dynamic safety stock) in the range of coverage profile (see Figure 6.17).

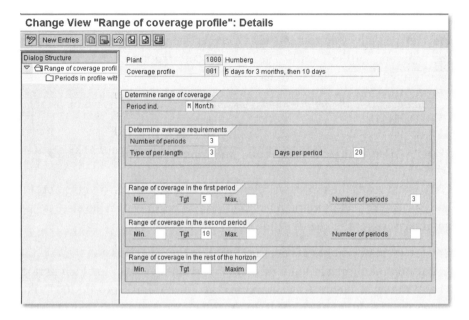

Figure 6.17 my SAP ERP Range of Coverage Profile—Customizing

▶ **Periods (month, week, or period in the planning calendar)**
The periods are calendar periods; they are calculated from the calendar start of the period. A week period, for example, is calculated from Monday to Sunday, while a month period is calculated from the first calendar day to the last calendar day of the month.

▶ **Number of periods** used to calculated the average daily requirements

▶ **Period lengths**
- ▸ *Work days* are defined using the factory calendar.
- ▸ *Calendar days* are defined by the Gregorian calendar.
- ▸ You can define *standard days* so that 20 days are always considered when calculating the monthly average.

From the parameters you set, the system determines the **number of days** that should be used as the basis for calculating the average daily requirements. For example, if you set "week" as the period, "standard days" for the period length (five days), and the value 2 as the number of periods, the result is 10 days. The combined requirements are spread over 10 days.

The system then calculates the **sum of requirements** that fall in this period. This calculation always uses all the requirements of the current period, even if the planning run occurs when part of the period lies in the past. For example, if the planning run occurs in the middle of a month, the calculation of the average daily requirements also includes the requirements scheduled at the beginning of the month. The average daily requirements can be calculated using the following formula:

Requirements in the defined number of periods / number of days within the total period length

Step 2: Calculating the minimum, maximum, and target inventory levels

The system reads the ranges of coverage set in the range of coverage profile and calculates the minimum, maximum, and target inventory levels. The target inventory level is the dynamic safety stock.

You can maintain **ranges of coverage for up to three periods** and then set different minimum, maximum, and target ranges of coverage for each period. The example in Figure 6.18 shows a range of coverage profile (001) that allows for two different intervals. Interval 1 shows a safety range of coverage of five days for the first three months. After the first three months, the safety range of coverage is 10 days.

In addition to the ranges of coverage for the three periods, you can also define **deviating ranges of coverage** for specific periods. It is a good idea to do this if you need to schedule a higher level of safety stock at certain times—perhaps in the months before Christmas because of the increased demand over the holiday.

During the planning run, the system checks for date-related ranges of coverage for the dates for the MRP elements (requirements, plan orders, and so on). If it finds date-related ranges of coverage, it uses the deviating values. If there are no date-related ranges of coverage for the dates, the system uses the values that you maintained for the three periods.

The system calculates the inventory for each period using the following formulas:

*Minimum inventory level: average daily requirements * minimum range of coverage*

*Target inventory level (= dynamic safety stock): average daily requirements * target range of coverage*

*Maximum inventory level: average daily requirements * maximum range of coverage*

You assign the range of coverage to the material in the material master record (in the **MRP 2** view, go to the **Net Requirements Calculation** field group, and then the **Range of Coverage** field). From the SAP menu, select **Logistics · Materials Management · Material Master · Material · Change · Immediately**, and then select the **MRP 2** tab.

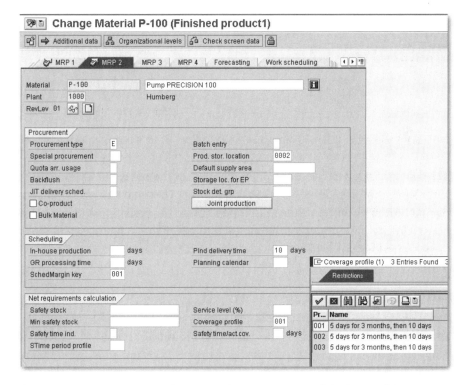

Figure 6.18 mySAP ERP Material Master, MRP 2—Assignment of the Range of Coverage Profile

Step 3: Checking the MRP elements

During each planning run, the system checks every MRP element (requirements, plan orders, and so on) to see if the available quantity is below the minimum inventory level.

If a requirement consumes more than the minimum inventory level, the system generates a procurement proposal and measures the procurement quantity so that the available quantity is once again at the target level (the level of the dynamic safety stock).

If the quantity exceeds the maximum inventory level, it is adjusted accordingly for non-fixed procurement proposals. An exception message is issued for a fixed procurement proposal.

Step 4: Calculating the dynamic safety stock

Table 6.3 provides an example of a dynamic safety stock calculation.

Range of coverage	Days	Daily requirements	Inventory (days * daily requirements)	Available quantity	Order
Maximum	8	18 units	144 units	62 units	46 units (replenish to the target)
Target	6		108 units		
Minimum	4		72 units		

Table 6.3 Sample Calculation of the Dynamic Safety Stock in the Range of Coverage Profile

The dynamic safety stock is considered as part of the net requirements calculation; it is not scheduled as a gross quantity. The quantity of an existing planned order is therefore increased depending on availability. If the warehouse already has enough of the material to cover the dynamic safety stock, the system does not generate an additional planned order.

Safety Time

As illustrated in Figure 6.19, the safety time or actual range of coverage guarantees that the warehouse stock can cover the requirements of a specified number of days. It therefore serves as a time buffer and thus supplements the safety stock, which forms a quantity-based buffer.

The requirements are moved up (in a simulated manner) by the specified number of days. The stock receipts generated for these requirements in the planning run are scheduled earlier by the same number of days.

Figure 6.19 The Safety Time Guarantees Limited Requirements Coverage (Source: SAP)

An example: The planner specifies two days as the safety time (actual range of coverage). The requirements date is January 31. During the planning run, the system simulates moving up the requirements date by two days and generates a planned order with an ending date of January 29. But the actual requirements date (January 31) is not changed.

To use the safety time in mySAP ERP, from the SAP menu, select **Logistics · Materials Management · Material Master Data · Material · Change · Immediately**, and then the **MRP 2** tab. You must set the Safety Time indicator in the material master (**MRP 2** view, **Net requirements calculation** field group, **Safety time ind.** field) to determine if the safety time should be considered for all requirements or only for primary requirements.

You must also enter the number of work days that the requirements should be moved up in the **Safety time/act.cov.** field in the material master (**MRP 2** view, **Net requirements calculation** field group, **Safety time** field).

In certain periods, you might have to plan with an actual range of coverage that differs from the one you specified in the material master. To balance seasonal demand fluctuations, you can use the period profile for freely definable periods to specify a different actual range of coverage than the one indicated in the material master (see Figure 6.20).

You must then assign the profile in the material master (**MRP 2** view, **Net requirements calculation** field group, **STime period profile** field).

To reach this step, go to the SAP menu and select **Requirements Planning · Environment · Current Settings · Define STime Period Profile/Actual Range of Coverage**.

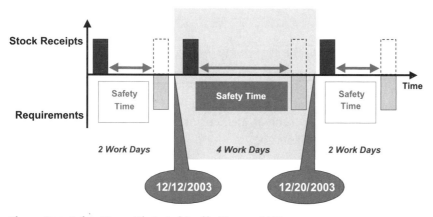

Figure 6.20 Safety Time with Period Profile (Source: SAP)

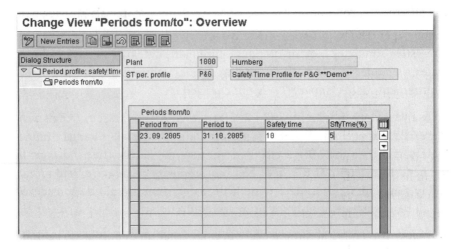

Figure 6.21 mySAP ERP Customizing—Safety Time Profile

You can also use the period profile to define a safety time that lasts less than one day. To do this, you must enter a percentage value in addition to the requirements lead time in the **SftyTme(%)** field (see Figure 6.21). The system then divides the daily requirements according to the percentage and brings these partial quantities forward by one more day. If you want to define a requirements lead time of 2.2 days, enter 2 (days) in the **Safety time** field and 20 (percent) in the **SftyTme(%)** field. The system then splits the daily requirements of 100 items with a requirements date of Sept. 9, 2005 as follows (see Table 6.4):

Requirements date moved ahead	Quantity
09/06/05	20 items
09/07/05	80 items

Table 6.4 Splitting the Daily Requirements (100 Items) into Two Modified Dates

The disadvantage of this procedure is that a procurement element is generated for each requirement. The system combines the required procurement quantities into one procurement element only if you work with weeks or months for the requirements.

Safety Stock Available for MRP

For every requirement that leads to a shortfall of the inventoy available for MRP, requirements planning generates a procurement element to procure the difference. From the SAP menu, select **Logistics · Materials Management · Material Master · Material · Change · Immediately**, and then select the **MRP 2** tab.

You can define the level of the safety stock in the **MRP 2** view (**Net requirements calculation** field group, **Safety stock** field) of the material master for each plant or in each MRP segment of each MRP area. The safety stock reduces the quantity available to MRP.

Requirements planning replenishes the safety stock with stock receipts in the event of a shortfall, as indicated in Figure 6.22. The same applies if the safety stock falls short by a very small amount in relation to its level. This type of safety stock is independent of the requirements quantities. It therefore has a static nature. The safety stock is displayed in its own line in the list of current requirements and stocks and in the MRP list.

You can define the portion of the safety stock available to MRP for each MRP group in the **Customizing**, **Requirements Planning** node and the **Defining the Safety Stock Availability** step (see Figure 6.23). A percentage is defined in relation to the level of the safety stock indicated in the material master data. In SAP customizing, select **Implementation Guide · Production · Requirements Planning · Planning · MRP Calculation · Set Range of Coverage Profile**.

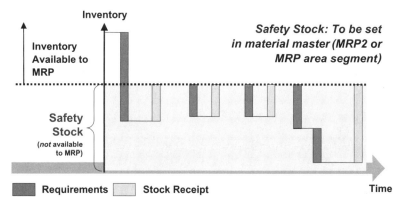

Figure 6.22 Example of Safety Stocks Available and Unavailable to MRP and the Related Stock Receipts (Source: SAP)

A new procurement proposal is generated only if the available portion of the safety stock is insufficient. The procurement proposal brings the level up to that of the safety stock, as shown in Figure 6.24. Suggested orders are not generated for very small shortfalls.

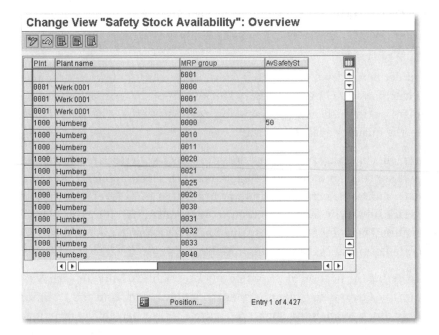

Figure 6.23 mySAP ERP Customizing—Safety Stock Availability

This approach reduces the administrative effort, and all planning become less intensive. This means of making safety stock partially available is a tremendous advantage in inventory management, because it enables companies to use safety stock more effectively and thereby reduce inventories.

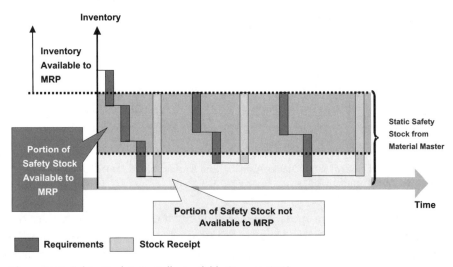

Figure 6.24 Safety Stock Is Partially Available (Source: SAP)

6.5.2 Optimization Potentials in Safety Stocks

To manage safety stocks as efficiently as possible, consider the following significant opportunities for optimization:

Complex and involved master data maintenance for safety stock
Safety stock is entered in mySAP ERP for each material master record. The planner often has to maintain several hundred material master records. However, the work doesn't end there. The safety stock level requires constant monitoring and, if necessary, must be modified. The multiplicity of master data causes this work.

To alleviate the problem to some extent, material groups are created. The safety stock in each material group is identical, or even set at the same level for all materials; however, these approaches do not adequately reflect a real-life situation. Usually, the amount of safety stock created is too high for materials for which a shortfall had to be posted, or for materials that the planner regards as endangered, or, in the worst case, for an entire material group.

Complex and involved maintenance of the reorder point
A procurement order is triggered when the reorder point is reached. The safety stock should cover any uncertainty about the replenishment lead time. But because two different master data fields must be maintained, monitored, and possibly changed here, the maintenance effort involved increases exponentially for the planner. Therefore, values are often simply combined in one field. For example, only the safety stock that contains the reorder point is maintained. The safety stock is therefore higher than necessary, as is the average stock.

Static safety stock
Safety stock is static. It does not automatically change over time, only when the planner adjusts it. If the planner adjusts the safety stock, this adjustment affects the present and the future. But in the future, it cannot adjust itself (i.e., the safety stock is never dynamic) and it does not work with a dynamic requirements situation. The requirements change, but the safety stock remains the same and therefore it cannot handle short-term and significant requirement fluctuations. Consequently, stockouts result.

Assuming the normal distribution as a basis
The normal distribution of the requirements is used as the basis for calculating safety stock. But normal distribution is not always the case in daily work.

The effort it takes the MRP controller to determine the distribution type is usually too great. Therefore, there is always some uncertainty when calculating the safety stock. We recommend that you calculate the distribution type at least once a year, based on historical data.

Forecast quality

In order to determine your optimal safety stock level, the quality of your forecast must be high. If the forecast is poor, this has a negative affect on the safety stock calculation. The safety stock may not be able to cushion the uncertainties of the market. The first step is to increase the quality of the forecast. An important factor here is the selection of the correct forecast procedure. The choice of a specific procedure depends on the regularity of the requirement. Please see Chapter 4, *Demand Planning and Forecasting*, for more detailed information on sales planning and forecasts.

Transparency of costs

Safety stock calculation includes the selection of the service level. And the service level, in turn, depends on the costs of storage and stockouts. On a day-to-day basis, it's difficult to even determine the storage costs. And in general, you can only estimate stockout costs. Here, too, it's important for you to determine the costs regularly and carefully to increase the quality of your safety stock calculation.

6.5.3 Optimization with SAP APO

Because safety stocks are generally required for various production plants or distribution centers, you can select a safety stock method for each location production in the product master.

SAP APO provides two methods for planning safety stock:

▶ Standard safety stock planning
▶ Enhanced safety stock planning

In the standard method, the planner must specify certain information to calculate the safety stock. In the enhanced method, however, the safety stock is determined automatically based on the service level, the current requirements forecast, and historical data.

The standard method rest completely on the experience of the planner. With the enhanced method, the system suggests the amount of safety stock based on scientifically proven algorithms.

Standard safety stock planning is used to build up warehouse inventory according to the safety stock values that you set based on your past experience with the location product master. You can select from various methods. Unlike enhanced planning, this approach does not consider a forecast error. The safety stock value is static and time-dependent.

The lowest, flat line in the upper illustration in Figure 6.25 shows an absolute safety stock. It is static and describes the same level for all periods that follow.

The middle curve in the lower illustration shows a relative safety stock. It is defined in days (target range of coverage) and the same amount of material is always procured, depending on the requirements situation, to cover the target range of coverage, say, 10 days. In other words, orders are always placed to fill the inventory for 10 days.

As shown in the upper illustration of Figure 6.26, the enhanced method first creates the deviation bandwidth between the actual demand (the angular line) and the requirements forecast (the curve in the middle). The second step (shown in the lower illustration) adds the safety stock requirements to the overall requirements, in line with mean absolute deviation (MAD). The safety stock is therefore dynamically adjusted to the MAD (upper curve).

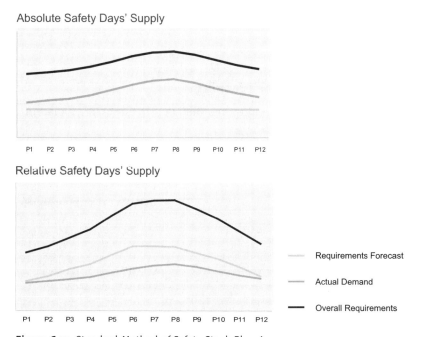

Absolute Safety Days' Supply

Relative Safety Days' Supply

Requirements Forecast

Actual Demand

Overall Requirements

Figure 6.25 Standard Method of Safety Stock Planning

Determining the Deviation Bandwidth, MAD

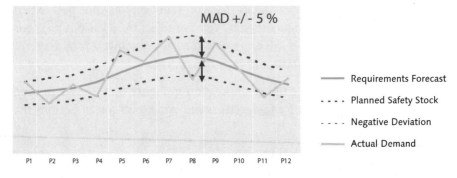

Dynamic Adjustment of the Safety Stock to
Current Mean Absolute Deviation, MAD

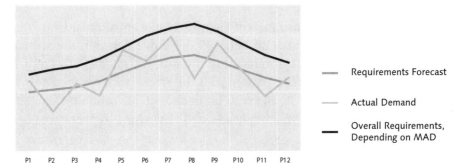

Figure 6.26 Enhanced Method of Safety Stock Planning

6.5.4 Standard Safety Stock Planning

You can change the safety stock values manually on the interactive planning desktop in Supply Network Planning.

The standard methods are distinguished by the consideration of time and are based on safety stock information that the planner enters into the system:

	Time-independent (static)	Time-dependent (dynamic)
Safety stock	SB—safety stock	MB—safety stock (time-dependent maintenance)
Safety range	SZ—safety range	MZ—safety range (time-dependent maintenance)

Table 6.5 Standard Methods of Safety Stock Planning in SAP APO

	Time-independent (static)	Time-dependent (dynamic)
Maximum from safety stock and safety range	SM—Maximum from safety stock and safety range	MM—Maximum from safety stock and safety range (time-dependent maintenance)

Table 6.5 Standard Methods of Safety Stock Planning in SAP APO (cont.)

The following standard methods are available (see also Table 6.5):

▶ SB—Safety stock from the location product master

▶ SZ—Safety range from the location product master

▶ SM—Maximum from SB and SZ from the location product master

▶ MB—Safety stock (time-dependent maintenance)

▶ MZ—Safety range (time-dependent maintenance)

▶ MM—Maximum from SB and SZ (time-dependent maintenance)

SB, SZ, and SM are static methods. Their parameters are set independently of time in the location's product master (**Lot Size** tab). MB, MZ, and MM are dynamic methods. Their parameters are set depending on time during interactive Supply Network Planning (SNP) safety stock planning.

You can therefore define the safety stock with a safety range of coverage or as a maximum from the safety stock and the safety range. If you create a maximum, you can adjust the amount of safety stock dynamically to the flow of requirements as long as it does not fall below the defined level of safety stock.

Static Methods in SAP APO

SB—Safety stock from the location product master
This method is used in the Production Planning (PP) area if the **Safety Stock** and **SB Methods** fields are maintained in the location product master.

From the SAP APO menu, select **SAP APO · Master Data · Product · Product**. In the product master, select the **Lot Size** tab and enter **MB** in the **Safety Stock Method** field (see Figure 6.27).

You must also set a key figure (see Figure 6.28) in **Model/Planning Version Management**—in the **Take Safety Stock into Account** field of the plan version in the **PP/DS** area. You can call this screen by following menu path **APO · Master Data · Planning Version Management · Model and Version Management**.

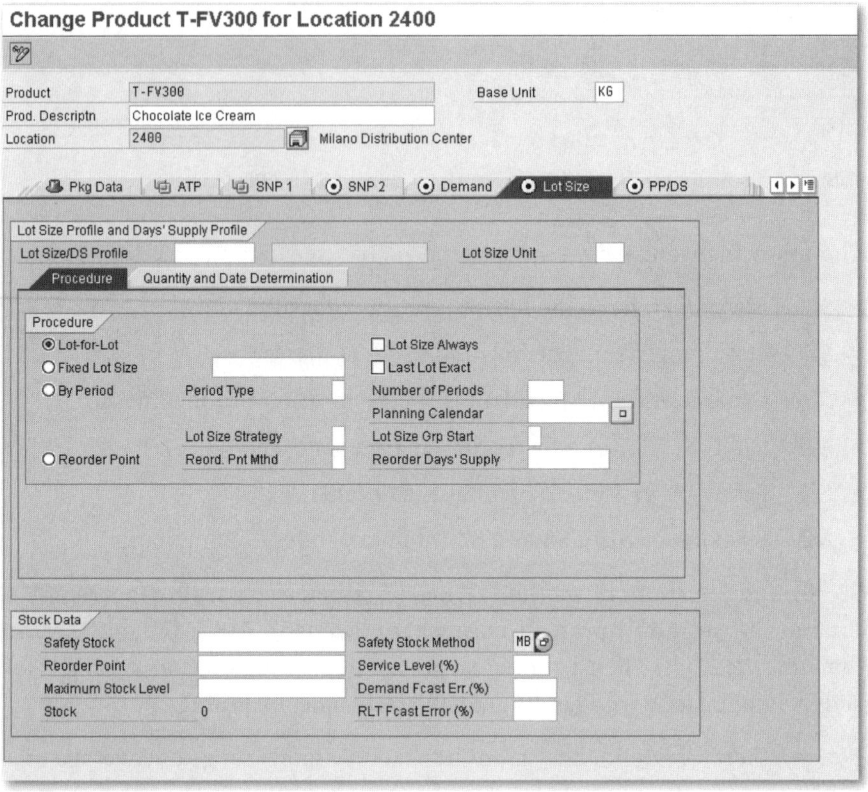

Figure 6.27 SAP APO Product Master—Safety Stock Method

The safety stock is the quantity that should cover unexpectedly high requirements in the coverage period. To cover requirements, planning creates an order in the amount of the safety stock. The starting date of the plan order is the current date, provided the strategy settings allow this. The system does not consider the offset from the strategy settings. The order creation takes the resource capacities into account if the strategy calls for it. You can generate an excess coverage alert during safety stock planning.

SZ—Safety range from the location product master
You must maintain the **Safety Days' Supply and Safety Stock Method** fields if you wish to consider using this standard method. Select **SZ** as the **Safety Stock Method**.

The safety days' supply is the number of business days between the availability date of the newly created stock receipt element and the requirements date of a requirements element.

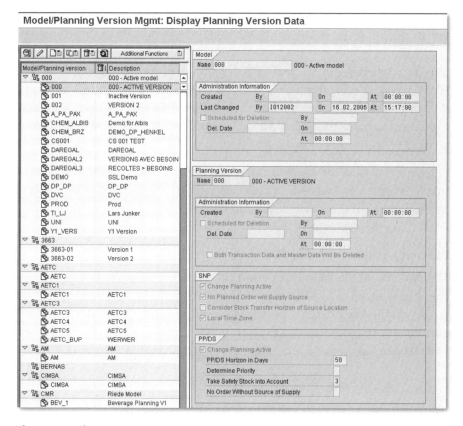

Figure 6.28 Planning Version Management in SAP APO

In mySAP ERP, only whole days can be specified for the safety days' supply. But in SAP APO, you can specify fractions of days. Two decimal points are permitted. For example, you can enter 0.5 days for 12 hours or 0.33 days for 8 hours (more exactly: 7 hours, 55 minutes, and 12 seconds). A business (work) day corresponds to 24 hours.

The location's production calendar serves as the basis for scheduling. During planning, the requirements elements are pushed into the past (virtually) by the amount of the safety days' supply. This situation is used as a basis for generating orders.

Periodic lot sizes are based on the original dates of the requirements. The safety days' supply is not used to distribute the requirements over the periods. But the generated requirements coverage is changed by the amount of the safety days' supply. However, for technical reasons, planning with continuous requirements considers the safety days' supply during the distribution of the requirements across the periods.

SM — Maximum from SB and SZ from the location product master

PP/DS planning with this safety stock method uses the SB and SZ methods. No "maximum" is created from both procedures. To execute these methods, you must maintain the **Safety Stock, Safety Days' Supply**, and **Safety Stock Method** fields.

In technical terms, the safety stock is determined first, and the safety days' supply is considered second, because the safety stock should also be adjusted by the amount of the safety days' supply.

Dynamic Methods in SAP APO

The dynamic methods analyze period-related safety ranges and safety stocks. The data is mapped in SNP as key figures. In PP/DS, the dynamic methods can access the key figures if the **SNP Planning Area** is specified in **SAP APO Customizing** of PP/DS under **Display Global Parameters and Default Values**. The planning area must contain the key figures shown in Figure 6.29.

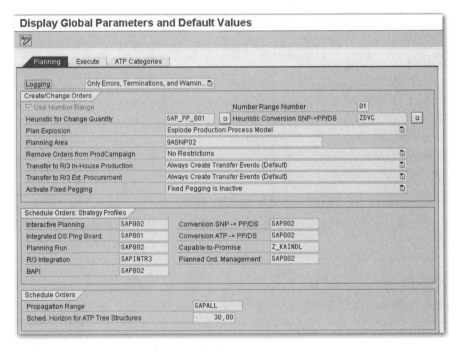

Figure 6.29 SAP APO Customizing — Global Parameters

MB — Safety stock (time-dependent maintenance)

Safety stock is calculated here much like it is in the SB method, but the period-dependent value is used instead of the **Safety Stock** field from the location master data.

If the dynamic safety stock in a period is greater than in the previous period, a virtual requirement that represents the quantity difference is generated. An appropriate stock receipt element covers the virtual requirement in the planning run.

If the dynamic safety stock decreases from one period to the next, fewer stock receipt elements are created for the requirement elements in the period with the smaller amount of safety stock—corresponding to the quantity difference. In the product view, you can see that the requirements are partially covered with the excess safety stock.

Figure 6.30 illustrates the dynamic safety stock in SNP interactive planning, in the **Safety Stock (Planned)** field. Follow menu path **SAP APO · Supply Network Planning · Planning · Interactive Supply Network Planning**.

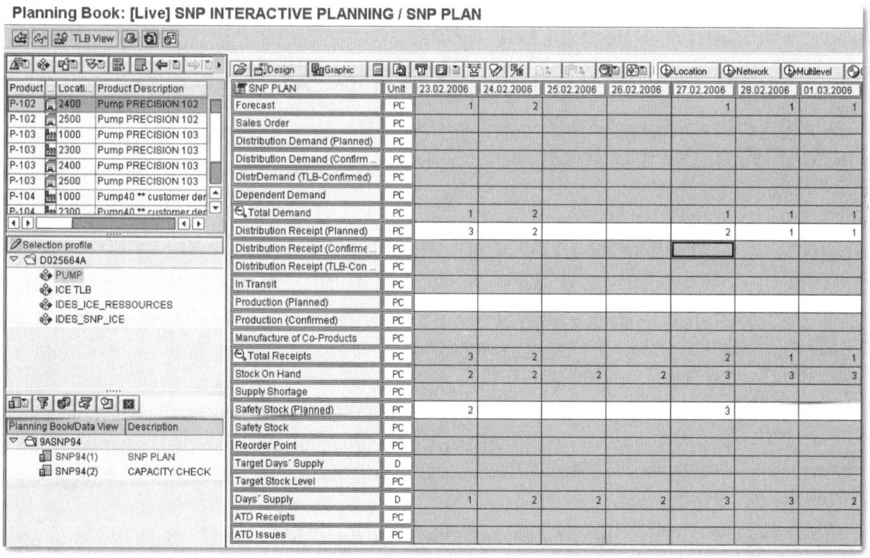

Figure 6.30 SAP APO Interactive Supply Network Planning (SNP) with Key Figures for Dynamic Safety Stock

In the figure, you can see a sample requirement for 1 unit on 02/23/06 in the **Forecast** row (week 8), and an entry for 2 units in the **Safety Stock (Planned)**

row. And you can see the related stock receipt in the **Distribution Receipt (Planned)** row: 3 (1+2).

In week 9, the requirements are 3, and the safety stock has increased by 1 to a total of 3. Therefore, you now see a stock receipt of 2 (1 + 2). The **Stock On Hand** level is now 3.

MZ — Safety days' supply (time-dependent maintenance)

The safety stock here is determined much like it is in the SZ method, but the period-dependent safety ranges are used instead of the safety ranges from the location product master. Execution is similar to that of the SZ method, but the requirements of a period are moved by the period-dependent safety days' supply.

MM — Maximum from MB and MZ (time-dependent maintenance)

Much like safety stock method SM, this method executes methods MB and MZ after each other. PP/DS planning first considers the MB method and then the MZ method.

Using Standard Methods in SAP APO

You enter the relevant data in the **Safety Stock**, **Safety Stock Method** (available methods: SB, SZ, SM, MZ, MB, and MM), and **Safety Range** fields in the **Lot Size** tab in the location product master.

If you want to use methods MZ, MB, or MM, you must use the SNP standard planning area **9ASNP05** and standard planning session **9ASNP_SSP** (or a planning area and planning session based on them) that contain key figures **9ASAFETY — Safety Stock** (planned) and **9ASVTTY — Safety Days' Supply** (see Figure 6.30).

If necessary, you can also modify the safety stock values after the planning run on the interactive planning desktop in Supply Network Planning.

Advantages and Disadvantages of the Standard Methods

The standard methods are relatively uncomplicated algorithms that planners will find easy to understand and use. Planners can easily trace the results and are usually already familiar with the methods.

To use the standard methods, planners must store the appropriate parameters in the material master data. If one planner is responsible for a relatively large number of materials, a huge amount of maintenance is required. This amount is difficult to estimate because the parameters themselves must be monitored and adjusted from time to time.

In reality, it's impossible to monitor or maintain the parameters for individual materials. Instead, it's easier to work with material groups and define the same parameters for all the materials in a group. If a stockout occurs, the planner resets (upwardly) all the parameters (the reorder points or safety stocks, in this case) of the entire material group. A hidden increase in stock levels is thereby preprogrammed.

An additional disadvantage is that the safety stocks depend entirely on the planner's estimate. This approach is not supported by the IT system.

6.5.5   Enhanced Safety Stock Planning

The standard methods are solely based on the experience of the planner, whereas with the enhanced methods, the system suggests the amount of safety stock. The enhanced methods are based on the following assumptions:

▶ The requirements are regular, which means they are present in almost every period. The requirement quantities are significantly larger than zero, or they do not fluctuate too wildly. The following rule of thumb applies:

Standard deviation / average value < 0.5

You can assume that there will be a normal distribution of forecast errors. This assumption usually does not apply to spare parts, because they usually have sporadic requirements.

▶ Stockouts can be resupplied later. In other words, no requirements are lost.

▶ Upstream links in the supply chain can always supply downstream links completely. Planners can take alternate measures to avoid potential stockouts that are not covered by safety stock (rush transports, for example).

▶ All uncertainties within the supply chain are statistically independent of each other.

▶ The average value of a forecast error is practically zero. For the most part, overestimates and underestimates counterbalance each other. The forecast procedures in use therefore may not show any significant, systematic error.

If one or more of the assumptions noted above do not apply at all or apply only somewhat in your scenario, the calculated safety stocks can deviate from the correct values. As a result, the actual service level can deviate from the target service level.

Safety stock planning in Supply Network Planning therefore allows you to consider the supply side of your supply chain. In other words, you have the option not only to consider the forecast and actual requirements, but also to consider the deviations between the order and the actual delivery.

Time-independent warehouse stock generally depends on the following elements:

1. **Method of safety stock planning**
   The target service level is based either on the percentage of fulfilled orders or on the volume of fulfilled orders. For example, if you want to define the target safety stock as a percentage of fulfilled orders, a partial fulfillment is unacceptable and is regarded as an unfulfilled order. But the target warehouse stock is calculated based on the assumption that back orders can cover unfilled orders so that no sales are lost and the requirements are regular.

   The replenishment procedure in use does not influence safety stock planning. The replenishment procedure is set in the location product master. If you select a reorder point method, the reorder point quantity is calculated based on the target days' supply from the location product master. If you select an order cycle method, the target days' supply is regarded as an order cycle.

2. **Forecast requirements and historical variability of the requirements**
   The requirement for a product in a location is the total amount of the primary requirements in the location and the secondary requirements in all downstream locations.

   Calculation of the safety stock takes into account the derived requirements variability from demand planning and past forecasts (forecast error of the requirements). The system also considers the forecast error of the requirements that you might have defined in the location product master.

   During the creation of the safety stock for finished products, safety stock planning follows the requirements from the location (such as a distribution center) to the customer level. The system considers incoming quota arrangements.

During the creation of the safety stock for components, the system calculates requirements based on the explosion of the BOM components and the primary requirements of the finished products.

3. **Expected replenishment lead time and historical variability of the replenishment lead time**

The replenishment lead time (RLT) of a product in a location represents the amount of time needed for replenishing the product from an upstream safety stock location. Safety stock calculation considers the expected replenishment lead time based on the production time, the time needed to process goods issues, transportation time, and the time needed to process goods receipts. In addition, the system also considers the variability of the replenishment lead time determined in the past.

Safety stock planning considers the replenishment path from the location where the safety stock is stored up to the next upstream safety stock location. The critical replenishment path is the path with the longest replenishment time because the safety stock in one location should cover the variability or the replenishment lead time in the worst-case scenario.

The variability of the replenishment lead time (forecast error of the RLT) is calculated on the basis of two of the key figures that you defined. One key figure is the RLT planned in the past; the other is the actual RLT. The system also considers the forecast error of the RLT that you might have defined in the location product master.

Safety stock is calculated for each period. It is planned only for a location's products.

Determining the Service Level

The starting point of determining the service level is the service level that you should maintain by carrying the amount of safety stock you have calculated. You can categorize it as follows, depending on the business process:

▶ **Stockout-oriented (alpha service level)**
The service level percentage states that no stockout is expected in x % of the periods within the planning period.

▶ **Stockout-oriented (beta service level)**
The service level percentage states that x % of the expected total customer requirements can be satisfied within the planning period.

Table 6.6 contains an example for calculating the stockout or occurrence of a stockout in enhanced safety stock planning in SAP APO.

Period	1	2	3	4	5	6	7	8	9	10
Expected requirements	100	100	100	100	100	100	100	100	100	100
Stockout	0	0	0	0	0	10	0	0	0	10
Occurrence of a stockout	–	–	–	–	–	X	–	–	–	X

Table 6.6 Sample Calculation of a Stockout in Enhanced Safety Stock Planning in SAP APO

The formula for calculating the stockout:

Total of stockouts: 20 -> beta service level:
1 – (20 / 1000) = 98%

The formula for calculating the occurrence of a stockout:

Total of stockout occurrences: 2 -> alpha service level:
1 – (2 / 10) = 80%

To decide what service level to use, determine if subsequent delivery of a stockout involves stockout-dependent or stockout-independent costs. If the majority of the costs of a subsequent delivery are stockout-independent (fixed) costs, we recommend an alpha service level. If the majority of the costs of a subsequent delivery are stockout-dependent (variable), we recommend a beta service level.

Determining Forecast Quality

Along with service level, forecast quality is important for the calculation of safety stock. You can consider a forecast error on the requirements side and on the supply side. Use the descriptions of key figures in Table 6.7 as a basis for your calculations.

Requirements Side	Supply Side
Key figure for the planned requirements quantity	Key figure for the planned procurement time
Key figure for the actual requirements quantity	Key figure for the actual procurement time

Table 6.7 Key Figures for Determining the Forecast Error

The forecast error is calculated by determining the plan vs. actual deviation of the related key figures. The standard plan vs. actual deviation is interpreted as the forecast error. With this approach, a forecast error is determined from the historical data and assumed for future forecasts. To properly deal with the dynamics of future processes, it helps to interpret the forecast error as a relative error. In other words, the relationship of the forecast error and the forecast (variation coefficient) is recorded—instead of just the forecast error. The example in Table 6.8 illustrates this approach.

If the forecast error does not depend on the forecast, an increasing forecast leads to the unexpected result that the level of safety stock goes down— because the forecast error decreases in relation to the forecast. A relative forecast error therefore makes more sense than a constant forecast error in a dynamic environment.

Period	1	2	3	4	5
Requirements forecast	100	1,000	1,000	100	100
Forecast error if the standard deviation is constant	10	10	10	10	10
Forecast error if the variation coefficient is constant	10	100	100	10	10

Table 6.8 Calculating the Forecast Error

If a procurement forecast error exists (forecast error of the replenishment lead time), the requirements forecast error is adjusted with the assumption that the two forecast errors are independent of each other.

You can also enter the requirements forecast error and the replenishment lead time directly into the location product master. We recommend direct entry in the following cases:

▶ No historical data exists (because a new product is involved, for example).

▶ The scope of the historical data is so small that you cannot calculate a statistically significant forecast error.

▶ The forecast error can be seen as a constant.

You can also use the forecast error to determine the accuracy of the forecast, the forecast error can also be calculated exactly. It describes the expected deviations between the forecast requirements quantity and the requirements quantity actually realized. The calculation is based on historical forecast quantities and actual quantities. The historical forecast error that you determine is projected onto future forecasts. It is referred to as a *mean absolute forecast error* or mean absolute deviation (*MAD*).

To properly deal with future forecasts, it helps to interpret the forecast errors as relative forecast errors. In other words, the relationship between the forecast error and the forecast is calculated, instead of just the forecast error. This relationship is called the *mean relative percentage forecast error*, mean relative deviation, variation coefficient, or mean absolute percentage error (*MAPE*). The relative (i.e., percentage) forecast error is weighted with the amount of the requirements forecast and is therefore converted into an absolute (i.e., number) forecast error.

Calculating the Safety Stock

Calculating the safety stock here follows the example of the AS (Alpha service level) policy, as shown in Table 6.9.

Service Level	Safety Factor	RLT	Relative Forecast Error	Safety Stock
50.01%	0.0003	1	100	0.04
80.00%	0.8416	1	100	119.02
90.00%	1.2816	1	100	181.24
95.00%	1.6449	1	100	232.62
98.00%	2.0537	1	100	290.44
99.00%	2.3263	1	100	329.00
99.50%	2.5758	1	100	364.28
99.90%	3.0903	1	100	437.03
99.99%	3.7191	1	100	525.96

Table 6.9 Calculating the Safety Stock

The result is the following formula for calculating the safety stock:

$$SS = k * \sigma_{rel} * \sqrt{\lambda + 1}$$

Assuming that the forecast error and the replenishment lead time remain constant (a constant of k and σ), a decreasing forecast error affects the safety stock directly. It is expressed in a restatement of the formula:

$$\sigma_{rel} = SS / k * \sqrt{\lambda + 1} \quad \sigma_{rel} = SS / constant$$

Figure 6.31 illustrates the results. A forecast error change results in a proportional safety stock change. Lowering the forecast error by 20% also lowers the amount of safety stock by 20%.

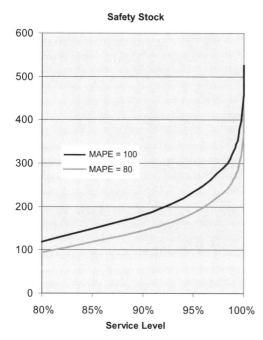

Figure 6.31 Example of the Effect of the Forecast Error on Safety Stock

▶ **Inventory policy**
The inventory policy used in SNP requirements planning also has a significant influence on the algorithm for calculating the safety stock. Therefore, you must distinguish between two different inventory policies, as shown in Figure 6.32.

▶ **Order cycle policy** (black line)
An order decision is made depending on the time; procurement can be triggered only for all t periods.

▶ **Reorder point policy** (grey line)
A reorder point decision is made depending on the warehouse stock. In other words, procurement can be triggered if warehouse stock goes below a specific level, s (reorder point).

Four model-based safety stock methods with model support result from both interpretations of the service level:

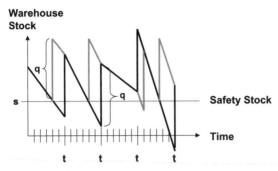

Figure 6.32 Example of Inventory Management with an Order Cycle Policy (Black) and Reorder Point Policy (Gray) (Source: SAP)

	Order Cycle Policy	Reorder Point Policy
Alpha service level	AT	AS
Beta service level	BT	BS

Table 6.10 Enhanced Safety Stock Methods in SAP APO

The preconditions for the use of these methods include the following:

▶ The requirements trend of the product is regular (in contrast to sporadic requirements).

▶ Stockouts are delivered subsequently: as in a back-order case (as opposed to a lost sales case).

In the context of these preconditions, safety stocks can be calculated at any point in the supply chain or for each period of the planning stage.

The workflow of a safety stock method in SAP APO is as follows:

▶ From the SAP APO menu, select **SAP APO · Master Data · Product · Product**, and go to the product master. Select the required safety stock method in the **Lot Size** tab of the **Safety Stock Method** field. The following methods are available for safety stock planning: **AT, AS, BT,** and **BS**.

▶ Enter the service level for the location product for which you are planning in the **Service Level (%)** field. The interpretation of the value entered here depends on the safety stock method you have selected.

▶ If the relative forecast error is almost constant, or if historical plan versus actual data is unavailable, you can enter an estimate of the relative forecast error in the location product master data. Enter the forecast error in the **Forecast Error Requirements (%)** field and the replenishment lead time in the **Forecast Error RLT (%)** field. You can calculate such a forecast error estimate with this formula:

*Sigma_D / Mue_P * 100%*

Sigma_D is the standard deviation of the time series (forecast value vs. actual value). The variable Mue_P is the average forecast value.

You should let the system calculate the forecast error from historical data if it is available.

▶ In the **Target Range** field, enter the number of days that the warehouse inventory and planned stock receipts should cover the known requirements of a product. If you select an order cycle method, this value is interpreted as an order cycle.

▶ In the APO easy access menu, select **Supply Network Planning · Planning · Safety Stock Planning**. The **Safety Stock Planning** screen is displayed.

You can see the large window of SAP safety stock planning in Figure 6.33 (first section) and Figure 6.34 (second section). The following paragraphs explain the important fields of both sections in order.

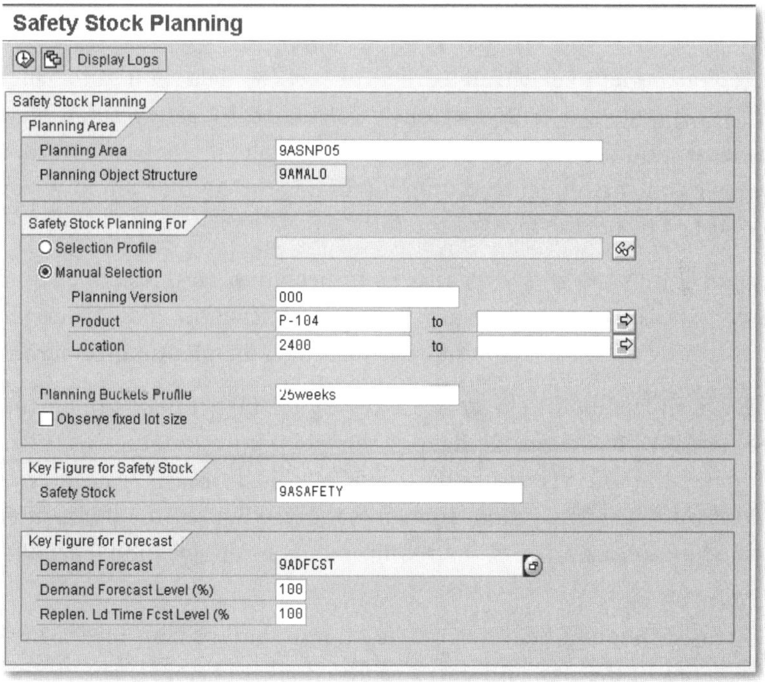

Figure 6.33 SAP APO: Enhanced Security Planning, Screen 1

The upper portion of the **Safety Stock Planning** screen includes the filter criteria for selecting the objects used in safety stock planning: planning area, planning object structure, and planning version.

▶ In the **Safety Stock Planning For** field group, enter the planning objects you want to plan for: which products should be planned in which locations.

▶ If you use safety stock method **BS**, you can use the **Observe fixed lot size** field to indicate whether the system should consider the fixed lot size in the location product master when determining the procurement quantities.

▶ In the **Safety Stock** field, select the key figure to store the results of safety stock planning (the calculated safety stock).

▶ In the **Demand Forecast** field, select the key figure that contains the forecast demand. (This is the demand that covers safety stock planning.) The key figure is normally **9ADFCST**, which must be assigned to planning object structure **9AMALO**.

▶ In the **Demand Forecast Level (%)** field, you can change the requirement forecast that you want to use to calculate the safety stock. For example, if you have information that the forecast in sales planning is too high or too low, you can increase or lower the level of the forecast.

▶ In the **Replenishment Lead Time Forecast Level (%)** field, you can change the replenishment lead time previously calculated by safety stock planning. You can find this value in the log. For example, if you have information that the replenishment lead time forecast is too high or too low, you can increase or lower the level of the forecast.

The lower portion of the window contains information on the sources used to calculate the uncertainties. Here too, you must first set the filter criteria to select the planning area, the planning structure, and the planning version.

▶ In the **Realized Demand** field, select a key figure that contains the actual realized demand. Based on the data of this key figure, safety stock planning valuates the uncertainty of past requirement forecasts. An entry in this field is optional. The system considers the key figure only if you have not defined a forecast error of the requirements in the location's product master.

▶ In the **Planned Demand** field, select a key figure that contains forecast figures generated in the past. An entry in this field is optional. The system considers the key figure only if you have not defined a forecast error of the requirements in the location product master.

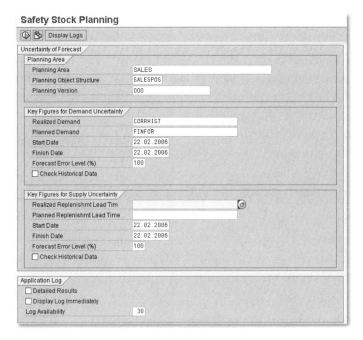

Figure 6.34 SAP APO: Enhanced Security Planning, Screen 2

▶ The *difference* between the realized and planned demand helps determine the variability of the demand forecast.

▶ In the **Start Date** and **Finish Date** fields, enter the period for which the forecast error should be calculated.

▶ If you assume that your forecast accuracy will improve in the future, you can enter a percentage in the **Forecast Error Level (%)** field that corresponds to the forecast level. For example, you can determine that the forecast error in the future will be only 80% of the past forecast error.

▶ If you activate the **Check Historical Data** flag, the system checks to see what periods of historical data are available from the specific key figure when calculating the forecast error in the specified period. The system then considers the historical data only after this period when calculating the forecast error.

▶ In the **Realized Replenishment Lead Time** field, enter a key figure that contains the actual replenishment lead time. Safety stock planning must also valuate the uncertainty of the expected replenishment lead time. An entry in this field is optional. The system considers the key figure only if you have not defined a forecast error of the requirements lead time in the location product master. If you do not enter a key figure here and have not set a forecast error, the system assumes that the replenishment lead time does not involve any uncertainty.

▶ In the **Planned Replenishment Lead Time** field, enter a key figure that contains the replenishment lead time planned in the past. An entry in this field is optional. The system considers the key figure only if you have not defined a forecast error of the replenishment lead time in the location product master. If you do not enter a key figure here and have not set a forecast error, the system assumes that the replenishment lead time does not involve any uncertainty.

▶ Set the **Application Log** flag if you want to display a log of the results.

You can display the calculated safety stock as a key figure in interactive SNP planning and if necessary change it manually or copy it into another planning version. You can also use the calculated safety stock in **PP/DS** and in **capable-to-match (CTM) planning**.

Advantages and Disadvantages of the Enhanced Methods

One *advantage* of the enhanced methods of determining safety stock is that the security stocks are optimally adjusted to various levels of demand. The safety stock is no longer stored statically in the master data. It is geared towards actual demand. This approach means that fluctuating demand and procurement situations are automatically taken into account.

Another advantage is that complicated and involved processes for configuration or maintaining master data are no longer necessary. The system makes the optimal setting individually for each material master.

And yet another advantage of the enhanced safety stock methods is the consideration of the current replenishment lead times.

One *disadvantage* of the enhanced methods is that planners cannot immediately trace the results. Instead, they must work with the result more intensively. And because this procedure is usually new to planners, they need more time to familiarize themselves with it.

To understand the results, planners must understand the enhanced methods and their relationship with forecast accuracy.

The enhanced methods of safety stock planning provide a significant opportunity to optimize inventory if they are used correctly. Therefore, we absolutely recommend their use.

Safety stock planning also offers allows you to achieve a specific service level by creating safety stock for all semifinished and finished products in the corresponding plants and distribution centers across the entire supply chain.

In the context of safety stock planning, two essential questions must be answered:

1. At what levels within the supply chain should safety stock be carried?
2. What amount of safety stock is necessary to be at a level that stores safety stock?

For a simple supply chain that consists of one vendor, two production plants, two distribution centers, and one customer, deciding the levels at which safety stock should be carried is very complex because of the possible number of combinations (2^n). The example given here contains 64 possibilities. Because of the large number of options, you should make the best possible use of the planners' experience and give them the opportunity to simulate selected planning scenarios.

In general, for any supply chain structure, dynamic, multilevel safety stock planning represents a very complex decision-making process. Therefore, you should use high-performance heuristics. Such heuristics focus on algorithms for single-level, time-independent safety stock planning that can be linked to multilevel, time-dependent supply chain planning by adjusting the input parameters.

The system must adjust the forecast and the forecast error for the demand and procurement sides.

▶ In terms of the demand side, the system first determines all the product locations that are supplied from the product locations that carries safety stock. In the next step, all forecasts and forecast errors are projected onto the product locations that carries safety stock to calculate the safety stock, while considering all quantities and time relationships.

▶ In terms of the supply side, the system first determines all the product locations that supply the product that carries safety stock. That step is repeated until a location product that carries safety stock or an external supply in the supply chain is found. Next the critical supply path is determined by calculating the maximum replenishment lead time. Finally, all the forecasts and forecast errors along the critical path are projected onto the product location that carries safety stock to plan the safety stock.

In fixing the lot sizes, there is generally a conflict of interest between logistics and production. This chapter shows you how to optimize lot sizes, what strategies you can use, and how you can leverage mySAP ERP and SAP APO options.

7 Lot Sizes

Conflicts will always arise between logistics and production, or between logistics and procurement regarding the lot size with which a product should be manufactured, or a raw material should be procured. Generally, logistics seeks small lot sizes to minimize storage costs and retain flexibility. Production, on the other hand, requires certain minimum lot sizes to meet its targets in order to optimize both setup costs and capacity utilization.

You can tackle this problem by using an optimized lot-sizing policy. For such a policy to work, you must be familiar with the required lot size strategies and ensure that you assign them to the right products. mySAP Enterprise Resource Planning (mySAP ERP) and SAP Advanced Planner and Optimizer (SAP APO) have several options that you can employ for just this purpose. We'll look into these options later on in this chapter.

7.1 How Do Lot Sizes Affect Stocks

The lot sizes principally influence two critical areas:

▶ **The manufacturing costs**
The manufacturing costs are composed of the material and production costs and the overhead costs. The production costs, in turn, consist of the direct production costs and the production overhead costs. The fixed costs of production (setup costs) as part of the direct production costs must be set against the variable costs of stockholding and capital commitment. The optimal lot size should therefore be determined in relation to the total costs.

▶ **The lead times**
Here, it is important to determine the lot size so that the overall lead time for all orders can be minimized in the production in a single period.

Based on these two critical areas, in the first case, you can see that the lot sizes affect the stock costs, and in the second case, lot sizes affect the inventory quantities. If the lot size is small, setups are performed on a regular basis and setup times account for an increasing amount of the lead times. Fast throughputs are therefore hindered by setup times; however, the lead time is also high if the lot is very large, because a great deal of time has to be expended on the processing. Therefore, you can expect a minimum lead time between these two extremes.

For example, with weekly requirements, you must decide whether you want several weekly requirements to be grouped into one production order (one "lot"), so that you can both produce and store these requirements during the grouping period at the same time. In this case, you can then serve several weekly requirements from the stock. Alternatively, you can decide not to group the weekly requirements, and instead to re-issue the requirement each week as a separate production order. This will lead to higher setup costs, but lower stockholding and capital commitment costs.

Weekly production orders mean no storage costs, or very low storage costs; however, they require weekly setup costs for machines to switch from one production order to the next. Conversely, the creation of large lots that group several weekly requirements implies higher storage costs, but lower setup costs. These costs contain the direct setup costs, the indirect setup costs that arise when bottleneck machines cannot be used productively, and the costs for machine startup.

You'll also find yourself deciding on lot-size formation when external procurement orders arise. Here, the fixed order costs must be set against the storage costs. If several orders are summarized, the order costs remain constant while the storage costs escalate. If you order the individual purchase requisitions separately, each order will have fixed costs, but the storage and capital commitment costs will fall, because smaller volumes can be stored.

In short, we can say that the lot size definitely impacts the following areas in your company:

▸ **Sales**
The lot sizes affect the pricing when selling products.

▸ **Procurement**
The lot sizes affect the pricing for purchasing articles; in specifying minimum purchase quantities (for instance, a lot size of 100 pieces or a multiple of this).

▶ **Production**

The lot sizes pay a role in selecting the following:

▷ Bill of Materials (BOM) and routing in mySAP ERP, both of which are used as a basis for production orders

▷ Production Process Model (PPM) in SAP APO, which is used as a basis for planned orders and production orders

▷ Alternative to a multiple BOM that is to be used

▷ Activity sequence to be used for alternative sequences in the routing.

We'll look at the static procedures, and then the periodic procedures, and finally at the optimizing procedures in mySAP ERP. There are only minimal differences between the procedures in mySAP ERP and SAP APO. Apart from our discussion of the periodic procedures, we will therefore not provide a separate explanation for SAP APO.

7.2 Stochastic (Static) Lot-Sizing Procedure in mySAP ERP and SAP APO

Lot-sizing procedures are divided into stochastic and deterministic lot-sizing procedures. *Deterministic* lot-sizing procedures work on the basis that future requirements are known because of forecasts. Here, planning is performed on the basis of past experience.

Stochastic lot-sizing procedures, on the other hand, work on the basis that future requirements, both in terms of the requirement volume and the timing, are unknown. Different requirements in different periods are not taken into account. Due to this uncertainty, planning is not possible and the ongoing monitoring of stocks is vital. Additionally, reorder point methods (control point) and reorder cycle methods (control cycle) are frequently employed. These are discussed in detail in Chapter 5, *Material Requirements Planning*. For both stochastic methods, it is also important to establish what order quantity is to be procured when the new order is triggered. The lot size is then exclusively formed based on the quantities entered from the relevant material master record.

Figure 7.1 shows the three different criteria by which lot sizes can be calculated in SAP:

▸ Exact lot size

▸ Fixed lot size

▸ Replenishment up to maximum stock level

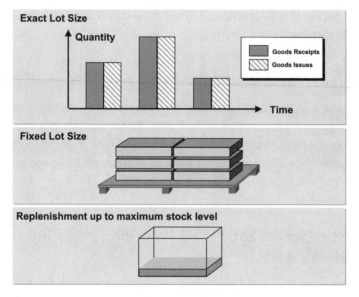

Figure 7.1 Lot-Sizing Using Static Lot-Sizing Procedures (Source: SAP)

7.2.1 Exact Lot Size

In undercovering a material for which the criterion of exact lot sizes applies, the system applies the undercoverage quantity (requirement minus available warehouse stock) as a lot size in its calculation. The planned warehouse stock is then reached for the corresponding requirement date. This procedure is also described as the *Lot-for-Lot procedure*. Planning is day-based, which means that requirement quantities that arise on the same day are summarized as one procurement proposal. Therefore, an order proposal is not generated for every requirement on the same day. This procedure minimizes the stockholding costs, but it generally results in higher ordering costs. Because only daily summaries are used, you cannot generate process-related (hour-or shift-related) procurement proposals.

The exact lot sizes are the most commonly used lot size, because they don't generate any stocks in addition to customer requirements. They are therefore used, in particular, in make-to-order production and in make-to-stock production.

The exact lot size is adjusted if rounding profiles or minimum lot sizes are used.

To plan using exact lot sizes, in the SAP menu go to **Logistics · Production · Master Data · Material · Change · Immediately** and then enter the **EX** indicator for the exact lot size in the **Lot size** field for the material in the material master (**MRP 1** tab) (see Figure 7.2).

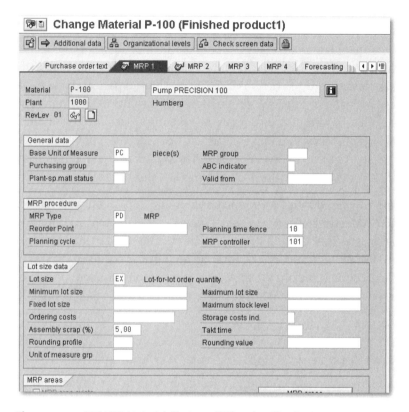

Figure 7.2 mySAP ERP Material Master—MRP 1—Lot Size Settings

7.2.2 Fixed Lot Size

Understandably, fixed lot sizes are chosen for a material only if particular technical characteristics, such as pallets of a certain quantity or tanks of a certain size, require a fixed lot size.

In undercovering a material for which the criterion of fixed lot sizes is relevant, the system applies the fixed lot size that is defined in the material master record in its calculation. If the quantity of a fixed lot size is too small to eliminate the undercoverage, several lots are scheduled in the amount of the fixed lot size for the same date, until there is no more undercoverage.

For a fixed lot size of five pieces, for example, too many orders could be generated for a sales order for 500 pieces. In this case, you can define a threshold value so that if this value is exceeded, a material will get a termination message if too many procurement proposals are formed for one date and one material.

For a fixed lot size of 500 pieces and a purchase order of five pieces, 500 pieces will be manufactured/ordered. The fixed lot size therefore builds up stocks beyond the actual customer requirements. Sometimes this is actually desirable, for instance, if restrictions like the machine capacity or the packaging unit for a material (e.g., the production quantity fits exactly onto one pallet, one skeleton container, etc.) are to be taken into account. If you don't want a build up of stocks, you must define a threshold value above the days' supply that displays the excessively high lot size to the material requirements planning (MRP) controller or the production scheduler.

You can enter the fixed range for the material in the SAP menu via **Logistics · Production · Master Data · Material · Change · Immediately** and there in the material master (**MRP 1** tab), in the **Lot size** field. In the **Lot size data** section, choose the **FX** indicator and choose the quantity of the fixed lot size in the **Fixed lot size** field. In our example, we have defined a fixed lot size of five pieces. For every lot size that is formed, 1 x 5 to n x 5 is thus defined as the lot size.

7.2.3 Fixed Lot Size with Splitting and Overlapping

This setting allows you to define that a fixed or periodic lot size should be subdivided into partial quantities, and that these partial quantities should not be produced at the same time, but rather that production should be overlapping. This lot-sizing procedure is useful if the actual periodic requirement incurred, or the quantity to be manufactured for a particular date is very large, but production is designed to handle only smaller quantities.

7.2.4 Replenishment up to Maximum Stock Level

In the lot-sizing procedure *Replenishment up to maximum stock level*, the lot size that the system uses in its calculation corresponds to the difference between the available warehouse stock and the maximum stock defined in the material master record.

This procedure is used if the warehouse is to be filled up to its maximum capacity. This can be useful if, for example, you can only store a certain quantity due to storage restrictions (tanks or silos in the chemical or consumer goods industry). For example, if a manufacturer of foodstuff needs chocolate icing to produce confectionaries and stores this product in a silo, she will always use this lot-sizing procedure when she fills out an order.

To do this, in the SAP menu go to **Logistics · Production · Master Data · Material · Change · Immediately** and choose a maximum stock level in the **MRP 1** view in the **Maximum stock level** field.

7.2.5 Calculating the Lot Size

In consumption-based planning, the lot-sizing procedure is only valid for reorder point planning. The lot size is calculated depending on the type of reorder point planning. We distinguish between:

▶ **Reorder point planning without taking external requirements into account**
Here, if there is an undercoverage, the lot-sizing procedure creates a procurement proposal whose order quantity corresponds to the difference between the maximum stock defined in the material master and the current warehouse stock and the existing fixed receipt elements:

Maximum stock – current warehouse stock – existing fixed receipt elements = lot size

▶ **Reorder point planning taking external requirements into account**
Here, additional requirements are included in the calculations; in conjunction with the *Replenishment up to maximum stock level* lot-sizing procedure, the requirements planning attempts to accomplish two goals:

  ▷ The requirements must be covered.

  ▷ The maximum stock level that has been set must not be exceeded.

The requirements dates are not taken into account here. The total of all requirements is calculated. The lot sizes are calculated in two steps and by using two different formulas. First, formula 1 is calculated; then, formula 2 is calculated; and finally, the larger of the two lot sizes is applied. If variant 1 is used, you can create an order of up to 14,000 pieces.

Table 7.1 shows you an example for calculating the lot size for reorder point planning taking external requirements into account.

Reorder point planning taking external requirements into account	
Formula 1	**Sample data**
Maximum stock	*10,000*
– Current stock	*1,000*
– Fixed receipts	*0*
= Lot size	*9,000*
Formula 2	**Sample data**
Reorder point	*4,000*
+ total of the requirements in the replenishment lead time	*5,000*
– Current stock	*1,000*
– Fixed receipts	*0*
= Lot size	*8,000*
Variant 1	**Sample data**
Maximum stock	*10,000*
+ total of the requirements in the replenishment lead time	*5,000*
– Current stock	*1,000*
= Lot size	*14,000*

Table 7.1 Example for Calculating the Lot Size for Reorder Point Planning

7.2.6 Evaluating Stochastic Procedures

The advantages of stochastic procedures are:

▶ They are easy to use.

▶ They have a simple logic for determining the lot size.

▶ Using their parameters makes changing the lot size very easy.

The disadvantages of stochastic procedures are:

▶ They require a greater maintenance effort because the master data has to be maintained for each material. This usually results in many materials being handled in exactly the same way, because generally the MRP controller won't have the time to maintain and monitor the parameters separately for each material. He or she will therefore form material groups.

This often leads to higher stocks, because most safety features are built into the parameters to ensure that no material in this group ends up being "out-of-stock."

▶ The parameters are decided based on past experience and usually aren't optimized or determined automatically by the system. This leads to increased costs, because the parameters that are set (lot sizes, checkpoints, expected balances...) have a distinct influence on the lot-sizing costs and on the stockholding and stockout costs. Using one's "intuition" is a very inaccurate way of managing which parameters are employed.

▶ The rigidly set parameters do not adjust in line with the fast-changing requirements. As soon as the MRP controller notices this problem, an exceptional situation has already occurred in production or procurement with resulting costs.

▶ Stochastic methods ignore fluctuating prices or promotions/special offers. With special offers, in particular, out-of-stock situations frequently arise because the additional quantities cannot be procured at such short notice using stochastic methods.

Based on these various advantages and disadvantages, stochastic methods are therefore only relevant for BX, CX, and CY materials (see Chapter 3, *Inventory Analysis*).

7.3 Deterministic (Periodic) Lot-Sizing Procedures in mySAP ERP and SAP APO

7.3.1 Periodic Lot-Sizing Procedures

With deterministic procedures, we differentiate between procedures with and without economic (cost-minimizing) lot sizes. The procedures that don't take costs into account are known as *practitioner rules*, such as the weekly lot size, fixed coverages, or minimum/maximum lot sizes. With deterministic lot-sizing procedures, the requirement quantities of one or several periods are summarized to form one lot size. This is why they are referred to as "periodic lot-sizing procedures." You can define any number of periods that you want to group into a single procurement proposal.

In mySAP ERP, the periods can comprise several days, weeks, or months, depending on the planning calendar. The system will generate the availability date for periodic lot-sizing procedures on the first requirement date of the period; however, you can also specify that the availability date should be moved to the beginning or to the end of the period. The availability date is the date (including the goods receipt processing time) on which the material must be made available again.

Figure 7.3 Lot-Size Creation for Periodic Lot-Sizing Procedures (Source: SAP)

The following different types of periodic lot-sizing procedures exist:

▶ **Daily lot size**

All requirement quantities within a day or any chosen number of days are grouped to form a lot size.

To plan using the daily lot size, for example, in the SAP menu go to **Logistics · Production · Master Data · Material · Change · Immediately** and then enter the **TB** indicator for daily lot size in the **Lot size** field for the material in the material master (**MRP 1** tab). For the weekly lot size use **WB**, and for the monthly lot size use **MB**.

▶ **Weekly lot size**

All requirement quantities within a week, or any selected number of weeks, are grouped to form a lot size.

▶ **Monthly lot size**

All requirement quantities within a month or any selected number of months are grouped to form a lot size.

▶ **Lot sizes with flexible period lengths**

All requirement quantities within a fixed or freely selectable number of periods that can be flexibly defined are grouped as one lot size. You define the period length in the same way here as you do for the posting periods. The number of periods corresponds to the number of posting periods. This lot size is also known as a period lot size.

▶ **Lot sizes with freely definable periods**

All requirement quantities within a fixed or freely selectable number of periods that can be flexibly defined are grouped as one lot size. You define the number of periods and their length in the same way here as you do for the Production Planning and Detailed Scheduling (PPS) planning calendar. These periods are not linked to the posting periods. This lot size is also known as a period lot size.

You can interpret the start of the planning calendar period as an availability date or as a delivery date.

If you selected **material requirements planning** as the replenishment type and set a periodic lot-sizing procedure by the planning calendar, in the SAP menu go to **Logistics · Production · Master Data · Material · Change · Immediately** and in the **MRP 2** tab, in the **Planning calendar** field, specify which calendar should be used as the basis. Here, the beginning of the period is interpreted as the availability date.

If you want to interpret the beginning of the period as the delivery date, define the delivery cycle with the planning calendar entered here. This specifies the days on which the supplier will deliver the material. The delivery cycle will be useful in the following situation, for example: scheduling and ordering are performed each Monday and Tuesday. The materials that are ordered on Mondays are delivered on Wednesdays; however, the materials that are ordered on Tuesdays are not delivered until Friday.

You can enter the delivery cycle in addition to the planning cycle. To do this, in the SAP menu, go to **Logistics · Production · Master Data · Material · Change · Immediately** and select a planning calendar there in the **MRP 1** tab in the **Planning cycle** field.

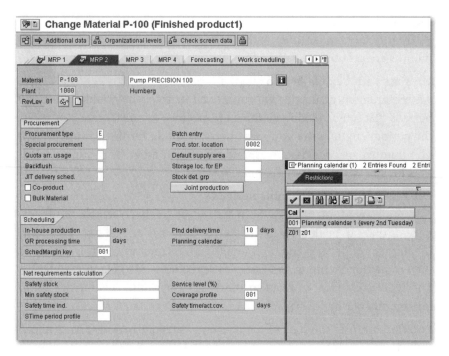

Figure 7.4 Lot-Size Creation With Planning Calendar

7.3.2 Fixed Ranges in mySAP ERP

Fixed ranges are a deterministic rule that we encounter very frequently during application. The range consists of the remaining number of days for which a material is available, or must be available. It is then established that the requirement has to be covered by a firmly defined number of periods.

The range is defined by the planner as a planned number of days, on the one hand, so that requirement fluctuations can be smoothed out. If the range is not met, this will create corresponding procurement proposals if they are required. On the other hand, the planner must be able to use the range to identify how many days a material will continue to last. To do this, the planner must be allowed to establish the current range at any time. In SAP, the range is calculated automatically.

Fluctuating requirements quickly lead to increased costs and an unfavorable stock policy. If requirements are very high, high storage quantities are ordered without taking the stockholding costs into account. Therefore, smaller order quantities could prove to be significantly less expensive. For small requirements, the fixed ranges mean that small volumes will be ordered, even though high fixed costs would make larger lots cheaper.

The advantages of the fixed ranges are:

▶ The lot sizes are adjusted to reflect the requirements.

▶ They are easy to use.

▶ They offer a simple logic for determining the lot size.

The disadvantages of the fixed ranges are:

▶ Greater requirements fluctuations lead to increased costs.

▶ More maintenance is required, because the range still needs to be maintained for each material master.

You can use various methods to calculate the range in the requirements planning in SAP.

Statistical Range of Coverage Calculation with Range of Coverage Profile

You define the minimum, maximum, and target range for certain periods in the range of coverage profile.

The range of coverage profile is defined in Customizing under **Implementation Guide · Production · Requirements Planning · Planning · Lot-Size Calculation · Maintain Rounding Profile**, as you can see in Figure 7.5.

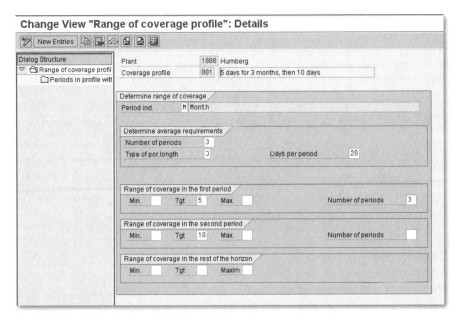

Figure 7.5 Range of Coverage Profile in mySAP ERP Customizing

You can maintain ranges of coverage for up to three periods and define different maximum, minimum, and target ranges for each period. The fixed range of coverage is always given in days in SAP. In the example shown in Figure 7.5, a lot size is given for a fixed range of coverage of five days for the first three months. A fixed range of coverage of 10 days then applies.

In addition to the ranges of coverage for the three periods, you can define different ranges of coverage for certain periods. This is useful if, for example, you have to schedule a higher safety stock due to increased demand in the months before Christmas.

To do this, in the SAP menu go to **Logistics · Production · Master Data · Material · Change · Immediately** and in the material master in the **MRP 2** tab, assign the range of coverage profile to the material in the **Range of coverage profile** field, as you can see in Figure 7.6.

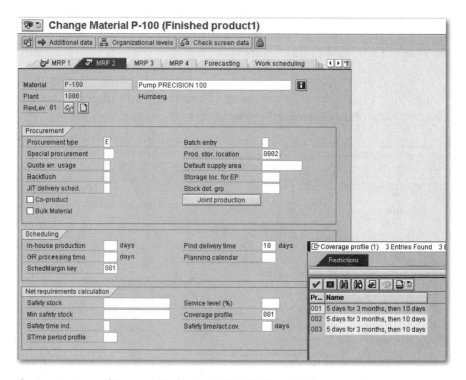

Figure 7.6 Range of Coverage Profile in mySAP ERP Material Master

The system uses the specified range of coverage values to calculate the minimum, maximum, and target stock based on average daily requirements. If the available quantity is less than the minimum stock, a procurement proposal is created that allows the system to fill up again to the target stock. This is how a requirements-oriented dynamic safety stock is created.

The stock calculation for the corresponding period is performed based on the following formulas:

Average daily requirement = Requirement in the specified number of periods/number of days within the entire period length

Statistical range of coverage = Available quantity at the relevant time/average daily requirement

Minimum stock = Average daily requirement * minimum range of coverage

Maximum stock = Average daily requirement * maximum range of coverage

Target stock = Average daily requirement * target range of coverage

With the minimum and maximum range of coverage, you can establish an interval for calculating the dynamic safety stock. The system checks whether the statistical range of coverage is under the minimum value. If it is, the safety stock is calculated again during the next planning run, starting with the target range of coverage as your basis. If the maximum range of coverage is exceeded, an exception message is issued.

An example for statistical range calculation:

▸ Sample data for the average daily requirement:

   ▹ Requirement for the 1st period: 1,000 pieces

   ▹ Requirement for the 2nd period: 3,000 pieces

   ▹ Requirement for the 3rd period: 4,000 pieces

   ▹ Planning period: Week

   ▹ Period length: 5 days

   ▹ Number of periods: 3

   ▹ Sample data for the statistical range calculation

   ▹ Target range of coverage for period profile 1: 2 days
      Length of the period profile 1:2 weeks

   ▹ Target range of coverage for period profile 2: 3 days
      Length of the period profile 2:3 weeks

▸ Calculation of the average daily requirement:

(1,000 + 3,000 + 3,500)/(3*5) = 7,500/15 = 500

▶ Calculation of the dynamic safety stock:

*Average requirement * Range of coverage in period 1*
*500 * 2 = 1,000*

*Average requirement * Range of coverage in period 2*
*500 * 3= 1,500*

▶ Result: For the first two weeks after the MRP date, 1,000 pieces of safety stock are scheduled. For the following three weeks, 1,500 pieces of safety stock are scheduled.

Safety Time/Actual Range of Coverage

You define the safety time/actual range of coverage in the material master as a planned number of days that the warehouse stock should be able to handle, without new receipts being added. The system simulates bringing the existing requirements forward by the specified number of days and creates procurement proposals that fit the schedule, so that the receipts for the material take place before the actual requirement date. This ensures that the warehouse stock will still be sufficient, even if requirements fluctuate.

Days' Supply and Receipt Days' Supply

The days' supply for a material specifies how long a material will continue to last based solely on the current plant stock.

The receipt days' supply for a material indicates how long the stock will last if anticipated receipts are also taken into account. You can define two different receipt days' supplies. For example, you can define that for receipt days' supply 1, all possible receipt elements should be taken into account, but for receipt days' supply 2, only the receipt elements that you can be sure of (i.e., shipping notifications and production orders) should be considered.

Based on these ranges of coverage, the planner can identify whether a material requires action to be taken. Both of these ranges of coverage are calculated by the system during the planning run and displayed in the requirement planning evaluations.

Actual Range of Coverage

The actual range of coverage indicates how long the quantity of a material that is available on a particular date or in a particular period can cover the requirements that fall in the subsequent periods. It is given as a number of days.

The actual range of coverage is calculated by the system during the planning run for all periods, and is displayed in the period totals in the requirements planning evaluations and in the planning table for repetitive manufacturing.

7.3.3 Period-Specific Fixed Ranges of Coverage in SAP APO

As you can see in Figure 7.7, you can enter the ranges of coverage for each period directly into the planning folder in SAP APO. In theory, you can also do this in the flexible planning in mySAP ERP; however, there, you are not in the requirements planning environment, as you are with SAP APO. Flexible planning is only a rough-cut planning in which stocks are not yet taken into account. In SAP APO, the ranges of coverage are determined based on current sales orders and current stocks. Planning in SAP APO therefore takes into account the ranges of coverage by period for operative planning, whereas operative planning in mySAP ERP takes into account only the static ranges of coverage from the material master.

Splitting and overlapping are also possible for all periodic lot-sizing procedures. Here the system will, by default, generate the availability date for periodic lot-sizing procedures on the first requirement date of the period; however, you can also specify that the availability date should be moved to the beginning or the end of the period.

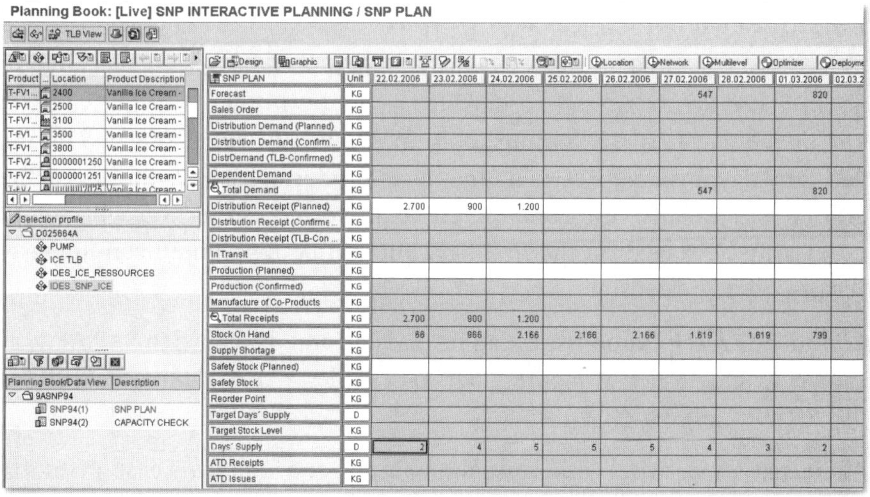

Figure 7.7 Period-Specific Ranges of Coverage in SAP APO

7.3.4 Additional Lot-Sizing Procedures in SAP APO

In SAP APO, you can also use other periodic lot-sizing procedures:

▶ **Shift lot size**
All requirement quantities within a shift or any chosen number of shifts are grouped to form a lot size.

▶ **Hourly lot size**
All requirement quantities within an hour or any chosen number of hours are grouped to form a lot size.

These procedures allow you to have goods (such as perishable products, for example) delivered by your supplier at a specific hour, for a particular shift, or several times a day, and to build this requirement right into the planning stage. In the food industry, for example, fresh items have to be delivered several times a day. A lot-size creation of less than one day is therefore necessary in order to plan the delivery adequately and accurately.

These procedures increase the transparency in your supply chain, because they plan receipts and issues more accurately and can identify exceptional situations more quickly.

Figure 7.8 shows the APO product master. In the SAP APO menu, go to **Master Data · Product Master** and go to the **Lot size** tab. Select a period type on the right-hand side of the screen in the **Period Type** field using the **F4 Help**.

7.3.5 Continuous Input and Output

In repetitive manufacturing, it is quite common for large lots of a material to be produced across several periods, for example, 1,000 pieces in five days. The total quantity of 1,000 units (output) is generally not completed on the very first day; instead, a certain quantity is produced each day, for example, 200 units. Similarly, the components required for production will not all necessarily be staged on the first day, but will be distributed continuously across several periods.

Continuous receipts and issues can be planned and displayed in SAP APO, as shown schematically in Figure 7.9. This enables a cost-optimized MRP for the receipts and issues.

Three cases can arise with continuous input and output. These cases are described below using examples.

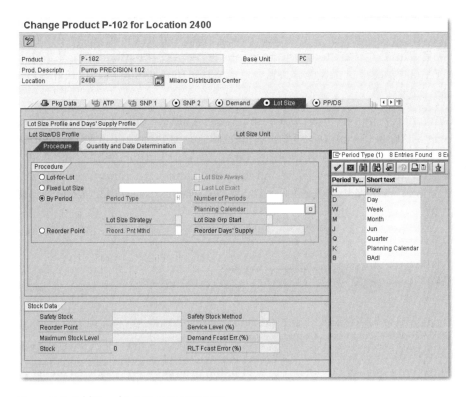

Figure 7.8 Additional Lot Sizes in SAP APO

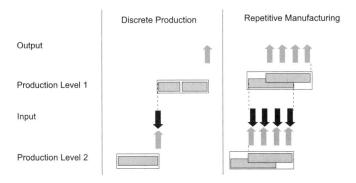

Figure 7.9 Continuous Input and Output in SAP APO (Source: SAP)

Discrete Input—Continuous Output

For the finished product FERT01, there is a discrete input on 08/10/00 of 1,000 pieces in the form of a purchase requisition from a distribution center as shown in figure 7.11. To meet this requirement, a planned order for this exact quantity is generated on 08/09/00. For the FERT01 product, the exter-

343

nal procurement indicator is set in the **distribution center**; in the **plant** location, this indicator is on **in-house production**; and in the PPM for FERT01, the **C** indicator is set to continuous for the output. The production duration for 1,000 pieces is two days. There is a 1:1 relationship between all production stages.

Without continuous input and output, you would see only the planned order over 1,000 pieces on 08/09/00. With continuous input and output, the system calculates the output quantity for each point in time, while taking into account the start and end date and the production restrictions (capacity, production time window, breaks, etc.). See the receipts/issues diagram in Figure 7.10.

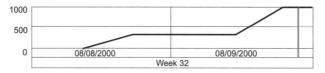

Figure 7.10 In the Receipts/Issues Diagram: Discrete Input—Continuous Output (Source: SAP)

The output quantity can be displayed in the **product view: single elements** to the second, and can be displayed in the **product view: periodically** at bucket level (see Figure 7.11). For 08/08/00, we obtain a cumulated output quantity of 400 pieces and for 08/09/00, we obtain a cumulated output quantity of 600 pieces.

These two "continuous" quantities, in turn, form an input for the next planning level (input for HALB01), where the continuous output quantity is calculated and displayed according to the same principle.

Product View: Periodic		Un	08.08.2000	09.08.2000	10.08.2000	11.08.2000
FERT01 / Finished Product						
	Available quantity	PC			1000	1000
	Total requirements	PC				
	Purchase requisition	PC			1000	
FERT01 / Finished Product						
	Available quantity	PC	400			
	P Ind. ind. reqmts	PC				
	Total requirements	PC		1000-		
	Planned order	PC		1000		
	Distributed	PC	400	600		

Figure 7.11 Periodic Product View: Discrete Input—Continuous Output (Source: SAP)

Continuous Input—Continuous Output

HALB01 is a dependent requirement for FERT01. In the Production Process Model (PPM) for FERT01, the product HALB01 is labeled as continuous input, and in the PPM for HALB01, the product FERT01 is labeled as continuous output. Continuous output quantities are generated to cover the requirements, based on the continuous input quantities (dependent requirements). The symmetrical process between cumulated requirements and receipts in Figure 7.12 results from the 1:1 relationship between FERT01 and HALB01.

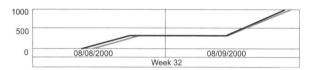

Figure 7.12 In the Receipts/Issues Diagram:
Continuous Input—Continuous Output (Source: SAP)

In the periodic product view, for the HALB01 on 08/08/00, we obtain a cumulated output quantity of 400 pieces as a dependent requirement; for 08/09/00, we obtain a cumulated output quantity of 1,000 pieces as a planned order.

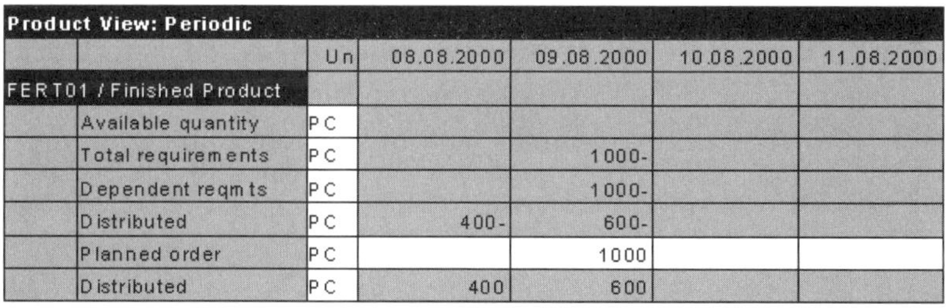

Product View: Periodic						
	Un	08.08.2000	09.08.2000	10.08.2000	11.08.2000	
FERT01 / Finished Product						
Available quantity	P C					
Total requirements	P C		1000-			
Dependent reqmts	P C		1000-			
Distributed	P C	400-	600-			
Planned order	P C		1000			
Distributed	P C	400	600			

Figure 7.13 Periodic Product View: Continuous Input—Continuous Output (Source: SAP)

Continuous Input—Discrete Output

In the PPM for HALB01, the product ROH01 is marked as continuous input, which produces the course of the continuous dependent requirement for ROH01. In the product master of ROH01, "E" for external procurement appears as a procurement alternative, that is, the system creates two discrete purchase requisitions of 400 and 600 pieces. In the receipts/issue diagram in Figure 7.14, the continuous requirement progression of ROH01 is shown in red and the discrete receipt of ROH01 is shown in green.

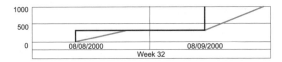

Figure 7.14 In the Receipts/Issues Diagram:
Continuous Input—Discrete Output (Source: SAP)

In the periodic product view, a cumulated output quantity of 400 pieces is obtained for the ROH01 on 08/08/00 as a dependent requirement, and for 08/09/00 an output quantity of 600 pieces in the form of a purchase requisition.

Product View: Periodic						
	Un	08.08.2000	09.08.2000	10.08.2000	11.08.2000
FERTC1 / Finished Product						
Available quantity	P C				
Total requirements	P C		1000-		
Dependent reqmts	P C		1000-		
Distributed	P C	400-	600-		
Purchase requisition	P C	400	600		

Figure 7.15 Periodic Product View: Continuous Input—Discrete Output (Source: SAP)

7.3.6 Summary

Overall, we can say that the deterministic procedures that do not factor cost generally lead to increased costs, because the ordering costs and stockholding costs are not balanced out. Working on intuition alone, the material requirements planning (MRP) controller will only rarely find the optimal ordering costs and stockholding costs.

For this reason, we recommend those deterministic procedures that try to find economic lot sizes (cost-minimizing lot sizes), because this is the only way to find the financially viable lot sizes.

Unfortunately, these procedures are seldom used in current practice. The MRP controller usually makes decisions regarding production and procurement lots. However, MRP controllers are often so busy with day-to-day operations that they simply don't have the time to grapple with such methods. Furthermore, sufficient help is not available, although most ERP and advanced planning and scheduling (APS) systems do support economic lot-sizing procedures. Generally, these procedures are not mentioned when the system is introduced, because most external consultants are not familiar with them and because there is usually neither the time nor the budget to explain these procedures in further detail to the MRP controllers. The most common reason for opting against using economic lot-size calculation is probably due to the more complex determination methods, which the MRP controller would prefer not to adopt.

For these reasons, often dynamic lot-sizing problems are solved by using static lot-sizing procedures, although these procedures fail to provide any optimization that addresses the cost factor. The MRP controllers primarily define the lot sizes intuitively, based on fixed order and purchase order volumes, or based on defined ranges of coverage and past experience. Employing economic lot sizes first requires an appreciation of the underlying logic, which, in most cases, demands strong encouragement through training and experience.

7.4 Optimal Lot-Sizing Procedures in mySAP ERP and SAP APO

7.4.1 Taking Costs into Account in Economic Procedures

With the static and periodic lot-sizing procedures, the costs that arise from the stockholding and the setup, or the purchasing transaction, are not taken into account. With the deterministic lot-sizing procedures that take costs into account, we also talk of "economic" or "optimal" lot-sizing procedures.

The goal of optimizing lot-sizing procedures, on the other hand, is to choose the lot size in such a way that the total minimal costs accrue. These are composed of:

▸ Material or production costs

▸ Ordering costs (setup or order costs)

▸ Stockholding costs

▸ Stockout costs

You should note that only the variable components of these costs could be included in the lot-sizing decision, because the fixed costs—such as the personnel and operating resources—cannot be reduced at short notice. It is a relatively complex issue to define what costs should be included in the lot-sizing process. On the one hand, you must determine how to separate decision-relevant cost types and non-decision-relevant cost types. On the other hand, you must ensure that these costs are precisely established and assigned in relation to their source. Therefore, let's look at these cost elements in a little more detail.

Material Costs

As part of the order quantity planning, the material costs must be evaluated with the cost prices. These costs are composed of the net purchase prices (gross purchase prices minus the discounts and markups for small volume purchases) and the purchasing costs that vary with quantity (e.g., transport costs, insurance costs, packaging costs, or storage and stock removal costs).

For production quantity planning (for in-house production), the material costs are assessed as manufacturing costs. These costs are composed of the individual material costs, the material overhead costs, the individual production costs, the production overhead costs, and other miscellaneous costs.

Ordering Costs

The ordering costs are independent of the order quantities and are incurred with every new ordering transaction. These costs are composed of the personnel and material costs for the posting and offer process, the order placement, deadline monitoring, goods receipt and quality control, posting of the goods receipt, storage, auditing and the payment directive. Transport costs can also be fixed, if they are incurred with every order, regardless of the order quantity. These costs can only be accurately determined with a detailed activity-based costing system. In practice, approximate values are used, which are determined in the cost center accounting. The costs for each order are derived from the following calculation:

Order costs for each order = Order costs per period / number of orders in the period

The order costs are usually determined on a monthly basis and are checked for any variances. The fixed order costs for each order, on the other hand, are fixed only if the number of orders for each period does not change significantly.

Production Costs

You can determine the lot-size-independent production costs (known as setup costs) by adding the changeover costs between two production orders and the startup costs that may arise when you begin to process an order. The changeover costs arise due to installation, redesigning, or cleaning work performed at the workstations in production. Also included under the umbrella of production costs are the replacement of tools, the provision of task lists, or the familiarization of personnel.

Stockholding Costs

The stockholding costs are costs for the storage and maintenance of materials during warehousing. Such costs arise when requirement quantities are purchased or produced early (i.e., before their actual requirement date), and have to be stored in the warehouse until the requirement date. The longer the storage duration and the higher the material value, the higher the stockholding costs. The storage costs are determined by the ratio between the stockholding costs (costs from the warehouse cost centers and the capital commitment for the average warehouse stock) and the average warehouse stock for the previous year:

*Stockholding costs = ((Storage costs + imputed interest) * 100) / average warehouse stock*

Stockout Costs

The stockout costs contain profit reductions that occur because the required materials cannot be delivered in the quantity needed, or cannot be delivered on time to production or to the customer. These costs can be materials that have not even been sold, or markdowns if deadlines are missed. The stockout costs also include costs for rescheduling at short notice, express goods due to shortfall quantities, and higher costs for alternative materials, overtime, or penalties.

Cost Optimization

Since the stockholding costs and the ordering costs show different kinds of cost development, depending on the lot size, the lot sizes need to be optimized. This problem is illustrated by the following example of a purchaser:

If the purchaser orders on a regular basis, he will have low storage costs, but high ordering costs due to the high number of order transactions. If he orders only rarely, the ordering costs will be low, but the storage costs will be high, because the materials ordered before the requirements date have to be stored in the warehouse and costs will thus accrue for a long period of time.

We start on the basis of the first material shortage date determined from the net requirements calculation. The material shortage quantity that exists at this time is considered to be the minimum procurement quantity. The system then adds successive shortage quantities to this lot size until, via the particular cost criterion, optimum costs on which the procedure is based have been established.

The various optimizing lot-sizing procedures differ from each other both in the type of minimum cost and in the consideration of constant or fluctuating requirements. The classic Andler method (also known as the Harris method) is based on a constant material requirement. The "dynamic" procedures consider variable requirements. The best-known procedures here are part-period balancing, the cost-offsetting procedure, and the Groff procedure. These procedures are heuristics that approach the optimal conditions. The Wagner and Whitin procedure finds the exact optimum. All of these methods can be reproduced in SAP and will be discussed in more detail below.

7.4.2   Andler Lot Size (Harris Method)

The Andler lot size is an optimization method that requires constant requirements (statically), with the objective of minimizing the total stockholding costs (variable costs) and the setup costs (fixed costs), as shown in Figure 7.16.

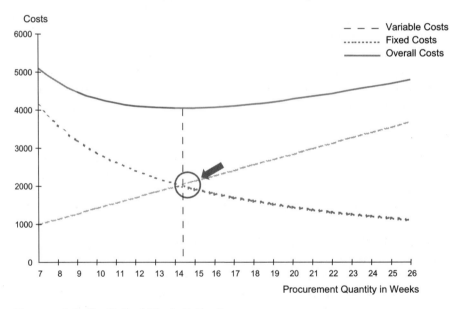

Figure 7.16 Andler Method (Harris Method)

You can derive the following characteristics from the formula to determine the optimal lot size: The more valuable the commodity (high price) or the more expensive the storage (high stockholding price), the smaller the lot size. The higher the setup costs, the bigger the lot.

The optimal lot size is subject to the following prerequisites:

▶ The unit price is independent of the procurement quantity.

▶ The requirement is known and constant if, for example, the monthly requirement is equal to one-twelfth of the annual requirement.

▶ Stockout costs are not allowed.

▶ The distribution of the warehouse issues is constant over time. The goods issues fluctuate only slightly around a constant level, which means that they are constant over time.

▶ The delivery time is effectively zero.

▶ No provision is made for minimum order quantities.

▶ A material can be ordered independently from other materials.

▶ The costs for the storage and the orders can be determined with sufficient accuracy.

Looking at these prerequisites, you can see where the weaknesses are in the Andler lot-size formula. The following secondary conditions are not considered:

▶ Other products have no influence on the lot size of the product considered.

▶ No restrictions arise from the capacity utilization of production.

▶ There are no by-products (integrated MRP).

▶ There is enough space and capital to obtain and store the optimal lot size.

▶ Fluctuating requirements are not considered.

▶ Variable acquisition prices, for instance, due to volume discounts, have no impact on the lot size that is determined.

▶ Andler also fails to consider delivery times of more than zero.

The Andler method assumes a closed planning period, for example, the annual requirement must be known. Under the given conditions, a true optimization is therefore possible. But, this means that the Andler method is only a static optimization procedure. The dynamic methods, on the other hand, work partly with an open, moving planning horizon, while the optimal lot size is determined by systematic trial and error. Mathematically speaking, the dynamic methods can only be described as approximation procedures. If requirements are constant, they all deliver the values that are identical to those of the Andler calculation, and therefore are no worse than the Andler method. Furthermore, in reality, requirements are very rarely constant. For these reasons, and the reasons already discussed, we should dispense with the Andler method and adopt the dynamic lot-sizing procedures instead.

The idea behind the dynamic procedures, contrary to the Andler method, is as follows. The total costs represent a minimum if the order costs are equal to the cumulated storage costs. Here, you work from the first period requirement for which the total costs are calculated. The order quantity is then extended by one period requirement in each case (the period requirement cannot be divided) and the resulting cost change is determined. This is continued until the lowest costs are found. We will now look at the other dynamic methods.

7.4.3 Part-Period Balancing (Cost-Balancing Method)

The part-period balancing method (part-period method or cost-balancing method) uses the characteristic of the traditional lot-sizing formulas that at the minimum cost, the variable costs (storage costs) are equal to the ordering costs.

With the part-period balancing method, successive requirement quantities are repeatedly grouped to form a lot, based on the material shortage date, until the total of the storage costs that have increased, as a result of the lot increase, is equal to the ordering costs (balancing between quantity-independent and quantity- and time-dependent costs).

Table 7.2 shows you an example for calculating the part-period balancing, given the following assumptions:

▶ The price is 10.00 Euro.

▶ The ordering costs are 100.00 Euro.

▶ The storage cost percentage is 15%.

Using the part-period balancing method, you can see that the optimal lot size in this example is 3,000.

In SAP, you must enter the **PP** indicator for part-period balancing for the material in the material master under **Logistics · Production · Master data · Material · change · immediately** and then in the **MRP 1** tab in the **Lot size** field, and you must also enter the **Ordering costs** and the **Storage costs indicators** (see Figure 7.17).

Requirement Date	Storage Duration	Requirement Quantity	Lot Size	Storage Costs	Total Storage Costs
06. Jul	0	1,000	1,000	0.00	0.00
13. Jul	7	1,000	2,000	28.77	28.77
20. Jul	14	1,000	3,000	57.53	86.30
27. Jul	21	1,000	4,000	86.30	172.60

Table 7.2 Part-Period Balancing—Calculation

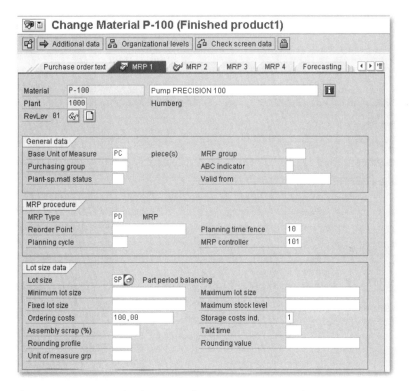

Figure 7.17 Part-Period Balancing in the mySAP ERP Material Master

The ordering costs are the costs that arise with every order or production order, regardless of the lot size, in addition to the order price or production costs.

The storage costs indicator defines the storage cost percentage. This indicator considers the costs incurred in proportion to the storage quantity and unit price. It relates to the average storage value. It is taken as constant for the duration of the coverage time. The values are usually between 15% and 35%.

The storage costs indicator is defined in SAP Customizing under **Implementation Guide · Logistics · Production · Requirements Planning · Planning · Lot-Size Calculation · Check Lot-Sizing Procedure · Maintain Storage Costs Indicator** for each storage location/plant combination. Several storage cost rates can be preset for each combination. Figure 7.18 shows an example in which a different **storage cost rate** applies for the Hamburg plant (1,000) than for the Berlin plant (1,100).

The part-period balancing method does not determine an optimum. It just approaches it. In particular, in the case of fluctuating or constant requirements, other economic lot-sizing procedures achieve a better result.

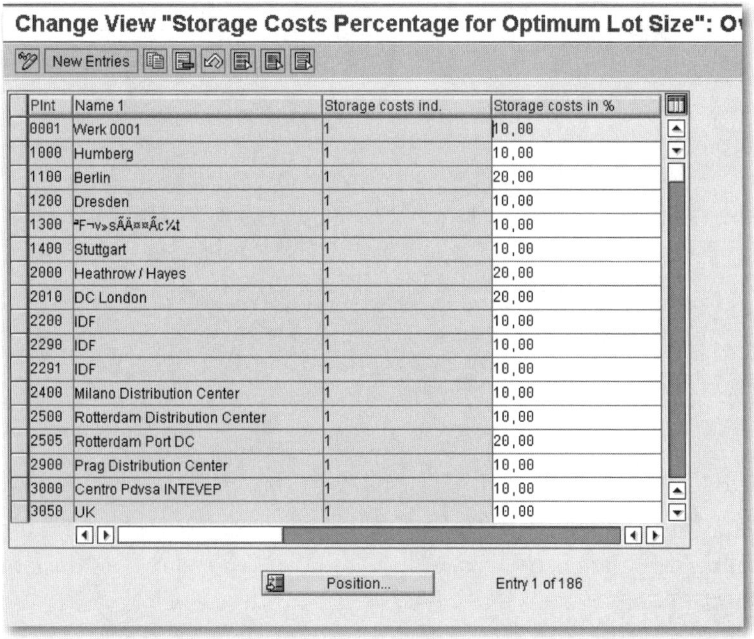

Plnt	Name 1	Storage costs ind.	Storage costs in %	
0001	Werk 0001	1	10,00	
1000	Humberg	1	10,00	
1100	Berlin	1	20,00	
1200	Dresden	1	10,00	
1300	"F¬v»sÃÄ==Ãc¼t	1	10,00	
1400	Stuttgart	1	10,00	
2000	Heathrow / Hayes	1	20,00	
2010	DC London	1	20,00	
2200	IDF	1	10,00	
2290	IDF	1	10,00	
2291	IDF	1	10,00	
2400	Milano Distribution Center	1	10,00	
2500	Rotterdam Distribution Center	1	10,00	
2505	Rotterdam Port DC	1	20,00	
2900	Prag Distribution Center	1	10,00	
3000	Centro Pdvsa INTEVEP	1	10,00	
3050	UK	1	10,00	

Position...   Entry 1 of 186

Figure 7.18 Storage Costs Indicators in mySAP ERP Customizing

7.4.4   Least Unit Cost Procedure

The goal of the least unit cost procedure is to minimize the unit costs of each lot to be formed. To do this, based on the material shortage date, the system groups together successive requirement quantities to form a lot size until the total costs per unit form a minimum value. The total costs here are the total from the ordering costs and the entire storage costs.

Table 7.3 shows you an example for calculating the least unit cost, given the following assumptions:

► The price is 10.00 Euro.

► The ordering costs are 100.00 Euro.

► The storage cost percentage is 15%.

If we divide the entire costs by the order quantity (i.e., the total of the individual requirements), you get the unit costs that can be influenced, which are then minimized during the least order cost procedure. The unit costs initially drop to a minimum and then climb again. The quantity to be ordered is equal to the total of the requirement values, up to the period with the lowest unit costs. The procedure is continued until a higher value is reached than the last one calculated, that is, it continues even if the values are the same.

Requirement Date	Storage Duration	Requirement Quantity	Lot Size	Storage Costs	Total Storage Costs	Unit Costs
06. Jul	0	1,000	1,000	0.00	100.00	0.100
13. Jul	7	1,000	2,000	28.77	128.77	0.064
20. Jul	14	1,000	3,000	57.53	186.30	0.062
27. Jul	21	1,000	4,000	86.30	272.60	0.068

Table 7.3 Least Unit Cost—Calculation

In the example in Table 7.3, the optimal lot size is 3,000 units.

In SAP, you must enter the **LU** indicator for least unit cost for the material in the material master under **Logistics · Production · Master data · Material · change · immediately** and then in the **MRP 1** tab in the **Lot size** field. You must also enter the **Ordering costs** and the **Storage costs indicator** (see Figure 7.17).

Again, with this method, the optimal solution is not fully reached; instead, it is merely approximated. Of the optimal lot-sizing procedures, the least unit cost procedure is the most frequently used method, after the Andler method. However, even here, other lot-sizing procedures give better results for fluctuating or constant requirements. We would refer here, e. g., to the work of Knolmayer and Wemmerlöv.

7.4.5 Groff Lot-Sizing Procedure

The Groff lot-sizing procedure is predicated on the fact that, based on the classical lot-sizing formula, at the minimum cost, additionally incurred storage costs are equal to the ordering cost savings (see Figure 7.19).

Additional storage costs that arise from an increase in the lot size are set against the resulting ordering cost savings. Based on a certain period, the system will then continue grouping requirement quantities together to form a lot until the increase in the average storage costs per period is higher than the reduction of the ordering costs for each period.

The Groff procedure is identical to the Silver Meal method if the marginal storage costs per period are precisely described.

In the following example, you can see that, based on Groff, the optimal lot size is 1,000, because the ordering costs saved are equal to the additional storage costs incurred.

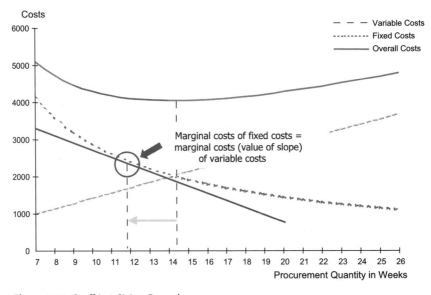

Figure 7.19 Groff Lot-Sizing Procedure

Table 7.4 shows you an example for calculating the least unit cost, given the following assumptions:

▶ The price is 10.00 Euro.

▶ The ordering costs are 100.00 Euro.

▶ The storage cost percentage is 15%.

Requirement Date	Storage Duration	Requirement Quantity	Lot Size	Ordering Costs Saved	Additional Storage Costs:
06. Jul	0	1,000	1,000	0.00	0.00
13. Jul	7	1,000	2,000	1.79	2.05
20. Jul	14	1,000	3,000		
27. Jul	21	1,000	4,000		

Table 7.4 Lot-Size Calculation Using the Groff Procedure

In SAP, go to **Logistics · Production · Master Data · Material · Change · Immediately** and then, in the **MRP 1** view in the **Lot size** field, enter the **GR** indicator for the Groff lot-sizing procedure and the **Ordering costs** and the **Storage costs indicator**.

Splitting and overlapping are also possible for all optimal lot-sizing procedures. Here the system will, by default, generate the availability date for optimal lot-sizing procedures on the first requirement date of the period; however, you can also specify that the availability date should be moved to the beginning or the end of the period.

On average, the Groff procedure is around 1% higher than the costs of the exact procedure of Wagner and Whitin, which will be introduced below. While Groff does not determine an optimum value, unlike the heuristic lot-sizing procedures already outlined, the Groff procedure produces better results for fluctuating or constant requirements than, for instance, the part-period balancing procedure, or the least unit cost procedure.

7.4.6 Dynamic Lot-Size Calculation

Unlike the Andler lot-sizing procedure, which can determine an optimum through the completed planning period, the dynamic procedures are based on a dynamic planning period and the optimal lot size is determined by systematic trial and error. Mathematically speaking, they are therefore described as approximation procedures. Like the part-period balancing and the Groff procedure, they draw on the Wagner and Whitin procedure; however, they are not genuine optimization procedures, but merely heuristic procedures that approach the optimum values.

With dynamic lot-size calculation, based on the material shortage date, the system continues to group together requirement quantities to form a lot until the additional storage costs accrued are higher than the ordering costs. Dynamic planning calculations are very similar to the part-period balancing, both in terms of their parameters and decision criteria and concerning their technical implementation. In both cases, the additional storage costs resulting from a lot grouping are compared with the fixed procurement costs, and a new lot is created if the fixed procurement costs are exceeded. The difference between the two methods is that the part-period balancing checks the total storage costs of the grouped periods against the fixed procurement costs, while the dynamic planning calculation only compares the additional costs for each individual period to be grouped.

During dynamic lot-size calculation under capacity restrictions, planning is no longer performed for one part in isolation, but rather the entire part spectrum of the net requirement is considered. In particular, the capacity restrictions for production and storage are observed.

Table 7.5 shows an example for the dynamic lot-sizing procedure, given the following assumptions:

▶ The price is 10.00 Euro.

▶ The ordering costs are 100.00 Euro.

▶ The storage cost percentage is 15%.

Requirement Date	Storage Duration	Requirement Quantity	Lot Size	Storage Costs	Total Storage Costs
06. Jul	0	1,000	1,000	0.00	00.00
13. Jul	7	1,000	2,000	28.77	28.77
20. Jul	14	1,000	3,000	57.53	86.30
27. Jul	21	1,000	4,000	86.30	172.60

Table 7.5 Lot-Sizing Calculation Using the Dynamic Lot-Sizing Procedure

In the above example, the optimum is determined with the lot size 4,000.

In SAP, you must enter the **DY** indicator for least unit cost for the material in the material master under **Logistics · Production · Master data · Material · change · immediately** in the **MRP 1** tab in the **Lot size** field. You must also enter the **Ordering costs** and the **Storage costs indicator**.

However, with all optimal lot-sizing procedures, you must ensure that the information on the underlying storage costs and ordering costs is determined and monitored as accurately as possible. If these costs change, the material master setting must also be checked and changed if necessary. Master data discipline is therefore vital here.

7.4.7 Optimal Lot-Sizing Procedure in SAP APO

SAP APO also provides all previously described lot-sizing procedures. There, the procedures are assigned to the APO product master through the assignment of a planning heuristic (see Figure 7.20).

Go into the **PP/DS** tab in the **APO product master** and press **F4** to choose a heuristic in the **Product Heuristic** field.

In the **APO product master** in the **Procurement** tab (see Figure 7.21), you can store both a cost function and procurement costs for the calculation. The system places higher priority on the cost function. If none is maintained, the entry for **Procurement Costs** is maintained.

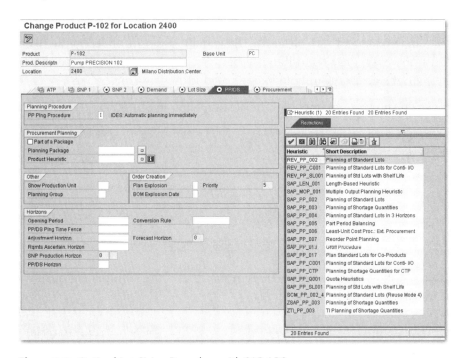

Figure 7.20 Optimal Lot-Sizing Procedure with SAP APO

The parameters of the cost function are defined using the **Parameter** button. For the **Groff procedure** and **Part-period balancing** heuristics, it's immaterial which procurement type you choose for the cost function.

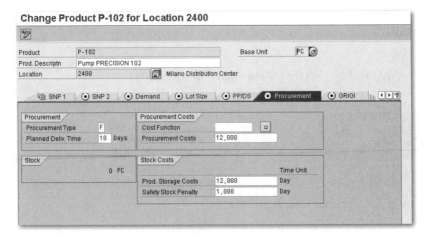

Figure 7.21 Cost Function for the Optimal Lot-Sizing Procedure in SAP APO

The heuristic function is divided into four columns. In the first two columns, you enter the area for which the cost definition is valid. The **From** value is used inclusively; the **To** value is used exclusively. For each validity area, you can define fixed and variable costs. The variable costs are added to the fixed costs; however, only the difference between the beginning of the validity area and the actual quantity to be evaluated is used as a multiplier.

Table 7.6 shows an example for the cost function in SAP APO.

From	To	Fixed Costs	Variable Costs
1	10	0	1
10	20	10	0.9
20	999999999.999	19	0.8

Table 7.6 Cost Function for the Optimal Lot-Sizing Procedure in SAP APO

Table 7.7 shows you the calculation of the costs if the requirement quantity of the material is 5, 12, or 20 units:

Requirement	Fixed costs	Variable costs	Result
5 units	0	5 (5 * 1)	5
12 units	10	1.8 ((12–10)*0.9)	11.8
20 units	19	0 ((19–19)*0.8)	19

Table 7.7 Example for the Cost Function in SAP APO

In mySAP ERP, you cannot store this type of cost function. SAP APO considers the costs at this point much more closely. In this way, you can use a customer-specific planning heuristic to implement additional optimal lot-sizing procedures.

7.4.8   Comparison of Lot-Sizing Procedures in SAP

The grouping of requirement quantities to form one lot size can be influenced by additional restrictions in the material master record: First, by specifying limit values (minimum lot size, maximum lot size). These values are taken into account during the lot-size calculation, that is, the lot size is either rounded to the minimum lot size, or the system prevents a grouping in excess of the maximum lot size. Secondly, you can influence lot size by specifying a rounding value, which allows you to stipulate that during the lot-size calculation, the lot size will be a multiple of an order unit (for example, the pallet size, if deliveries are only made in full pallets).

7.5   Restrictions in the Lot-Size Calculation

In all cases, the ultimate objective of order- and lot-size calculation is to minimize costs. In a subsequent step, we must now also consider the restrictions in the lot-size calculation (i.e., what we could not add as parameters to the algorithm). These restrictions are of greater significance and ultimately make up the criteria that will determine how you calculate order quantities.

1. **Company-specific restrictions**
   Production- and process-related conditions of the production area lead to technically limited maximum order quantities. The reasons for this are space requirements (storage space, space for incoming goods inspections, intermediate storage in front of the machine) and the limited available machine and equipment capacity. Furthermore, in order to avoid excessively high capital commitment and therefore liquidity restrictions, there is a capital limitation. Finally, a maximum allowed coverage time is fixed when determining risk assessment, thereby taking into account the importance of the product (maximum coverage).

2. **Product-related restrictions**
   A maximum coverage of the product is also frequently set for its storage, based on characteristics of the product (for example, its shelf life, how perishable it is, etc.).

3. **Supplier-related restrictions**
   The supplier often demands a minimum purchase quantity (e.g., a batch) or a minimum order value. Furthermore, the supplier-side also has packaging units and production units. Finally, quantity scales are also derived from the type of discount structure offered.

4. **Transport-related restrictions**
   Certain transport units (maximum transport quantity), the predetermined transport type, and loading and unloading options for containers may require us to deviate from the optimal lot size.

5. **Market trends and trends in production organization**
   Market trends are moving toward higher numbers of variants, that is, a process organization for process-oriented production with small lots. Therefore, in addition to the ordering and storage costs, other cost elements have to be factored into the equation (average processing time, storage requirement, number of express orders, process disruptions, flexibility). Later, we will look at the effects of lot sizes on stock-oriented production control again.

Other weaknesses to the lot-size formulas that are not considered:

▶ The effect of the lot size on the lead time

▶ The ability of the supplier or of in-house production to deliver

▶ Size/capacity of the storage space

▶ Shelf life of the goods

▶ Liquidity of the company

SAP estimates that the difference between the "optimal result" of the Wagner and Whitin procedure and the suboptimal result, for instance, the Groff heuristic, is approximately 1%. The economic lot-sizing procedures can therefore be used without any significant disadvantage. The Wagner and Whitin procedure can be implemented in SAP APO with a customer-specific heuristic.

All lot-sizing procedures—the stochastic, periodic, and also the optimal procedures—can only optimize product for product. In the case of multi-phase production, the system will therefore only optimize the production phase planned by the scheduling. The lot sizes of the dependent requirements change accordingly, and the requirements dates are adjusted. For example, if lots are grouped at the higher-level phase, you might infer that the dependent requirements must be available closer in time and in greater quantities. Increased storage costs are then incurred at this level.

Nevertheless, experience shows that using optimal lot-sizing procedures enables you to reduce stocks and make work much easier for your MRP controllers.

7.6 Selecting Lot-Sizing Procedures

In SAP, you can select from among many different lot-sizing procedures. You must first perform an ABC analysis so that you know where your potential is and can implement specific measures for your materials. To choose the right lot-sizing procedures, you need a simulation of the corresponding lot-sizing procedures; alternatively, SAP offers many different setting options, which are listed in Table 7.8.

LS Procedure	mySAP ERP Key Figure	SAP APO Key Figure	ABC-XYZ Matrix								
			AX Part	AY Part	AZ Part	BX Part	BY Part	BZ Part	CX Part	CY Part	CZ Part
Statistical lot sizes											
Exact (with and without splitting)	EX/LL	EX/LL	X	X	X	X					
Fixed	FX/FK	FX/FK					X	X	X	X	
Maximum stock	MS	MS									X
Periodic lot sizes											
Continuous input/output	Not available	SAP_PP_C001	X				X		X		
Hourly lot size	Not available	H	X				X				
Shift lot size	Not available	H	X				X				
Daily lot size	DS	D		X			X		X		
Weekly lot size	WS/W2	W					X	X	X		
14-day lot size	Planning calendar	K						X		X	
Monthly lot size	MB	M							X	X	X
Quarterly lot size	Planning calendar	Q							X		X

Table 7.8 Overview for Selecting the Correct Lot-Sizing Procedure in SAP

LS Procedure	mySAP ERP Key Figure	SAP APO Key Figure	ABC-XYZ Matrix								
			AX Part	AY Part	AZ Part	BX Part	BY Part	BZ Part	CX Part	CY Part	CZ Part
Economic lot sizes											
Groff	GR	SAP_PP_013	X	X		X	X				
Dynamic LS	DY	Customer-specific heuristic or optimization workbench	X								
Part-period balancing	PP	SAP_PP_005					X	X	X	X	X
Least unit cost LS	LC	SAP_PP_006		X			X			X	

Table 7.8 Overview for Selecting the Correct Lot-Sizing Procedure in SAP (cont.)

If you want to optimize your lot sizes, proceed as follows:

1. Run an ABC analysis to classify your materials.

2. Then, run an XYZ analysis to discover how constant or fluctuating is the demand for your product.

3. Create an ABC-XYZ matrix.

4. Using your financial controlling, determine the storage costs and ordering costs for your materials. This is important in case optimal lot sizes will be used.

5. Use different lot-sizing procedures for your materials and simulate their application, if necessary. Note the use of the lot-sizing procedures shown in Table 7.8 in the ABC-XYZ matrix. If you're using the selection criteria from Table 7.8, a simulation will usually not be necessary.

6. Choose an appropriate lot-sizing procedure and define the corresponding settings for each material in SAP.

7. Using the logistics information system in mySAP ERP or a data warehouse in mySAP Business Intelligence (mySAP BI), introduce a corresponding analysis system to allow you to immediately identify any changes in the requirement or stock behavior.

Planners must pay particular attention to production, with all of its uncertainties. This chapter shows you how to handle bottlenecks, material buffer stocks, and resource problems when it comes to planning.

8   Production

In real life, scheduled and actual deadlines of production orders often deviate from one another. The reasons for this are varied: disruptions to the production process, machine failures, ill personnel, or material bottlenecks. In particular, a lack of transparency in the production process—from order intake to confirmation to delivery to the customer—poses a general planning problem.

8.1   How Do Backlogs in Production Affect Stocks?

An order usually travels through several work centers (resources) during the production process. As a rule, at least one of these resources (i.e., machines or personnel) always constitutes the bottleneck. A bottleneck can also change during a production order.

Bottleneck capacity is usually precisely planned and the orders are specially monitored at the delicate location. Deviations and faults in the production process always have the greatest affect on bottleneck resources and can delay the entire process. Then, so-called *backlogs*, which are orders for which the planned start deadline or planned end deadline has already come and gone, can occur. When this happens, the planner is faced with the following various challenges:

Due to the fact that orders can no longer be processed according to schedule, waiting queues form on the machine because the inflow is greater than the outflow. This lengthens the lead times of the orders. Planned deadlines of future orders can no longer be met. Parts that were once important are suddenly no longer needed, and parts that were thought unimportant are now missing, so the more important parts can no longer be differentiated from the less important parts.

Buffer stocks form at the bottlenecks, because orders have to wait to be processed. This can cause delays on non-bottleneck machines, because they have to wait for the delayed order or operation. Large components of the production are affected by only one such backlog.

As a result of extended production lead times, processing flexibility is reduced and short-notice sales orders can no longer be responded to as quickly as required. Transparency is also reduced due to the increased number of waiting queues in front of the machines and the increased buffer stocks in the production. In short, the ability to deliver is reduced.

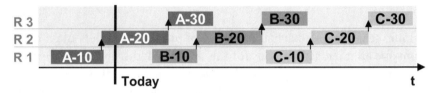

Figure 8.1 Example of a Planning with Item Backlog

Figure 8.1 depicts a typical backlog situation. R1 to R3 represents the resources (work centers) on which three orders (A, B, C) are being produced, with three operations each.

Operation A-10 and the start deadline of operation A-20 are in backlog; that is, operation A-10 should have been completed by this time and A-20 should have begun. If the production was initiated immediately, operation A10 would have to be shifted to the Today line on the time axis. This would mean that operations A-20 and A-30 would also be assigned new deadlines. Because the resource R1 is occupied due to the operation A-10 being shifted, operation B-10 must also start later. The operations B-20 and B-30 would also then have to be moved. Consequently, the backlog of operation A-10 means the following:

▸ Most or all of the order deadlines are unrealistic.

▸ Resource loads are incorrect because order deadlines are no longer correct.

▸ Under certain circumstances, order sequences are incorrect and must be corrected.

▸ Priority shifts cause capacity and material bottlenecks in other orders.

▸ Required dates for purchasing are no longer correct.

▸ Missing parts occur unforeseen.

- Overtime hours cannot be employed efficiently.

- An unnecessarily long commitment of capital occurs due to the forced idle and wait times.

- Just-in-time deliveries must be secured with high safety stocks.

- The lack of transparency has to be compensated for with an enormous controlling expense.

- The entire planning situation has to be adapted to the current situation.

- Production planners and schedulers can now only react. They no longer have room to negotiate for anticipatory production planning, which can, in the long-term, erode morale among all personnel involved.

The Cost Factor of Idle Time

Figure 8.2 shows the lead time of an order across several production stages.

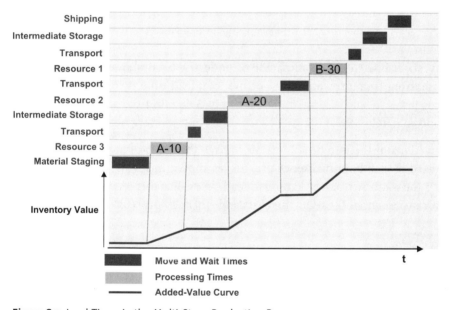

Figure 8.2 Lead Times in the Multi-Stage Production Process

Idle times, such as temporary storage or transport times between the individual processing stages, form the largest portion of the total lead time. The line in the lower part of the diagram runs in parallel to how the inventory value develops. The inventory value rises with the processing time, because the actual value creation only takes place here. The rest of the time, the inventory value remains constant. With a reduction of the entire processing time, the capital would be transacted faster, that is, the return on investment (ROI) would increase. In other words, the existing capital could be used faster, thereby reducing the need for outside capital.

Figure 8.3 illustrates the potential that is created by preventing backlogs and idle times.

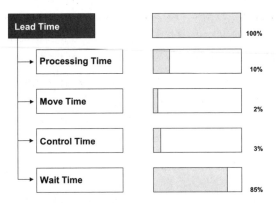

Figure 8.3 Components of Lead Time in the Production Process

Investigations in the manufacturing industry have shown that the actual processing time uses only 10% of the total lead time, while the move time uses just 2%, and control time uses only 3%. Idle time alone accounts for approximately 85%.

If we look at the idle time in detail, we see that 75% of the total idle time is caused by a suboptimal work process, as shown in Figure 8.4. Backlogs are also the main reason for extended lead times. For this reason, there is a significant potential for reducing costs and stocks in process optimization.

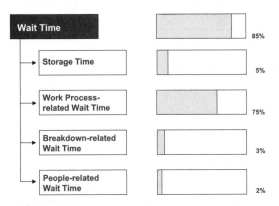

Figure 8.4 Components of Idle Time in the Production Process

The Cost Factor of Backlogs

Backlogs create a false view of capacity: Utilization of capacity always exceeds 100% in the current week, and even surpasses 300%. This means that a preview of the capacities that are being utilized (i.e., which capacities and how many) is not possible with backlogs in production. This is an enormous disadvantage, especially if seasonal or temporary workers are employed, with short notice periods and availability times. With a good capacity forecast, these variable costs could be reduced or optimally managed.

Furthermore, backlogs lead to production having a high share of goods in process. This means that many orders have been started, but have not been completed. Many stocks therefore tie up unnecessary capital and storage space.

To resolve backlogs, additional orders must be pushed through production, in addition to rush orders. This inevitably leads to smaller lots in production and increased setup costs, which represent a large, lot size-independent share of the variable production costs. A setup optimization could reduce the variable production costs here.

Strategies for Cost Reduction

Production Managers can turn to various strategies to minimize total production costs. Fixed costs cannot be reduced offhand, because this would often amount to a reduction in personnel. Through improved utilization, however, new investments in more machines can be prevented, or, at least protracted. In the variable area, improved utilization of capacity can be achieved through the reduction of backlogs. More orders can be produced, which, in turn, lowers the variable production costs. By reducing idle times, the total lead time is shortened and so-called *work-in-process stocks* automatically decrease.

You cannot avoid backlogs entirely. There will always be situations of exceptions in production that require you to respond. Most backlogs, however, don't occur due to exceptional situations, but rather due to suboptimal planning in advance. Production plans are not usually optimized today, and there is a lack of transparency across all production stages.

The reason why backlogs already occur in the planning process will be explained in the following section. Then, we'll define the requirements for a backlog-free production plan, and conclude by showing you how to arrive at such a production plan. In addition, we'll present several steps on how you can proceed in your production optimization.

8.2 Why Do Backlogs Occur in Production Planning?

8.2.1 The Cause: The MRP-II Concept

The mySAP ERP system provides integrated solutions for different branches within a company. The framework extends over sourcing, manufacturing, warehousing, and sales of products. Accounting and controlling support the processes. The focus here is on one's own company, in close context with suppliers and customers. The core of an ERP system in the supply chain area rests with the material requirements planning—the MRP-II planning. Here, a planning of the entire product structure is carried out, based on customer needs; and orders and production orders are created correspondingly.

Figure 8.5 shows how the MRP-II logic is generally implemented in ERP systems today.

Planning Against Infinite Resources

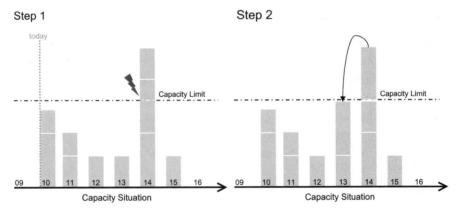

Figure 8.5 MRP-II: Planning in Two Steps

With MRP-II, the material requirements are planned in the first step (material requirements planning) and the machines' capacity requirements are calculated. The results are a capacity load profile of the resources. Furthermore, the planner will determine that several resources are overloaded (bottleneck resources). In the second step of planning, an attempt is made to minimize or completely resolve these capacity bottlenecks (finite scheduling). If finite scheduling is carried out individually for all production stages, the planner must initially carry it out for the first production stage. Production orders are rescheduled with this step, which inevitably leads to deadline shifts for dependent orders. A new material requirements planning for the second production stage is triggered, and, subsequently, the finite scheduling must then be triggered. This process must be repeated for all production stages of a production process.

Because this process in the MRP-II concept is very lengthy and time-consuming, it is rarely used in practice, especially in the case of short-notice changes, where one would have to start from the beginning.

8.2.2 The Evolution: From MRP to APS

In the first generation of MRP systems, the respective Bill of Materials (BOMs) were resolved through the BOM processor for material requirements planning and the material requirements were determined. In doing so, only the quantities and deadlines for materials were planned. There was no resource allocation, and order processing existed only partially or not at all.

The Problem With MRP-II

In most cases, independent individual plans that were not synchronized with one another were created at the respective planning and implementation levels. The individual planning steps were carried out sequentially: First sales planning, then material requirements planning, and finally capacity requirements planning.

This led not only to long processing times in planning, but also to the realization of contrary goals, which did not allow for a uniform and coordinated planning: While production wanted to fully utilize capacity, safeguarding the ability to deliver through building inventories was at the forefront for sales and distribution. Often, already issued procurement or production orders were deferred again in the last planning step by production control in order to optimize the process sequence of orders in accordance with manufacturing criteria. Consequently, available capacity was not considered until late in the planning process, while all prior planning steps assumed infinite production capacity. More precise planning and production information from external suppliers and partners could also not be included in the planning.

Further Development of the MRP-II Concept

Additional production resources were considered in the planning stage in the expansion of the simple MRP concept, along with the MRP-II Concept. Material requirements planning continued to be important, but additional steps—such as capacity requirements planning and scheduling—could be carried out sequentially after this MRP planning step.

Requirements planning across several plants and distribution planning were carried out in other planning systems.

The MRP-II planning philosophy had the following disadvantages:

▸ Long planning duration due to sequential execution of planning steps

▸ Outdated planning results due to long planning cycles

▸ Static lead times increased the total lead time and led to what became known as "lead time syndrome"

▸ Planning and scheduling with unlimited resource availability

▸ Poor utilization of capacity without being able to resolve bottlenecks to optimize capacity

▸ Special manufacturing principles (such as job shop manufacturing) are insufficiently supported

Further development toward MRP-II planning with the help of control stations, third-party Advanced Planning and Scheduling (APS) systems, and concepts such as "order release with load limitation" also proved ineffective in resolving the structural planning deficits.

Ultimately, the aforementioned shortfalls led to the development of a new generation of planning systems: the supply chain management systems (SCM systems). Information will now be processed and available in real time; the Internet will be used for the exchange of information. SAP followed this approach and, with mySAP Supply Chain Management (mySAP SCM) and the software component SAP Advanced Planner and Optimizer (SAP APO), developed a complete APS system in which concurrent material and capacity requirements planning and, furthermore, true optimization options, are available. Another clear advantage lies in the close real-time integration with the backend system mySAP ERP.

8.3   Reduction of Backlogs

8.3.1   Realistic Production Plans

Characteristics of a Good Plan

Before we consider the process for determining a production plan, we will specify the criteria against which a plan must be evaluated. The following characteristics distinguish a good production plan:

▸ The production plan must be robust.

▸ The production plan must be technically feasible.

▸ The production plan must conform to the target criteria of the company.

▸ You should consider the service level and customer service.

▸ Inventory stocks must be reduced.

▸ Production flexibility must be retained.

▸ You must be able to maximize production output.

▸ Multi-stage production phases should be coordinated to one another.

▸ The planning should prevent backlogs in the production and be able to resolve them quickly and flexibly.

▸ The production plan should keep costs to a minimum, via setup optimization, for example.

Operational Criteria of a Good Plan

The following operational criteria and goals can be derived from these characteristics:

▸ Plan the degree of utilization of resources (maximum utilization of capacity).

▸ Determine the optimum sequence of orders (minimum setup time, minimum setup costs).

▸ Reduce setup costs and variable unit costs.

▸ Shorten order lead times.

▸ Minimize stockholding costs.

▸ Satisfy needs in a timely fashion (minimal belatedness).

▸ Maximize turnover (minimal belatedness).

Goal Conflicts

Unfortunately, several criteria or goals are contrary to one another:

▶ **Setup optimization versus short lead times and inventory reduction**
If throughput is to be high at bottleneck resources, it may only be set up infrequently and large lots must be produced. Large lots lengthen the lead times, cause production to be carried out sooner than necessary, and the stocks in the company grow.

▶ **Robustness versus short lead times and inventory reduction**
The demand for robustness can only be met with buffers. Buffers lengthen the lead times, cause production to be carried out sooner than necessary, and the stocks in the company grow.

No heuristics can automatically achieve a good compromise between these goal conflicts; the so-called *optimizer* is required here (see Section 8.4.3).

8.3.2 The Finite Production Plan

Characteristics of a Finite Plan

A finite production plan fulfills a necessary characteristic of a good plan, namely, the fact that it is technically feasible (i.e., the required production factors—resources and materials in particular—are available):

▶ Resources are not overloaded, because the actual capacities are taken into account during planning.

▶ Components are only consumed to the extent that these components are in inventory, or can be acquired in a timely manner.

▶ The product can be produced by the desired deadline, in accordance with all technical modifications. All plans, BOMs, and so forth, are complete, consistent, and allow for production.

▶ The required tools are available, because they are also checked for availability.

▶ Personnel is adequate and available with the right qualifications.

A finite plan does not necessarily have to be a good plan with regard to the other goals or evaluation criteria. It may not optimally coordinate the aforementioned goal conflicts with one another, either. For this, the optimizer is required.

Outlets in the Production Plan

In a complex production plan, situations may occur in which the system cannot fulfill the existing requirements, especially where there are insufficient or unrealistic specifications. To intercept these problems and still generate a feasible production plan, outlets must be defined that permit infringement against certain requirements. In this way, a suboptimal solution is found, but it represents the best solution under the given conditions.

Outlets are used, for example, when an order cannot be produced by the desired deadline due to insufficient resource capacity or material components that are lacking. The following outlets are possible:

- The planned order is not created. The customer order is not satisfied.
- The planned order is created late. The customer order is satisfied late.
- Alternative resources are utilized, despite higher unit costs.
- The product is outsourced.
- Overtime hours are performed.
- Orders are created as deallocated. Then, the aforementioned outlets must be manually checked to determine which of them, or other outlets, can be used.

A good production plan is further characterized by ensuring that such outlets are used as rarely and as selectively as possible. Selective utilization of outlets is considered to mean that in an overload situation of a bottleneck resource, the order with the lowest priority (rather than any arbitrary order) is deferred to a later date in the future.

MRP Heuristics and Finite Planning

The MRP heuristics traditionally used in mySAP ERP is unsuitable for finite planning, for the following reasons:

- The MRP heuristics does not achieve a good compromise between the conflicts of the finite planning goals. It does not have any goal function as is common with optimizers. Only with such a goal function can the algorithm determine how the different planning goals should be weighted against one another.
- The MRP heuristics does not carry out any setup optimization. With finite planning, the setup sequence is really coincidental to the current allocation of resources (with fixed planned orders and production orders), as

well as to the planning sequence of the products in the MRP heuristics. This is almost always suboptimal, however, and insufficiently utilizes resource capacity.

▸ The MRP heuristics normally carries out modification planning with a high reutilization mode. This means that products whose availability situation has not changed since the last planning are not rescheduled, either. As long as planning is done with infinite planning or the **Find Slot** planning mode, the planning orders for these products are not changed and the capacity commitments retain their deadlines; however, these commitments fragment the resources. The slots between the capacity commitments are often short, even if the resource is poorly utilized in the summation. The system can therefore find a slot for only products that are to be produced on the same resource.

▸ Planning in the MRP heuristics occurs in the sequence of the low-level code. If a resource is required for a finished product, as well as for an assembly contained therein, the resource is first encumbered by the planned orders of the finished product in the MRP heuristics. This can lead to insufficient capacity being available on the resource for the planned orders of the assembly.

▸ The MRP heuristics carries out planning product by product. If a product happens to be planned very late in the planning process, the chances that this product will find sufficient slots on the resource are reduced. So-called *loser materials* occur as a result.

▸ If the MRP heuristics are carried out with parallel processing, resources are allocated from several parallel dialog processes. Parallel resource allocations are not visible for the individual dialog process, which can result in allocating more resources than are needed.

In the above, several reasons were listed for preventing the system from finding suitable slots on the required resources for the transactions for new planned orders. If the system cannot find any slots, the following consequences are then imminent:

▸ As long as only backward scheduling is in operation, the planned order cannot be created. This serves not only to reserve the resource, however, but also and especially as a consumer for the raw materials. If freed capacities arise later (such as after a pre-production optimization), a new planned order could possibly be scheduled. Under certain circumstances, however, the raw materials and time needed to acquire them are then lacking.

▸ Once changed over to forward scheduling, you can defer the planned order far into the future under certain circumstances.

▸ If there are alternative infinite resources, the infinite resources are very frequently used. Utilization of the finite resources is rather poor in comparison.

In such a situation, you could attempt to achieve a better result through another strategy rather than through **Find Slot**. The following problems occur in doing so:

▸ If working with the insert or squeeze in modes, all steps that impede the resource's ability to plan a new planned order are shifted in the planning direction. This happens anew with every insertion process, which compromises the performance of the system enormously.

▸ All planned orders changed in this way must also be transferred to a connected R/3 system, which places a heavy load on the system.

▸ By shifting planned orders toward the present (this happens during backward scheduling), the component requirements are situated earlier. The planning of the components is no longer valid and must also be adjusted.

▸ By shifting planned orders toward the future (this happens if the insert mode is combined with forward scheduling), availability dates are shifted into the future and customer orders can no longer be covered in time. Typically, planned orders are deferred to a later date in the future by earlier scheduled products, thereby causing these products to become loser materials.

Consequently, the MRP logic is not suitable for the creation of a good production plan. Although it does exhibit a basic functionality for the creation of a production plan, it is still highly inadequate. A high degree of required manual effort and a certain degree of opacity are the result.

Resolving Backlogs

In SAP APO, you can create realistic production plans without backlogs with the help of finite production planning, synchronization of material and capacity planning, and a multi-level, coordinated material requirements planning. Through additional optimization, these can be coordinated with production costs and stocks to the best possible degree. Various simulation options allow for backlogs to be recognized in advance and to be prevented. With the support of the online alert monitor, backlogs that occur can also be recognized and resolved as quickly as possible.

With the SAP APO functionalities, you can avoid backlogs during planning and respond faster to exceptional situations. The planner can create a feasible production plan and then choose to act instead of merely react. He or she has the capability to quickly reschedule all dependent orders and recognize their implications. The planner can activate simulations proactively to prevent or prepare for risky situations. These versatile capabilities increase both transparency in the planning and production process, as well as flexibility in production. Additional advantages are:

▶ Shorter lead times of orders

▶ Lower buffer stocks in production

▶ Increase of maximum production capacities through improved utilization of resources

▶ Reduction of variable production costs

▶ Improved response capability for priority changes or additional customer requirements

▶ Improvement of ability to deliver and delivery reliability

You can see the result of planning without backlogs in Figure 8.6. Scheduling backlogs can be avoided from the outset. No order is delayed on any of the three resources, and consequently, there is no backlog.

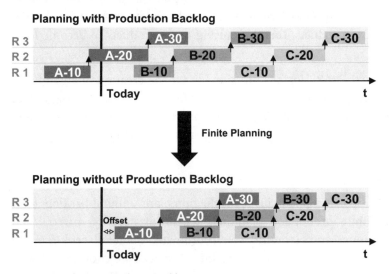

Figure 8.6 Planning Without Backlogs

8.4   Finite Planning and Optimization in SAP APO

No planning system absolves the planner from making decisions regarding which resources should be finite and which resources should be infinite. The planner is still accountable for finding the right mix of finite and infinite planning, as well as determining the right balance of optimization and manual intervention, in order to achieve shorter lead times and stock reduction.

Therefore, as a planner, you should check very carefully which resources must have finite planning and which resources must have infinite planning, and then determine the precise sequence of your planning process.

In the following sections, a practical example from the manufacturing industry is intended to show you the steps to take to best facilitate planning:

1. Infinite planning (MRP heuristics) for products that are produced on bottleneck resources is carried out, so that initial production jobs and orders are created.

2. Finite planning (optimization or resource heuristics) for the critical bottleneck resources is then carried out, so that their resource capacity utilization is optimized.

3. In a further step, the planning of the finished products is adapted to the modified resource allocation with the *Bottom-up* heuristics rescheduling, so that all further production stages are adjusted to the new deadlines that were created by Step 2.

4. Finally, infinite MRP heuristics is carried out again for all products that were not yet planned in Step 1.

In SAP APO, you can incorporate these four steps in a planning run. Upon starting, the steps are automatically processed in the background, in the sequence above. The subdivision is concealed from the planner; he or she sees only the individual planning step.

The following items are intended to describe the additional benefits of the SAP APO-PP/DS functionality in contrast to the ERP systems. In short, the question is how you can reduce and prevent backlogs and reduce stocks with SAP APO-PP/DS. We recommend that you examine the following areas of potential:

▶ Simultaneous, finite material and capacity requirements planning

▶ Planning heuristics

▶ Optimization methods and concepts

- Description of alerts and their forwarding
- Simulation
- Capable-to-Promise
- Embedding of superordinate and subordinate planning levels
- Separate planning tools in SAP APO PP/DS

8.4.1 Concurrent, Finite Material and Capacity Planning

Automatic Planning

A particular strength of the production planning and detailed scheduling function (PP/DS) in SAP APO lies in the simultaneous inspection of capacities as they relate to finite planning (in other words, the limited capacities) and the inspection for the availability of required materials.

The simultaneous material and capacity check can be carried out automatically during the planning of material requirements and at the time of order creation. The net requirements calculation is the first step in order creation that the system carries out during the automatic planning of a product. It is used for the calculation of unsecured product requirements. In order to then cover these unsecured product requirements, the system first sets the product requirements against the already existing acquisitions. The system then attempts to create stock receipts to cover unassigned deficit quantities. The net requirements calculation is also able to process criteria: Product acquisitions are merely assigned product requirements with corresponding criteria. This ability is called *characteristics-dependent planning* (CDP) in SAP APO.

The system calculates the quantities to be procured based on the requirements calculated in the net requirements calculation. The lot size calculation is controlled by minimum/maximum lot sizes, rounding values, target range, waste, inventory costs, and so forth. The goal of the lot size calculation is a minimization of the inventory and setup costs.

- Large lot sizes lead to higher inventory and lower setup costs.
- Small lot sizes lead to lower inventory and high setup costs.

During automatic planning, the system can create stock receipts for unsecured requirements either immediately or at the next planning run.

The system also carries out a supply source determination during this step. The system calculates the procurement type and selects a procurement alternative that can deliver the required quantity on time. If several procurement alternatives are maintained, the system uses the procurement alternative with the highest priority and the lowest costs. If none of the available procurement alternatives can deliver in time, the system creates the goods receipt for a later date.

The capacity review already takes place during the creation of a planned order. Contrary to mySAP ERP, the capability for an early simulation of planning scenarios is provided for in this way in SAP APO. Automatic planning is not available in mySAP ERP. There, it does not take place until the next MRP run. With SAP APO, you can respond significantly faster to planning changes, short-notice disruptions to production, or delayed deliveries by suppliers. The consequences of the changes or disruptions are visible immediately and you can quickly undertake appropriate countermeasures. This drastically increases the ability to deliver and reduces lead times. Backlogs are already prevented in planning, or can be immediately resolved.

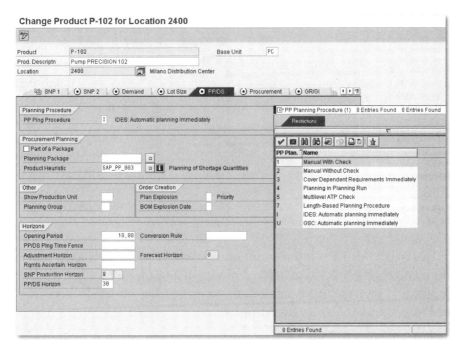

Figure 8.7 SAP APO Product File—PP/DS View

Figure 8.7 shows the product master data in SAP APO, which can be reached in the SAP APO menu under **Master Data · Product · Product Master**. In this view, you can enter the master data for the production planning and fine control. In the **Planning Procedure** section, you set whether you want to work with automatic planning. To do so, select the **Automatic Planning Immediately** entry in the **PP Planning Procedure** field located on the right side of the screen.

Pegging

Existing product receipts and product stocks that can cover the requirement are assigned to a product requirement through *pegging*. Pegging organizes the material flow across all low-level codes, beginning with procurement of components and raw materials, all the way to the delivery of a customer order, as shown in Figure 8.8.

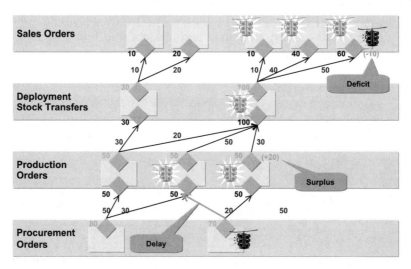

Figure 8.8 Pegging in SAP APO: Material Flow Organized Across All Low-Level Codes— Surpluses and Deficits Are Visible Immediately (Source: SAP)

Surpluses and deficits in the entire order network are immediately visible through pegging. In case of delayed receipt of an order for a superordinate production job, a deficit is immediately specified for this production order and for the higher-level customer order.

A differentiation is made between fixed and dynamic pegging. In **fixed pegging**, there is a permanent link between the consuming and the producing orders. The material flow relationship is fixed and is no longer changed during further planning steps.

Contrary to fixed pegging, in **dynamic pegging**, there is only a loose coupling between the low-level codes. Dynamic pegging is recalculated after every planning action and leads to another association of orders.

Fixed pegging and dynamic pegging have several advantages and disadvantages:

▶ One advantage of fixed pegging is that a link between an acquisition element and an outgoing element assigned once is retained, even if other acquisition and outgoing elements change. This represents an enormous advantage, particularly for individual productions. Orders can be sent through the entire production, with their resources across all production stages, without changing the resource. In this way, you can ensure that production is carried out for only a specific customer order in one production job. Contrary to mySAP ERP, fixed pegging associations can also be changed manually, if there is an actual need.

▶ One advantage of dynamic pegging is that a more favorable planning situation is achieved through the redistribution of receipt quantities to product requirements after a change to a receipt or requirement element.

▶ Dynamic pegging also enables lot creation and the recalculation of lots after requirements changes. If working with weekly lots, for example, and the requirements change within a week, heuristics can calculate the new receipt element based on the total of requirements in the period.

▶ Another important advantage of dynamic pegging is in its flexibility for allocating consumers and resources. In this way, stocks can be optimally utilized.

▶ A disadvantage of dynamic pegging is the need for constant recalculation of the pegging network. In complex pegging networks, an n:m relationship is quickly created between several orders from a 1:1 relationship between consuming and producing orders. The scheduling results from the re-planning of such pegging networks are very difficult to retrace.

▶ A distinct advantage of pegging lies in the transparency it enables for production and MRP. Customer orders, production jobs, and purchase orders can always be traced across all production stages, top-down or bottom-up, even in a customer-anonymous make-to-stock production. The consequences of a delayed delivery on the affected production and customer orders are recognized quickly. Information on the current realistic delivery date of a customer order can therefore be provided at any time. Because there is no pegging in mySAP ERP, SAP APO creates enormous transparency within your production, regardless of how many production levels with which you work.

You can determine whether you plan with fixed or dynamic pegging in the **Pegging** section in the **Planning Strategy** screen (see Figure 8.9).

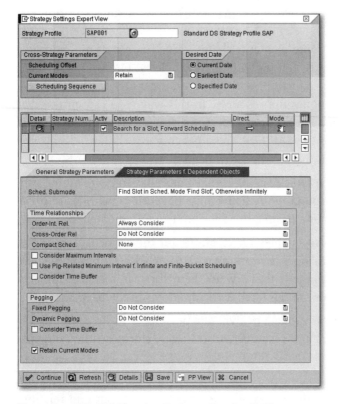

Figure 8.9 SAP APO Planning Strategy—Pegging Settings

The pegging links between incoming and outgoing elements can be viewed at the following locations in SAP APO:

Product View—Elements Overview
The quantity of a receipt that is not required or the quantity of a requirement that is not covered is shown for each receipt or requirement element in the **Surplus/Shortfall** column. This gives you a quick overview of the surplus or shortfall for a material in the overview display. In addition, you can see alerts, if any are present (see Figure 8.10, second column). Because the example in the figure works with exact lot sizes, an incoming or outgoing item does not create a surplus or shortfall here.

Product View—Context
The finished product requirements that are covered from a selected receipt element on any production level are shown in the context display, along

with what receipt elements are required for the raw materials. This means that you see all relevant pegging information for the allocation of individual orders here. In the figure, the requirements for the planned order 202587 (i.e., the purchased requisition) are covered by planned order 128481, which is one production level lower. This planned order is covered from the stock level.

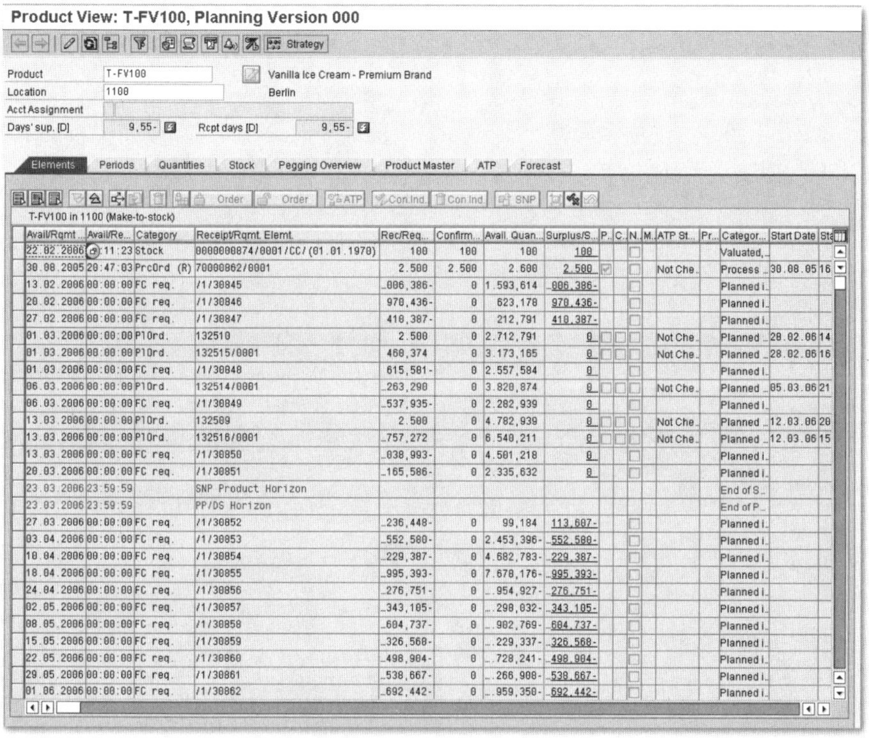

Avail/Rqmt...	Avail/Re...	Category	Receipt/Rqmt. Elemt.	Rec/Req...	Confirm...	Avail. Quan...	Surplus/S...	P..	C..	N..	M..	ATP St...	Pr...	Categor...	Start Date	Sta
22.02.2006	:11:23	Stock	0000000874/0001/CC/(01.01.1970)	100	100	100	100							Valuated,..		
30.08.2005	20:47:03	PrcOrd (R)	70000862/0001	2.500	2.500	2.600	2.500					Not Che..		Process ..	30.08.05	16
13.02.2006	00:00:00	FC req.	/1/30845	806,386-	0	1.593,614	806,386-							Planned i..		
20.02.2006	00:00:00	FC req.	/1/30846	970,436-	0	623,178	970,436-							Planned i..		
27.02.2006	00:00:00	FC req.	/1/30847	410,387-	0	212,791	410,387-							Planned i..		
01.03.2006	00:00:00	PlOrd.	132510	2.500	0	2.712,791	0					Not Che..		Planned ..	28.02.06	14
01.03.2006	00:00:00	PlOrd.	132515/0001	460,374	0	3.173,165	0					Not Che..		Planned ..	28.02.06	16
01.03.2006	00:00:00	FC req.	/1/30848	615,581-	0	2.557,584	0							Planned i..		
06.03.2006	00:00:00	PlOrd.	132514/0001	263,290	0	3.820,874	0					Not Che..		Planned ..	05.03.06	21
06.03.2006	00:00:00	FC req.	/1/30849	537,935-	0	2.282,939	0							Planned i..		
13.03.2006	00:00:00	PlOrd.	132509	2.500	0	4.782,939	0					Not Che..		Planned ..	12.03.06	20
13.03.2006	00:00:00	PlOrd.	132516/0001	757,272	0	6.540,211	0					Not Che..		Planned ..	12.03.06	15
13.03.2006	00:00:00	FC req.	/1/30850	038,993-	0	4.501,218	0							Planned i..		
20.03.2006	00:00:00	FC req.	/1/30851	165,586-	0	2.335,632	0							Planned i..		
23.03.2006	23:59:59		SNP Product Horizon											End of S..		
23.03.2006	23:59:59		PP/DS Horizon											End of P..		
27.03.2006	00:00:00	FC req.	/1/30852	236,448-	0	99,184	113,607-							Planned i..		
03.04.2006	00:00:00	FC req.	/1/30853	552,580-	0	2.453,396-	552,580-							Planned i..		
10.04.2006	00:00:00	FC req.	/1/30854	229,387-	0	4.682,783-	229,387-							Planned i..		
18.04.2006	00:00:00	FC req.	/1/30855	995,393-	0	7.678,176-	995,393-							Planned i..		
24.04.2006	00:00:00	FC req.	/1/30856	276,751-	0	954,927-	276,751-							Planned i..		
02.05.2006	00:00:00	FC req.	/1/30857	343,105-	0	298,032-	343,105-							Planned i..		
08.05.2006	00:00:00	FC req.	/1/30858	604,737-	0	902,769-	604,737-							Planned i..		
15.05.2006	00:00:00	FC req.	/1/30859	326,568-	0	229,337-	326,568-							Planned i..		
22.05.2006	00:00:00	FC req.	/1/30860	498,904-	0	728,241-	498,904-							Planned i..		
29.05.2006	00:00:00	FC req.	/1/30861	538,667-	0	266,908-	538,667-							Planned i..		
01.06.2006	00:00:00	FC req.	/1/30862	692,442-	0	959,350-	692,442-							Planned i..		

Figure 8.10 SAP APO Product View—Elements

The advantage of the context view lies in the multilevel, cross-material view. For example, you can see all purchase orders, production and planned orders of a specific customer order, or all orders of the entire production levels of a material. Using this context view, you can quickly respond in case of exceptions, particularly in multilevel production processes. This view is not available in mySAP ERP.

Alert Monitor

In the Alert Monitor, the surpluses and shortfalls of location products are displayed.

Order / Resource	ReqElement	Ver	Rec/ReqQty	ReqPegQty	ActPegQty	T	Require...	Rqmnt ...	AvailDay	Avail.Ti...	P	Source	Target	P..
FC req. /1/29851			2-	0	0		10.02.2006	00:00:00	09.02.2006	12:00:00	0	2500	2500	P-1
PurRqs 202587/000010	FC req. /1/29851		220	2	2	D	10.02.2006	00:00:00	09.02.2006	12:00:00	0	1000	2500	P-1
PlOrd. 128481	PReqRel 202587/		150	150	150	D	09.02.2006	07:02:00	09.11.2005	09:08:35	0	1000	1000	P-1
DepDmd 128481/0001			150-	0	0		02.11.2005	11:25:43		00:00:00	0	1000	1000	102
DepDmd 128481/0002			150-	0	0		02.11.2005	11:25:43		00:00:00	0	1000	1000	102
DepDmd 128481/0003			150-	0	0		02.11.2005	11:25:43		00:00:00	0	1000	1000	102
DepDmd 128481/0004			150-	0	0		02.11.2005	11:25:43		00:00:00	0	1000	1000	102
SNP:PL-ORD 202599/1	PReqRel 202587/		167	1	1	D	09.02.2006	07:02:00	30.01.2006	23:59:59	0	1000	1000	P-1
SNP:PL-ORD 200107/1	SNP:DepDmd 20:		3.636	167	167	D	30.01.2006	00:00:00	13.01.2006	23:59:59	0	1000	1000	102
PurRqs 10021446/00001	SNP:DepDmd 20		10	10	10	D	12.01.2006	00:00:00	09.12.2005	18:27:45	0		1000	102
Stock /0001/CC	SNP:DepDmd 20		1.523	1.240	1.240	D	12.01.2006	00:00:00	22.02.2006	13:25:06	0		1000	102
SNP:DepDmd 200107/2			2.386-	0	0		12.01.2006	00:00:00	09.12.2005	18:27:45	0	1000	1000	102
SNP:PL-ORD 200097/1	SNP:DepDmd 20:		3.696	167	167	D	30.01.2006	00:00:00	13.01.2006	23:59:59	0	1000	1000	102
Stock /0001/CC	SNP:DepDmd 20		2.105	2.105	2.105	D	12.01.2006	00:00:00	22.02.2006	13:25:06	0		1000	102
SNP:DepDmd 200097/2			1.591-	0	0		12.01.2006	00:00:00		00:00:00	0	1000	1000	102
PlOrd. 128476	PReqRel 202587/		100	59	50	D	09.02.2006	07:02:00	09.11.2005	09:07:59	0	1000	1000	P-1
DepDmd 128476/0001			100-	0	0		02.11.2005	11:25:07		00:00:00	0	1000	1000	102
DepDmd 128476/0002			100-	0	0		02.11.2005	11:25:07		00:00:00	0	1000	1000	102
DepDmd 128476/0003			100-	0	0		02.11.2005	11:25:07		00:00:00	0	1000	1000	102
DepDmd 128476/0004			100-	0	0		02.11.2005	11:25:07		00:00:00	0	1000	1000	102
PrdOrd (C) 60000862	PReqRel 202587/		10	10	10	D	09.02.2006	07:02:00	30.11.2005	23:59:59	0	1000	1000	P-1
OrdRes 60000862/0001			10-	0	0		30.11.2005	13:59:59		00:00:00	0	1000	1000	102
OrdRes 60000862/0002			10-	0	0		30.11.2005	13:59:59		00:00:00	0	1000	1000	102
OrdRes 60000862/0003			10-	0	0		30.11.2005	13:59:59		00:00:00	0	1000	1000	102
OrdRes 60000862/0006			10-	0	0		30.11.2005	13:59:59		00:00:00	0	1000	1000	102

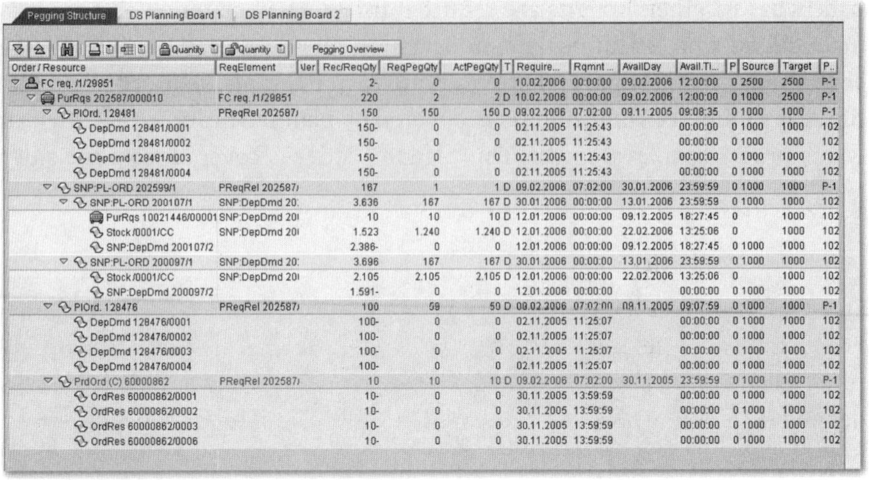

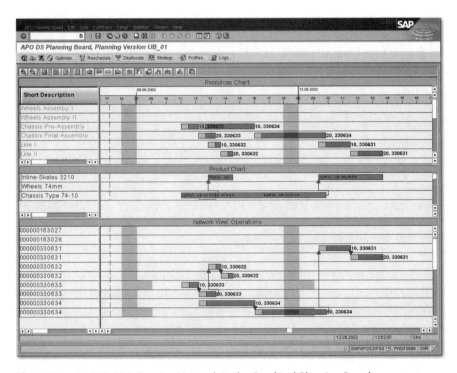

Figure 8.11 SAP APO Product View—Context

Figure 8.12 An SAP APO Pegging Network in the Graphical Planning Board

Graphical Planning Board

Dependent objects can be shifted along with an operation shift on the graphical planning board (see Figure 8.12). You can recognize the dependent orders by the green lines connecting the orders. Dependent objects can also be orders from other production levels, if they are connected with the shifted operation via pegging relationships and if it is set in the strategy profile that pegging relationships are to be observed.

8.4.2 Planning Heuristics (PP/DS Planning Run)

What Are Heuristics?

Standard heuristics are available within the SAP APO components Planning Production and Detailed Scheduling (PP/DS) for the production planning run. Heuristics are algorithms that can be used to resolve planning problems, depending on the planning focus for products, operations, or resources. Because these algorithms and strategies are based on experience, conjecture, or hypotheses, they merely increase the probability of finding a solution. There is no guarantee for finding a solution, to say nothing of finding a good solution. Nevertheless, heuristics are well suited for a whole range of planning problems. A considerable advantage—versus optimizing procedures, for instance—lies in the comparably simple transparency of the results and the better performance.

Heuristics are differentiated into:

▶ Detailed scheduling heuristics

▶ Customer-specific heuristics

We will not describe all heuristics here; however, we will name the most important heuristics for inventory optimization, as well as several others that mySAP ERP doesn't offer.

▶ **Production planning heuristics**
   The heuristics for production planning include several for lot-sizing procedures, process control, and for service functions (see Figure 8.13). The heuristics cover requirements with the help of lot-sizing procedures. They are available for in-house produced products, as well as outsourced products.

▶ **Detailed scheduling heuristics**
   The heuristics of detailed scheduling serve to schedule planned and production orders. The planning focus is on resources and operations. Examples of such heuristics are the reduction of lead time and the resolution of backlogs.

Production planning heuristics are explained in greater detail in the following sections so that their areas of application are better understood.

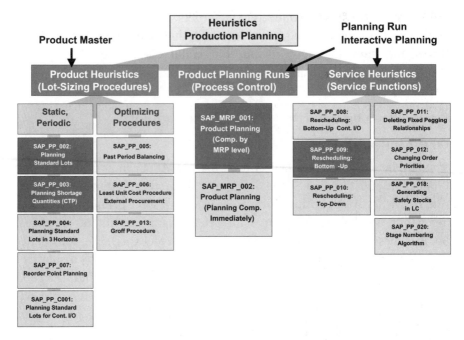

Figure 8.13 Overview of Several Heuristics in SAP APO Production Planning (Source: SAP)

Product Heuristics

Product heuristics define algorithms for the planning of materials. The individual steps of a planning run (source determination, net requirements calculation, lot sizing, etc.) are implemented here. Product heuristics are particularly responsible for creating, changing, and clearing requirement coverage elements. There are the following product heuristics:

Planning standard lots (SAP_PP_002)

This algorithm carries out planning for covering product requirements and generates new receipts. It uses the lot-sizing procedures and settings from the product master. We do not recommend using SAP_PP_002 directly in a production planning run; however, if you want to call this heuristic, it is only advisable if there is a manageable number of products that are to be planned. Because the sequence in which the products are planned is random and does not follow the low-level codes, you should ensure that you do not plan header products and their components in the same operation. You should take into account all of these recommendations for all heuristics that cover requirements (other examples are SAP_PP_004, SAP_PP_005, and SAP_PP_C001).

Planning shortage quantities (SAP_PP_003)

With this algorithm, you can create receipt elements for product requirements where there are shortages and delete surplus receipt elements. The
system first carries out a dynamic pegging, in which it reallocates the fixed
and unfixed receipt elements to the requirements. In doing so, the system
takes into account characteristics (characteristics-dependent planning or
CPT) and receives fixed pegging relationships. The system then plans the
shortage quantities as follows or deletes surpluses.

Planning standard lots in three horizons (SAP_PP_004)

With this heuristic, you can create acquisition proposals for uncovered
requirements in up to three subsequent planning horizons, with different lot
sizing procedures.

*Heuristics for repetitive manufacturing (multi-resource planning
with SAP_REM_001 and SAP_REM_002)*

There are two basic heuristics for repetitive manufacturing. Both are for the
period-oriented planning on several resources and can be used for interactive as well as for background planning. You can start the heuristics on the
product planning board, on the DS planning board, and also in the order
view. Both heuristics create planned orders for existing requirements and
allow for the resource capacities available per period in doing so. The uniform multi-resource planning (SAP_REM_001) evenly distributes the
planned orders across all resources. Conversely, the multi-resource planning
for the primary resource (SAP_REM_002) first attempts to utilize a preferred
resource, and then the alternative resources, up to 100%. If an alternative
resource is no longer available, the resources of the previous period are utilized. If there are overloads in the first period, the orders are distributed
across the resources of the subsequent periods. With the help of this heuristic, you can compensate for seasonal fluctuations within a time period that
would lead to surpluses and shortages in capacity planning over time. This
planning functionality, which is not available in mySAP ERP, means an
improved utilization of resources, especially for seasonal production. Figure
8.14 shows the initial situation for the following sample scenario: Products 1
and 2 can only be produced on the resources L1 and L3, where L1 is the primary resource. Product 2 can only be produced on the resources L2 and L3,
where L2 is the primary resource. All three resources can produce a maximum of 100 pieces per week. In weeks 1 and 5, there is a capacity overload
due to a seasonal demand.

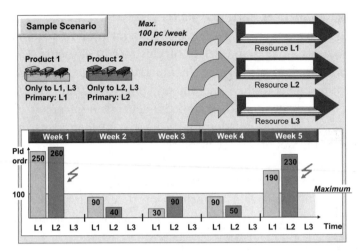

Figure 8.14 Example of Multi-Resource Planning in SAP APO—Initial Situation (Source: SAP)

In the first step, the heuristic (SAP_REM_002) attempts to utilize the primary resources. The secondary resources (here, resource L3 for product 2) are then utilized. An attempt is then made to utilize first the primary and then the secondary resources in the previous weeks, in a backward wave (see Figure 8.15). Here, then, the surplus requirements of 30 pieces from product 2 are relocated to the primary resource L2 in week 4. For product 1, this means that the surplus planned order of 90 is shifted first to the primary resource L1 for 10 pieces, and then on to the secondary resource L3 in the amount of 80 pieces.

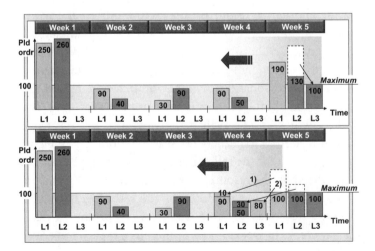

Figure 8.15 Example of Multi-Resource Planning in SAP APO—Backward Wave (Source: SAP)

The same logic is now applied to the surplus capacity requirements in the current week. These cannot be shifted backward, only forward. Of the 150 surplus pieces of product 1 from week 1, 10 pieces are relocated to the primary resource L1 in week 2, then 100 pieces to the secondary resource L3 in week 2 and the last 40 pieces to the primary resource L1 in week 3.

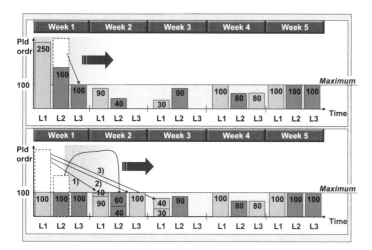

Figure 8.16 Example of Multi-Resource Planning in SAP APO—Forward Wave (Source: SAP)

Heuristics for campaign planning

Production campaigns are used primarily in manufacturing where products are manufactured on production systems. Between the design of different production passes or before standstill, these systems must be changed over or cleaned. Often, manufactured products are not only put into final storage but also intermediate storage, if they are to be used by a subsequent production phase, for example. These setup or cleaning processes, as well as storage, can be very costly. There is a difference between single and multiple product campaigns. A product campaign is equivalent to the quantity of material that is produced without interruption on a production line of a process stage, or the quantity of material that can be packaged on a packaging line. At the production level, the campaign is the equivalent of a total of several passes. A *pass* is the quantity of material that can be produced in one manufacturing process. Before you can use the products in a subsequent campaign, they must undergo a major setup and cleaning process. The quantities of materials of a material group are only interrupted by small setup and cleaning periods within a multiple product campaign.

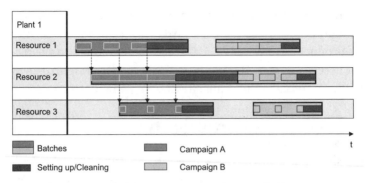

| | Batches | | Campaign A |
| | Setting up/Cleaning | | Campaign B |

Figure 8.17 Campaign Planning in SAP APO (Source: SAP)

In Figure 8.17, you can see the multi-stage campaign A, which is carried out on three resources. At each stage, it again consists of three individual passes (orders) and a cleaning job at the end of the campaign. In this way, the cleaning costs are distributed across all three orders and the planning of all orders takes place centrally via the campaign. In SAP APO PP/DS, the campaign planning can be called and carried out from the DS Planning Board. Figure 8.18 shows the campaign in the upper resource view and the three accompanying orders in the lower order view.

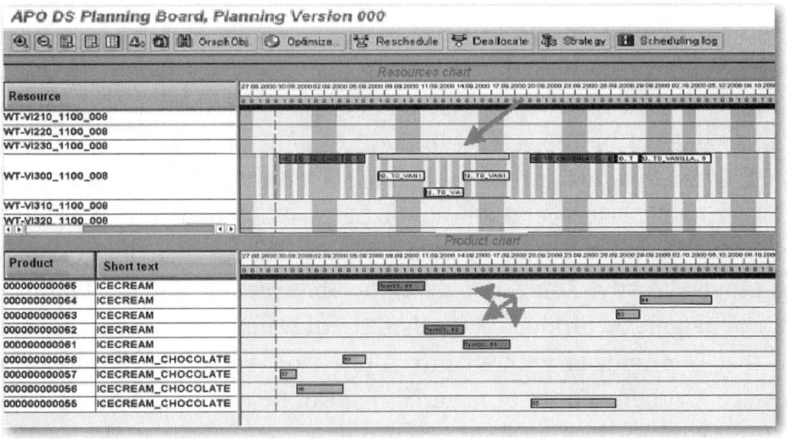

Figure 8.18 Campaign Planning in SAP APO PP/DS—DS Planning Board

The goal of campaign planning is to weigh setup and storage costs against each other. Therefore, frequent changing of the production system can reduce storage costs, but can result in high setup costs. On the other hand, if changeovers are carried out as little as possible, this can reduce setup costs, but higher storage costs can result.

With these heuristics, you have the most important planning functions for production campaigns at your disposal. Neighboring orders that produce the same product, or have the same setup group, can be collected into a production campaign. Consequently, you need only one setup order for all orders of a production campaign. Production campaigns can be optimally created and planned in SAP APO, in contrast to mySAP ERP.

Heuristics for Push Production

The goal of the push production is to consume surplus raw material. A typical push material, for example, is milk. The shelf life of the raw material of milk expires, but the final products of cheese and butter last longer. With push production, surplus milk can be prevented from having to be destroyed. Receipt elements and inventories of a raw material are brought to a meaningful use.

The following reasons can account for raw material surpluses:

▶ No consumer is available for a certain quantity of a push material. Because the expiration date will run out, however, it must be decided what will be produced in what quantity in order to consume the unused material.

▶ The receipt elements were created by a procurement planning heuristic that rounded to minimum lot sizes, fixed lot sizes, or rounding quantities.

▶ After fixing the receipt element, demand has decreased. The procurement planning heuristic can no longer adapt the receipt element to the reduced requirement quantity.

▶ Your company processes milk or operates in recycling and therefore has only restricted influence on the supply of raw materials.

▶ You pursue the goal of processing raw materials for possible finished products, even without customer orders. For perishable raw materials, in particular, the arrival of customer orders cannot be delayed.

▶ The surplus raw material is difficult to store and endangers the environment.

The production plan is therefore not modified based on a demand for target products, but rather it is based on a not yet used offering of raw materials or semi-finished products. Additional material components are usually required to utilize such a product or such a resource. These are then planned, as in the past, according to the pull principle.

You can access the push production function from the product view (**Transaction · SAP · APO · RRP3**) via the **Goto** menu or from the Alert Monitor for excess alerts, by clicking the right mouse button.

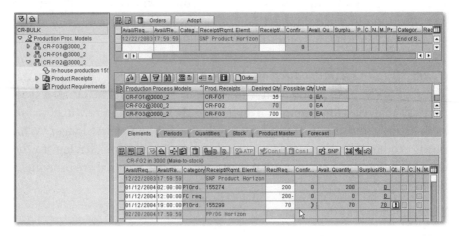

Figure 8.19 Push Production in SAP APO PP/DS

In Figure 8.19, you can see three tables in the right half of the screen. The product excesses are displayed in the upper-most. Highlight the surplus that you want to use and click on the **Adopt** button. The possible products that can be manufactured from the raw material are displayed for you in the center table. A possible quantity is displayed for each product. Enter the required quantity for a product and click on the **Orders** button. A planned order is created—or several, if you have set a fixed or maximum lot size in the product master. These new planned orders consume the raw material for which a surplus was determined. The new planned orders are then displayed in the bottom table. The total of the required quantities should not be larger than the possible quantity; otherwise, an additional requirement for the surplus raw material will be created.

Heuristics for multiple output planning (SAP_MOP_001)

Multiple output planning (MOP) complements the order generation in the area of production planning and detailed scheduling (PP/DS) in that it enables the planning of a production in which one product is divided (cut, split, etc.) into multiple products. In the example in Figure 8.20, film reels with the dimensions 3 m x 10,000 m (so-called jumbos) are split into spool reels of 3 m x 500 m.

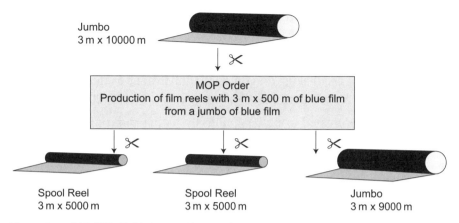

Figure 8.20 SAP APO Multi-Output Planning (MOP; Source: SAP)

In comparison to the standard PP/DS function, MOP provides the following advantages:

▶ Optimized selection of production receipts that are intended to cover an order

▶ Offcut determination

▶ Evaluated criteria of additional receipts

In the following sections, we'll explain the practical example shown in Figure 8.21 for the MOP. In this example, the fictional company Film Manufacturing, Inc. produces films for various applications with different finishes and colors. Multiple output planning can also be applied to other scenarios, of course (i.e., in the paper, textile, or steel industries, for example, or for the graduation of cables, tree trunks, metal blocks, etc).

The films are customized according to customer request. Self-adhesive film with the following finishes and colors is sold as a trimmed roll, for instance:

▶ Finish

▷ Matte

▷ Glossy

▷ Writable

▶ Color

▷ Transparent

▷ White

▷ Blue

The dimensions can be determined by the customers themselves. The production of trimmed rolls proceeds as follows:

1. Jumbos are first manufactured from backing material, varnishes, and other components, making film rolls with dimensions of at least 4,000 mm x 5,000,000 mm and a maximum of 4,000 mm x 15,000,000 mm.

2. Spool reels are created from the jumbos by rolling and trimming. A spool reel is generally 2,000 to 4,000 mm wide and 5,000 to 200,000 mm long.

3. The spool reels are divided into trimmed rolls. A trimmed roll can be 10 to 2,000 mm wide and 5 to 200,000 mm long.

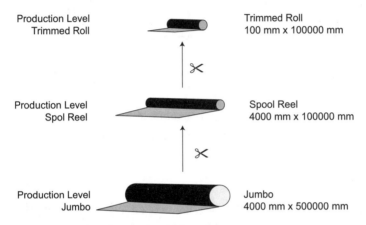

Figure 8.21 Practical Example, MOP

The MOP planning process looks like the following:

1. A customer orders 37 trimmed rolls of self-adhesive film, with the following characteristics:

   ▶ Dimensions: 100 mm wide and 100,000 mm long

   ▶ Finish: Matte

   ▶ Color: Blue

   You have created a customer order in the mySAP ERP system with actual product requirements. This customer order is automatically transferred into the SAP APO system for planning with the help of the SAP APO Core Interface (CIF). There, the SAP APO system starts the multiple output planning, via the production planning and detailed scheduling (PP/DS) function or the Available-to-Promise (ATP) inspection:

   The stocks shown in Table 8.1 are available for self-adhesive film with these requirements.

Production Level	Stock	Free Product Receipts
Trimmed roll	—	—
Spool reel	1 spool reel; Dimensions: 3,500 mm x 75,000 mm	—
Jumbos	1 jumbo; 4,000 mm x 5,000,000 mm	2 jumbos; Dimensions: 4,000 mm x 15,000,000 mm

Table 8.1 Practical Example, MOP—Inventory Information

2. The SAP APO system first searches via the stock search at the trimmed roll production level for product receipts that can cover the requirement quantity.

   Because no inventories or free product receipts exist at the production level for the requirements from the customer order, the inventory search is extended to the previous production stage. The requirement/inventory comparison analyzes the need for the spool reel pre-material (here: 3,700 mm x 100,000 mm) and forwards this information to the inventory search.

3. The SAP APO system attempts to determine a suitable product receipt at the spool reel production level with the information from the requirements/inventory comparison.

   There is a stock of a spool reel with matte, blue, self-adhesive foil at this production level, but this is only 75,000 mm long instead of the required 100,000 mm. The SAP APO system continues the inventory search at the previous production level. The requirements/inventory comparison again analyzes the requirements for the jumbo pre-material (here: 3,700 mm x 100,000 mm) and transfers the information to the inventory search.

4. The SAP APO system attempts to determine a suitable product receipt at the jumbo production level.

   A stock of one jumbo roll and two free product receipts for jumbos that meet the requirements exist at this production level.

   The SAP APO system decides via the requirements/inventory comparison which jumbo should be used to cover the customer requirements. In the customer-based logic of the requirements/inventory comparison, it is specified that the smallest jumbo should be used. Therefore, the SAP APO system chooses the jumbo with the dimensions of 4,000 mm x 5,000,000 mm.

5. The APO system creates an order for the production of a spool reel with 100,000 mm of length and pegs this order with the jumbo identified by the inventory search.

The remainder of 4,000 mm x 4,900,000 mm is put into free inventory (i.e., warehoused) as a spool reel.

6. The SAP APO system then creates an order for the production of 37 trimmed rolls with 100,000 mm of length and 100 mm in width. This order is pegged (for production) with the product receipts of the first order.

The remainder of 300 mm x 100,000 mm is put into free inventory as a trimmed roll.

7. The product receipt for this order of 37 trimmed rolls is pegged with the customer order.

In addition, advanced lot-sizing procedures are available in SAP APO, which allow for cost viewpoints (inventory and ordering costs). Please refer to Section 7.4 for a detailed explanation of the lot-sizing procedures.

In planning multiple materials, an additional process control is required to define the planning sequence, for example (MRP stages). These tasks are managed by additional heuristics—the MRP heuristics. For that reason, product heuristics should not be used directly in the planning run; instead, they should be integrated in an MRP heuristic.

MRP Heuristics

MRP heuristics represent the process control for the product heuristics. Contrary to product heuristics, with which only one material is typically planned, the MRP heuristics are for planning many or even all materials of one plant. An MRP run should be carried out in SAP APO with an MRP heuristic.

Because different materials can use different product heuristics, MRP heuristics represent a kind of clamp around the individual product heuristics. When we speak of an MRP planning run in SAP APO, we mean both of the following heuristics:

Planning according to MRP levels (SAP_MRP_001)
You can carry out planning according to MRP levels in the production planning run. These apply globally for all planning versions of a supply chain model and are determined using the master data. Note that the MRP level

determination is carried out for the complete supply chain in SAP APO. In mySAP ERP, it is carried out only in reference to the plant. In SAP APO, depending on the heuristics settings, the transport relationships are also considered when determining the MRP levels. The MRP level is therefore also an attribute of the location product and model in SAP APO. In mySAP ERP, the MRP level is a characteristic of the material and is independent of the plant. For this reason, cross-plant planning is possible in SAP APO, whereas mySAP ERP imposes restrictions here. The service heuristic **SAP_PP_020 (stage numbering algorithm)** must be carried out before the first planning according to MRP levels and always at the start of a production planning run, if the MRP levels of the selected location products have changed.

Automatic planning (SAP_MRP_002)

With this algorithm, you can initiate planning by product by immediately taking into account the required components. This procedure enables equitable planning of finished products and components. The production planning run is scheduled using a corresponding variant as a batch job or started online. With the help of the variant, the planning range and additional planning parameters are specified, such as the **Time Profile** to be used (see Figure 8.22).

Production Planning Run

Settings for Heuristic | Strategy

Global Settings

Planning Version	000
Time Profile	SAP001
Propagation Range	SAPALL
Simulation Version	

Control Parameters

☐ Display Logs

Processing Steps

Step	Function/Heuristic	Profile	Cust.ID	Obj.	Save	Select.Crit.
01	Stage-Numbering Algorit...			4	☑	⇨
02	Product Planning (Comp. ...	SAP001		4	☑	⇨
03	Rescheduling: Bottom Up			4	☐	⇨
04					☐	⇨
05					☐	⇨
06					☐	⇨
07					☐	⇨
08					☐	⇨
09					☐	⇨
10					☐	⇨

Figure 8.22 Settings for an MRP Planning Run in SAP APO

It is important that the individual heuristics and their processing sequence are listed here. In the example in Figure 8.22, the stage numbering algorithm, which determines the MRP levels, is carried out first in the **Function/Heuristic** field. The product planning according to MRP levels is then carried out. Finally, a rescheduling is carried out bottom-up, in which the pegged requirements are deferred so that receipts can be covered in a timely fashion.

Service Heuristics

In addition to the heuristics already mentioned, there also exist the *service heuristics* in the standard version. The two relevant service heuristics here synchronize the material flow.

Heuristics rescheduling: bottom-up (SAP_PP_009) and heuristics rescheduling: bottom-up for Conti-IO (SAP_PP_008)

These two bottom-up heuristics shift pegged requirements so that they can be covered on time by the existing receipts. The rescheduling algorithm: *Bottom-Up for Conti-IO* is used for continuous receipt and requirement elements. Customer orders and planned primary requirements are not shifted. To correctly carry out the planning via a supply chain, all components must be planned at the highest MRP level—that is, at the lowest BOM level—then at the next BOM level, and so forth, until the finished product. The goal of the continuous input/output is to plan the component production or component outsourcing continually to the secondary requirements (such as is the case with long orders). The continuous input/output is accurate to the second.

A single "virtual" continual input secondary requirement is always created (see Figure 8.23), even if the order runs throughout several days. Depending on the lot-sizing procedure, planned orders are created for the assembly. Example: A planned order for a finished product A has an order length of 10 days, as well as a secondary requirement quantity of 40 pieces. In this case, a "virtual" secondary requirement with a quantity of 40 pieces is created. If the lot-sizing procedure *Daily Lot Size* is selected for the assembly, one planned order of four pieces is created per day.

Heuristics rescheduling: top-down (SAP_PP_010)

This heuristic reschedules all receipts so that they cover the given requirements. Stocks are not shifted. To ensure that the functionality is correct across several MRP levels, you must integrate the stocks in the MRP heuristic SAP_MRP_001.

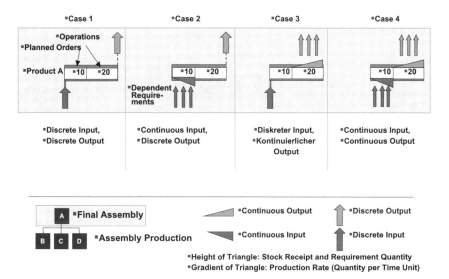

Figure 8.23 Continuous Input/Output (Source: SAP)

The procedure must be carried out just as you did for heuristic SAP_PP_009. To properly carry out the planning via a supply chain, all components must first be planned at the highest MRP level—that is, at the lowest BOM level—then at the next BOM level, and so forth, until the raw material.

Changing order priorities (SAP_PP_012)

If receipts and requirements are changed or newly created, the system automatically carries out a dynamic pegging, in which it reallocates the receipts to the requirements. Receipt and requirement elements can then be linked with different order priorities through a pegging relationship. With this algorithm, you can adapt the priorities of receipt elements to the priorities of the allocated requirement elements. The algorithm determines the requirement elements, which are designated to the receipt element via a fixed or a dynamic pegging relationship, for each receipt element. The algorithm then determines the highest order priority (the lowest numerical priority value) of the allocated requirement elements and allocates this order priority to the receipt element.

The service heuristics described here neither create new orders, nor change existing orders with regard to quantity. Supply source and resource changes cannot be carried out. To utilize the product and MRP heuristics, you must select a corresponding product heuristic on the right half of the screen in Figure 8.24, in the **SAP APO Product Master** in the **PP/DS** view, in the **Procurement Planning** section, in the **Product Heuristic** field.

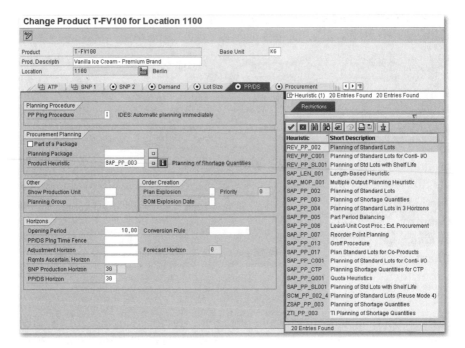

Figure 8.24 SAP APO Product Master—Product Heuristics

Detailed Scheduling Heuristics

The detailed scheduling heuristics are responsible for planning and re-planning existing operations (or orders). In the standard version, the following detailed scheduling heuristics are available:

Backlog resolution (SAP002)

With the detailed scheduling algorithm for backlog resolution, you can resolve the backlog on the selected resource in the DS Planning Board and in the mass detailed scheduling; that is, reschedule operations that are located before the current point in time (+/– offset time). The system first deallocates these operations, and then subsequently reschedules them.

Lead time reduction (SAP004)

With the detailed scheduling algorithm for lead time reduction, you can reduce the lead time of orders on selected resources in the DS Planning Board and in the mass detailed scheduling. To do so, the system fixes the selected resources and, therefore, all operations that are located on these resources. Starting from each fixed operation, it re-plans the other operations of the affected order so that the time intervals between the individual operations of the order are set as small as possible.

Aggregation of orders on container resources (SAP_PI_001)

With the detailed scheduling algorithm **Aggregate Orders** (**Container Res.**), you can bundle previously selected orders into one order. A container resource is used in production for temporary storage of various products. Only one product can be found in the container at a specific point in time. Filling and removal can take place via several actions. From the planning viewpoint, the container is allocated with a defined product quantity for a specific period. The container resource has storage capacity in addition to production capacity. The characteristics of the container are determined by the fill level description. The fill level is characterized by the **Minimum Production Quantity**, the **Maximum Stock Level**, and the **Allowed Remaining Quantity**. The maximum stock level defines the maximum quantity of the product that can be located in the container. The **Minimum Production Quantity** defines the minimum quantity of the product that must be filled in a container. It can only be used if the container resource is used for production. The **Allowed Remaining Quantity** defines the maximum quantity of the product that may be in the container, if the product is to be filled into it.

The examples in Figure 8.25 show the stock and the allocation of differently applied container resources.

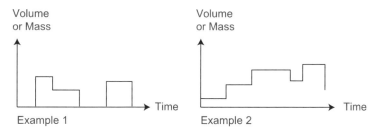

Figure 8.25 Allocation of Container Resources (Source: SAP)

In Example 1, a container resource is used for production. The product is then emptied from the resource at various times, or all at once. The container must always be completely emptied before it is used again.

In Example 2, a container resource is used for temporary storage. The product is filled or removed from the container resource at various times. The container does not have to be emptied completely before the product is refilled.

Figure 8.26 shows the fill level of the container resource and the related stock growth.

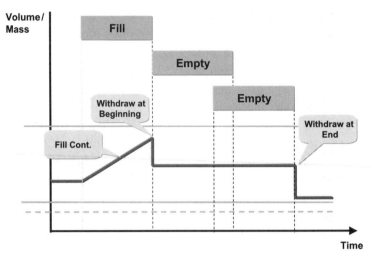

Figure 8.26 Stock Growth of a Container Resource (Source: SAP)

You can display the material quantity that is found in a container resource on the **APO DS Planning Board**, as shown in the lower part of Figure 8.27, which is where you can see the container's incoming and outgoing items. The related orders are displayed in the center; the resource utilization is displayed in the upper part of the figure.

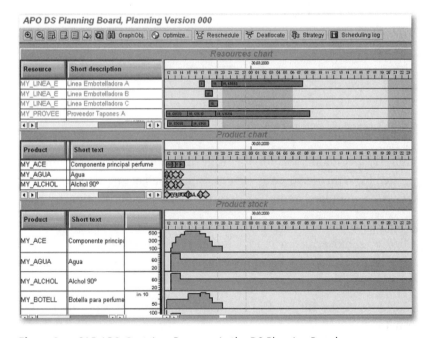

Figure 8.27 SAP APO Container Resource in the DS Planning Board

Violations of the container resource's inventory characteristics can be displayed via the **Alert Monitor**. The following alerts can be displayed there:

▶ **Inventory < 0**
The quantity of product in the container resource is below zero.

▶ **Minimum product quantity not reached**
The product quantity that was filled in the container is too low. This alert is only triggered if the stock is below the minimum production quantity after filling it with the product. No alert is triggered when removing the product, regardless of whether the stock in the container falls below the minimum production quantity.

▶ **Maximum quantity exceeded**
The stock in the resource exceeds the quantity defined as the maximum stock level.

▶ **Filling violates allowed remaining quantity**
Product was added, although the stock in the container is greater than the allowed remaining quantity.

▶ **Invalid mix**
Differing products were filled in a container resource.

Figure 8.28 lists all of the alerts that can be displayed for a container resource.

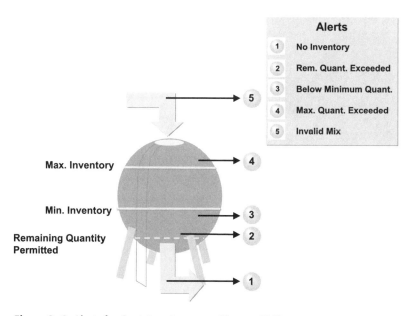

Figure 8.28 Alerts for Container Resources (Source: SAP)

Resources with stock properties have special constraints:

▸ Maximum stock level

▸ Minimum production quantity

▸ Allowed remaining quantity

These are only observed in SAP APO during planning, insofar as only alerts are written in the event of a violation of these constraints. Then, the planner has to manually establish compliance with stock properties, for example, on the DS Planning Board.

Heuristics for block planning (SAP_CDPBP_01 and SAP_CDPBP_02)

In some industries, such as the metal and paper industries, orders or operations are planned on different resources, not solely on the basis of their scheduled sequence, their priority and free capacity. Rather, for these systems, preliminary planning identifies which products (with which characteristics) and which types of products are to be aggregated and run jointly through the system. The main reason for this is usually that the processing of these aggregated products requires a similar system setup and changing setups requires a great deal of effort. In Figure 8.29, you can see orders for products that have to be painted in different colors. The orders are not planned to the next free resource according to their temporal sequence, but rather according to their color. Thus, the order entered most recently is planned as the second block on the resource (and not in the first block), which is responsible for painting orange-colored products.

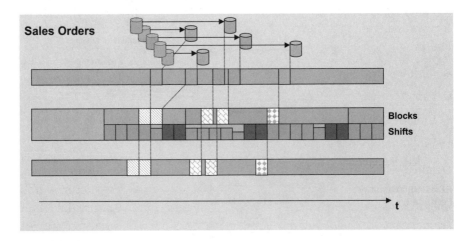

Figure 8.29 Block Planning (Source: SAP)

A *block* is a section of time in which a resource processes one or more products with the same characteristics. There are two ways in which to define the section of time: by the start and end time, or by the quantity of products to be processed. You can start this heuristic in the DS planning board, or in the production planning run. With it, you reschedule actions on block-planned resources if block characteristics have changed. You can adapt block limits of resources for which you have carried out block planning with *buckets* to the load situation.

The algorithm processes the block cycles one after another in the set scheduling horizon, beginning with the time of execution. For each cycle, it is first checked whether an adjustment of the block limits is necessary or possible. The adjustment is necessary if at least one block has an overload in the continuous capacity view. An adjustment is possible if there is no block overload and the free capacity in the cycle can compensate for overloads. The start of the first block and the end of the last block of each cycle remain unchanged.

This causes an equalization of capacity utilization between the blocks of a cycle. Blocks with overload are extended and blocks with free capacity are shortened. The adjustment of the blocks takes place based on the relationship between the free capacity in the block and the free capacity in the cycle. Blocks with overload are extended so that their capacity offering just equates the capacity requirement of the actions in the block.

Stable forward scheduling

With this heuristic, you can carry out a multi-stage, finite planning to create a feasible production plan in the short-term horizon. You should use stable forward scheduling to resolve the following planning disruptions across several production stages:

▶ Backlogs

▶ Capacity overloads

▶ Violation of minimum clearances

▶ Violation of validity intervals of orders

Detailed scheduling heuristics do not create new orders, nor do they change existing orders with regard to quantity. **Planning strategies** determine how operations are planned with the help of detailed scheduling heuristics. These are described individually in the following sections. Their interaction with other strategy settings is also explained. Figure 8.30 provides an overview of the different planning strategies in SAP APO.

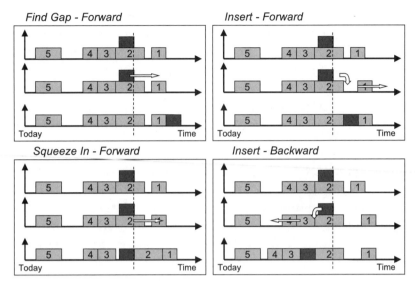

Figure 8.30 Planning Strategies in SAP APO (Source: SAP)

Infinite planning

This planning mode attempts to plan a new or rescheduled operation for the required point in time, without considering the existing resource load. This planning mode is not used on capacity-relevant resources. Furthermore, this planning mode is used in the PP heuristics and in the MRP heuristics because finite planning is only possible to a limited degree when creating an order.

Find slot

In this finite planning mode, the system attempts to plan the new or rescheduled operation in the next possible slot in the planning direction, as shown at upper left in Figure 8.30. The slot must be sufficiently large and there must be ample capacity available. This planning mode is used only to search for a suitable slot in an existing planning situation, without changing the planning situation (exceptions are sequential-dependent setup actions). It is primarily used on the DS Planning Board and in the sequence heuristics. It is suitable for the order system only to a limited degree, because only sufficiently large slots can be used and, therefore, the existing capacity of smaller slots cannot be fully exploited.

Insert operation

This planning mode is used to insert an operation at a specific position in an existing allocation. The specified preferred deadline is drawn upon to determine the position. If an operation is already planned for the required deadline, the operation that is to be inserted is planned before (backward planning direction; see Figure 8.30 lower right) or after (forward planning direction; see Figure 8.30 upper right) this operation. The operations before or after that point are shifted in the planning direction, if necessary.

The scheduler must attempt to comply with the new operation sequence that is specified by the re-planning deadlines for each resource. This planning mode is therefore solely intended for use on the DS Planning Board, where it can be used to bring into sequence the operations on a finite resource. Through compact planning, the other operations of the order can be adjusted to the allocation of the finite resource with regard to scheduling. Using this planning mode is not useful in the order system. For one thing, there is the problem of the sequence specification on several resources. For another, massive orders that have already been confirmed can be shifted by this planning mode and may possibly have their required deadlines violated.

Squeeze in operation

In this finite planning mode, the system attempts to insert a new or rescheduled operation into the existing allocation for the required deadline, even if the slot in the allocation is too small. If the slot is too small, the system shifts the neighboring operations in both planning directions (see Figure 8.30, lower left). This planning mode was developed so that the user can place an operation on a resource precisely with the required timing.

In this mode, the planner can shift individual operations via drag and drop on the DS Planning Board. It is not useful, however, to specify a precise deadline for several operations. Normally, schedulings influence one another reciprocally, so that changes made by the scheduler lead to shifts of already planned operations. This causes the deadline specifications of these operations to be lost. This planning mode should therefore find only very limited use. For these reasons, this planning mode is also unsuitable for the creation of orders (see also Insert Operation).

Insert operation and close slot until end

This planning mode represents an extension of the insert operation planning mode. Its primary goals are sequence building and sequence compliance. In addition, allocation on the planned resource should be kept as slot-free as possible. The same limitations apply here as for the insert operation planning mode. The system attempts to insert a rescheduled operation at the required spot. The system then attempts to close slots in the resource allocation in the planning direction—starting from the original deadline of the operation. Slots are only closed to the start or end of an affected block in block planning. The system begins with the first slot in the planning direction, then attempts to close the next slot, and so forth. This process is cancelled if a step cannot be shifted—if this operation is fixed, for example, or because allocation relationships to other operations cannot otherwise be maintained. The sequence of operations and their resource allocations are not changed with this planning strategy.

Compact planning and finite planning submodes

The goal of compact planning is to keep the lead time of an order as short as possible. This is done by dispatching operations with their minimum clearances. In using compact planning, SAP recommends planning rescheduled operations finitely (finite planning mode) and planning dependent operations either infinitely or deallocated. With this setting, a midpoint scheduling is carried out around the resource that is to be planned.

Maximum clearances and finite planning

The goal of maximum clearances is to prevent two sequential operations from being planned as far away from one another as possible. Observation of maximum clearances can lead to this problem with multiple planning, analogous to planning with the finite planning submode. The problem occurs mainly when multiple finite resources are bottleneck resources with dense allocation. Not only must a free slot be found for the operation that is to be rescheduled, but also one must be found for the dependent operation. This makes it difficult for the scheduler to re-plan the operations so that both operations find a slot and still fulfill the maximum clearance. Therefore, SAP recommends that maximum clearances only be considered when it is absolutely required by the process. Violations of maximum clearances can be displayed in the Alert Monitor, if this is specified in the alert profile.

Planning sequence

The planning sequence specifies the sequence in which the operations are to be planned or re-planned. As a result, it does not usually reflect the sequence of operations on the resource according to the scheduling. The planning sequence only has a direct influence on the sequence of operations if all operations are planned or re-planned for the same deadline; that is, if the "Earliest Deadline" or "Entered Deadline" options are set in the strategy profile. However, restrictions such as resource allocations, fixed actions, downtime, uninterruptible activities, and blocks can lead to the planning sequence deviating from the sequence of operations according to the scheduling.

Because there is only one planning sequence per strategy profile, it applies for all strategies of the strategy profile. When using several strategies with different planning directions, it no longer makes sense to use the planning sequence for sequence formation, since different planning directions would require different planning sequences to achieve the same sequence of operations on the resource. SAP therefore recommends that the planning sequence be used for sequence formation on only one resource. Furthermore, it is recommended that the sequence planning be carried out on all operations of the resource or, in the case of block planning, only on the operations of a block.

Non-working times

The goal of planning in non-working times is primarily to complete orders that were begun before a break or a weekend, and must absolutely be completed. By planning in non-working times, the problem can be solved in a simple fashion (without changing the working times in the resource) with overtime hours. Planning in non-working times may only take place manually. Only the planner can determine how long work may be performed after working hours are over.

Interruptibility

The interruptibility of actions influences the scheduling of orders. An uninterruptible action can only be dispatched in work times between breaks and weekends. For an uninterruptible action that is longer than a work period without a slot, this scheduling restriction can result in the operation not being planned at this spot. In a worst-case scenario, the operation is not planned until the end of the resource offering. To resolve this problem, adjust the uninterruptibility in the plan. SAP recommends that operations be defined as uninterruptible if the modeling allows it.

Customer-Specific Heuristics

If the standard tools cannot satisfy the customer-specific scenario, you can define individual heuristics by using the **Heuristics Framework**. From a technical point of view, all heuristics consist of a number of parameters and a functional component with a defined interface. This interface is the same in all heuristics function components. This allows a customer-specific heuristic to be easily integrated in the standard planning environment (interactive planning, planning run, etc.).

8.4.3 Optimization Methods and Concepts

Optimization Goals

Production deadlines and resource allocations of operations are optimized to meet the following goals:

▶ **Total lead time**

The total lead time is the time required for the processing of all orders in the optimization interval, that is, the lead time of the entire production program. The optimizer attempts to shift all operations as far as possible to the left edge of the optimization interval, resulting in the allocation for all current orders as being very dense and the resources allocated for the future being as freed up as possible.

▶ **Setup times**

The setup time is the total of all setup times of the operations in the optimization horizon. These setup times are therefore times that are required for setting up the resources between orders or operations. They are differentiated into static and dynamic setup operations. Dynamic setup operations are dependent on the operation processing sequence; static operations are independent of sequence. Setup optimization is therefore only useful if the optimizer can influence the setup times via the sequence of operations. The goal here is to minimize setup times and thereby improve the utilization of machine capacity.

▶ **Setup costs**

Setup costs are costs that are incurred when setting up machines. The related setup cost rates are maintained and called from the setup matrixes, like the setup durations. Setup costs should only be called upon in the following cases:

▷ The costs for a "setup" time unit are dependent on the operation sequence. If the setup costs are proportional to the setup times, an optimization according to setup times would suffice.

▷ The setup times must be evaluated differently on different resources.

In determining setup costs, only the relations between the setup costs need to be observed. The absolute amount has no meaning, except that they must be aligned with the other goals via the weightings in the goal function.

Example: Setup costs in the amounts of 0 (no material change), 20, and 40 would have the same effect on the sequence as setup costs in the amounts of 0, 1 and 2. High costs can be better reproduced via the goal weight, which would have to increase by the factor of 20 in this case.

▶ **Delay costs**

Delay costs are costs that are incurred through a delayed completion of orders, such as costs for non-delivery to customers Minimization of the maximum delay costs is useful in order to avoid or at least reduce particularly large or expensive delays. This can contribute to an improvement in customer satisfaction, as well as to delivery reliability. The total of the delay costs is calculated as follows:

Total of delay costs = Σ (delay (order) * delay costs (priority (order))

Minimization of delay costs and setup times are the most commonly used optimization goals.

▶ **Mode costs**

An activity can often be carried out on different resources, called "alternative modes" in the work plan (production process model; PPM) and in optimization. These modes are allocated in the production process model with priorities that reflect specific action-resource combinations and that are intended to steer automatic planning in the right direction. Mode costs, therefore, are costs that are incurred due to a shifting of a production operation to another action or resource. Fixed and variable costs are considered here. The total of the mode costs is calculated based on the allocated modes of the PPMs of all orders in the optimization horizon:

Total of mode costs = Σ (fixed costs (priority ($mode_{mode, PPM}$)) + variable costs (priority ($mode_{mode, PPM}$)) * net duration ($mode_{mode, PPM}$))

The operational ideas behind optimization with mode costs are:

▷ Fixed mode costs reduce the number of actions in modes with low priority on the resources.

▷ Variable mode costs reduce the allocation duration in modes with low priority on the resources.

Here, the user must know the cost driver: the number of actions, the allocation duration, or both.

Because there is often an unmanageable number of combined possibilities for the planning of actions when optimizing these goals, one option that best meets the operational goals must be selected. This selection process is carried out by the system automatically and is called optimization.

Optimization Algorithms

An optimization procedure is essentially suited to find a good solution, depending on the planning problem. There are two different kinds of optimization procedures:

▶ **Genetic algorithm**
The genetic algorithm is suitable for planning problems for which not only feasible but also optimal solutions must be found. A typical application for this procedure is the formation of a setup-optimized sequence of operations.

▶ **Constraint propagation**
The constraint propagation procedure focuses on solving complex planning problems whereby many dependencies and constraints must be considered.

Optimization in SAP APO PP/DS

The DS Planning Board is best suited for interactive optimization, as it can display the production plans. You cannot specify whether the new optimized plan should be accepted until leaving the planning board or saving the planning results. Optimization generally takes place only with the resources that were marked on the DS Planning Board. The *Optimizer* is called via the functions menu or the **Optimize** button, without automatically starting optimization. You will then be requested to specify the **Optimization Horizon** or to confirm the proposed values, as shown in Figure 8.31.

The system then displays the user interface for the interactive optimization. There you can either accept the suggested **optimization profile** or modify it interactively. In the optimization profile, you can adjust how you want to weight the individual **target criteria**, for example. In Figure 8.32, you can see that the total of the setup times has been weighted at 38.46 %. In the other sections, you can adjust parameters for order and resource processing, for additional strategies, for the optimization horizon, and for other settings.

The duration of the optimization run can be adjusted in the **Maximum Runtime** field. The following generally applies: The longer the runtime, the greater the probability that a good solution will be found. There is no basic rule for the timing setting, however. It may happen that no solution can be found with a relatively high time setting, but a very good result is achieved with a repeated run with the same time setting. With exceptions, a shorter runtime can even lead to a better result than a higher time setting.

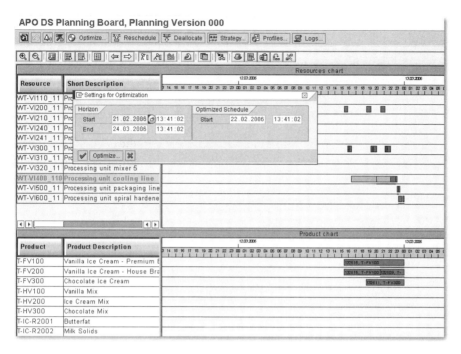

Figure 8.31 Calling the Optimizer in SAP APO

In carrying out optimization, different time settings are tested with different numbers of actions and the results are depicted schematically. Time settings of several hours are thoroughly viable in operating practice. Even with a high time setting of several days, the optimizer would not find a better solution after several minutes, which would be recognizable on the curve progression of the graphic illustration and on the value of the target criterion in the optimization environment.

The **Objective Function** is the primary point of orientation for the entire optimization. Its total value consists of the sum of the individual values multiplied together with the respective weighting factors. The optimizer's goal is to minimize this value.

Optimization can be carried out according to up to six different criteria. In allocating values for weighting criteria, you must ensure that the relations of individual criteria correspond with each other. For example, the total lead time should be the lead time for all planned orders; it will therefore always exceed the total of all setup times by a multiple degree. If this relation were not considered in weighting goals, the optimization results would be distorted.

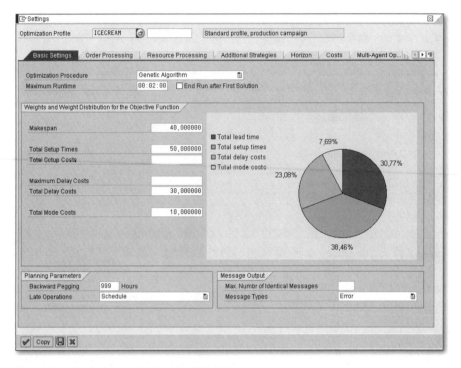

Figure 8.32 Optimization Settings in SAP APO

The following example is provided to clarify the problem for you: Optimization is to be carried out according to two criteria: total of lead times = 100 hours and total of setup times = 20 hours. Both goals are intended to have the same priority. Nevertheless, the weighting for both criteria cannot be set to the value of 5 (meaning 50%) in the optimizer. That would only be correct if both criteria had the same number of hours. The weighting must therefore be set to 1 for the total lead time and to 5 for the total number of setup times.

Using Setup Optimization

To optimize the capacity of bottleneck resources, the portion of the offering time that is pure production time should be as high as possible, while the portion that is idle, standstill, and setup times should be as low as possible. With the "total of setup times" optimization goal, this can be achieved. To do so, planned and production orders are arranged so that as few changeovers are required as necessary. Figure 8.33 illustrates this operation.

Setup times cannot usually be brought to their theoretical minimum, because a series of competing goals prevents the optimizer from doing so.

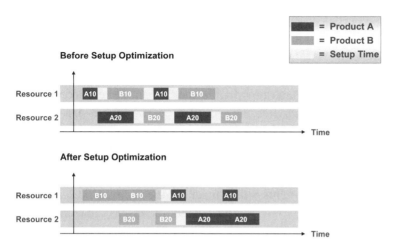

Figure 8.33 Setup Optimization (Source: SAP)

Figure 8.34 shows two order sequences. The upper sequence is the one with the shortest setup times—the so-called *setup-optimized order sequence*. The lower sequence is the one with the smallest stocks. The diamonds represent the requirement deadlines. There are three different requirement deadlines for product A, for example. To optimize the machines, the setup times for product A are minimized in the upper sequence. Consequently, however, all three orders for A are already completed by the first requirement deadline and the pre-produced quantities of orders 2 and 3 have to be put into stock. If setups are rarely carried out, orders or operations are removed increasingly further from their requirement deadlines and stocks can increase.

Figure 8.34 Goal Conflict in Setup Optimization (Source: SAP)

The goal conflict between the stocks and setup cannot be resolved by the system on its own. You must provide the system with instructions on how the optimization of both goals should be prioritized and weighted.

Machine Failure

A machine can go down, whether planned or unplanned, for a certain period of time. This machine failure, as well as its consequences for planning, must be represented in the system. For this purpose, the machine failure duration is defined in the system. A capacity overload is created in this period, and must be resolved in the subsequent step. The failure times are stored in the resource master data on the **Failure Times** tab. You can also call the master data from the DS Planning Board by double-clicking on the resource. Downtimes are depicted in dark gray on the SAP APO DS Planning Board.

When downtime occurs, all planned and production orders in the downtime period are shifted to the end of the downtime period, regardless of their status, and dispatched there infinitely. In order to generate a new finite program, either manual adjustments can be made, or the optimizer can be used. Use of the optimizer is recommended if the planning task is too complex for a manual solution. The optimizer can calculate a replacement program, which is appropriate to the target function that best fulfills the optimization criteria.

Integration of External Optimizers

When integrating external, customer-specific optimizers, you have the following options:

▸ Connection of an external optimization using Business Application Programming Interfaces (BAPIs)

▸ Integration of an external optimization in the SAP APO system using the Optimization Extension Workbench (APX)

The **Optimization Extension Workbench** is used if the optimization methods are to be applied in relation to special characteristics, which are only important for certain companies or industries (such as dimensions, weight, or temperature).

If you want to use external optimization that is already configured for connection to the SAP APO system via APX by the manufacturer, the required interface configuration is specified by the external optimization. Proceed according to the instructions of the manufacturer of the external optimization.

If you want to connect an external optimization in proprietary development to the SAP APO system with APX, you need to have good skills in the following areas: SAP RFC and BAPI technology, Microsoft ActiveX and OCX technology and ABAP. Furthermore, you should be very familiar with the SAP APO components to which the optimization is to be connected.

8.4.4 Alerts and Their Forwarding

Disruptions such as resource overloads or transgression of the delivery date cause problems in the integrated supply chain, as well as fluctuations in actual values. The Alert Monitor can display these problems and plan actual deviations when they occur in planning, for example. The alert categories that are to be displayed are specified in the Alert Monitor profile. Alerts can be allocated to a processing cycle in the Alert Monitor and forwarded to workflow scenarios.

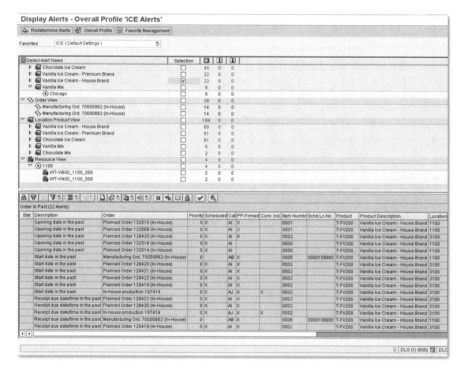

Figure 8.35 SAP APO Alert Monitor

The Alert Monitor window in Figure 8.35 consists of the following screen areas:

In the **view selection** (upper left), you can determine if alerts are to be displayed based on objects (such as location products) or specific alert types.

In the **object selection** (below left), a list of all objects, which have an alert in the category selected in the view selection, is displayed. Choose the objects for which you need more detailed information.

In the **display area** (right), the system shows the list of all selected alerts. The following functions are available to you:

You can process alerts, such as hiding, forwarding, or sending them as a document. You can sort, filter, print, and export the list, or change the layout.

Depending on the respective alert type, you can navigate to the corresponding application functions via the alert's context menu in order to resolve the planning problem that caused the alert.

8.4.5   Comparing Planning Results

Supply chain management represents the entire logistics chain, from the supplier through the production and distribution facilities to the customer. To recognize the effects of planning changes for the entire supply chain, it is necessary to carry out simulations. This also applies to short-term changes in the area of production planning and capacity scheduling. Effects on material requirements planning can also be recognized by simulating alternative resource allocations or changes to the master data.

The goal in doing so is to achieve the optimum order sequence or the optimum resource utilization. The lowest production fixed costs can also be a goal of the simulation. Simulation tools are therefore important instruments for planning support, because they allow complex interrelationships to be tested and analyzed in advance. This protects companies not only from increased costs, but also from production failures, conventional penalties due to poor or incomplete delivery, or downtime due to lack of available material components. The dynamics and complexity of production planning can therefore be optimally coordinated with each other with the help of the simulation. The production planner can intervene proactively in the production planning and is not just a reactive initiator of an independent production. The complicated network of all master data and orders can be represented in a simulation and dynamically investigated and evaluated, both qualitatively and quantitatively.

With the help of simulation, you can answer the following questions, for example: What if …

▶ all orders were produced by the desired deadline with the shortest lead time possible?

▶ a machine has planned downtime in the 11th calendar week?

▶ a shop floor area changes over the shift operation during a vacation period?

▶ a personnel pool is reduced from five to three in the month of May?

▶ an urgent order additionally needs to be processed?

▶ an order was planned and another was brought forward instead?

Note that the simulation does not solve your problems by itself. If used incorrectly, the result is a cost-intensive playing field that does produce detailed findings, but cannot resolve the planning situation.

The **Plan Monitor** is used to determine the current scheduling quality and to compare different versions or time periods in planning. It is a tool with which production planners can evaluate the quality of a production plan before it is approved for implementation. To do so, the characteristics of a plan are evaluated in relation to specific objects, versions, and time periods, and points scores are allocated to the results. You can define your own guidelines for calculation of the points scores or use standard aggregations (such as the total or average value).

The results can be displayed in a table and a graphic, as shown in Figure 8.36.

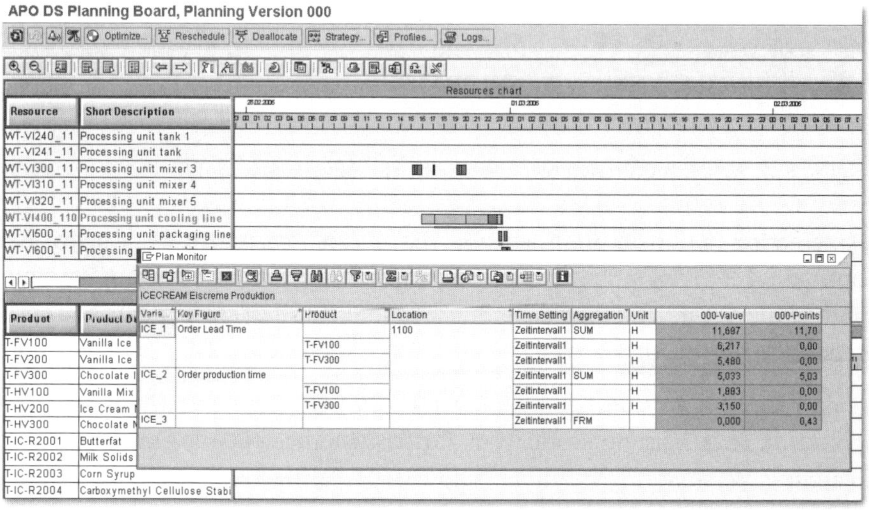

Figure 8.36 SAP APO Plan Monitor

The plan monitor compares the simulation version (000-Value and 000-Points columns) with the planning version (Value and Points columns) and evaluates the results accordingly. The product lead time and product setup time characteristics are selected in the figure.

A **supply chain model** that is the basis of all planning functions in SAP APO and includes master data exclusively is defined in SAP APO. The simulation can be carried out on this basis and compared with the actual planning situation. Through SAP APO's model and version management, you can construct several planning versions for a supply chain model (see Figure 8.37).

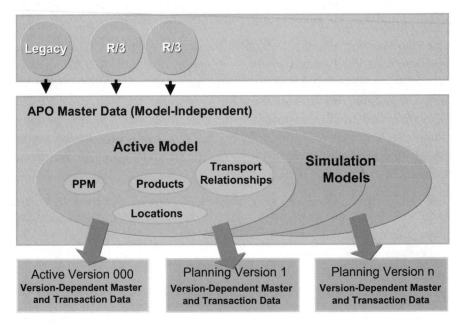

Figure 8.37 Model and Version Management in SAP APO (Source: SAP)

By creating these different versions, you can investigate all aspects and options of a given supply chain scenario with different planning datasets, and simulate the effects of different parameters. You can also create several models for simulation.

Each planning version contains master data and transaction data, such as products, locations or Production Process Models (PPMs). In an inactive planning version, for example, simulated planned independent requirements can be increased and the production can be planned in agreement with these increased demands. After planning in one or more planning versions, the planning results can be compared with one another. The planning of the shortlist (active version) can then be approved for transfer to the implementation system.

All of the master data approved for planning must be allocated to the active model and the active planning version—that is, the model 000 and the planning version 000—in the production system. Master data that is transferred out of SAP R/3 is automatically allocated to the active model and the active planning version.

Production planning and detailed scheduling (PP/DS) provide you with simulation versions that are each based on a set of the planning data. You use these versions to simulate different plans, such as different sequences or the selection of alternative resources, for example. By using interactive planning, heuristics, or optimization, you can create different plans without changing the data in the planned version. With the Plan Monitor and the evaluation of performance characteristics, you can compare different simulated versions. You can also unload simulated versions and proceed with the planning. Lastly, you can accept the best plan into the operative planning version.

Simulations are available in mySAP ERP only to a very limited degree. Conversely, SAP APO offers you many advantages through the simulation of planning changes: remainders can be recognized and resolved in advance; the order sequence can also be improved without optimizers; and the effects of changes to purchase or sales orders can be perceived early. Required or desired changes can therefore be prioritized based on simulations.

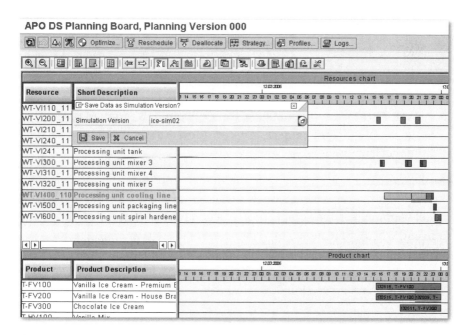

Figure 8.38 Simulation on the DS Planning Board—Saving a Simulation Version

In Figure 8.38, you can see the simulation being called from the **Graphical DS Planning Board**. If you change something on the planning situation, but have not yet saved it, the changes are not yet active. To save the changes in a simulation version, you only need to supply a name for the simulation version. If the simulation version will be used for productive operation, it must be activated. To do so, click on the **Save** button, and the input screen shown in Figure 8.39 is displayed.

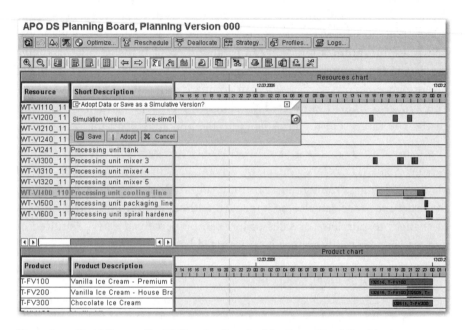

Figure 8.39 Simulation on the DS Planning Board—Adopting a Simulation Version

In the **SAP APO Menu** under **Master Data · Planning Version Management**, or in the Supply Chain Engineer, you can allocate several planning versions to a supply chain model (see Figure 8.40).

On the left-hand side, you can see the models and their allocated planning versions. On the right-hand side, you can see detailed information for each model-planning version combination, such as who created the model or version, and whether the model or version should be deleted. Furthermore, you can make specific settings globally in the planning version, such as the PP/DS horizon. In the example above, the PP/DS horizon in model 000 was specified for the planning version 000 to 50 days.

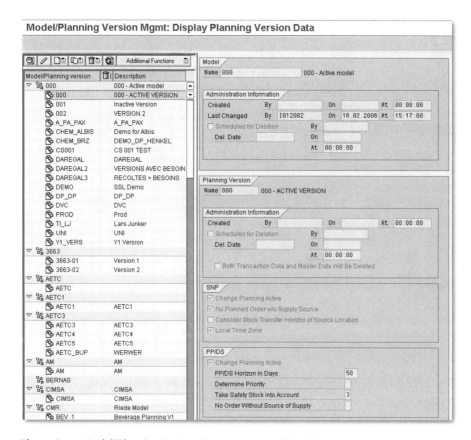

Figure 8.40 Model/Planning Version Management in SAP APO

8.4.6 CTP: Capable-to-Promise

Capable-to-Promise (CTP) is a global availability testing procedure that is integrated in the production planning and detailed scheduling (PP/DS) function.

You use this procedure if you have to give your customers a reliable delivery date when entering the sales order (see Figure 8.41). With the help of CTP, you can carry out an ATP availability test for the desired product when creating the sales order, and initiate PP/DS immediately in the case of incomplete availability. This then creates PP/DS planned orders or order requests for the quantity missing at each production level. When creating the planned order, the system checks the capacity availability of the most important resources, as well as the availability of the components according to the PP/DS logic. From the availability deadlines of the procurement proposals, the system can then determine the confirmation date for the customer order.

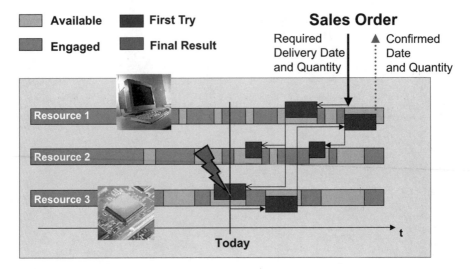

Figure 8.41 Capable-to-Promise (CTP)—Process Flow (Source: SAP)

You can use the CTP process for short-term and medium to long-term production planning, whereby the newly accrued demand only needs to be planned.

The CTP procedure is adjusted in the **ATP Check Instructions**. There, the **Availability Check First, Then Production** option can be set in the **Start Production** field, as shown in Figure 8.42. The production check as the first step can also be omitted. Then, the check is made immediately after the CTP procedure.

The order confirmation process still runs via telephone in many companies today. If a sales order cannot be delivered from inventory, sales must first consult with production. This delays the confirmation process, so that the customer order is usually either confirmed immediately according to a roughly determined delivery date, or the customer is called back after consultation between sales and production. Thanks to the CTP procedure, sales orders can be confirmed immediately, with a realistic deadline. Especially in make-to-order production, you can achieve a competitive advantage and increase your ability to deliver through CTP.

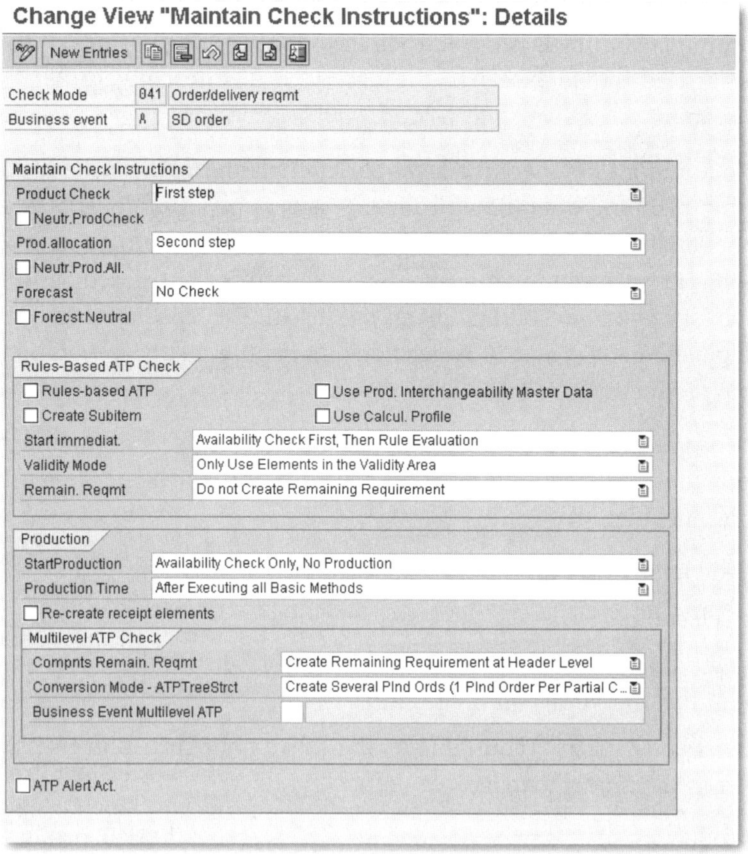

Figure 8.42 Updating the ATP Check Instructions in SAP APO

8.4.7 Embedding Superordinate and Subordinate Planning Levels

Functionalities in SAP APO have a close integration with each other. The cross-plant network planning (SNP—Supply Network Planning) undertakes decisions via the tactical planning and supply source determination. The strengths of SNP lie in the choice of supply source under consideration of the costs, for one thing, and in the rough determination of the production date under consideration because of sourcing and inventory costs, for another. With SNP, you can determine what will be produced when and where. The "when" cannot be more precise than a planning period and does not take into account any sequence-dependent setup.

A rough capacity plan represents the basis for planning in-house production. This is referred to as SNP planning in APO. The goal of SNP planning is more than just the precise modeling of all technical feasibility conditions; rather, it is the planning of resources and component requirements in advance. In this advance planning, planning is referred to in terms of planning periods. Planning can be carried out precisely to the day in SNP. Alternatively PP/DS allows for planning precisely to the second.

The PP/DS is found at the operative level of detail planning. It can tie in to plant-spanning planning operations from the tactical planning level above with the functionalities of sales planning (DP) and plant-spanning network planning (SNP). Pre-planning requirements can therefore be planned appropriately. The strengths of PP/DS planning lie in the consideration of sequence-dependent setup and in restrictions that apply for the generation of producible production orders.

If SNP is used, the created plan must be detailed later. Aspects of planning that were not considered in SNP must be observed and amended after the fact. Examples include:

▸ Sequence-dependent setup

▸ Resource selection

▸ The exact production time within the planning period and, therefore, the sequence of the operations on the resource

▸ Components and capacity requirements that were not planned in SNP in order to keep the model manageable there

If the SNP production plan is to be detailed or implemented, the SNP production plan must be transferred into a PP/DS production plan.

In contrast to mySAP ERP, SAP APO provides the following advantages of integrated planning between SNP and PP/DS here:

▸ SNP planning considers the results of PP/DS planning. The PP/DS production orders are considered in SNP as fixed acquisition elements, while the PP/DS secondary requirements are considered as fixed requirement elements.

▸ The SNP planning considers the capacity consumption of PP/DS orders on mixed resources. If applicable, the SNP planning observes the setup conditions that result from PP/DS orders.

▸ A product can be planned through the settings of the SNP and PP/DS planning horizon, both by SNP as well as by PP/DS. There should be clear responsibilities here, but both sides can intervene if necessary, in case of extraordinary disruption.

▶ Secondary requirements from SNP planning can be covered by a PP/DS acquisition element or vice versa.

▶ A controlled transition to PP/DS planned orders takes place for the planned orders created by the SNP planning.

Time fences are product-specific

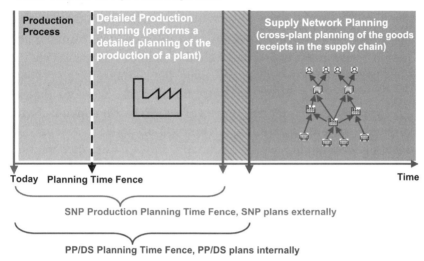

Figure 8.43 Planning Horizon in SNP and PP/DS (Source: SAP)

In Figure 8.43, you can see that the division between the superordinate level—cross-plant planning—and the subordinate level—production planning—is controlled by different horizons. The production orders are planned at the plant level within the SNP horizon; within the PP/DS horizon, the planned orders are planned in cross-plant planning. The hatched horizon applies for both planning areas.

SNP creates no orders within the SNP production horizon. The SNP production horizon can therefore be used to separate the responsibilities for planning between the supply network planning (order outside of the SNP production horizon) and the production planning and detailed scheduling (order within the SNP production horizon).

The PP/DS planning is carried out within the PP/DS horizon. The PP/DS planning does not normally create orders outside of this horizon. The optimizer has the capability, however, to manually create orders there or to defer orders (out of the PP/DS horizon), if there is not sufficient capacity available within the PP/DS horizon, for example.

In addition to the transformations on the product (production, relocation, resorting, receiving, delivery), accompanying actions that are subject to administration are also carried out on the implementation level. These actions are supported by implementation systems, such as papers being printed out for production (i.e., production orders). The link between SAP APO and mySAP ERP is made through the **Core Interface (CIF)**, a real-time planning interface between the planning and implementation system.

Only those data objects that are required for the respective planning and optimization processes are transferred from the complex data quantity of the R/3 system to APO. Both the initial data supply (initial transfer) and the supply of the APO with data changes (change transfer) take place via the CIF interface. Typically, the master data objects of the APO are not identical with those of the R/3 system. Instead, the relevant R/3 master data is mapped to corresponding planning master data of the APO in the master data transfer. The R/3 system thereby remains the leading system for the master data. Only special APO master data for which there are no corresponding counterparts in the R/3 system are created directly in APO. For this reason, master data is also regularly transferred to SAP APO, while the movement data is transferred in real time, and is therefore permanently available in both systems, as shown in Figure 8.44.

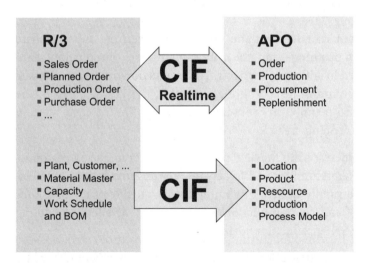

Figure 8.44 Data Transfer via CIF in SAP APO (Source: SAP)

Planning is not necessarily carried out for all materials in APO. It is conceivable that the planning of critical materials takes place in APO, while less critical materials (such as consumption-controlled purchased materials) continued to be planned in R/3. Materials that are planned in APO may not be planned again in R/3; the planning result is transferred directly from APO in the form of planned orders to R/3. Nevertheless, secondary requirements must be determined in R/3 for materials that have a parts list (normally as a result of requirements planning). Therefore, assign these materials the dispatch character **X0** with the dispatch procedure **X** (without dispatch, with parts list resolution). The dispatch character **ND**, for "No dispatch," is not suited for materials planned in APO, since it does not allow for a BOM explosion in R/3. In the integration model, the dispatch character **X0** also lends itself to be used for selection of the materials relevant for APO. Generally, you should exercise caution when separating materials into APO and non-APO relevant materials. For shrewd planning in APO, you must ensure that all materials integral for the planning process are also actually planned in APO. Consider capacity planning: If the capacities are to be planned in APO for the various resources, all materials whose productions access these resources must also be planned in APO.

8.4.8   Separate Planning Tools in APO PP/DS

Periodic Display

Within the interactive planning, an additional, universal planning tool is available to you in APO—in addition to the DS Planning Board and the product view—with the **Product Planning Board**. With the help of the product planning board, a production plan can be created and the results of a planning run can be evaluated. It is a tool for operative planning and for the planning of production quantities.

The product planning board is particularly well suited for repetitive manufacturing, because materials and their utilization can be planned simultaneously on the lines/resources. It also supports both product planning and capacity requirements planning. Because it also enables the planning of outsourced components, it simultaneously provides an interface for outsourcing controllers.

In repetitive and flow manufacturing, planning and control are period-oriented and quantity-oriented. For that reason, the product planning board is processed periodically and provides a temporal and quantified overview of products and production lines.

In the product planning board, the planner can input, change, or rearrange production quantities directly to alternative resources (Figure 8.45, bottom right). The planner can check the production quantities at a glance and determine the current capacity utilization of the production line and the current availability of the products produced on it (Figure 8.45, upper right).

Because planning is frequently shift-based, the product planning board also has functions that enable the distribution of product quantities across shifts. It is also possible to define a flexible period grid. There, different periods follow one another sequentially, such as two days in shifts, three weeks in days, two months in weeks. You can also define your own periods and display them in the product planning board.

Furthermore, you can use the product planning board for planning and procuring components; that is, the procurement planner can monitor the stock and demand level, and change or create order requests, delivery plan classifications, and recalls directly on the product planning board. SAP also provides its own standard suggestion profile for him or her, which he or she can select for configuration of the product planning board.

The following functions can be called from the product planning board:

- Heuristics, for automatic planning
- PP/DS optimizer
- Alert Monitor
- Plan Monitor
- DS Planning Board

The product planning board additionally enables a periodically aggregated view of production and outsourcing.

Selection of the resources and products for which planning is to be carried out takes place in the navigation tree of the product planning board (see Figure 8.45, upper left). The navigation tree enables the display of alerts, as well as simple navigation through the supply chain and the parts lists. It can be grouped according to location, planner, resources, goals and sources.

There is a flexible selection of charts (see Figure 8.45, lower left):

- Product overview
  - Periodic
  - Individual elements
  - Quantity graphic

- Resource view
  - Periodic
  - Individual elements
- Production view
  - Periodic
  - Individual elements
- Optimizer
- Heuristics
- DS Planning Board
- Alert Monitor
- Plan Monitor
- Backlog processing
- Delivery plans (sales and distribution)

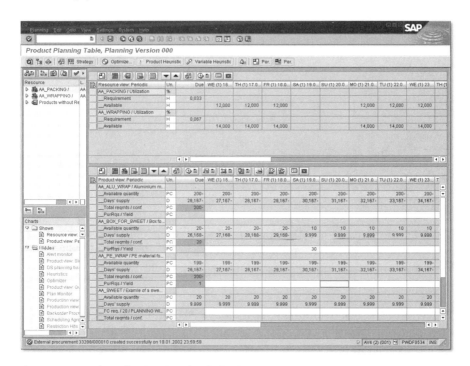

Figure 8.45 Product Planning Board in SAP APO

Graphical Display

Various time-related aspects of planning can be displayed graphically in the charts of the **DS Planning Board** (Figure 8.46), such as the chronological position of operations on the resources (upper chart), the development of resource utilization over time, or pegging relationships between orders (lower chart).

You call the DS Planning Board directly in the area menu of the production planning, in order processing, or in the product planning board.

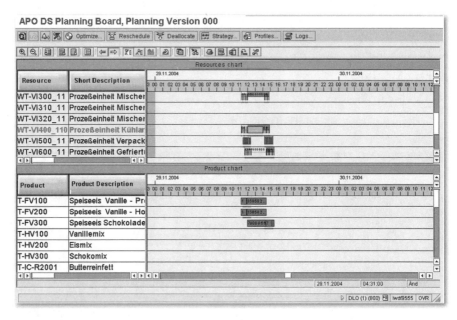

Figure 8.46 Graphical Planning Board in SAP APO

Planning problems, such as sequence or deadline problems, can be solved interactively on resources in the DS Planning Board. Various planning functions and heuristics are also available, in addition to manual planning via drag and drop.

When calling the DS Planning Board, the system automatically creates a copy of the current planning version, a so-called *simulation version*. The application is planned in this version based on the status of the planning version at the time the board is called. While you're editing the simulation version with the DS Planning Board, however, the planning version can change. Other planners call operations back, for example, or create orders. If you want to work with the latest planning status, you must update the simulation version. When updating, the system integrates the planning data from the planning version with a higher priority into the simulation version.

Several tools to identify planning problems are also available to you in the DS Planning Board, such as the Alert Monitor, the Plan Monitor, as well as various evaluation methods, such as for resource utilization or for work-in-process stocks. You can resolve planning problems with the following measures:

▶ Plan or re-plan operations or orders via drag and drop

▶ Plan or re-plan operations or orders with the help of detailed scheduling heuristics, such as with sequence planning or backlog resolution

▶ Change the capacity offering and the planning parameters of resources

▶ Create or change orders

If you want to know tomorrow where you're going to be the day after tomorrow, then you need to start looking at what yesterday can teach you about today. Controlling is key to the optimization of processes, and this holds true in inventory management. This chapter explains how you can control and monitor your inventory and logistics processes.

9 Inventory Controlling

The high level of complexity of logistics systems and increasing performance requirements are driving the need for target-driven planning, management, monitoring, and coordination of the various subdivisions within logistics. You can use logistics controlling to accomplish these tasks. The primary objectives of logistics controlling are:

▸ Constant monitoring of economic feasibility based on target vs. actual comparisons of costs and services

▸ Collecting, aggregating, and providing decision-relevant information

Another important element of logistics controlling is inventory management, which is discussed later in this chapter.

9.1 Why Inventory Monitoring?

In the past, companies usually implemented logistics processes in self-contained functional areas. This department-based thinking led to isolated views of the logistics services process. For example, reducing costs in one functional area may increase costs in another area of the same company. Interdependencies must also be considered, for example, those between inventory and other logistics services, such as service level or lead times (as described in Chapter 6, *Service Level and Safety Stocks*, and Chapter 8, *Production*). Therefore, the interactive aspects of logistics controlling and of inventory controlling in the context of inventory management, and their effect on other performance key figures, must be considered. It is also important to define and apply key figures consistently throughout the entire company to ensure comparability. Inventory controlling is essential for avoiding sub-optimal isolated solutions and for integrated and process-oriented management of the supply chain process.

A number of relevant key figures are explained here, using the example of purchase order planning. Purchase order planning is used to release raw material and manufacturing supplies at the individual suppliers' sites. The scope of services is essentially determined by the number of different suppliers. The following is a list of suitable performance key figures for measuring the fulfilment rate of the task at hand:

▶ Number of A, B, and C items to be planned

▶ Number of suppliers

▶ Number of items to be serviced

▶ Number of new items and new suppliers

▶ Number of special items

▶ Number of complaints

▶ Stockout figure

▶ Number of person hours worked

Logistics controlling therefore serves two purposes: it is used for long-term price determination and price correction, and it allows the MRP controller to detect and eliminate trouble spots and vulnerabilities. The goals of inventory controlling include:

▶ Optimizing inventory costs

▶ Minimizing administrative costs

▶ Defining and monitoring planning parameters

▶ Defining target values

9.2 An Introduction to Logistics Controlling

The goal of logistics controlling is to analyze, measure, and evaluate the performance of the logistics processes within a company's supply chain.

Current literature on the subject discusses individual instruments for supply chain controlling, such as the key figures of the Supply Chain Operations Reference (SCOR) model.

The existing self-contained supply chain controlling concepts are rudimentary. The approaches of, e. g., Kaplan/Norton and the Supply Chain Council (SCC) offer procedures for creating systems of key figures. However, only the SCC's approach addresses the entire supply chain.

To use key figures successfully in logistics controlling, you must understand what key figures are and how they can be used. Key figures are numerical values that deliberately condense a complex reality to provide information about quantitatively measurable facts and relationships. The mathematical/statistical form is frequently used in business literature as a systematization characteristic as a means of systematizing key figures. It divides key figures into absolute figures and relative indicators, as shown in Figure 9.1. Absolute figures include coefficients, totals, differences, and products. Statistically calculated measures, such as average value, are also assigned to the category of absolute figures.

Relative indicators comprise relative figures, classification figures, and index figures. To form classification figures, unequal values of the same type are placed in a relationship with one another. Relative figures are relations of values of different types that have a logical relationship with each other. The values of classification figures and relative figures are all based on the same period. Relations of similar values based on different periods are called index figures. They measure the value against a base value, indicating significant deviations over time.

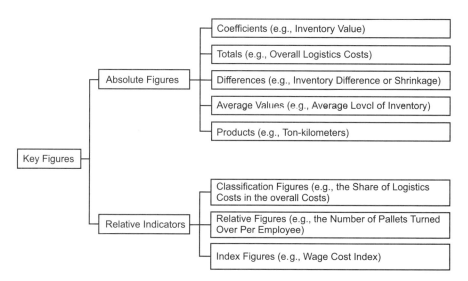

Figure 9.1 Mathematical/Statistical Differentiation of Key Figures

In addition to using the mathematical/statistical form, you can use various business-related criteria to differentiate between different key figures. These criteria include the information basis, the focus, the approach, and the object range. The information basis indicates where the key figure originated, such as in the balance sheet or the profit and loss statement, for example. If key figures are differentiated on the basis of their focus, they can be classified as **profitability** and **liquidity key figures**, for example. Liquidity level 1 is an example of a liquidity key figure. It indicates what percentage of short-term liabilities is attributable to cash and cash equivalents. Return on equity is an example of a profitability key figure. It is defined as the quotient of the net income over equity.

Key figures can be classified as normative or descriptive, depending on their use. Normative target figures are used as future-oriented target variables, while descriptive actual key figures describe facts in the past that require further processing or a decision.

Individual key figures generally have limited significance, because the information they contain is condensed to such a large degree. There is also an associated risk of misinterpretation because important details and contexts may be lost. Using a large number of key figures can provide a considerably improved representation of complexity at an operational level. However, this often produces a maze of "hieroglyphics," which are complex, prevent a clear view of the essential facts, and are uninformative. *Supply chain information systems* can solve this dilemma. An information system comprises a set of elements (key figures) and a set of relationships between these elements. A collection of individual key figures alone does not constitute an information system. Therefore, an information system provides complete information about business-related facts and contexts.

9.3 The Information System of the Supply Chain Council

The information system of the Supply Chain Council (SCC) represents a system for measuring processes or their performance in accordance with the systematization characteristic *type of activity to be measured*.

The Supply Chain Council is an international, non-profit initiative. It was established in the USA in 1996 by Pittiglio, Rabin, Todd & McGrath consultants (PRTM), Advanced Manufacturing Research (AMR), and 69 other companies. Since then, 450 institutions and companies have become members of the SCC. The initiative's goal is to develop and endorse the SCOR model as a cross-industry standard process reference model for supply chain management (see Supply Chain Council, 1999).

The SCOR model enables standardized representation or modelling of real intercompany business processes within the supply chain. It also allows users to perform benchmarking and to analyze best practices based on best-in-class conversions. Benchmarking allows companies to determine where they stand in relation to their competitors based on the results of the member companies of the Supply Chain Council. Examples of best practices can be found in the Integrated Supply Chain Benchmarking Study from PRTM.

The integrated supply chain of the SCOR model comprises the entire value-added chain, that is, all flows of material, goods, and information, from the supplier's supplier to the customer's customer.

The SCOR model consists of *three modeling levels,* which represent increasing degrees of detail.

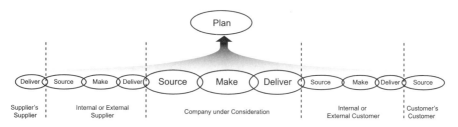

Figure 9.2 Level 1 of the SCOR Model (Source: SCOR)

Figure 9.2 shows the first level of the SCOR model, where the supply chain model is created. It comprises four core processes: *plan, source, make,* and *deliver.* The "plan" process extends along the entire value chain and includes assigning resources, aggregating and prioritizing demand requirements, order distribution, and rough-cut capacity planning for all products and value paths in the supply chain. In addition, infrastructure planning, such as make-or-buy decisions or long-term capacity and resource planning, is part of this process. The "source" process includes the delivery, receipt, quality control, and storage of a material, as well as vendor evaluations and vendor contract management. The "make" process, meanwhile, comprises staging the required material, manufacturing and testing the products, releasing the products, as well as packaging and intermediate storage. Machines, production plans, product quality, and short-term capacity are all included in the infrastructure of the make process. The "deliver" process includes sales order management, storage and distribution of finished products, and management of distribution channels.

Management of the required infrastructure is also integrated into each of the four core processes. In addition to the description and definition of the scope of the task within the supply chain, the company's competitive objectives are also defined at the first level.

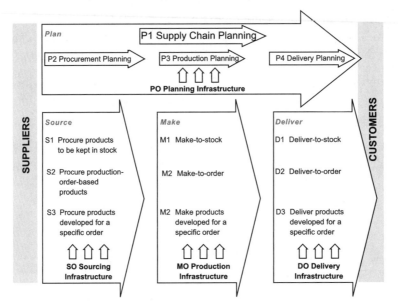

Figure 9.3 Level 2 of the SCOR Model (Source: SCOR)

At the second level, the supply chain is configured using the 17 standard process categories shown in Figure 9.3. The configuration of the supply chain reflects the company's strategy in relation to its processes.

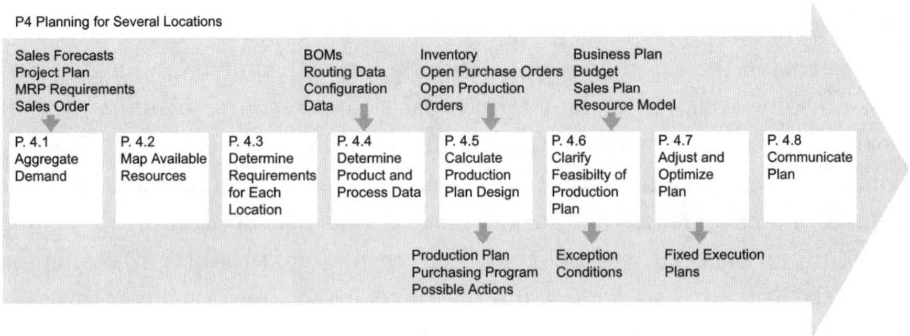

Figure 9.4 Level 3 of the SCOR Model (Source: SCOR)

At the third level, shown in Figure 9.4, each of the process categories defined at the second level can be refined for specific industries by mapping the sub-processes or process elements. In addition, the incoming and outgoing process information, diagnosis key figures (process key figures), best practices, and available tools, such as the entity relationship model, are identified at this level. There is also a fourth level that can be added to the SCOR model, in which the company's supply chain strategy is implemented by describing and customizing the process components.

The key figures of the information system, which is based on the SCOR model, are based on the individual modeling levels. The key figures of the first modeling level provide an overall view of the supply chain and are assigned to various perspectives according to the balanced scorecard (BSC) approach. The **Supply Chain SCORCard**, shown in Figure 9.5, comprises the customer perspective, which is broken down into the categories of service level, flexibility, and response time, and the company perspective, which is broken down into the categories of costs and assets. Assigning the individual key figures to these perspectives ensures equilibrium between the objectives with in the BSC approach. Supply chain management defines the objectives for the individual key figures, taking strategy into account in each case.

SCORCard for Top Management (Level 1)	Customer View		Company View	
	Service Level	Flexibility & Response Time	Costs	Assets
Service Level	✓			
Order Processing Performance • Ability to Deliver • Order Processing	✓			
Error-Free Order Processing	✓			
Supply-Chain Response Time		✓		
Production Flexibility		✓		
Total Supply-Chain Management Costs			✓	
Value-Added Productivity			✓	
Warranty Costs			✓	✓
Cash-to-Cash Cycle Costs				✓
Range of Coverage				✓
Asset Turnover				

Figure 9.5 SCORCard—Cost and Performance Key Figures at the Management Level (Source: SCOR)

The management key figures (cost and performance key figures) of the SCORCard can be used as tools for managing the supply chain, for example, by tracking monthly changes in the service level.

The specific key figures of the second level (performance key figures) and the third level (diagnosis key figures) can indicate reasons for changes. The diagnosis key figures are based on the plan, source, make, and deliver processes and are assigned to these three categories: *supply chain complexity*, *supply chain configuration*, and *supply chain management*. Figure 9.6 provides an overview of the key figures that are included in the second and third levels of the SCOR model.

Level 2: Performance Key Figures		Level 3: Diagnosis Key Figures		
		Supply Chain Complexity	Supply Chain Configuration	Supply Chain Management
Cycle Time / Quality / Customer Satisfaction / Costs				
Plan	> Requirements/Demand Planning Costs > Costs of Financing and Planning the Supply Chain > Range of Coverage	> % of Order Changes > Number of Stock Material Items That Can Be Ordered > Total Output > Stockholding Costs	> Total Output per Channel > Number of Channels > Complexity of Channels	> Planning Cycle > Forecast Accuracy > Range of Coverage of Obsolete Products > Regenerative Planning Cycle > Method of Order Entry
Source	> Material Costs > Range of Coverage > Procurement Cycle	> % of Expenses for Material Additions by Distances > Range of Coverage of Raw Materials	> Material Purchase per Region > % of Material Purchasing Costs by Distances > Complexity	> Vendor Delivery Performance > Payment Period > % of Received Individual Parts with Cycle Time < 8 Weeks > Percentage for Plan Reduction without Additional Costs
Make	> Warranty Costs > Ability to Deliver > Production Cycle Time	> Number of Stock Material Items That Can Be Ordered > Total Output by Type > Output Increase Flexibility	> Production Process Steps per Region > Capital Turnover	> Added Value (%) > % in Stock, % Order-specific, % Sales Order-specific > Repair and Rework Times
Deliver	> Ability to Deliver > Order Management Costs > Delivery Performance > Order Processing Cycle Time > Forecast Accuracy per Channel > Error-Free Order Processing	> Number of Orders, Items, and Deliveries per Channel > % Returns > % Repeated Returns	> Delivery Destinations by Region > Number of Channels	> Published Delivery Time > Number of Error-Free Invoices

Figure 9.6 Performance and Analysis Key Figures (Source: SCOR)

The main advantage of the SCC's approach is the standardization of processes, supply chain terminology, and key figures. The reference model improves communication between partners in the supply chain in relation to strategies, processes, and key figures. Standardization also provides a basis for benchmarking and for the identification of best practices in the supply chain.

However, the SCC's approach does have disadvantages, including the lack of transparency for evaluating the cause-and-effect relationships or the links between the different key figures. In particular, no explicit connection can be identified between the SCORCard and the performance key figures. Another disadvantage is that not all key figures can be clearly identified. This flexibility may hinder benchmarking or limit its significance. Finally, the objective and subjective information requirements are not explicitly taken into account.

9.4   Problems with Data Collection

The main advantage of key figures is their ability to summarize large amounts of complex data into meaningful values. However, this involves the challenge of retrieving the most important data from all of the available information. Various problems must be overcome when determining the correct data basis:

▶ **Key figure inflation**
   Too many key figures are created whose significance is ultimately too low compared with the effort involved or is already covered by other key figures.

▶ **Key figure errors**
   The basic data used to create key figures must be accurately specified and defined in detail. Key values must be specified to ensure comparability over time and across different areas in the company. Otherwise, incorrect figures, which may occur over time, or different interpretations of the same key figures in different areas of the company could result in wrong decisions.

▶ **Lack of consistency among key figures**
   Using several key figures in an information system should not produce inconsistencies. Values should only be linked to one another if they are connected. A lack of consistency may also result in serious errors in decision-making.

▶ **Key figure control issues**
   In general, key figures should only be created if their values can be controlled when deviations occur. Key figures can be controlled directly or indirectly. With key figures that are controlled directly, a target value can be controlled by selecting one or more action variables. This is not possible with key figures that are controlled indirectly.

▶ **Understanding causal relationships**
   It is important to know how a process affects a key figure, and which parameters or decisions can be used to influence a key figure. Only in this

way can the relevant departments and persons in the company strive to improve the key figures.

▶ **Connecting target systems to the information system**
The target values must be integrated into the company's target system so that everyone in the company can work on improving the relevant targets.

▶ **Implementing an early warning system for key figure monitoring**
An early warning system that alerts relevant departments and persons to exceptional situations on both a regular and an as-needed basis is required to ensure that key figure monitoring follows standard rules and, most importantly, that it is automatic.

9.5   Important Inventory Key Figures

The most important key figures for inventory optimization are presented below and are illustrated by some practical examples.

9.5.1   Range of Coverage

The "range of coverage" key figure provides information about the current inventory level relative to demand. It indicates how long the inventory will last based on an average daily demand (see Figure 9.7).

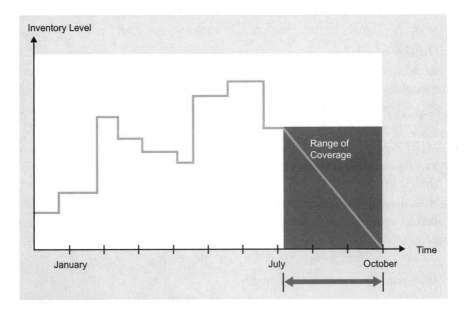

Figure 9.7 Range of Coverage Key Figure

Figure 9.7 shows the development of the inventory level over time. For the (future) period of July to October, the future requirement is subtracted from the current inventory level. This gives you the range of coverage key figure.

An analysis using this criterion allows you to select materials with an overly extensive range of coverage and therefore adjust to the changed consumption situation. The analysis uses the following formula:

consumption range of coverage: current inventory level / (average consumption/day)

required range of coverage: current inventory level / (average requirement/day)

The warehouse range of coverage should be evaluated for each item or, if the items are of the same type, for each item group. Therefore, providing a material range of coverage for the entire inventory does not make sense in most cases, because the items in the inventory often cannot be compared with one another. The pattern of their supply and demand differs too significantly for a range of coverage to be calculated for all items.

The following questions must be answered when determining the range of coverage:

▶ Which period is to be analyzed (day, week, month)?

▶ Over which period are the consumption values to be calculated?

▶ Is the average consumption to be calculated on the basis of past values or future requirements?

In the case of seasonal items, the consumption period should include at least one full season. The material range of coverage should be the same at the start and the end of the season.

It is also important that you compare the target range of coverage with the actual range of coverage on a regular basis and adjust both where necessary.

Range of Coverage/Replenishment Lead Times Matrix

In the range of coverage/replenishment lead times (RLT) matrix, the range of coverage and the replenishment lead times of items are compared, as illustrated in Table 9.1.

	RLT	Range of Coverage							
		No inventory	Up to 7 days	7–14 days	15–20 days	21–60 days	61–110 days	No consumption	Total
Replenishment Lead Times	Up to 14 days	9	18	22	35	33	34	52	203
	15–20 days	3	22	25	56	88	41	66	301
	21–60 days	0	26	28	26	143	48	33	304
Replenishment lead times	61–110 days	1	30	31	17	14	35	45	173
	No data	27	28	17	19	0	31	23	145
	Total	40	124	123	153	278	189	219	1,126

Table 9.1 Comparison of Range of Coverage and Replenishment Lead Times

This comparison allows you to evaluate inventories. The selected fields in the table indicate where there is potential for optimizing your inventory, in particular where the replenishment lead times are shorter than the range of coverage. In the fields highlighted in dark gray, the replenishment lead time is significantly longer than the range of coverage. In this case, you must verify the replenishment lead time and ensure that stockouts do not occur.

Range of Coverage/Consumption Quantities Matrix

If you compare the range of coverage with the consumption values of the individual materials, as is illustrated in Figure 9.8, you can very easily differentiate between "productive" and "unproductive" items.

Items with a consumption value of zero and a very large range of coverage (shown on the left in the figure) are generally slow-moving items. Items with a consumption of value of zero and a range of coverage of zero (shown in the top left section of the figure) have been identified as dead stock in this example. Items with a very large range of coverage (shown in the bottom right section of the figure) are referred to as "unproductive items." In this case, there may very likely be potential for optimizing your inventory. The target range of coverage should be verified for these items. Items with a very small range of coverage and a relatively high level of consumption are referred to as "productive items." They are likely to show a very high level of inventory turnover. MRP controllers should closely monitor these items.

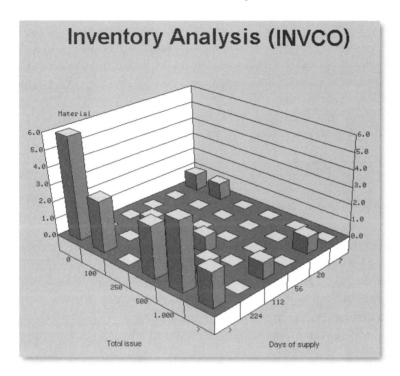

Figure 9.8 Range of Coverage/Consumption Quantities Matrix

9.5.2   Inventory Turnover

The inventory turnover key figure indicates how often an average inventory is turned over within a defined period (see Figure 9.9). Therefore, this key figure refers to the past. The inventory turnover is calculated as the quotient of the cumulated consumption (the top line in the diagram) over the average inventory level (the dotted line in the diagram).

An analysis based on this key figure allows you to select slow-moving items. It provides a basis for evaluating the efficiency of the tied-up capital in the past, for example. The capital turnover of an inventory is as follows:

(inventory turnover =) total consumption / average inventory

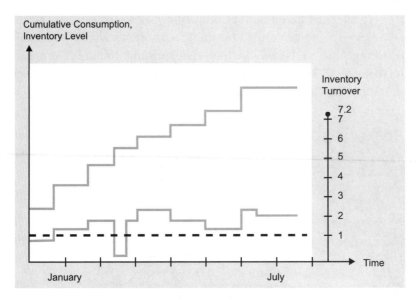

Figure 9.9 Inventory Turnover Key Figure

The greater the value, the more economically feasible stockholding becomes. This is because the required inventory level decreases as the rate of turnover increases. Total consumption ultimately reflects the company revenue. The sales volume should normally rise as consumption increases. Therefore, to improve this key figure, the volume of sales must increase at a faster rate than the inventory, or the inventory must be reduced while the sales volume remains static.

An example: With annual sales of 10 million and an inventory of 1 million, the inventory turnover is 10. If annual sales were increased to 11 million by means of a price increase of 10%, and if the inventory level remained unchanged, the inventory turnover would be 11. However, the physical quantities do not change. If you measure the inventory turnover in items, it amounts to 10 in both cases, with or without a price increase. Since inventory turnover is an inventory key figure, you should measure it in items.

9.5.3 Slow-Moving Items

Slow-moving items are materials that have not been consumed for a long time (see Figure 9.10). In this diagram, the consumption curve indicates that there has been no consumption from approximately the end of May until the end of August.

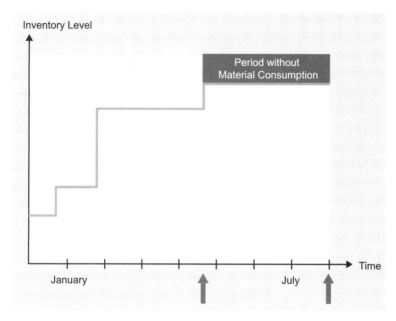

Figure 9.10 Slow-Moving Items Key Figure

An analysis of this key figure allows you to select materials that are not currently being used. These materials incur unnecessary costs. Using this key figure, you can therefore detect and eliminate unnecessary stock.

The slow-moving items key figure compares the **value of last consumption** and **days without consumption** key figures.

The days without consumption key figure is the number of days that have elapsed since the date of the last consumption. If a material has high values for both the value of last consumption and days without consumption key figures, action is required.

You should distinguish between the different types of materials (raw materials, semifinished products, and finished products) in the analysis of slow-moving items. In addition, you should use the ABC classification system. Therefore, you can prioritize and adjust items that have a high material value first.

It is important to filter out spare parts before the analysis, because these are subject to different provisioning strategies. For example, in many cases, companies must ensure that spare parts are available for long periods due to maintenance obligations, even if no consumption of those spare parts has been detected for a long time.

9.5.4 Inventory Value

An analysis with this key figure is based on the value of the valuated inventory of a material, and allows you to select materials with a high level of material tie-up (see Figure 9.11). The progression of the curve indicates the inventory value of the selected material and the average inventory consumption (indicated by a dotted line).

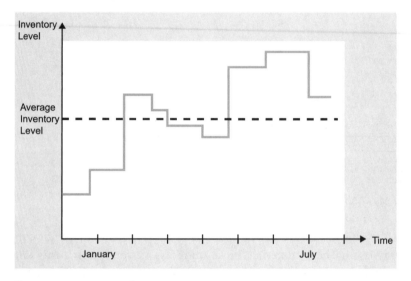

Figure 9.11 Inventory Value Key Figure

You can use the current or average inventory for the analysis. The current inventory value is based on the product of the inventory and the current price. The average inventory value is based on the product of the average inventory level and the current price.

9.5.5 Dead Stock

Dead stock refers to part of the inventory that has not been moved for a defined period of time in the past (see Figure 9.12). In the figure below, dead stock is highlighted in grey. This inventory was not used in the selected period.

The value of the dead stock is the product of the dead stock and the current price. An analysis of the dead stock key figure allows you to select materials with inefficient inventory levels. If a material has an excessively high inventory level, this is detected, and important control parameters, such as safety stock, can be checked.

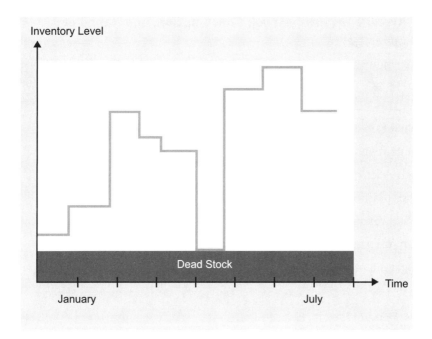

Figure 9.12 Dead Stock Key Figure

The period considered in the analysis of dead stock should be at least one year. The difference between dead stock and safety stock can be regarded as potential for inventory optimization. Dead stock generally occurs in the following cases:

▸ When planning cycles are too long

▸ When safety stock levels are too high

▸ When lot sizes are too large

▸ When replenishment lead times are incorrect

▸ When procurement is not in line with requirements

Sort the results of the dead stock analysis by increasing inventory value. Then compare the dead stock quantity with the relevant control parameters, such as safety stock, lot sizes, safety times, rounding values, or minimum lot sizes. Finally, compare your suppliers' actual delivery times for your purchased parts, because dead stock is often caused by early deliveries.

9.5.6 Average Inventory Level, Consumption, and Range of Coverage

These key figures are required in order to compare key figures with one another to assess the inventory situation. They are used in the following key figures:

- Absolute range of coverage
- Absolute inventory level
- Safety stock
- Reorder point
- Absolute consumption
- Maximum inventory level
- Replenishment lead times
- ...

The average inventory level (see Figure 9.13) is calculated using the following formula:

(opening inventory level + n closing inventory levels for the month) / (n + 1)

The formula for calculating average consumption is as follows:

total consumption quantity / number of total consumptions

The formula for the average range of coverage is shown below:

average inventory level / (average total consumption/day)

The average inventory level is the sum of the opening inventory level and the closing inventory level in the analysis period, divided by 2. The average total consumption is calculated as the quotient of the total consumption divided by the number of days in the analysis period (see Figure 9.13).

You can divide materials into different classes based on the **value of average inventory at receipt** and **range of coverage of average inventory** key figures. This allows you to identify connections between the two key figures and to locate problem areas, such as the materials that have the highest values based on both key figure values. You can also determine which materials tie up the most capital. In addition, you can compare the safety stock with the average inventory level and detect any major discrepancies.

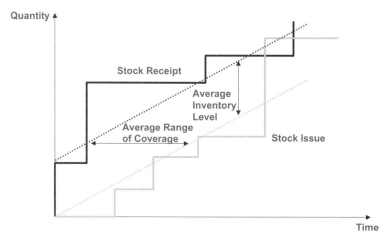

Figure 9.13 Average Range of Coverage and Average Inventory Level Key Figures

9.5.7 Receipt Value of Valuated Inventory

The receipt value of the valuated inventory is calculated as the delivered quantity of inventory valuated with the standard price or with the moving average price. In the case of a goods receipt for a purchase order, the receipt value is calculated from the delivered quantity valuated with the purchase order net price. If an invoice has been posted for the purchase order before the goods receipt, the invoice price is used for valuation.

9.5.8 Safety Stock Buffer

The **range of coverage of average receipt** and **range of coverage of average inventory level at receipt** key figures represent the safety stock buffer and are compared in the analysis.

Avoiding stockout situations is an important objective of inventory management. There are two strategies you can use to achieve this goal:

▶ A high safety stock level, and therefore also a high average inventory level at receipt

▶ A large lot size, and therefore also a large range of coverage at receipt

If you decide to use the first strategy, you should check to see if the lot size, and therefore also the average inventory level at receipt, can be reduced.

If you decide to use the second strategy (for costs reasons, for example), you should consider reducing the safety stock level, and therefore also the average inventory level.

You must closely monitor characteristic values that show high values in relation to both key figures (i.e., the range of coverage of average receipt and the range of coverage of average inventory level at receipt) : If you have both a large lot size (range of coverage of the average receipt) and a high safety stock level (range of coverage of average inventory at receipt), your planning is faulty. If you have a large lot size, a low safety stock level is generally sufficient, and if you have a high safety stock level, a smaller lot size is sufficient. Therefore, you should only use one of the strategies described above, that is, either a large lot size or a high safety stock level.

9.5.9 Safety Stock

To optimize your inventory from a safety stock point of view, the **value of average inventory at receipt** and **inventory factor** key figures are compared.

The **inventory factor** is calculated as the quotient of the average inventory level at receipt divided by the safety stock. Ideally, it should be 1.

To optimize your inventory while also taking into account the safety factor, it is useful to reduce the average inventory at receipt to the safety stock level. In the ideal scenario, the average inventory at receipt and the safety stock key figures are identical. If the average inventory at receipt is greater than the safety stock, too much stock is being held. If it is lower than the safety stock, there is a risk of shortage. To optimize the average inventory at receipt, you should ask yourself the following questions:

▶ Does the lead time in the material master correspond to the actual lead time?

▶ Does forecasting or planning produce realistic requirements?

With reorder point planning, a purchase order is always triggered once the inventory level drops below the reorder point. The reorder point is the sum of the safety stock and the consumption in the delivery time period. If, for example, the average inventory at receipt is consistently greater than the safety stock, this may indicate that the delivery times have not been estimated correctly, that an order was placed too early, or that the safety stock level is too high.

Take notice of materials that differ significantly from each other with regard to the two key figures and that have an inventory factor significantly higher than 1. This indicates that there is room for improvement, particularly in terms of the consumption forecast or delivery time settings.

9.5.10 Inventory Level at Receipt

In this analysis, the **range of coverage of average inventory at receipt** and the **value of average inventory at receipt** key figures are compared.

If a goods receipt regularly occurs when there is still a large quantity of material in the warehouse, a disproportionately high average inventory level accumulates, which results in high costs.

However, the inventory level at receipt can only be assessed in relation to consumption. The range of coverage of the average inventory at receipt is therefore a critical key figure.

An unnecessarily high inventory level at receipt occurs if material is procured or goods are produced prematurely. The following checks should be performed to identify the cause of an excessively high inventory level at receipt:

▶ Does the lead time in the material master correspond to the actual lead time?

▶ If safety stock is entered manually: Can the safety stock be reduced?

▶ If the safety stock is calculated: Is the defined service level justified?

▶ Does forecasting or planning produce realistic requirements?

Materials for which both a large range of coverage of the average inventory at receipt and a high value of average inventory are indicated have high inventory levels at receipt as measured by consumption, and should therefore be examined in more detail.

9.5.11 Lot Size

For this key figure, the **range of coverage of average inventory** and **value of average inventory** key figures are compared.

If a material is ordered or produced in excessively large lot sizes, this results in an excessively high average inventory level, which causes unnecessary costs. However, the lot size must be analyzed in relation to consumption. A high level of consumption justifies a large lot size. Therefore, you need a key figure that takes both lot size and consumption into account: the **range of coverage of average receipt in days** key figure. If the range of coverage of the average receipt is too large, the lot size, and therefore also the average inventory, can be reduced.

Of particular interest here are materials that have the highest values in relation to both key figures, in other words, materials that have a large range of coverage of average receipt and show a high average receipt value. In this case, you should reduce the lot size, because, with a high receipt value, the existing lot size has resulted in a high inventory value, and therefore a high level of capital tie-up.

9.6   Tools for Inventory Analysis

9.6.1   LMN Analysis

The LMN analysis is similar to the ABC analysis, except items are classified according to volume rather than value. This analysis is therefore also known as the inventory volume analysis:

▶ L = large-volume item

▶ M = medium-volume item

▶ N = small-volume item

In both material requirements planning and logistics, you want to know whether a small-volume item (such as a bolt) or a large-volume item (such as an engine) is being put away, planned, or transported. If, for example, the range of coverage analysis indicates that a C item should be planned with a range of coverage of five months, the MRP controller would also provision a corresponding quantity for a large-volume item in accordance with the range of coverage strategy. However, this does not make much sense from a logistics point of view. The number of slow-moving items would increase on a huge scale and, in the worst case scenario, there would no longer be sufficient storage capacity for A or B items. It is therefore important to perform the LMN analysis in addition to the ABC analysis. The logic in the LMN analysis is the same as in the ABC analysis.

9.6.2   Flowcharts in Production

Flowcharts were developed by Prof. Wiendahl. They are based on the same display format as cumulative quantities. A flowchart with key figures is shown in Figure 9.14.

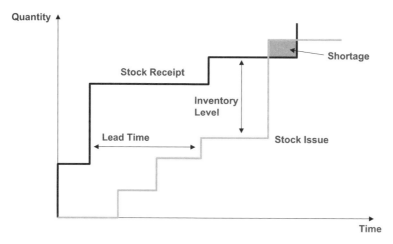

Figure 9.14 Flowchart—Key Figures in Production

Starting with the opening inventory, all goods receipts and goods issues are entered for each stage. The lead time is the horizontal distance between the issues curve of the source resource and the receipts curve of the target resource. The inventory level is the vertical distance between the receipts curve and the issues curve of an item, item group, or an entire assortment.

If the receipts curve is higher than the issues curve, there is a surplus. If the issues curve is higher than the receipts curve, there is a shortage. Management targets can be compared with actual performance using flowcharts, which indicate whether targets have been achieved.

On-time delivery performance can be evaluated by comparing the target and actual dates of receipts, as shown in Figure 9.15.

Negative areas indicate a delay, while positive areas indicate early deliveries, which cause what is referred to as a "time buffer."

The flowchart also shows whether MRP, production, and logistics are working in sync with one another. It provides an overview of departments and companies and is particularly useful for virtual partners. Once buffers between partners are identified, they can be minimized to reduce risks. The lead time can be visualized along the entire supply chain and compared with the delivery time, as shown in Figure 9.16.

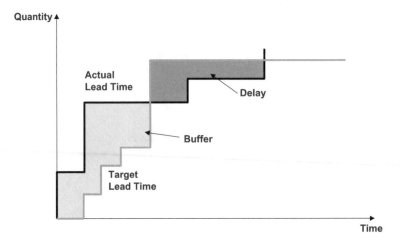

Figure 9.15 On-Time Delivery Performance Flowchart

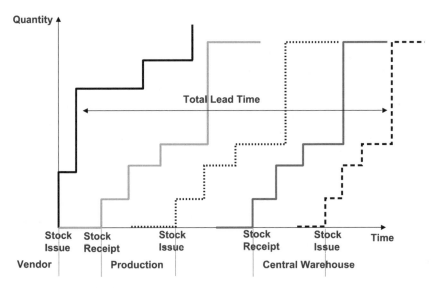

Figure 9.16 Total Lead Time Flowchart

9.6.3 Procurement and Consumption Cycles

The synchronization of the procurement and consumption cycles for specific items can be monitored and fine-tuned on an ongoing basis. The "procurement cycle" refers to the timespan in which items are procured (for example, every 14 days). The "consumption cycle," meanwhile, refers to the timespan in which the items are consumed (for example, once a week). Figure 9.17 shows a sample comparison of the procurement and consumption cycles.

Consumption Cycle

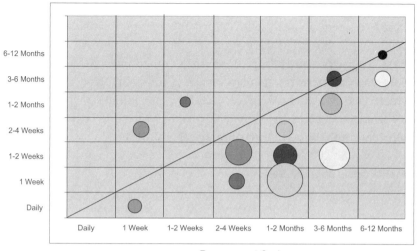

Procurement Cycle

Figure 9.17 Procurement and Consumption Cycles

The procurement cycle is shown on the x-axis in the chart, and the consumption cycle is shown on the y-axis in the chart. The size of the circles indicates the number of items. Most items show a consumption cycle of one week. However, each item is only procured once every one to two months. In most cases, the reason for this is the bundling of individual purchase orders into a collective purchase order to minimize purchasing costs.

This type of matrix allows you to quickly identify where action needs to be taken in inventory management and material requirements planning. In the case of items located above the diagonals, that is, items whose consumption cycle is longer than their procurement cycle, MRP procedures should be checked. In practice, it is common for MRP procedures to remain unchecked for several years at a time, even though consumption patterns have most likely changed.

If most of the items are located below the diagonals (as in the example), ABC analysis should be used to determine whether this group includes A items. A items should be procured in parallel with consumption whenever possible. In other words, these items should also be on the diagonals in the chart where possible, or, in certain isolated cases, even above the diagonals.

9.7 Inventory Monitoring in mySAP ERP

In mySAP ERP, you can analyze inventory information relating to inventory controlling in the Logistics Information System (LIS). In the SAP menu, select **Logistics · Logistics Controlling · Inventory Controlling · Standard Analyses**. Here you can perform standard analyses for your plant, storage locations, materials, and batches. Figure 9.18 shows the initial screen of material analysis, which you access from the SAP menu by selecting **Logistics · Logistics Information System · Standard Analyses · Material**.

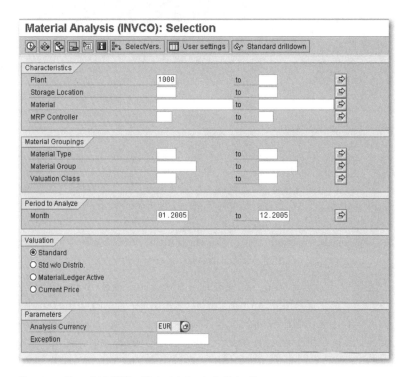

Figure 9.18 mySAP ERP—Material Analysis Selection

In the **Characteristics** field group, you enter the characteristics you want to select for your analysis. You can restrict the selection by plants, storage locations, materials, or batches. In the example shown here, all materials belonging to plant 1000 are selected.

In the **Material Groupings** field group, you can restrict your selection further, by selecting materials that belong to a specific material group, for example.

The **analysis period** you select indicates the period for which you want the analysis to be performed.

To calculate the inventory values, in the **Valuation** field group you must indicate how the inventory value is to be calculated in the analysis. Standard valuation is used in the example shown here.

Finally, you can also specify the **analysis currency** and indicate whether the system should alert you as soon as pre-defined threshold values are exceeded (exceptions). Figure 9.19 shows the result of you inventory analysis.

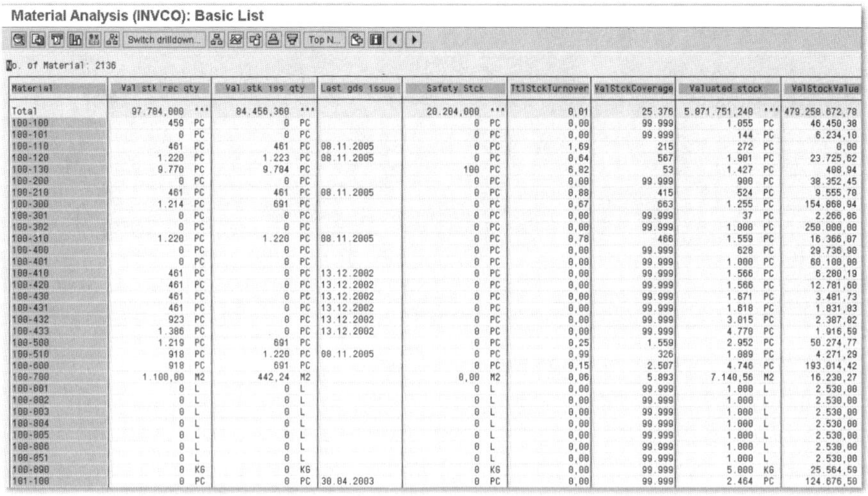
Material Analysis (INVCO): Basic List

Switch drilldown... Top N...

No. of Material: 2136

Material	Val stk rec qty	Val.stk iss qty	Last gds issue	Safety Stck	TtlStckTurnover	ValStckCoverage	Valuated stock	ValStockValue
Total	97.784,000 ***	84.456,360 ***		20.204,000 ***	0,01	25.376	5.871.751,240 ***	479.258.672,78
100-100	459 PC	0 PC		0 PC	0,00	99.999	1.055 PC	46.450,38
100-101	0 PC	0 PC		0 PC	0,00	99.999	144 PC	6.234,10
100-110	461 PC	461 PC	08.11.2005	0 PC	1,69	215	272 PC	0,00
100-120	1.220 PC	1.223 PC	08.11.2005	0 PC	0,64	567	1.901 PC	23.725,62
100-130	9.770 PC	9.784 PC		100 PC	6,82	53	1.427 PC	408,94
100-200	0 PC	0 PC		0 PC	0,00	99.999	900 PC	38.352,45
100-210	461 PC	461 PC	08.11.2005	0 PC	0,88	415	524 PC	9.555,70
100-300	1.214 PC	691 PC		0 PC	0,67	663	1.255 PC	154.868,94
100-301	0 PC	0 PC		0 PC	0,00	99.999	37 PC	2.266,86
100-302	0 PC	0 PC		0 PC	0,00	99.999	1.000 PC	250.000,00
100-310	1.220 PC	1.220 PC	08.11.2005	0 PC	0,78	466	1.559 PC	16.366,07
100-400	0 PC	0 PC		0 PC	0,00	99.999	628 PC	29.736,90
100-401	0 PC	0 PC		0 PC	0,00	99.999	1.000 PC	60.100,00
100-410	461 PC	0 PC	13.12.2002	0 PC	0,00	99.999	1.566 PC	6.280,19
100-420	461 PC	0 PC	13.12.2002	0 PC	0,00	99.999	1.566 PC	12.781,60
100-430	461 PC	0 PC	13.12.2002	0 PC	0,00	99.999	1.671 PC	3.481,73
100-431	461 PC	0 PC	13.12.2002	0 PC	0,00	99.999	1.618 PC	1.831,83
100-432	923 PC	0 PC	13.12.2002	0 PC	0,00	99.999	3.015 PC	2.387,82
100-433	1.386 PC	0 PC	13.12.2002	0 PC	0,00	99.999	4.770 PC	1.916,59
100-500	1.219 PC	691 PC		0 PC	0,25	1.559	2.952 PC	50.274,77
100-510	918 PC	1.220 PC	08.11.2005	0 PC	0,99	326	1.089 PC	4.271,29
100-600	918 PC	691 PC		0 PC	0,15	2.507	4.746 PC	193.014,42
100-700	1.100,00 M2	442,24 M2		0,00 M2	0,06	5.893	7.140,56 M2	16.230,27
100-801	0 L	0 L		0 L	0,00	99.999	1.000 L	2.530,00
100-802	0 L	0 L		0 L	0,00	99.999	1.000 L	2.530,00
100-803	0 L	0 L		0 L	0,00	99.999	1.000 L	2.530,00
100-804	0 L	0 L		0 L	0,00	99.999	1.000 L	2.530,00
100-805	0 L	0 L		0 L	0,00	99.999	1.000 L	2.530,00
100-806	0 L	0 L		0 L	0,00	99.999	1.000 L	2.530,00
100-851	0 L	0 L		0 L	0,00	99.999	1.000 L	2.530,00
100-890	0 KG	0 KG		0 KG	0,00	99.999	5.000 KG	25.564,59
101-100	0 PC	0 PC	30.04.2003	0 PC	0,00	99.999	2.464 PC	124.676,50

Figure 9.19 Material Analysis—Key Figures View

A range of inventory key figures is shown, including the total consumption, the current inventory quantity, the date of the last issue, the average range of coverage in days, the average inventory level, the current material range of coverage, and the inventory turnover. If you press the **More Key Figures** button, you can display any number of other key figures.

You can also display detailed information in graphical form or as a table. In addition, you can navigate directly from this screen to the inventory overview in Inventory Management.

For the key figures specified above, you can display a receipts diagram, an issues diagram, and a diagram showing the development of the inventory level for a characteristic value. To do this, select the receipts/issues diagram from the **Goto** menu. This diagram provides an overview of the development of the inventory level and the cumulated issues and receipts data for each material, as shown in Figure 9.20.

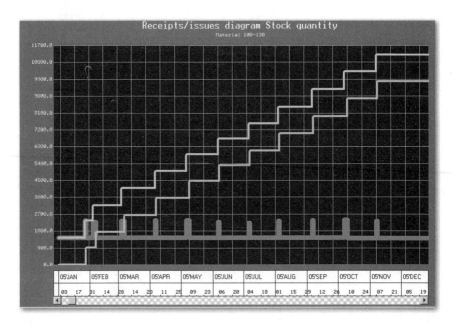

Figure 9.20 Receipts/Issues Diagram in mySAP ERP

For each characteristic value, you can display a table containing the inventory movements for the key figures listed above. The table indicates the movements that have taken place within the analysis period of the standard analysis. For each day in this period, you can simply double-click to display the individual movements that have taken place on that day, along with the corresponding document numbers. You can double-click on the document number to navigate directly to the document.

The following key figures can also be displayed as a table:

▶ Opening inventory

▶ Average value

▶ Minimum

▶ Maximum

▶ Closing inventory

▶ Last consumption

▶ Average range of coverage

▶ Inventory turnover

▶ Zero stock

▶ Percentage of dead stock

This detailed analysis is shown in Figure 9.21.

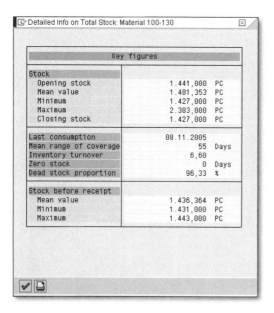

Figure 9.21 mySAP ERP—Detailed Information on the Selected Material

10 Afterword

If the previous chapters have raised your interest, and you want to reduce unnecessary safety stock in your company without compromising your ability to deliver at any time, you should perform a *value assessment to optimize your inventory*. A value assessment enables you to both save costs and keep your customers happy.

To support the analysis of your planning and material requirements planning (MRP) processes, here's a recommended procedure to identify optimization potentials and determine concrete measures.

The Focus of a Value Assessment

A value assessment focuses primarily on business analyses, but also includes SAP-related topics in its considerations. A value assessment is carried out in the following areas:

▸ Forecast and demand-planning process

▸ Material requirements planning and inventory management

▸ Distribution

▸ Production

▸ Inventory monitoring

The aforementioned areas are introduced and described in a potentials workshop that examines their influence on the inventory. At this time, the core topics are identified and prioritized. Then, an individual analysis of the actual status per core topic is done so that we can identify and evaluate the existing potentials. Finally, we develop and describe proposals for a new implementation.

The Goals of a Value Assessment

▸ Analysis and prioritization of the potentials and core areas of inventory optimization

▸ Analysis of the potentials in the identified priority area of inventory optimization including a description of the cost reduction

▸ Gaining information on the ability to make forecasts regarding your products based on a report of your forecast accuracy potentials, for example

- Design of optimized company-specific forecast models
- Determining key performance indicators (KPIs) for representing and controlling the stock situation

The Contents of a Value Assessment

Potentials workshop
- General description of the core areas (materials requirements planning, forecast, production, inventory management, distribution, and inventory monitoring) and their influence on the inventory
- Prioritization of potentials and core areas
- Assessment of forecast and demand-planning process
- Evaluation of the forecast basis and identification of areas of improvement
- Determination and definition of optimal forecast models
- Examination of forecast accuracy and recommendations for increasing the accuracy

Assessment of material requirements planning (MRP) and inventory management
- Identification and evaluation of your material requirements planning parameters (reorder point, safety stock, lot sizes, etc.)
- Evaluation of your MRP strategies
- Recommendations for organizing your inventory management
- Recommendation of inventory key figures for your products

Assessment of the distribution
- Identification and evaluation of the ability to deliver, the service level, and the delivery reliability
- Examination of your replenishment strategies and collaborative inventory management scenarios
- Assessment of tracking and tracing potentials in the distribution processes

Assessment of the production
- Assessment of lead times
- Evaluation of master data and lot size strategies

- ▶ Discussion of scheduling strategies
- ▶ Determining the potentials of set-up optimizations

Assessment of inventory monitoring

- ▶ Identification and definition of inventory key figures that enable you to control your processes
- ▶ Development of rules for an automatic control of your inventories
- ▶ Discussing inventory controlling tools (ABC analyses, XYZ analyses, etc.)
- ▶ Examination of stock receipt and stock issue lines

Performing a Value Assessment

A team of experienced experts, with business and SAP know-how and extensive SCM knowledge, perform the assessment of your inventories. Depending on the initial situation, the assessment takes approximately two to three weeks. The results are then presented in a final meeting.

The Results of a Value Assessment

- ▶ Statement on the potentials in the identified core areas
- ▶ Information on the ability to make forecasts for your products
- ▶ Report on the forecast accuracy potentials
- ▶ Optimized, company-specific forecast models
- ▶ Documented potentials and concrete recommendations for taking actions regarding inventory management from process and IT-related viewpoints
- ▶ Suggestion for the implementation of an inventory monitor including the corresponding KPIs

To perform a value assessment to optimize your inventories, please contact:

Marc Hoppe
SAP Systems Integration AG
Email: marc.hoppe@sap.com
Mobile: +49–160–908–21606

Appendix

A   Literature

Armstrong, J.: Principles of Forecasting, A Handbook for Researchers and Practitioners, Norwell: Kluver Academic Publishers 2001

Armstrong, J.; Collopy, F.: Integration of Statistical Methods and Judgment for Time Series Forecasting: Principles from Empirical Research, in: Wright, G.; Goodwin, P.: Forecasting with Judgment, Chichester: Wiley 1998

Ballou, R.: Business Logistics Management, 3. Edition, London: Prentice-Hall 1992

Emde, W. B.: Analyse und Prognosemethoden in der rechnergestützten Absatzplanung, Köln: Wison-Verlag 1977

Forrester, J. W.: Industrial dynamics, The MIT Press, Cambridge, Massachusetts, cited according to: Lee, H. L.; Padmanabhan, V.; Whang, S.: Information distortion in a supply chain. The bullwhip effect, in: Management Science, Vol. 43 (1997), No. 4, pp. 546–558

Gilchrist, W.: Statistical Forecasting, London: Wiley-Interscience 1976

Hartmann, H.: Bestandsmanagement und -controlling, Gernsbach: DBV 1999

Hoppe, M.: Collaborative Planning and Development, in: Supply Chain Management, No. 2/2003, IPM 2003

Jenkins, G. M.: Practical Experiences with Modelling and Forecasting, St. Helier: Time Series 1979

Kaplan, R. S.; Norton, D. P.: The Balanced Scorecard. Translating Strategy into Action, Boston: Harvard Business School Press 1996

Kleti, J.; Brauckmann, O.: Manufacturing Scorecard, Wiesbaden: Gabler 2004

Knolmayer, G.; Mertens, P.; Zeier, A.: Supply Chain Management auf Basis von SAP-Systemen, Berlin: Springer Verlag 2000

Lilien, G.L.; Rangaswamy, A.: Marketing Engineering. Computer-Assisted Marketing Analysis and Planning, New Jersey: Prentice Hall 2002

Makridakis, S.: Forecasting, Planning and Strategy for the 21st century, New York: Free Press 1990

Makridakis, S.; Wheelwright, S.; Hyndman, R.: Forecasting, Methods and Applications, New York: John Wiley & Sons 1998

Martin, A. J.: Distribution Resource Planning, New York: Wiley 1995

SAP Documentation: SAP APO Rel. 4.0/4.1 — *help.sap.com*

SAP Documentation: SAP ERP Rel. 4.7 — *help.sap.com*

Seifert, D.: Collaborative Planning and Replenishment, Bonn: Galileo Press 2002

Silver, E.; Meal, H.: A Heuristic for Selecting Lot-Size Quantities, in: Production and Inventory Management Journal Issue 14 (1973), pp. 64–77

Supply Chain Council: Supply Chain Council & Supply Chain Operations, Reference (SCOR) Model Overview, *http://www.supply-chain.org/html/scor_overview.cfm*, Pittsburgh 2004

Tempelmeier, H.; Günther, H.-O.: Produktion und Logistik, Berlin: Springer Verlag 2003

Wagner, M.: Demand Planning, in: Stadtler, H.; Kilger, Ch.: Supply Chain Management and Advanced Planning, Heidelberg: Springer 2000

Wemmerlöv, U.: A comparison of discrete single stage lot-sizing heuristics with spezial emphasis on rules based on the marginal cost principle. Engineering Costs and Production Economics 7, pp. 45–53

B   The Author

 After finishing his studies in business administration at Fachhochschule Nordostniedersachsen in Lüneburg, Germany, and at John Moores University in Liverpool, England, Marc Hoppe joined CAS AG, Germany, as an SAP developer in the logistics and production planning areas. Later, he became a logistics consultant and was responsible for implementing national and international SAP R/3 projects. Since 1998, he has worked as a Supply Chain Management (SCM) consultant at SAP SI AG. Marc Hoppe is responsible for the business-relevant and IT-based implementation and optimization of SCM processes, as well as the re-engineering of entire supply chain processes. In 2001, he became Consulting Director for SCM, and since 2003, he has managed additionally the Supplier Relationship Management (SRM) unit. Marc Hoppe consults for large corporations such as Siemens, Unilever, Gillette, Philips, Deutsche Telekom, and Philip Morris, as well as medium-sized companies like G+H Isover or Fertiva. He has published numerous works on inventory optimization.

If you have any questions regarding inventory optimization, or if you want to share your comments on this book, you can contact the author:

Email: marc.hoppe@sap.com
Fax: +49–6227–782–5664

Index

Learn how to integrate SAP SRM with other core SAP components

Uncover key insights on strategies, functionalities, and methodologies

695 pp., 2007, 69,95 Euro / US$ 69,95
ISBN 978-1-59229-068-0

Enhancing Supplier Relationship Management Using SAP SRM

www.sap-press.com

Sachin Sethi

Enhancing Supplier Relationship Management Using SAP SRM

This book will help readers leverage valuable insights into strategies and methodologies for implementing SAP SRM to enhance procurement in their companies.

Tips and tricks, changes brought about by 5.0 and customization will be woven in throughout the book. It will provide detailed information on integration and dependencies of mySAP SRM with core SAP components like MM, IM, FI and HR.

Gain a comprehensive understanding of SAP Warehouse Management

Learn the basics before fully exploring the functionality within each part of SAP WM

approx. 504 pp., 79,95 Euro / US$ 79,95
ISBN 978-1-59229-133-5, July 2007

SAP Warehouse Management: Functionality and Technical Configuration

www.sap-press.com

Martin Murray

SAP Warehouse Management: Functionality and Technical Configuration

This comprehensive reference guide for SAP Warehouse Management (WM) first introduces you to the fundamental aspects of this important module. Then, get an in-depth understanding of the functionality of WM and learn best practices for how to configure it. This detailed functionality and technical configuration guide includes all key aspects of WM, including WM Master Data, Stock Replenishment, Picking and Putaway strategies, as well as Storage Unit Management. Readers quickly gain a complete understanding of WM and its interaction with other SAP Supply Chain modules, making this book a truly indispensable resource.

Effectively analyze supply chain processes, inventory and purchasing

Avoid the hassle of custom ABAP reports by using LIS

Up-to-date for ECC 5.0

328 pp., 2007, 69,95 Euro / US$ 69,95
ISBN 978-1-59229-108-3

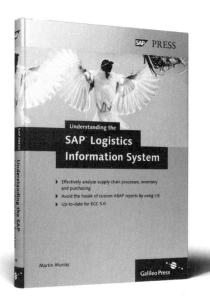

Understanding the SAP Logistics Information System

www.sap-press.com

Martin Murray

Understanding the SAP Logistics Information System

Gain a holistic understanding of LIS and how you can use it effectively in your own company. From standard to flexible analyses and hierarchies and from the Purchasing Information System to Inventory Controlling, this book is full of crucial information and advice.

Learn how to fully use this flexible SAP tool that allows you to collect, consolidate, and utilize data. Learn how to run reports without any ABAP experience thus saving your clients both time and money.

Apply SAP SD to your own company's business model and make it work for you

Learn all aspects of SD functionality and essential technical details

365 pp., 69,95 Euro / US$ 69.95
ISBN 978-1-59229-101-4

Effective SAP SD

www.sap-press.com

D. Rajen Iyer

Effective SAP SD

Get the Most Out of Your SAP SD Implementation

From important functionalities to the technical aspects of any SD implementation, this book has the answers. Use it to troubleshoot SD-related problems and learn how BAdIs, BAPIs and IDocs work in the Sales and Distribution area. Understand how SAP SD integrates with modules like MM, FI, CO, and Logistics. Whether you're looking for in-depth SD information or need advice on implementation and upgrades, this practical guide is an invaluable reference.

A single source of MM-related
information, including
MM Master data, Purchasing,
Inventory Management and
Financial integration

Understand how MM works and
how it relates to and integrates
with other SAP modules

504 pp., 2006, 69,95 Euro / US$
ISBN 1-59229-072-8

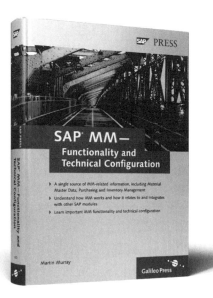

SAP MM—Functionality and Technical Configuration

www.sap-press.com

Martin Murray

SAP MM—Functionality and Technical Configuration

This book includes all aspects of SAP Materials
Management (SAP MM), including MM Master Data,
Purchasing, Inventory Management, and Financial
Integration. The book also addresses cross-appli-
cation topics that are relevant to MM, such as
document management, batch management, and
classification. Using practical examples and case
studies, this book will give readers a comprehensive
understanding of SAP MM, how it works, and how it
interacts with other SAP modules.

**Configuration and application
of APO-DP and APO-SNP**

Business principles made easy

**Functions, use, customization,
and master data parameters**

**Fully up-to-date for
SAP SCM 5.0**

440 pp., 2007, 69,95 Euro / US$ 69,95
ISBN 978-1-59229-123-6

Sales and Inventory Planning
with SAP APO

www.sap-press.com

Marc Hoppe

**Sales and Inventory Planning with
SAP APO**

This comprehensive reference shows you how
to best use the cross-company modules APO-
DP and APO-SNP in your supply chain, for a
wide variety of tasks such as carrying out
accurate forecasts and optimally utilizing the
means of transport.

A comprehensive manual
for discrete manufacturing
using SAP PP

Processes and customizing
made easy

All-new 2nd edition—fully updated
and extended for mySAP ERP 2005

477 pp., 2007, 69,95 Euro / US$ 69,95
ISBN 978-1-59229-106-9

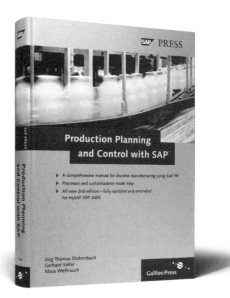

Production Planning and Control with SAP

www.sap-press.com

J.T. Dickersbach, G. Keller, K. Weihrauch

Production Planning and Control with SAP

Basic principles, processes, and complete customization details

This book provides readers with a concise and easy-to-follow description of the production planning and control processes in SAP. Expert insights provided by the authors help consultants, implementation teams, and production employees learn how to master the processes and customizing features of SAP PP (release mySAP ERP 2005). This comprehensive reference covers all major production planning and control aspects as well as key details on mySAP SCM (APO) integration—all bolstered by volumes of examples and a complete glossary.

Master the functionality of
SAP Auto-ID Infrastructure 4.0

Best practices to implement
SAP solutions for RFID in
your supply chain

Expert insights on implementation
and in-depth business
process details

104 pp., 2006, 68,– Euro / US$ 85,–
ISBN 1-59229-081-7

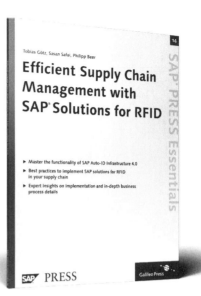

Efficient Supply Chain Management
with SAP Solutions for RFID

www.sap-hefte.de

T. Götz, S. Safai, P. Beer

Efficient Supply Chain Management with SAP Solutions for RFID

SAP PRESS Essentials 14

This SAP PRESS Essentials guide shows you how you can optimally implement SAP Auto-ID Infrastructure 4.0 in the supply chain. The basic principles of RFID technology are introduced as you are provided with a detailed description of the solution's functionality— with a specific focus on goods receipt and goods issue processes. You'll quickly discover how you can improve the flow of goods by improving the flow of information. The highly detailed process steps are well illustrated in many screenshots, useful both for an integrated SAP ERP/SAP R/3 system, as well as a standalone solution. Master data maintenance and monitoring are outlined as well as the key technical requirements, interfaces and integration requirements. In addition, the unique guide also analyses results from a variety of pilot projects.

deloitte.

deloittenet . com

1. Username : US_ RDonehudi

2. Passwor : Ezilan396

3. left Send   Menu

Take a Course : DLC → Pin → 140579

Certificate
Hart ✓